Religious Transformations
in the Early Modern Americas

THE EARLY MODERN AMERICAS

Peter C. Mancall, Series Editor

Volumes in the series explore neglected aspects of
early modern history in the western hemisphere.
Interdisciplinary in character, and with a special
emphasis on the Atlantic World from 1450 to 1850,
the series is published in partnership with the
USC-Huntington Early Modern Studies Institute.

RELIGIOUS TRANSFORMATIONS

—— IN THE ——

EARLY MODERN AMERICAS

EDITED BY

Stephanie Kirk and Sarah Rivett

PENN

UNIVERSITY OF PENNSYLVANIA PRESS

PHILADELPHIA

Published by
University of Pennsylvania Press
Philadelphia, Pennsylvania 19104-4112
www.upenn.edu/pennpress

Printed in the United States of America on acid-free paper
10 9 8 7 6 5 4 3 2 1

Library of Congress Cataloging-in-Publication Data

Religious transformations in the early modern Americas /
edited by Stephanie Kirk and Sarah Rivett. — 1st ed.
    p. cm. — (The early modern Americas)
  Includes bibliographical references and index.
  ISBN 978-0-8122-4654-4 (hardcover : alk. paper)
  1. Christianity—North America.   2. Christianity—
South America.   3. North America—Church history.
4. South America—Church history.   5. Missions—North
America.   6. Missions—South America.   7. North
America—Religion.   8. South America—Religion.   I. Kirk,
Stephanie L.   II. Rivett, Sarah.   III. Series: Early modern
Americas.
  BR510.R45 2014
  277.06—dc23
                                            2014013134

CONTENTS

Introduction
Stephanie Kirk and Sarah Rivett   1

PART I. COMPARISONS

Chapter 1. Religions on the Move   25
J. H. Elliott

Chapter 2. Baroque New Worlds: Ethnography and Demonology
in the Reformation and Counter-Reformation   46
Ralph Bauer

Chapter 3. Martín de Murúa, Felipe Guaman Poma de Ayala,
and the Contested Uses of Saintly Models in Writing Colonial
American History   79
David A. Boruchoff

PART II. CROSSINGS

Chapter 4. Transatlantic Passages: The Reformed Tradition
and the Politics of Writing   109
David D. Hall

Chapter 5. Dying for Christ: Martyrdom in New Spain   131
Asunción Lavrin

PART III. MISSIONS

Chapter 6. Believing in Piety: Spiritual Transformation
Across Cultures in Early New England   161
Matt Cohen

Chapter 7. Return as a Religious Mission: The Voyage to Dahomey
Made by the Brazilian Mulatto Catholic Priests Cipriano Pires
Sardinha and Vicente Ferreira Pires (1796–98)   180
Júnia Ferreira Furtado

Chapter 8. Jesuit Missionary Work in the Imperial Frontier:
Mapping the Amazon in Seventeenth-Century Quito   205
Carmen Fernández-Salvador

PART IV. LEGACIES

Chapter 9. "Reader . . . Behold One Raised by God": Religious
Transformations in Cotton Mather's *Pietas in Patriam: The Life of
His Excellency Sir William Phips, Knt.*   231
Teresa A. Toulouse

Chapter 10. Between Cicero and Augustine: Religion and
Republicanism in the Americas and Beyond   252
Sandra M. Gustafson

Notes   265

List of Contributors   331

Index   335

Acknowledgments   351

Introduction

STEPHANIE KIRK AND SARAH RIVETT

From 1492 through the revolutions of the late eighteenth century and early nineteenth centuries, Christianity took hold in the Americas. Subjected to persecution or seized with evangelical fervor and the promise of spiritual fulfillment in new settings, friars, lay converts, ministers, secular clergy, and nuns moved across the Atlantic Ocean in pursuit of the life that they believed to be dictated by their faith and of a place free from what they perceived to be the corruptions of European society. Upon arriving in Boston, Salvador da Bahia, Quito, Jamestown, or Mexico City, spiritual seekers formed convents, colleges, congregations, Praying Towns, missions, and *reducciones* in order to implement their religious ideas into practice and facilitate the social organization of settlement. *Religious Transformations in the Early Modern Americas* takes a spatial perspective on religious history, tracing geographical movements and population dispersals as they were shaped by the providential designs and evangelizing impulses of European empires. Christianity changed as a result of Atlantic transit into new forms of faith, ecclesiology, and theology. The collision of European traditions with American environmental and cultural realities, the reinstitution of religious hierarchy in colonial settings, and the challenge of indigenous cultures and new population configurations engendered religious reinvention.

Many of the religious communities that formed in the Americas exhibited a spiritual quest to replicate the primitive church of Christian antiquity and to further their respective agendas for reform. The native populations that European missionaries encountered served an integral role in the aspiration to fulfill Christian designs. Protestants and Catholics who traveled to the Americas studied indigenous religion intensely with the aim of reaffirming the purity of their own. Europeans described indigenous peoples variably as *tabula rasa* awaiting the salvific force of Christ, descendants of the ten lost tribes, or worshippers of pagan idols who had merely fallen away from their core Christian identity.[1] Yet time and again, either consciously or by virtue of an opposing worldview, native populations did not fit easily into these Christian categories.[2] Christian Indians also persisted with the practice of indigenous forms of belief, ultimately undermining doctrinal and missionary authority.[3]

Numerous missionary accounts attempted to fit American Indians into a Christian cosmos. In his 1541 *Historia de los Indios de la Nueva España* [*History of the Indians of New Spain*], one of the first Franciscans to arrive in Mexico, Fray Toribio de Benavente, more commonly known by his Nahua name of Motolinía, claims God "punished" the newly conquered lands of New Spain with ten severe plagues. The Jesuit José Acosta's *Historia natural y moral de las Indias* [*Natural and Moral History of the Indies*],[4] published in 1590, reports that the idolatry practiced by the Indians was a product of diabolical delusion and provides evidence of the New World as an apocalyptic battleground between God and Satan.[5] The Dutch geographer Joannes de Laet's *Nieuwe wereldt, ofte, Beschrijvinghe van West-Indien* (1625) traces the ancient origins of the "savages" who lived in New France through a commentary on their language.[6] Citing Jean de Léry on Brazil and Acosta, the French Jesuit Marc Lescarbot observed in 1609 of the Mi'kmaq in Acadia: "our savages make a fire and leap over it, as did the ancient Canaanites, Ammonites, and sometimes the Israelites."[7] In 1650, Thomas Thorowgood's *Jews in America* argues that the "Americans descended from Sem."[8] Time and again, through ethnographic observations matched to scriptural passages and through linguistic connections between American Indian and ancient languages, early travelers to the New World attempted to suture biblical history and Christian antiquity to the new sights, sounds, and civilizations that they encountered.

Religious writing in and about the Americas often straddled a desire to adhere to ancient authority alongside the compulsion to account for the new. Acosta's *Natural and Moral History* is in many ways the urtext for a pattern repeated across two centuries of European attempts to balance the precarious tension between the novelty of discovery in the Americas and the authority of antiquity. Pliny's *Natural History* and the Bible are Acosta's two most important but ultimately inadequate source texts. While Pliny could attribute "the varieties of the human race" to the "ingenuity of Nature," made as "toys for herself and marvels for us," Acosta did not have this playful luxury.[9] In Acosta's account, there was nothing marvelous or playful about human variety, for all had to be understood within a framework of providential design. Acosta's expandable use of scripture accommodates natural wonders, hidden resources, and human practices as phenomena previously inaccessible to biblical authors became newly revealed. In Acosta's *History*, writing is central to both the project of colonization and to the task of transforming experiential discovery into Christian truths. Occasionally, American Indians supplied Acosta and the Jesuit priests, natural philosophers, and theologians with what they were looking for—affirmation of their own deeply held religious convictions and faith-based certainty of God's design. But even while affirming Europeans' own preconditioned beliefs, native populations taught missionaries and settlers something else. Missionary encounters redefined faith, theology, and pious practices, reshaping Christianity into new forms that then reentered a pattern of Atlantic circulation. When news from the New World traveled back to Europe, ancient Christian truths came repackaged in a new light.

Imperial activities in the Americas gave European nations new energy and dynamism. When Charles II chartered the Royal Society in 1662, he outlined his effort to "extend not only the boundaries of Empire, but also the very arts and sciences," envisioning a national agenda for the increase of knowledge that was also connected to the colonial enterprise in the New World.[10] Yet religious ventures in the Americas also exhibited a fractured hierarchy of authority. The activity of the Society of Jesus in New France upheld a utopic vision of spiritual renewal that was cut off from the politics of the Old World.[11] Meanwhile, in New Spain the relationship between the Spanish Crown and the Jesuits underwent sweeping changes over time. During the sixteenth century the Jesuits' actions were deeply bound up with the promotion of the crown's interests, but by the late seventeenth century the Society of Jesus and its interests had become creolized, and conflict with the Spanish authorities and the imperial project became more and more frequent.[12] Puritans fled Old England for New to escape religious persecution but also because they believed that their king and brethren were headed in the wrong spiritual direction and that their religious mission was to redeem God for England.[13] While codifying the national borders and giving shape to Atlantic empires, the motivation for religious journeys to the New World often challenged long-standing structures of authority and religious as well as secular traditions.

The Americas offered a paradoxical enticement for religious immigrants. On the one hand, the land was imagined as a clear and uncontaminated space, ripe with the promise of spiritual renewal. On the other hand, Europeans envisioned vast native populations patiently awaiting conversion, whose recent pagan past provided the impetus for both evangelical fervor and spiritual renewal.[14] The supposed enclosed and pristine space of the convent, for example, offered the setting for the display of exemplary female values in a newly found American paradise. Spanish and French nuns made the arduous Atlantic crossing[15] in order to found convents that would house decorous New World virgins whose purity spoke to the Church's ability to promote female exemplarity in even the most challenging of environments.[16] The Mendicant orders and later the Jesuits founded missions and *reducciones* in many rural and remote regions of Latin America. During the early stages of the evangelization project, the Franciscans, Dominicans, and Augustinians founded large missionary complexes in Mexico and Peru incorporating churches, open-air chapels, schools, and monastery buildings. In the later colonial period, the Jesuits built missions in a variety of geographically removed regions, including the jungle area on the border of present-day Brazil, Paraguay, and Argentina, which they named El Paraguay. By the date of Jesuit expulsion in 1767, the Society ran thirty *reducciones*, or mission towns, where the Guaraní Indians lived, worked, and prayed and received protection from slave raiders. Puritan congregations in New England allowed laymen as well as women new forms of spiritual self-discovery as they orally translated the evidence of grace recorded upon their souls into communal knowledge and a corporate identity that fashioned itself as a spiritual beacon to the world.[17] By the 1650s, Praying Towns began to appear alongside congregational communities, exhibiting a homologous structure of worship, testimony, and church membership.[18] In each case, the Americas provided a setting for spiritual clearing, a way to imagine and refashion forms of piety believed to more closely approximate the primitive Christian church, while also bringing the communion of saints, whether of Roman Catholic or radical Protestant orientation, closer to an imminent moment of millennial fulfillment. In Catholic and Protestant doctrine, the communion of saints bound the faithful on earth to a commitment of spiritual solidarity, which believers understood to be a visible representation of the mystical body of Christ in heaven.

The need to differentiate doctrinal terms through overinflated rhetorical divisions often masked underlying theological parallels between Reformation and Counter-Reformation advocates.[19] The opening sentence of William Bradford's *Of Plymouth Plantation* reflects this rhetorical mask through a language of apocalyptic battle prophesized to take place in the New World under the auspices of reclaiming ancient, primitive Christian purity: "It is well known unto the godly and judicious, how ever since the first breaking out of the light of the gospel in our honorable nation of England, (which was the first of nations whom the Lord adorned therewith after the gross darkness of popery which had covered and overspread the Christian world), what wars and oppositions ever since, Satan hath raised, maintained and continued against the Saints, from time to time, in one sort or other."[20]

While fixated on stopping the spread of the competing Christian faith, both Roman Catholics and Reforming Protestants also came to the Americas with the commensurate aim of establishing new godly kingdoms. To such Europeans, the Americas could be a staging ground for the continuation of an apocalyptic battle between God and Satan. While anticipating the litany of "bloody death and cruel torments" that would mark the path of the righteous through the necessity of martyrdom and Indian wars, ultimately Europeans believed that the "churches of God" and Christian truth would prevail.[21] For all European Christians, the spiritual journey to the Americas marked a homecoming of sorts through an attempt to reclaim the "ancient purity" of an original sacred essence and to reimagine religious community before the onslaught of apocalyptic battles that characterized the sixteenth and seventeenth centuries.

However, just as the authority of the ancients could not be maintained in the face of new experiences, lands and populations, missionaries, ministers, secular priests, and theologians in the early Americas failed to realize this "ancient purity" and "primitive order."[22] In place of millennial reclamation of the ancient church, Christianity experienced a religious reinvention, which often stemmed from the clerical need to institute New World orthodoxy and manage the threat of dissent or heresy—particularly when that threat presented itself in the form of women's religious practice and writing or through the need to suppress or correct American Indian and African interpretations of Christian doctrine. Whether in a rural Mexican mission or a New England congregation, migration patterns to the Americas often led to spiritual disappointment and even despair that had to be managed alongside the need to uphold hopes for spiritual renewal and millennial fulfillment.[23] The European journey across the Atlantic and into the psychological and literal wilderness of the New World became an allegory for the journey of the soul. The particular resonances of time, place, and communities of Africans and American Indians profoundly impacted the Eurocentric ideals that had motivated these journeys. Upon arriving in the Americas, religious individuals necessarily traded a portion of their Old World identity for colonial American selves. Religious identity in the early modern Americas reconstituted itself through a particular confluence of interaction with foreign landscapes, native tribes and complex indigenous civilizations, and new models of community and social interaction.

*   *   *

From the moment of Columbus's arrival in the Americas in 1492 to the loss of Spain's last colonies of Cuba, Puerto Rico, and the Philippines in 1898, Spanish imperial politics became inextricably intertwined with the politics of religion. In the first entry of the *Diario* Columbus directed to the Catholic monarchs, Isabel of Castile and Ferdinand of León, the Genovese navigator framed his expedition in terms of previous Christian triumphs the king and queen had enjoyed: "Whereas, Most Christian, High, Excellent, and Powerful Princes, King and Queen of Spain and of the Islands of the Sea, our Sovereigns, this present year 1492, after your Highnesses had terminated the war with the Moors reigning in Europe, the same having been brought to an end in the great city of Granada, where on the second day of January, this present year, I saw the royal banners of your Highnesses planted by force of arms upon the towers of the Alhambra."[24] Columbus himself would take similar royal banners to the Americas, where he would unfurl them to the undoubted puzzlement of the indigenous Tainos who witnessed his actions: "At two o'clock in the morning the land was discovered, at two leagues' distance; . . . they found themselves near a small island, one of the Lucayos, called in the Indian language Guanahani. Presently they descried people, naked, and the Admiral landed in the boat, which was armed, along with Martin Alonzo Pinzon, and Vincent Yanez his brother, captain of the Nina. The Admiral bore the royal standard, and the two captains each a banner of the Green Cross, which all the ships had carried; this contained the initials of the names of the King and Queen each side of the cross, and a crown over each letter."[25]

The Spanish Crown undertook the financing of the evangelical mission in the New World, and in return the monarchy enjoyed the *Real Patronato* of the Roman Catholic Church in its American territories. The papacy granted the *Patronato* to the Spanish Crown through the promulgation of a series of key bulls in which it awarded Spain sovereignty over the lands it had conquered, as well as control over the religious benefices there. Spain's sovereigns thus enjoyed an unprecedented degree of control over the Church in their dominions.[26]

Under the auspices of the Spanish Crown, large numbers of religious men immigrated to the New World, determined to bring the word of God to those they deemed "pagan." Isolated priests and monks had accompanied many of the conquistadors on their expeditions, the first being the Hieronymite monk, Fray Ramón Pané, who travelled with Columbus on his second voyage and undertook alone the fraught process of indigenous conversion as detailed in his *Relación acerca de las antigüedades de los indios* [*Account of the Antiquities of the Indians*]. Following the completion of the conquest of Tenochtitlan in 1521, Hernán Cortés petitioned Charles V, the Holy Roman Emperor, for help with the evangelization of the latter's new subjects. At the end of the fourth of his five *Cartas de relación* [letters of relation], Cortés pleads with the emperor for the assistance of ordained men: "Each time I have written to Your Sacred Majesty I have told Your Highness of the readiness displayed by some of the natives of these parts to be converted to our Holy Catholic Faith and to become Christians."[27] He discards an earlier plan he and others had made for the sending of bishops, now favoring the Mendicants who would live from tithes with which they might support themselves and build monasteries and churches. Cortés expresses concern that bishops and other Church dignitaries would bring with them the corruption he saw as endemic in the Old World Church: "they [bishops] will only follow the customs which, for our sins, they pursue these days, of squandering the goods of the Church on pomp and ceremony, and other vices, and leaving entailed estates to their sons and kinsmen."[28] Such practices, common in the Spanish Church, worried Cortés, would serve only to make a mockery of the evangelization process. To this end he requested that two "principal persons" in the Order of St. Francis and that of St. Dominic should come to Mexico, invested with the power to consecrate churches and confer holy orders, for example. These purer and less contaminated messengers of the Holy Word, as Cortés apparently conceived of the Dominicans and Franciscans, would not only be able to evangelize the Indians, but also minister to the Spanish who, resident in the Americas for both present and future, found themselves so far from both the "Church of Rome" and "the proper remedies of our consciences."[29]

The Franciscans who arrived in Mexico City in 1523 were the first religious order the pope officially dispatched to the New World as agents of the evangelization process. Almost immediately, the friars began the process of institutionalizing Christianity as envisioned by Cortés in his letter to Charles V. In 1527 they built the first European-style school, San José de los Naturales, where the friars catechized and educated the sons of Indian nobles in the Catholic tradition.[30] Other orders arrived subsequently to build on the work begun by the Franciscans.[31] The Mendicant orders and the Jesuits saw themselves as replicating the work of the primitive church of late antiquity, as well as early medieval saints who brought Christianity to the remote rural regions of Europe. The most ardent manifestation of this belief came from the Franciscans who, influenced by the apocalyptic writings of the twelfth-century Cistercian Abbott Joachim Fiore, believed his designated Third Age would be found in the newly conquered and soon-to-be converted Americas. The Franciscans' "optimistic millenarianism" fought off constant challenges from both other orders as well as from within its own ranks.[32] This representation, even in its initial stages, caused both concrete and discursive difficulties as a land of idolatry and its subjects were to be transformed into an exemplary Christian space. On the surface, their success was great; Motolinía himself claimed that the Franciscans had baptized approximately five million Indians between the years of 1524 and 1536. While these figures have been disputed both by scholars of the time such as Bartolomé de Las Casas as well as current sources, the Franciscans did indeed conduct mass baptisms that allowed them to claim huge numbers of indigenous subjects for the faith.[33] The depth of these conversions is hard to measure as Indians incorporated Christian systems into already established religious practices to produce syncretic versions of the religion the friars imparted to them. Franciscans missionary practices became acculturated with the ancient ways in which indigenous peoples related to their gods.[34] In fact, in the viceroyalty of Peru powerful ancestral rituals associated with mummification of the dead persisted despite the best efforts of extirpators of idolatries.[35] Extirpation processes followed hard on the heels of the "crumbling optimism" of Franciscans during the second half of their evangelization efforts. After decades of mass baptisms and other conversion practices, they could no longer adhere to the belief that the indigenous peoples worshipped false idols through ignorance but instead realized that they clung willfully to demonic cults. The Indians "were no longer innocent pagans but rather Christians sinning against the faith."[36]

Differences in theology and evangelical methodology existed among the different Mendicant orders, the Jesuits, and the secular clergy who ministered to and evangelized the indigenous populations. All believed without question that God had chosen the Spanish Crown to bring the Indians into the Christian fold, and the tensions that existed among them, especially in the early period of the evangelization, speak to the high stakes attending the conversion of the conquered. The confrontation of the Spanish invention of America as a sacred proto-Christian territory with what they saw as the confounding and labile nature of indigenous faith created an anxious and competitive environment for the members of the religious orders who labored there. It is important to remember, moreover, that as we speak of the institutionalization of Christianity in the New World and of the "Church" in general, we are not speaking of a monolithic entity.[37] Disputes between the Mendicants in the early part of the process—particularly between the Dominicans and the Franciscans—as to how best to evangelize the natives manifested themselves acutely in a 1555 letter Motolinía wrote to Charles V, criticizing Las Casas. Motolinía, the Franciscan, accuses Las Casas, the Dominican, of jealousy and of a catalogue of sins against the faith and the crown, including mistreating the Indians in making them his porters as he traveled throughout New Spain, of relentless self-promotion, and of failing to baptize new converts. The Franciscan concept of rebuilding the primitive church in the Indies that imbued their conversion efforts was further hampered by other male religious groups consolidating their own power in the New World: "the sacred soil of America lent itself all too well to turf wars."[38] The secular clergy began to consolidate their own power in the sixteenth century, although they did not rise to dominance until the eighteenth century with the advent of the Bourbon Dynasty in Spain and the reforms they implemented in Spanish America. The greatest upset to the Franciscan vision, however, came in the closing decades of the sixteenth century, with the arrival of the Jesuits in Mexico City in 1572.

After many different attempts and false starts to obtain the presence of the Society in New Spain, the Jesuits arrived in Mexico in 1572.[39] It was not the activities of the mission field but rather the Christian humanist education of the white settler class that underwrote the arrival of the Jesuits in New Spain.[40] The Jesuits had resisted requests for their presence in New Spain for almost twenty years as they focused their energies on their mission to the East and on areas of the New World where other religious orders had yet to make an imprint. Their efforts to evangelize the natives in Florida, however, had resulted only in the killing of eight Jesuit missionaries in 1571, and led them to look toward New Spain as a possible site for their ministry.[41] In the same year as the Floridian tragedy, the *Cabildo* of Mexico City had written to Philip II requesting help with the education of young Spanish and Creole men whom they feared at risk of idleness and degeneracy for lack of grounding in

Latin and other important educational skills. Phillip responded by turning to the Jesuits, who were rapidly gaining fame for their expertise in education through their network of colleges in Europe and beyond. The Society replicated and expanded this educational project in colonial Mexico and in other colonies throughout Brazil and Hispanic America.

Jesuit colleges formed an important part of the Spanish urban landscape in the Americas. The Spanish used the foundation of their cities in the New World as the staging ground for the creation of Christian life in the colony.[42] Even before Philip II's Royal Ordinances of 1573 crystallized the details of urbanization, the Spaniards had shown their predilection for replicating European city life in the Americas. In what is known today as Cortés's first *Carta de relación*, his supporters tell of their leader's founding of the first city in Mexico, the Muy Rica Villa de la Vera Cruz. The letter's authors style themselves as the "Justiciary and Municipal Council" of the aforementioned city and describe Cortés's establishing of the city in Charles V's name, detailing the particular benefits this foundational act would bring to the emperor: "With great diligence he [Cortés] set about founding and settling a town . . . and appointed those whose names are signed at the bottom of this paper as alcaldes and regidores of the town, and received from us in Your Royal Highnesses' name the solemn vow customary in such cases."[43]

The institutionalization of the conquest via the founding of urban centers stands as the hallmark of Spain's intervention in the New World. In cities such as Cuzco and Mexico City they dismantled and refashioned indigenous polities into bastions of European values. Religious architecture in the form of parish churches, schools, colleges, monasteries, and convents stood as the most potent architectural reminder of the Spanish presence in the new cities with which colonizers hoped to replicate Spanish urban civilization in the New World. The first cathedral built in newly conquered Tenochtitlan was intended as only a provisional indication of Spanish dominance in religion and culture and was hurriedly constructed with stones from the Aztec Templo Mayor. Construction began with the arrival of the metropolis's first bishop, the Franciscan Friar Juan de Zumárraga, in 1524, and was completed ten years later.[44] Planning for a new cathedral began as the first building reached completion, clearly demonstrating the crown's desire to employ elaborately monumental sacred architecture in the service of the imposition of a new societal order and to provide a testament to the successes of the processes of evangelization. Construction on the Catedral Metropolitana de la Asunción

Figure 1. "Cathedral de México," 1858, Désiré Charnay, Getty Research Institute, Los Angeles.

de María that stands today in the *zócalo* in Mexico City began in the 1570s, and it would take over two hundred years to complete.[45]

Missions were an important part of Spanish and Portuguese religious identity and produced similarly monumental architecture designed to impact the neophyte Christians who gazed upon it. The Jesuits built extensive missions in the Brazilian Amazon region in the sixteenth and seventeenth centuries, although their progress and success in conversion was fitful and characterized by multiple hardships. The Maranhão region held the greatest concentration of Jesuit missions, and, in 1653 António Vieira, towering figure of the Latin American baroque, was named the area's Superior. His work in the Maranhão brought him into constant conflict with Portuguese slave raiders and settlers as the Jesuits sought to protect the Indians who lived within the mission complexes in *aldeias*, or Indian villages. Despite the enormous challenges missionary work presented, Vieira's vision of the Jesuits as a Society of Apostles ministering to the Indians held fast, and he rejected the emphasis on scholarly and educational work the Society carried out in their urban *colegios*, where they ministered primarily to the Creole population. At age eighty, living in retirement in Bahia, he became Jesuit Visitor in Brazil and used his position to convince Jesuit novices of his beliefs regarding their role. He preached two *Exhortações* at the Bahian college that, according to Thomas Cohen, can best be understood as "an intimate statement of Vieira's theory and methodology of mission."[46] In *Exhortacam I em vespora do Espíritu Santo* [*First Exhortation on the Eve of the Holy Spirit*] he urges them to turn their back on the scholarly life and to instead engage in the authentic apostolic work of the mission field: "And what greater honor (seeing that we are so attached to these *honorinhas*) and what greater honor than for me to enter with God into my part in the greatest work of His omnipotence? Who converted these gentiles? God and I. God with His grace, and I with my teaching. God entered into this work with His part and I with mine."[47]

Throughout the sixteenth century, the Protestant Reformation ideals of *sola scriptura* and *sola fides* fueled a variety of sectarian visions, united only through their collective indictment of Catholicism. While these transformations took place throughout Europe, the English initiated a new plan for state intervention in religious affairs through Queen Elizabeth's settlement of 1559, which mandated conformity with the Church of England. While this settlement facilitated a temporary resolution, the church's authority soon splintered further, as nonconforming Protestants clashed with the episcopal polity. Religious conflict intensified from the 1580s through the end of James I's reign through repeated appeals to antiquity and patristic evidence as a plea for further reform. Refusing to conform to the laws of church and state under the repressive regime of Archbishop Laud, Puritans and other radical Protestant sects left England in search of new lands and communities where they could practice their faith free from fear of persecution. The geographic expanse of the Reformation became an enticement for communal movements to Germany or the Netherlands and then eventually to America.[48]

In contrast to the Spanish, there was little regularity to the English communities established in seventeenth-century North America. Early Anglo communities were much less structured, each forging a corporate identity out of the wilderness through a general sense of a close-knit community.[49] Maintaining a looser structure of central authority than the Spanish, the English Crown issued patents, or land grants, according property rights to companies investing in colonial enterprises. Elizabeth I granted the first patent to

Humphrey Gilbert and Sir Walter Raleigh in 1578 to discover and settle "remote and heathen and barbarous lands."[50] In contrast to the vast financial engine that the Americas came to be for the Spanish Empire, the English viewed the colonies as serving multiple functions. The momentous publication of Thomas Harriot's *Brief and True Report of the Newfound Land of Virginia* (1588) succinctly encapsulates the colonial agenda of the British Isles in the late-sixteenth century. As one of the first eyewitness accounts of the New World, Harriot's *Brief and True Report* became an immediate success. It was reprinted in 1589 in Richard Hakluyt's *Principal Navigations* and then in a four-language edition, accompanied with Theodor de Bry's engravings, in 1590.[51] Divided into three sections, the text is part promotional tract of merchantable commodities, part catalogue of natural resources to be found in America, and part ethnography of the Carolinian Algonquian population. Written as an account of Sir Walter Raleigh's first colonial venture, the *Brief and True Report* faced the task of overriding the "envious, malicious, and slanderous reports" that were already circulating in England by the time Harriot returned in 1586. His aim was to restore the "the honor and benefit of [the English] nation" and in doing so, to make a good case for the benefits of colonization.[52] The *Brief and True Report* offers the potential investor a vision of a land ripe for cultivation.

As part of his promotional strategy, Harriot familiarized the unfamiliar. In his catalogue of resources "knowne to yeelde for victual and sustenance," he identifies several agricultural goods by their Algonquian name. "Wickonzowr," Harriot reports, is "called by us *Peaze.*" He explains that the English reader will find that these peas look much like English peas in form, but they are "far better" in "goodness and taste."[53] Harriot gives a detailed account of how the crop of peas might be cultivated: "their setting or sowing is after this manner." In the 1590 edition, de Bry's engraving accompanied the text to make this textual description visually familiar by presenting the reader with a bucolic scene of cultivation that the reader is then invited to emulate (Figure 2).

Harriot's ethnographic observations, "Of the nature and manners of the people," replicates the pattern of his two preceding sections on merchantable commodities and natural resources. He describes cultural difference in such as way as to render the Algonquians more recognizable to the reader, thus lessening the cultural divide.[54] In doing so, *The Brief and True Report* collapses the observed phenomenon into an intelligible frame of reference. In describing Algonquian homes, Harriot reports that "their houses are made of small poles made fast at the tops in rounde forme after the manner as is sued in

Figure 2. Theodor de Bry, *Admiranda narratio, fida tamen, de commodis et incolarum ritibus Virginiæ* (1590), Rare Books Library, Princeton University.

many arbories in our gardens in England."[55] After describing a manner of home building that the English reader would have perceived as entirely unfamiliar, Harriot compares the construction to an English arbor so that the reader has a point of reference. After numerous such comments on dress, habitation, war, and government, Harriot turns to religion as the solvent of universal humanism. Of the Algonquian's existing belief system, Harriot reports: "some religion they have already, which although it be farre from the truth, yet beyng at it is, there is hope it may bee the easier and sooner reformed."[56] Harriot warns the reader that that the native religion he is about to relate will seem entirely unfamiliar, while offering the reassurance that the fact of the Algonquian's faith makes them more susceptible to Christian conversion. Christianity thus becomes the umbrella term through which Harriot's observations on the nature and manner of the Algonquians can be massaged into purportedly universal recognition.

Harriot described a land replete with potential for plantation, commonwealth, and Christianity to prosper. Despite the financial setbacks of early English colonial efforts, the Virginia Company formed in 1606 under James I, instigating an intimate connection between clergy and colonization. Sermons became one of the principle means through which the company sought promotion. Several of England's well-known clergymen, such as William Crashaw, Samuel Purchas, and Alexander Whitaker preached about the moral riches to be found through the establishment of British commonwealths on the eastern seaboard of North America.[57] In 1613, Whitaker, for example, presented a vision of Virginia where "Magistracie and Ministrery are the strength and sinewes; nay the very life and being of a Christian body politique."[58] Integral to reinvigorating the English colonial project in the early seventeenth century, promotional tracts represented the land as ripe, plentiful, and either vacant or scantily inhabited by welcoming Indians.

An example of the English fantasy of an uninhabited land, John Cotton's *God's Promise to His Plantations* (1634) paints an eerily vacant picture of the land to be found in the New World. Cotton wrote this sermon before his own voyage to America. It presents a Puritan fantasy of an open and inhabitable wilderness that contrasts sharply with the detailed ethnographic accounts to be found in Acosta, Lescarbot, and De Laet, as well as in English writing by Hakluyt and Harriot.[59] In an imagined sermonic portrait of the New World, Cotton used the scriptural authority of 2 Samuel 7:10 to explain that God will clear the land by "making a Countrey, though not altogether void of Inhabitants, yet void in that place where they reside. Where there is a vacant place, there is liberty for the Son of Adam and Noah." Cotton establishes a direct typological link between the migration of seventeenth-century Puritans to the New World and the scriptural precedent of a vacant land where they may be "fruitful." Like Harriot and Whitaker, Cotton surmises that any "native People" who reside there will view the "foreign people" favorably. In doing so, Cotton willingly elided recent histories of war and violence such as the Indian massacre of 1622 that was reported in John Smith's *Generall Historie of Virginia* (1624).[60] This system of colonization based on royal patents and sponsoring companies meant that laws, social structures, and customs were imported from England, but without the proximity of the state and its various supporting institutions. When the Pilgrims and Puritans migrated in 1620 and 1630 respectively, they did so with the intention of contesting the power of the crown to mandate religious uniformity. They believed in a Calvinist-based religion that espoused a separation of church and state but that also privileged the spiritual authority of the individual to such a degree as to leave no clear signposts about how the disparate individuals practicing these faiths should form communities.

New religious communities appeared in Plymouth (1620), the Massachusetts Bay Colony (1630), and Rhode Island and Connecticut (1636). Collectively, they plotted to continue the work of the Reformation within the Anglo-American world as a way of reclaiming God for England. Close-knit communities were built around the individualized notion of faith, which then proliferated out from the individual to a sense of collective responsibility, corporate identity, and millennial fulfillment. Because the Puritans did not bring the authority of English law or ecclesiological polity with them, they were soon faced with the question of how to protect fragile communities of native newcomers from factionalism and conflict.[61] Protection from factionalism came in the form of an entirely new system of church governance and law.[62] In the 1640s, the congregational system developed out of a communal attempt to implement familiar religious convictions in an entirely unfamiliar setting. New England churches departed significantly from their Reformed counterparts in the Netherlands and the Low Countries by introducing the concept of a church covenant, or a contract between the elect and God, and spiritual testimony as a prerequisite for church membership. The consequences of these innovations in church practice were felt back home, as a sharp line divided Presbyterians and Congregationalists by 1643. While Presbyterians argued for a national church and a hierarchy that could mirror the structure of church bishops, Congregationalists insisted upon an autonomous visible church existing exclusively in local congregations.[63] These disagreements over church polity fueled different ways of imagining the Reformation of England's churches during the Civil War. Many Puritans returned home during this time.[64] Others turned their attention toward missionary endeavors.[65]

Anglo-Protestant missionaries, such as John Eliot, Roger Williams, and Thomas Mayhew viewed the successful conversion of American Indian populations as a culminating phase within the cycle of the New World errand.[66] The belief that all men were the sons of Adam and that history would eventuate in the second coming of Christ supplied Anglo-Protestant missionaries with a rationale for civilization and evangelization.[67] This vision was never realized in missionary practice. The ways that *Wôpanâak* audiences interpreted meaning often departed from the doctrinal intentions of Eliot, Thomas Shepard, and other missionaries.[68] One of Eliot's late missionary tracts, *Indian Dialogues,* constructs a conversation between three Indians, Penoowot, Waban, and Nishoukou. Modeling this text after the philosophical genre codified by Plato in the fourth century B.C.E., Eliot intended the *Dialogues* to be "instructive" rather than didactic, so that the Anglo reader would learn upon reading the text "what might or should have been said." Immediately, this tract introduces the ambiguity of meaning intrinsic to the process of translating Christianity to indigenous communities. Through a series of dialogues staged between Praying Indians and their unconverted kinsman, readers learned that the resistance to Christianity often came in the form of confusion over the relationship between matter and spirit: "If your praying to God do indeed teach you the true way of being rich, as you say, how cometh it to pass that you are so poor still?" Piumbuhhou, the "Learned Indian" within the "Indian Church," explains to his congregation that there is a difference between earthly and heavenly riches and that knowledge of God, grace, and Jesus is the greatest attainable wealth. Piumbuhou conveys this meaning by separating the Anglo-Protestant interpretation of scripture from the knowledge that may be gleaned through the autonomous interpretation of the Christian reader: "The Book of God is no invention of English-men, it is the holy Law of God himself, which was given unto man by God, before English-men had any knowledge of God." Piumbuhhou describes the Bible as a repository of ancient Christian wisdom, bespeaking a truth that transcends national as well as linguistic affiliation. Rather than supplanting indigenous belief with unwavering Christian truths, missionaries depended on a palimpsest of layered meaning.[69] Through a process that David Silverman calls "religious translation," missionaries filtered

Christian teachings through Wôpanâak religious ideas.[70] By the end of the seventeenth century, these elements of religious syncretism gradually revealed that the Wôpanâak could not be as easily enfolded into a Christian cosmos as Eliot had initially hoped. The combined force of King Philip's War, of a missionary enterprise that became in the 1680s too costly to sustain in relation to its achieved results, and of a Massachusett-English Christian world of fluctuating rather than fixed meaning caused Eliot to enter into a state of near despair and effectively ended the first phase of the Protestant mission to the American Indians.[71]

The presence of Africans brought forcibly to the Americas for economic gain further challenged theological commonplaces. In England, the Royal African Company was formed in 1660. Unlike missionary societies of the time, such as the New England Company for the Propagation of the Gospel, the Royal African Company members directed their financial efforts toward the transportation of bodies rather than the salvation of souls. A financial engine of the British Isles, the company supplied slaves to British colonies in Jamaica, Maryland, and Virginia.[72] Fearing that baptism would lead to manumission, the ministers and political elites stationed in these imperial outposts tended to oppose converting Africans and their descendants to Christianity.[73] This position had a religious justification in the Curse of Ham. According to Benjamin Braude, the link between this portion of scripture and the slave trade became increasingly prominent in England between 1590 and 1625, along with the rise of the slave trade and plantation system.[74] It was not until the 1700s and 1710s that clergy began to deny that baptism conferred manumission. Yet as ministers such as Cotton Mather made a case for the conversion of Africans in his *Negro Christianized* (1708), he did so by arguing that Christianity would in fact make slaves more productive. Similar arguments appeared before the British Parliament as proposed legislation. Until the first Great Awakening (1740), if conversion to Christianity was encouraged at all it was to make Africans more effective slaves. Following the mid-eighteenth-century revivals, however, the Christian conversion of peoples of African descent happened *en masse* through the efforts of George Whitfield and others. The writers that Vincent Carretta has grouped together as the "black authors" of the eighteenth-century Anglo world shared this Christian identity in common.[75] Phillis Wheatley, Olaudah Equiano, and Ukawsaw Gronniosaw began to deploy their Christian identities strategically in an effort to reconfigure the strict bifurcation between spiritual equality and social hierarchy that elite white members of the Anglo-Protestant world fought so ardently to uphold.

The traffic in African slaves in the Atlantic world imposed radical demographic, cultural, and religious transformations upon the early modern Americas as enslaved peoples from different tribal areas of the continent arrived in the major slave port cities of the New World. Between 1542, when Charles V's decree officially prohibited the enslavement of indigenous peoples, and 1550, records indicate the arrival of fifteen thousand African slaves into Spain's American territories.[76] In 1518 Charles V had decreed that all enslaved Africans must arrive in his American territories as Christians, although he issued no instructions regarding the details of how they would attain this status, and Africans came to Christianity in a variety of different ways.[77] Portuguese missionaries had been active in areas of central Africa, and the King of Kongo and some members of the region's population had converted to Christianity in 1491 and, in return for Portuguese assistance in local wars, provided them with captives for the slave trade.[78] Most African slaves, however, had conversion forced upon them after being captured or sold into bondage. Agents of the Portuguese Crown carried out perfunctory baptisms in ports and trading posts in Africa in order that those who survived the horrors of the Middle Passage would arrive in Spain and Portugal's American dominions as Christians. The Spanish Jesuit Alonso de Sandoval, who worked in the Colombian port city of Cartagena de Indias, criticized these types of baptisms in his 1627 treatise on African slavery, *De instauranda Aethiopum salute*. *De instauranda* offers a detailed look at different African ethnicities and languages and belief systems of the enslaved peoples who arrived in Cartagena to become enslaved subjects of the Spanish Crown. Sandoval denounces the mistreatment of slaves and includes the lack of Christian education offered to them before baptism in the slave ports among his critiques. He includes a letter from a fellow Jesuit, who reports: "I have testimony from the slave merchants themselves that in the Angolan port called Luanda, black slaves are simply lined up in the plaza one day before they set sail. . . . Up until this point they have been in prison. They do not learn the catechism and do not even know anything about God. . . . When the slaves are asked what they think baptism means, some say that it puts a spell on them so that the Spanish can eat them."[79]

Some Africans received religious education upon arrival in the Americas since royal ordinances mandated slave owners permit their slaves to attend church on Sundays and feast days and receive religious instruction. Despite the staggering demographic transformations the importation of African slaves wrought upon Hispanic America, there is little information regarding the evangelization and indoctrination of African slaves. This lack of information speaks to the general negligence with which church and crown approached the religious education of enslaved African peoples.[80] Africans and their descendants nonetheless actively transformed Christianity, leaving behind indelible manifestations that mark American Christianity to this day. Despite their exclusion from religious orders and other church institutions, Afro-Hispanic Christians formed their own Christian identities through the formation of groups such as confraternities. These types of local organizations permitted Afro-Christians to form their own communities of worship and social welfare in which Afro-Christian practices were woven into a structure originally imported from the metropolis.[81] Afro-Christian identity also operated in ways the church authorities could not have anticipated: Inquisition documents show how slaves strategically renounced Christianity and denounced themselves for blasphemy in order to call forth the protection of the Holy Office in the face of harrowing mistreatment by owners.[82]

*   *   *

This cross-disciplinary volume aspires to grasp the complexity and variety of the colonial world as it augmented, transformed, and challenged a range of Christian beliefs, while also maintaining nuanced attention to the particularities of a diverse range of communities and experiences. It is our hope that the interdisciplinary model and comparative methodological framework we outline here will suggest new ways of thinking about religious practice along a wider geographical axis and a greater chronological expanse, while also inviting further reflection on the participation of women, Native American populations, and the African diaspora in the transformation of religion in the New World.

The transformation of Christianity in the early modern Americas functions as the central organizing principle of this volume and provides a basis for our North-South hemispheric comparative analysis. Religion provides a provocative lens through which to view patterns of restriction, exclusion, and tension as well as those of acculturation, accommodation, and resistance in a comparative colonial context. The juxtaposition of New World religions across the hemispheric divide throws into relief the fervor with which church authorities attempted to establish New World communities of the faithful while at the same time controlling indigenous populations, subaltern Africans and their descendants, and disparate modes of female spiritual expression. Both doctrine and practice became vehicles for managing tensions between spiritual equality and social hierarchy. Meanwhile, through adherence to official and popular religious manifestations, these same communities of the faithful often exceeded the boundaries that church officials created for them as they shaped colonial societies.

As a topic of comparative analysis, religion produces challenges as well as opportunities. It provides a common basis of discussion across boundaries of discipline, field, language, and region, while also exposing the historical variances produced as Protestant and Catholic Reformation theologies defined themselves in opposition to one another. The formation of New World communities on both American continents, and the impact that these communities had on European, indigenous, and African religious traditions, presents new connections across what has been traditionally conceived of in scholarship as an Anglo-Protestant versus an Iberian-Catholic paradigm. While Catholics and Protestants formed their respective doctrines and theologies in a dialectic fashion throughout the early modern period, imperial religious enterprises in the New World were in many respects parallel endeavors. Each linked religious ideas and legal government to the organization and maintenance of a colonial community that also sought to extend its boundaries through missionary projects. Each also juggled commercial initiative with the embrace of moral tradition to engage in an ongoing project of adapting and refining religiously grounded visions of community with the experience of collective life in an unfamiliar place and among indigenous strangers, and, later on, a significant population of African slaves.

The aforementioned elements demonstrate trans-hemispheric continuities and fruitful inter-American points of contact concerning the formation of communities, the tension between liturgical practices and popular religious manifestations, and the control of resistant and marginalized groups of neophyte Christians that readers will find threaded throughout the essays contained in this volume. At the same time, the individual essays attend to specific dimensions of conversion, communal structure, and religious authority unique to the experiences of the Ibero-Catholic and Anglo-Protestant regions and thus avoid paving over real differences in the service of a seamless comparative model. While this volume reflects our attempt to map some general points of contrast and patterns of similarity in New World religious communities composed of different European nationalities and systems of religious belief, we also write from the perspective that we should proceed with this comparative methodological approach with caution, aware of its limitations as well as its possibilities. Important differences that accord with the political, economic, and religious climate of Old World countries should not be elided in the service of making general claims about New World discoveries, settlements, and patterns of colonization. While we aim to present a series of topics and themes that can speak to both the Iberian and Anglo experiences, we realize that the analysis presented in this framework offers only one slice of a more comprehensive picture.

In offering our comparative approach to religion we aim to elucidate a range of experiences within the rubric identified above. At the same time, through the juxtaposition of scholarship dealing with religious transformations from northern and southern hemispheres, we set forth a larger aim. We believe that there is historical significance to this conversation that extends beyond the need to produce new comparisons or to try to anticipate the future directions of our respective fields. This significance lies in the integral part that the study of early modern American religion plays in understanding the development of modernity. It is for this reason that we have chosen to focus primarily on the Anglo-Protestant presence in North America and the Ibero-Catholic presence in Latin America. The Ibero-Catholic and Anglo-Protestant division has perpetuated cultural stereotypes and scholarly paradigms of Anglo-Protestantism as bringing modernity to the New World, while Ibero-Catholicism promoted monolithic Christian conversion and repressive Catholic regimes. Part of our methodological aim in this volume is thus to revise this historical and cross-cultural inaccuracy, which has arisen partially out of the exceptionalist paradigm that has long shaped the myths associated with early American studies and out of the persistence of the tenets of the Black Legend in positioning colonial Latin American studies within the American academy.[83] One way in which to achieve this goal is to invite scholars together to talk about the topic of religion in their respective fields and disciplines. Such cross-disciplinary conversation contributes more knowledge of the religious experiences of the peoples contained within the geographic borders of each empire while also decoding some of the disciplinary concerns and terminologies that often render our work impenetrable or, in the worst case, irrelevant to those from other, seemingly related disciplines.

PART I

Comparisons

CHAPTER 1

Religions on the Move

J. H. ELLIOTT

In his *General History of the Indies*, published in 1552, Francisco López de Gómara famously observed: "The greatest event since the creation of the world (excluding the incarnation and death of Him who created it) is the discovery of the Indies."[1] It would take time to realize the full implications of Columbus's landfall, but Columbus himself had no hesitation in relating it to God's providential design for the salvation of the human race.[2] Future ages might see the event as marking a decisive moment in what would become the inexorable advance of Europe toward global domination, but for contemporaries and near-contemporaries it took its place in a spiritual, rather than a secular, interpretation of human history—an interpretation that moved in linear progression from the Fall of man to his ultimate redemption through Christ's suffering and sacrifice. In this great drama of sin and salvation, Christendom's discovery of a previously unknown world inhabited by millions of people who lived in benighted ignorance of the Gospel represented at once a challenge and a hope. The challenge was to bring to these peoples the truths of Christianity. The hope was that their conversion would hasten the return of Christ in triumph and the ending of the world.[3]

The priorities of the sixteenth century are not those of today, as Gómara's words remind us, and they serve as a helpful corrective to a historiography that tends to separate the religious from the more secular aspects of Europe's conquest and colonization of the Americas, and give the latter the primacy. Religious history needs to be more closely integrated with the history of the political and economic domination of the indigenous peoples of the Americas by European conquerors and colonists. Such an integration would, after all, be no more than a reflection of sixteenth-century realities. For those, whether Europeans or Native Americans, who experienced in their own lives the encounter of different civilizations, the division between the sacred and the profane was far from clear-cut. Even the most callous *encomendero* was likely to give at least fitful consideration to the state of his soul and his prospects for salvation, whatever his view of the Indians submitted to his charge. They, for their part, were as likely to be traumatized by the destruction of familiar spiritual signposts as by the new forms of labor service to which they found themselves subjected. On both sides of the encounter there were new relationships to be worked out, and major adjustments to be made. Conquerors and conquered, together with those who found themselves on the edges of the growing European intrusion into the hemisphere, had to come to terms with an American landscape that was new to all parties—a landscape in which the spiritual, the natural, and the human were inextricably interlinked.

Historians are faced with the problem of charting, understanding, and assessing the changes brought about on both sides of the Atlantic by the incorporation of the New World within the orbit of the Old. A focus on the process of change does not preclude an appreciation of the continuities, which in many instances may well have been greater, and more significant, than transformations that often were no more than superficial. But the Americas during the colonial period were a world in transition, and religion played a central part in that transitional process. It was a process, spanning three centuries or more, that involved three continents—Europe, America, and Africa—and one that cries out for study in a broad Atlantic context,[4] while not forgetting that its implications extend far beyond the Atlantic to encircle the globe. How much, for instance, was the Chinese rites controversy of the seventeenth century influenced by the experiences of the religious orders in America?[5]

The theme of this volume, *Religious Transformations in the Early Modern Americas*, raises four fundamental questions. First, how, and with what aspirations, did religious creeds and practices make the transatlantic crossing, and how were they modified as they adapted to their new American environment? Second, what was their impact and the extent of their influence on the beliefs and practices of the indigenous societies with which they came into contact? Third, what part did religion play in giving the emerging colonial societies their distinctive characteristics? Finally, what impact did religious developments in America have on the home country?

None of these questions is easily answered, and the fourth, in particular, has received far too little study. Would sixteenth-century Spain, for instance, have had more success in converting and assimilating its Morisco population if so many elite members of the religious orders had not devoted their energies to the conversion of the indigenous peoples of Mexico and Peru? Similarly, how did the departure to the New World of leading figures like John Winthrop and John Cotton affect the character of the Puritan movement in England, and how far were the upheavals of the English Civil War and the Interregnum influenced by the return of New England pastors anxious to build Jerusalem in their mother country?[26] For all the differences introduced by the transatlantic extension of their religious systems and beliefs, Spain and Spanish America shared, and continued to share, the same religious space, just as Britain and British America shared the same religious space. The same was true, in some degree at least, of continental European Protestant communities and their American extensions. Only in the African world was there a total rupture, since there was no communication between Africans separated by the ocean, and—at least until the end of the eighteenth century—no return journey.

Answers to these questions have to take into account important variations over both space and time. As they advanced into American space, the Spaniards came up against densely settled populations and sophisticated political organizations, both in Central America and in the Andes. The English, by contrast, established their settlements in sparsely settled regions, inhabited by small tribal polities. This meant that the process of settlement was likely from the beginning to assume different forms in the Iberian American and the Anglo-American worlds. For the same reason, relationships with the indigenous populations—numerically much larger in Iberian than British America—were likely to be different. All Europeans followed the Spanish example in lumping together the indigenous peoples under the brand name of "Indian." In fact Native peoples varied widely in terms of lifestyle and social organization, just as they also varied in their belief systems and ceremonial practices.

Differences in timing were also critical for the nature of the transatlantic transfer. When the English founded their Jamestown settlement in 1607, Spain's empire of the Indies was more than a century old, and the Iberian colonial societies were by then well established. Nowhere did the time lag have more significant consequences than in the realm of religion. That intervening century had seen the advent of the Protestant Reformation. The English, followed by the Dutch and the Scandinavians, brought with them across the Atlantic a Protestant version of Christianity with its own evolving characteristics and attitudes. The first Spanish friars and clerics to arrive in the New World had set sail from a Christendom that was at least nominally united. Now Christendom, and by extension Christendom overseas, was divided into two warring camps. The age of confessionalization brought a new militancy, a hardening of religious attitudes on both sides of the religious divide, and an enhanced concern with uniformity, discipline, and control. For all the importance of developments on the ground in America, events in the Old World dictated, and would continue to dictate, much of what happened in the New.

The differences in timing and environment inevitably complicate the task of drawing comparisons between the Iberian Catholic and the predominantly British Protestant New World. Over the period of a century filled with dramatic developments, there were bound to be major changes both in motivation and method. Yet if we observe the differences, we should also note the similarities. While the Protestant Reformation marks a major chronological divide, Protestantism and Roman Catholicism, in drawing on the same scriptures and early Christian Fathers, still had much in common, for all their doctrinal and ceremonial differences. The distinct parts of a disunited Christendom, interacting with each other, moved and would continue to move in broadly the same direction, even if at a different pace. By the eighteenth century, as the age of confessionalization yielded to the age of the Enlightenment, all churches and faiths, whether Catholic or Protestant, found themselves confronting the same challenge—the challenge of rationalism, scientific inquiry, and a growing secularization of values.

Bearing in mind both the continuities and the ruptures, what differences and similarities can be usefully identified in response to the first question, the nature of the transatlantic transfer? The Spanish Christianity transmitted to the Indies was a Christianity forged during the centuries of struggle to free the Iberian Peninsula from Moorish domination. The character it assumed as a permanent crusade against Islam gave it a militant and triumphalist edge, which from the fourteenth century onward found vivid symbolic expression in the annual celebration of the feast of Corpus Christi and the reenactment in dance form of the battles of Christians against Moors—a reenactment that would come to be repeated in the remotest villages of postconquest Mexico and Peru.[7] Coinciding as it did with the victorious completion of the Reconquista, Columbus's discovery of new peoples and new lands on the farther shores of the Atlantic strengthened the providentialist and messianic overtones already present in Spanish religion and gave it new direction and purpose, in the form of a global mission for the propagation of the faith and the encirclement and final overthrow of Islam.

If Spanish Christianity at the moment of discovery was shaped by its crusading heritage, it was also shaped by the movement for spiritual renewal that swept across late fifteenth and early sixteenth-century Christendom, giving impetus to reformist elements in the religious orders and encouraging reform of the Spanish church under royal leadership. The allocation by the papacy of the newly discovered lands to the Spanish and Portuguese crowns in return for a commitment to bring their pagan inhabitants within the Christian fold ensured that, from the earliest stages of conquest and colonization, Spain's religious mission became a state-sponsored and state-supported enterprise. As a result, during the centuries of Spanish rule in America, church and crown would work together in a mutually advantageous although often uncomfortable symbiosis.

But it was to the religious orders, and not to the secular clergy, that Hernán Cortés turned to undertake the massive task of evangelizing the millions of inhabitants of Mexico who had now became vassals of the Spanish crown. The arrival in New Spain in 1524 of Observant Franciscans—the Twelve Apostles— followed by the Dominicans and Augustinians in 1526 and 1533, placed a lasting imprint on Spain's enterprise of the Indies, even though the religious orders would be forced to give ground to the institutional church as the century proceeded. The early apostles of the Indies and several of their successors saw their mission as forming part of that movement for the spiritual renewal of Christendom to which they owed their missionary zeal.[8]

In the eschatological system that many of them held as an article of faith, the world was fast approaching its end.[9] But the prelude for the return of Christ in judgment would be the conversion of its peoples, and in the unbaptized millions of the New World's inhabitants the friars saw a harvest ripe for the gathering. Significantly, in 1531 the first of what were to be the many plays performed in post-conquest Mexico was entitled *The Last Judgment*, acted in Nahuatl by a cast of eight hundred Indian converts, and written by the Franciscan Fray Andrés de Olmos.[10] The millenarian expectations surrounding the European discovery of America immediately gave it a unique place in God's providential design, and this place was all the more important because, at first sight, the New World appeared to be uncontaminated by the vices of the Old. It therefore became sacred ground, a world in which Christianity could be implanted in the pure form of the primitive church. As such, it was a fit location for the building of the New Jerusalem. Not surprisingly, imported European books that included illustrations of an imagined reconstruction of Solomon's Temple in Jerusalem were to be found in the libraries of sixteenth-century New Spain, and served as a basis for attempts to build replicas in America.[11]

Spanish America therefore would become the scene for holy experiments, like Vasco de Quiroga's "pueblo-hospitals" of Santa Fe on the shores of Lake Pátzcuaro, and the later Jesuit missions in Paraguay.[12] But Spain's "enterprise of the Indies" was much more than a missionary enterprise. It was also an imperial project, and this required the imposition of the instruments and agencies of central authority, like viceroys, judicial tribunals, and all the apparatus of ecclesiastical government—bishops and cathedral chapters, parish priests, and tithes. By the end of the seventeenth century the church in Spanish America was organized into five archbishoprics and thirty bishoprics.[13] Although the religious orders managed to hold their own—they had some three thousand members in mid-seventeenth century New Spain, as against two thousand secular clergy[14]—the progressive institutionalization of religious life in the Indies, which also affected the religious orders themselves, brought it closer to the model of metropolitan Spain. But the church in America was always nearer to being a royal preserve in America than it was in Spain. No papal nuncio was allowed to set foot in the New World, and the ultimate authority rested with the Council of the Indies in Madrid.

The church as it developed in the Indies was a world away from the primitive Christian church that the friars had hoped to establish in their first flush of excitement as they set about baptizing thousands upon thousands of innocent souls. Every religious movement undergoes change as the process of institutionalization sets in, and what began as a missionary church in the Indies was no exception to the rule. A bureaucratic empire needs the support of a bureaucratic church, and this was all the more necessary when, as in Spain's empire of the Indies, the justification for its titles to land and dominion was based on its willingness and ability to accomplish its divinely ordained evangelizing mission. But the institutionalization of religion was accompanied by a decline in the initial fervor with which the mendicant orders first approached their evangelizing work. Increasing wealth and power undermined the original message of simplicity and poverty and gave the institutionalized church, and the religious orders themselves, a degree of independence that became a constant irritant to the agents of royal authority. The alliance of throne and altar was, and remained, the lynchpin of the system, but the regalist campaigns periodically launched by the crown, and pursued with increasing vigor in the eighteenth century, were a reflection of its perception that neither the religious orders nor the secular clergy were as amenable to royal control as they ought to be.[15]

Yet, in spite of church-state tensions, the Christianization of the Indies remained a resolutely state-directed enterprise, with the crown responding to the wishes of the papacy only in ways that it deemed appropriate, and in firm charge of ecclesiastical policy toward the New World. It met the costs of the transatlantic passages of members of the religious orders,[16] and it placed tight controls on emigration to America, restricting it to the king's Spanish subjects, and forbidding the passage of Moors, Jews, and, from 1552, of those who could not prove their purity of blood.[17] Spanish America was to become a bastion of orthodoxy, at least in theory if not necessarily in practice,[18] and the crown's determination to ensure that it remained so was further enhanced by the transatlantic transfer of the Inquisition, with the establishment of tribunals of the Holy Office in Lima in 1570 and Mexico City in 1571.

A comparison of the motivation and methods of the transfer of English religion to America with those involved in the transatlantic transfer of Spanish religion, suggests some striking contrasts, in spite of certain similarities. To establish their claims both against the indigenous population and against prior Spanish claims, English colonists needed some formal justification for their settlement and occupation of American land. Lacking the papal authorization enjoyed by the Spaniards, the English found their justification, like the Spaniards, in claims to be pursuing a divinely ordained mission. In the words of Richard Hakluyt the younger: "Now the Kings and Queens of England have the name of Defenders of the Faith; by which title I think they are not only charged to maintain and patronize the faith of Christ, but also to enlarge and advance the same."[19] It is not therefore surprising to find the Virginia Company deploying the religious argument in its defense of the founding of the Jamestown settlement. William Crashaw put it succinctly in a sermon delivered to the Virginia Company in 1610: "The high and promised end being plantation of an English Church and Common wealth, and consequently the conversion of heathen."[20]

But although the promoters of the English imperial project, like Hakluyt and Sir Walter Raleigh, envisaged the expansion of the Anglican church to America as integral to the project as a whole, the crown left it to the Virginia Company to make the necessary arrangements. Under Company auspices seven ministers went out in the first decade of settlement, and others arrived in the next few years. Following the reorganization of the Company in 1619, the General Assembly established the Church of England by law in Virginia, and made the dispositions for its financial maintenance that would last until the end of the colonial period, with ministers receiving a fixed income and a glebe. But no arrangements were made for the local ordination of ministers, and, although Charles I issued a high-sounding declaration in 1625 about imposing a "single form of public worship" in his dominions,[21] no bishop in England would be given responsibility for American affairs until 1691. As a result, the church in Virginia, with no episcopal support or supervision, was left very much to its own devices during these formative years, and slipped quietly under lay control, where it would remain.[22]

Whereas, then, we find in Spanish America a powerful and wealthy church and a crown maintaining close oversight over ecclesiastical affairs, we find just the opposite in British America. In England itself, at least before the Restoration, the Anglican church was a relatively weak institution, and this weakness was both reflected and magnified in the American colonies during the critical first century of colonization. The crown, for its part, was fitful and relatively ineffectual in promoting the interests of the established church overseas. It is an indication of the weakness of both church and crown in the colonies that, in spite of much talk, no Anglican bishop was appointed in British America before the coming of Independence. As a consequence, any colonist wishing to enter the ministry had to travel to England for his ordination. With no resident bishop to supervise the conduct of church affairs in the colonies, the colonial church, while attempting to follow the Anglican model in the home country, differed from it in several respects. In particular, it was much more subject to control by its congregations, since the vestry, the principal institution of church government at the local level, was very much under lay domination.[23]

The inability of crown and church to impose themselves on the English colonizing process in the way that they imposed themselves on its Spanish counterpart was a testimony to their domestic weaknesses. The early seventeenth-century English crown was confronted by an increasingly formidable parliament, and the church was confronted by the rise of Puritanism from within, and separatist movements from without. If British America were to be transformed into a sacred space, therefore, this was unlikely to be the result, as it was in Spanish America, of any state- and church-sponsored evangelizing mission. Instead, America's credentials as holy ground would be

gained by offering a refuge to those who found themselves the objects of religious discrimination at home or saw the opportunity to realize their spiritual
aspirations in an environment where they would be subject to no constraints
except those imposed by themselves.

The determination of crown and church in Spain to stamp out any hint
of heresy, and the restrictions imposed on emigration to the Indies, meant
that Spanish America would never become a religious refuge, other perhaps
than to those of Jewish ancestry, like the seven brothers of St. Teresa of Avila,[24]
who managed by one means or another to elude the ban. In England, on the
other hand, America was seen as a potential place of refuge for religious
minorities from the earliest stages of overseas expansion. Following the passage
of the act against recusants in 1581, Sir George Peckham seems to have envisaged the establishment of a colony in North America for English Catholics,[25]
an aspiration that would later be realized, if not very successfully, when the
Calverts received the seals and charter for the colonization of Maryland in
1632. It was the Protestant minorities, rather than the Catholics, who would
transform British America into an ideal laboratory for the performing of holy
experiments.

The Plymouth Colony was founded in 1620 by separatists in schism from
the Anglican church who had moved to Holland before deciding to move on
to America. The founders of the Massachusetts Bay Company in 1629, on the
other hand, still claimed to be in communion with the Church of England,
but looked to the open world of America to allow them the freedom to organize their worship and conduct their lives in a manner befitting the elect. To
achieve this, they set out to construct a form of godly discipline that had no
exact parallel in the Old World of Europe. Instead of the Presbyterian model
of church government followed in Geneva or Scotland, with its hierarchy of
structures and its regularized procedures for collaboration between the secular and ecclesiastical authorities, they developed a congregational system in
which each congregation, united by a covenant to which all members sub-
scribed, enjoyed absolute autonomy. Although there was to be close cooperation with the civil authorities, the colony's founders went to great lengths to
prevent any of the confusion of the temporal and spiritual power that, in their
view, fatally discredited the Geneva system. Benefiting from the absence in
the New World of the entrenched institutions, traditions, and legal systems
that tended to bedevil such experiments in England and continental Europe,
and developing a system of restricted church membership based on the practice

of testing prospective members for signs of grace,[26] they achieved their goal of creating what was, by contemporary standards, a godly society of great spiritual intensity.[27]

No doubt this New England way rested on a number of uneasy compromises, and could not be indefinitely sustained. From its early stages, there were many who remained outside it. Others disagreed with one aspect or another of its arrangements, as did Roger Williams, banished from the Massachusetts Bay colony in 1635 because of his wish for explicit separation from the Church of England. In Rhode Island he went on to found his own colony, designed to provide a place for "those who were destitute, especially for conscience's sake."[28] Protestant America provided the space in which those so minded were free to embark, like Roger Williams and Anne Hutchinson, on holy experiments of their own.

Not surprisingly, the emigration of Puritans to America, whether to New England or Virginia, began to attract the adverse attention of Archbishop Laud in the mid-1630s, but the government of Charles I had too many other preoccupations to place effective curbs on emigration, and some members even of Laud's own commission seem to have been untroubled by the potential consequences. As one of them, Lord Cottington, blithely remarked, there was no point in troubling oneself about the behavior of settlers who "plant tobacco and Puritanism only, like fools."[29] At about the same time, by contrast, the tribunals of the Inquisition were showing an increasing preoccupation with the presence of deviants—in this instance alleged Judaizers—in the viceroyalties of New Spain and Peru.[30]

In seeking to build a holy community in the American "wilderness"—a term that, with its strong biblical overtones, does not appear to possess an exact equivalent in the Hispanic world, but does seem to have had similar connotations for the Jesuits when they spoke of the *désert* of the forests of New France[31]—the Massachusetts Bay settlers offered a precedent that others would soon follow. The religious radicalism that erupted in England during the Civil War and its aftermath inevitably had repercussions in the overseas colonies, which remained in continuous communication with the mother country. The Quakers arrived in the Bay colony in 1656, and William Penn would embark on his own holy experiment on a much grander scale when he secured his charter for the founding of Pennsylvania in 1681. The Baptists, splintering off from the congregational churches of New England, coalesced into a church in 1665.[32] The Jews, permitted to return to England by Oliver Cromwell, established their famous synagogue at Newport in 1658.[33] By the end of the seventeenth century, the results of these various diasporas were plain for all to see. Sir Josiah Child, in his *A New Discourse of Trade* of 1693, would write that "whereas we in England vainly endeavour to arrive at a Uniformity of Religion, yet we allow an Amsterdam liberty in our plantations."[34] With no prohibitions like those that prevailed in Spain on the immigration of foreigners into England's transatlantic possessions, the religious patchwork that was already British America acquired further patches of many shapes and hues in the eighteenth century.

Pennsylvania in particular acted as a magnet of attraction for the persecuted of continental Europe. Not only British and Dutch Quakers, but Huguenots from France, Mennonites from the Rhineland, and Lutherans and Calvinists from southwest Germany flocked into the colony. The Atlantic was increasingly spanned by Protestant religious networks, and none was more efficiently organized than that of the German Moravians, whose communities in Europe and America kept in close touch with each other by their handwritten chronicle, the *Gemeine Nachrichten*.[35]

One of the most significant consequences of the establishment of these often highly charged religious communities was to perpetuate, in a Protestant setting, the millenarian and apocalyptic tradition that was the common inheritance of both Catholicism and Protestantism, and had first been carried to the New World by the Spanish Franciscans. When Thomas Prince argued in a sermon preached in 1740 that the Kingdom of God was advancing inexorably toward the conversion of millions across the nations, and that "when this whole globe shall thus be successively enlightened, then comes on the end of the present earthly scene,"[36] his words read like an eighteenth-century echo of the millenarian expectations of the sixteenth-century Franciscan Fray Toribio de Benavente, known as Motolinía. British America, with its multiplicity of sects emerging from radical Calvinism, offered fertile ground for eschatological hopes. They welled up in the periodical revivalist movements that characterized religious life in the British colonies, and inspired and excited thousands upon thousands in the Great Awakening.[37]

There was, however, one particularly significant difference between Spanish and British millenarianism—a difference that leads to the second of the three themes discussed in this essay, the impact of the transatlantic transfer on indigenous societies. The conversion of the Indians was integral to Spanish millenarian hopes. In the British American version, even where the evangelizing ideal was present, it played a much more muted part, and took second place in the providential scheme of things to the conversion of the

Jews.[38] In Virginia, in spite of the Virginia Company's professed intentions, Henrico College for the Christianization of young Indians emerged stillborn in 1619, and, with ministers in short supply, no systematic evangelizing program was begun. In New England, the Massachusetts Bay Company might take as its seal the image of an Indian begging the English to "come over and help us," but the mission not only came relatively late in the process of settlement, but also enjoyed, by comparison with the evangelizing effort in Spanish America, only limited support and success.

The differences between the achievements of the missionary enterprises in Spanish and British America, if achievement is measured simply by the number of converts relative to size of population, can be explained in part by the differences in settlement patterns and demographic characteristics. Nominally, at least, all the indigenous peoples of Spanish America were vassals of the crown and fell within the purview of the secular and ecclesiastical authorities, whereas in British America the bulk of the indigenous population lived either in the American interior or on the fringes of the colonial settlements, leaving relatively reduced and scattered Algonquian groups uneasily stranded within expanding white settlements. Although there were disagreements in Spanish America about the degree of coercion that should be employed to bring Indians into the Christian fold, Christ's command *compelle eos entrare*—"compel them to come in"—was a powerful rallying call, and the authorities had their ways of ensuring compliance. In particular, the policy of forced resettlement of large numbers of Indians into *reducciones* in both New Spain and Peru provided opportunities for the kind of religious indoctrination that would have been impossible if they had been left in their dispersed village communities.[39] Add to this the massive attempt, especially during the early days of conquest and colonization, to Christianize a pagan population; the commitment of the religious orders to ensuring the success of the enterprise; and the backing given to their efforts by the royal authorities, and it is obvious that, in any competition for converts, the English labored under severe disadvantages.

In 1649, in an attempt to promote the missionary enterprise in America, the Rump Parliament in England approved the founding of the Society for the Propagation of the Gospel in New England, but it depended for its activities on the voluntary contributions of the faithful.[40] This was as far as the English state would go. Dependent on voluntary effort for financial contributions, the English missionary enterprise was also dependent on the availability and willingness of ministers to engage in the task. But there was no superabundance of ministers, even in New England, and the character of New England Puritanism, as an exclusive rather than an all-embracing form of religion, was hardly conducive to an errand into the wilderness that included the conversion of the Indians as a major priority. The ministers were engaged in building a holy community, a church of visible saints, and their first duty was to see to the spiritual well-being of the elect. Nevertheless, some ministers, like John Eliot, whose "Praying Towns" can be seen as a kind of voluntary counterpart of the Spanish *reducciones*, did indeed engage in heroic labors and scored some notable successes. But much of their work was to be undone by King Philip's War in 1675–76, and thereafter the missionary endeavor flagged, although in some parts beyond Massachusetts Bay, praying Indians lived on.

It is plausible that Protestantism, with fewer of the external trappings of worship, had less of an appeal to many indigenous peoples than Catholicism, although historians may have exaggerated the dependence of seventeenth-century Protestantism, especially in its Puritan manifestation, on the printed, rather than the spoken word.[41] But Protestant and Catholic missionaries labored under many of the same difficulties—the problem, for instance, of finding precise equivalents for Christian terms in Native languages, and, above all, of understanding the mentality of indigenous peoples whose belief systems and forms of worship they found it impossible to equate with what they understood religion to be.

It is now widely acknowledged that "conversion" is itself a highly problematic concept.[42] As an expression of the aims and aspirations of a missionary church or society, it provides no objective criterion for measuring the point at which—or the degree to which—the desired transformation of an individual's inner life has actually been achieved. Yet if ambiguity and uncertainty cloud the notion of conversion, it remains clear that, when one belief system engages with another, each is likely to be forced into some degree of adaptation. In that sense, both are religions on the move. In conquest societies, like those covering large parts of Iberian America, it was possible to employ coercive methods that were generally not applicable in contact situations, of the kind that prevailed in much of British and French North America.[43] But while the forced acculturation that is possible in conquest societies may be able to change outward forms of behavior, for example, by forbidding polygamy or imposing new modes of dress, it is likely to run up against a series of buffers as soon as it attempts to enforce changes of religious practice, and, still more, of religious belief. Strategies of resistance by indigenous societies,

from the hiding of cult objects to every form of individual and collective dis-
simulation, have been extensively studied. The prolonged campaign for the extirpation of idolatry in Peru, for instance, had very mixed results. An Andean
village community in the Peruvian province of Cajatambo duly buried its
mummies in the churchyard when ordered to do so by the visitor general, but
promptly disinterred them as soon as he had left.[44] Yet these Andean communities were gradually being compelled by pressure and persuasion to adapt
their belief systems and practices to the requirements of the conquerors.
Moving to and fro between two different worlds, they slowly fashioned for
themselves a new religious cosmos that owed something to both.

The conquerors, however, also found it necessary to adapt their ideas and
rituals to their new environment. Typically the adaptation involved linguistic
concessions in order to convey complex Christian doctrines, accommodation
between the Christian liturgical calendar and indigenous calendars in an
attempt to appropriate pre-conquest feast days, and a careful selection of the
images and architectural forms best adapted to meet local requirements. In
sixteenth-century New Spain, for instance, the Mendicants, when building
their convent churches, appropriated the style of the Aztec central courtyard
that surrounded the temple pyramids, and incorporated it into a feature unknown in Europe—the four corner chapels, or *posas*, which could be used for
processional purposes to illustrate the four central mysteries of Christ's incarnation, passion, resurrection, and glorification.[45] In reality, accommodation
and selective adaptation were the order of the day not on one side of the religious encounter only, but on both sides.

Christian missionaries had all the more need to accommodate their beliefs and practices in order to win converts if they were unable to have recourse to the kind of physical and military pressure to which their fellow
evangelists could resort in conquest societies. If the Jesuits in French Canada
were more successful than the Puritans of New England in winning and
keeping converts to the faith, this was the result, at least in part, of their willingness to accommodate their religion to the expectations and practices of
the Huron. The Puritans, by contrast, have been described as "culturally inflex-
ible,"[46] displaying an intransigence that made it almost impossible for them to
meet the Wampanoag and Massachusett Indians on their own ground. Yet it
has to be said that, if the Jesuits were more culturally flexible than the Puritans, their flexibility was kept within tight bounds. Convinced of the universal
validity of their beliefs, it was as impossible for them as it was for the Puritans
to appreciate that their mental world was as much a construct as that of the

Huron or the Brazilian Tupis, whose belief systems they were so determined to replace with their own.[47]

But success or failure, whether in conquest or contact situations, depended on much more than the willingness or ability of missionaries and preachers to adapt their message to their audiences. Receptivity to the message of evangelists was determined by a whole variety of circumstances, from the particular characteristics of the belief systems of each indigenous community or tribe to the nature of the situation in which a community found itself, and its assessment of the degree to which it believed the message could be turned to some account. An infinite number of permutations and combinations lay along the spectrum that ran from rejection to acceptance.[48]

In general, it would seem true to say that peoples and communities were most willing to incorporate European notions of the divine into their own conception of the sacred when these appeared to offer a more effective recourse to supernatural agencies than what had previously been available to them, or else offered hope of restoring meaning and empowerment to lives turned upside down by traumatic change. Those with supernatural powers of healing were everywhere revered, and it was through their claims to a superior capacity in the exercise of such powers that French Jesuits or Spanish Mendicants could best hope to compete with shamans in the Canadian forests and with *curanderos* in the Andes, who in turn hoped to acquire new legitimacy through their association with Christianity.[49]

Since all societies, however, naturally tend to cling to their own "ways to the sacred,"[50] the chances of transformative impact were likely to be greatest where conquest had left a spiritual and ceremonial vacuum that was waiting to be filled. This seems especially true of sixteenth-century New Spain, where the friars were particularly successful in restoring ritual and ceremonial practices to disrupted lives, and in promoting those aspects of Christianity most likely to resonate among Nahua peoples, who had experienced the shattering of the old cosmic order. The Virgin Mary could be slipped into the place formerly occupied by the female deity Tonantzin, and the metaphors associated with the blood of Christ were easily transferable to a society rich in metaphors of its own about the sacrificial shedding of blood.[51]

Yet there was a line of demarcation between indigenous belief systems and Christianity that was impossible for even the most zealous of evangelists to cross. The obsessive concern of sixteenth-century Christendom with the diabolical powers of Satan was quick to make the transatlantic crossing to America. Human sacrifice, cannibalism, sun worship, and idolatry were seen as clear proof that the devil stalked the New World and held its inhabitants in his thrall. In the cosmic struggle between the forces of good and evil that shaped the worldview of Catholics and Protestants alike, there was no room for laxity. Whether in Puritan New England or in New Spain and Peru, the faithful had forever to be on their guard, alert to every sign of the machinations of the devil.[52]

In view of what they saw as the all too frequent backsliding of their converts—a backsliding that reflected the unwillingness or the inability of the Indians to adhere to the narrative written for them—sixteenth-century friars tended to become discouraged by the disappointing results of their efforts, and to impute their failures to Satan and his works. As a result, their optimistic assessment of the capacity of the Indians in the early stages of evangelization came to be replaced by a growing pessimism about the prospects for their genuine conversion. While this response was in part dictated by developments on American soil, it may also reflect the increasing emphasis on original sin to be found on both sides of the confessional divide in sixteenth-century Europe. If the first generation of friars—the generation that embarked on the evangelization of Mexico—displayed a genuine curiosity and openness when confronted with other civilizations, succeeding generations tended to have more rigid views, and to be more downbeat in their assessment of human nature in general and Indian nature in particular. The cumulative effect was to create a consensus that the best line of approach to the Indians was to treat them as wayward children, who stood in need of discipline and punishment from stern, if loving, fathers. Not surprisingly, the Indians responded to this lowering of expectations by retreating back into a world of their own.

This was more likely to be true of those who lived in the isolation of rural communities than those who became assimilated into urban life. Although different ethnic groups were assigned their own distinctive quarters in the cities and towns of Spanish America, daily life brought them into constant contact with each other. In seventeenth-century Lima, where attempts at segregation had visibly failed, Indians, Africans, and people of mixed race rubbed shoulders in crowded alley tenements, creating a multiethnic and multicultural society in which everything was exchanged, from devotional practices to magic remedies.[53] Urbanization, therefore, was likely to promote religious hybridity, but the power of the church made it a hybridity within the context of an overarching Christian culture.

In a city such as Lima, the church was an omnipresent institution. Its presence was manifested in the multiplicity of churches and convents spread

across the urban landscape, and in the vast and elaborate processions organized around the liturgical calendar—processions in which each social and
ethnic group had its own allotted place. A prime objective of the church in
Spanish America was to embrace all elements of colonial society within its
capacious fold. This would ensure the uniformity of faith and worship essential to salvation, planting them firmly within the corporate and hierarchical
structure of an ordered society that, in line with neoscholastic teaching, aspired to pattern the divine. It was a church that, as it evolved in Spanish
America, placed an enormous emphasis on display as the outward manifestation of the great enterprise in which it was engaged. Pageantry and ritual
provided forms of collective worship in which all could participate.

In the late 1780s, Crèvecoeur, famed as the "American Farmer," jotted
down some reflections on religion in Spanish America, which he had never
visited. "The solemn appearances of religion in South America," he wrote,
"dazzles the eyes of the beholders and involuntarily must inspire their hearts
with awful sentiments; there the Divinity appears oftener; miracles are daily
worked, which bespeaks its almighty arm; it seems more immediately to reside there than in our Protestant colonies; there it seems to communicate itself to mankind through a variety of channels which are entirely unknown
here." But he left his readers in no doubt as to where the advantage lay. "How
different," he continued, "how simpler, is the system of religious laws established and followed in this country; the awful judgements of the Deity and
its rewards promised, are held to mankind as an inducement to be good and
virtuous. The morality of the Bible is expounded as found in the sacred records as further extended by our Saviour. . . . Here religion does not consist
either in pomp or solemn rites. That of the heart is most acceptable to God."[54]

For all its crudity, the contrast drawn by Crèvecoeur between belief and
practice in Iberian America and British America represents an early approach
to the third question addressed in this essay: What part does religion play in
giving the emerging colonial societies their distinctive characteristics? It is
clear that in these two colonial Americas two very different systems stand
face to face. In Spanish America we find, in spite of all the tensions between
the secular clergy and the religious orders, a largely monolithic and state-
supported religious establishment, which could call on a whole range of instruments, from the confessional to the tribunals of the Inquisition, from
dominance over the educational system to prohibitions on the entry of books,
that enabled it to control not only the outward forms of worship and behavior
but also beliefs and attitudes. No doubt the control was often more nominal

than real. In reality, substantial numbers of prohibited books were smuggled into Iberian America through clandestine channels;[55] and in the vast spaces of America there were surely many more deviations from orthodoxy than those that came to the attention of the Inquisition.[56] Yet the constraints were there, and there can be no doubt that they inhibited, even if they could not entirely prevent, the open expression of alternative points of view.

By way of contrast, we find in British America by the eighteenth century a society in which no clerical establishment possessed the power or the authority to achieve a monopolistic control.[57] The Anglican church, even in colonies where its followers were in the majority, proved incapable of establishing the institutional structure that would transform aspiration into fact.[58] In New England, the congregational churches had struggled from the beginning to counteract the dissolving effects of space. For several decades ministers managed to hold the line through their exercise of strict religious discipline, but by the late seventeenth century the battle had visibly been lost.[59] The world around them was changing, as new sects took root, and as England itself officially sanctioned a degree of toleration with the passage in 1689 of the Toleration Act. Above all, there was an unresolved tension in Protestantism, especially in its Congregational form, between the aspiration to construct a holy community and the insistence that every individual should establish his or her own unmediated relationship to God.[60] The efforts of ministers to hold the community together through strong discipline and a rigid orthodoxy proved, in the end, to be counterproductive. The more they sought to impose control, the more internal division and dissent they fostered. In a physical environment that seemed to offer unlimited opportunity for personal advancement, and a spiritual environment that was being transformed into a marketplace for competing faiths, the individual, not the community, held the upper hand.

Although Puritan ministers were ultimately defeated in this battle of the faiths, they can, however, lay claim to have won a posthumous victory that may have mattered more. It was, after all, New England's version of the past that shaped the American Republic's image of itself. The Pilgrim Fathers, Plymouth Rock, and the City on the Hill became the icons of the society that won its independence from Great Britain in the late eighteenth century. The vaunted legacies of New England Puritanism—freedom, equality, individualism, and the notion of Manifest Destiny springing from the covenant between God and His chosen people—were to become the defining features of the new United States. Comparisons with Spanish America, or at least with the stereotyped images of it that the first English settlers carried in their mental baggage on the Atlantic crossing and that had remained largely constant ever after, only served to make the vision shine more brightly. Already when Crèvecoeur offered his comparisons between British and Spanish America, he left no doubt that, to his mind, religion lay at the very center of the differences between them. "Observe," he wrote, "the corner stone of every civil fabric [here], Toleration; this is the grand nerve which has fed and reared so many men in America."[61] Spain's dogmatic, priest-ridden religion had made its empire of the Indies a retrograde and oppressed society. The Reformed religion, on the other hand, and the toleration that was its by-product, had created the open and progressive society that British America had become.

How far can this contrast between a Protestant, British North America and a Catholic, Iberian South America stand up to scrutiny? There is no doubt that many aspects of the contrast have been overdrawn. Few historians, for instance, would now accept the notion of the Protestant work ethic in its Weberian form, and entrepreneurship was far from being confined to the northern half of the Americas. Similarly, the scholarship of recent years makes it necessary to qualify some of the starker traditional assumptions about the differentiation between a Bible-reading British America and a Spanish America woefully ignorant of the scriptures. Inventories of the deceased in three New England counties in the 1650s show that more than half of the households possessed no copy of the scriptures. Puritan ministers tended to place more emphasis on the living than on the printed word, and sermons and catechizing were central to their religious enterprise.[62]

This brought them closer in method and approach to the practices of their counterparts in Spanish America, where heavy reliance was equally placed on preaching and the catechism. In a newsletter of 1597, a Jesuit reported that "doctrine and catechism" were explained every afternoon to Indian congregations in the Peruvian town of Julí.[63] Throughout Spanish America, biblical stories figured prominently in sermons during the first phases of evangelization, and biblical texts were translated into Nahuatl.[64] On the other hand, while clerics and some laymen were allowed access to the Vulgate, the translation of the full text of the Bible in the vernacular was forbidden;[65] and, as the Counter-Reformation took hold, the authorities displayed a growing fear of the consequences of private interpretation of the scriptures.

The Bible can of course be read and used in many ways, but there remains a fundamental difference between the knowledge and exposition of selected biblical passages and a close and unrestricted reading of the scriptures based on personal choice. In North America, as in Europe, Protestants cherished their right of direct personal access to the word of God, and gloried in a faith that interposed no intermediaries between the individual and his or her Creator. The spiritual liberty that was central to the Protestant message had become deeply embedded in the collective consciousness of British colonial America by the middle decades of the eighteenth century. By the time of the American Revolution, freedom of conscience had come to be seen as an inalienable right,[66] and would formally be accepted as such in 1791, in the First Amendment to the Constitution of the newly created United States.

The extent to which Protestantism, and especially Protestantism in its Puritan manifestation, was responsible for the achievement-oriented individualism of the United States is, and will remain, a matter for debate. The sense of original sin, so deeply instilled into the overwhelmingly Protestant society of British America, acted as a powerful incentive to churches and communities to do all they could to ensure that the moral order and the common good should not be subverted by self-interest. But they would find it increasingly difficult to prevent the dike from being breached. As Crèvecoeur implied, it may have been the coexistence of a diversity of faiths, rather than the particular content of any single faith, that gave colonial society in British America on the eve of independence some of its most distinctive characteristics. Although in the second half of the eighteenth-century several sects succeeded, unlike the Anglican church, in imposing a degree of coercive authority over their followers,[67] the sheer multiplicity of competing faiths made mutual tolerance and its concomitants, freedom of thought and expression, essential for the maintenance of a measure of political control and social stability in late colonial society. One of the consequences of the recognition of the need for mutual tolerance was to leave individual men—and, to a lesser extent, individual women—with enlarged room for maneuver.

Under Spanish rule, central and southern America followed a different path. Faced with the enormous challenge of incorporating large indigenous populations into an expanding colonial society, a church that enjoyed a total monopoly over religious life pursued an integrationist policy designed to ensure that all members of the society, irrespective of social rank or ethnic background, should have their allotted space within a corporate, hierarchical ordering of society that should replicate, as far as possible, its perception of the divine. This integrationist approach achieved some remarkable successes, and helped to ensure that high degree of political stability that is one of the distinguishing features of the three centuries of Spanish imperial rule in

America. But there was a price to be paid. The insistence on absolute orthodoxy, the constraints on liberty of thought and expression, imposed limits on the possibilities for creative renewal within society at large. The attempts of historians and social scientists to chart an assumed road to modernity are likely to end in disappointment, since modernity, as we now realize, has many faces. But if we compare the religious character and experience of the Protestant and Roman Catholic worlds in colonial America, it would seem that Protestant America had a greater range of resources than Catholic America for confronting the enormous challenges that the winning of independence would bring in its wake.

CHAPTER 2

Baroque New Worlds

Ethnography and Demonology in the Reformation and Counter-Reformation

RALPH BAUER

During the sixteenth century, Europeans displayed varied, conflicted, and often contradictory attitudes about the religions of the peoples whom they encountered in the "Indies." Thus, while Christopher Columbus had famously claimed, in the (now lost) "Diario" written on his first transatlantic voyage in 1492 and paraphrased by the Dominican monk and defender of the Indians Bartolomé de Las Casas, that "they [the Arawak of the Bahamas] would easily be made Christians" as it appeared to him that "they had no religion," at the end of the sixteenth century the Spanish Jesuit José de Acosta, perhaps the most influential sixteenth-century historian of the New World, claimed that Native Americans did indeed have religion but that all Amerindian religions were certainly diabolic in origin and nature. Even though he noted certain similarities between European Christian and American pagan rituals, for him such similarities were evidence not of the Indians' faint memory of their "true" maker but rather of their diabolic imitations and perversions of Christian rites, originating from Satan's boundless pride in having himself worshipped in the New World like God was being worshipped in the Old. The fact that the New World had only recently been discovered was an indication of Satan's jealous guardianship of his dominion over the western hemisphere. But although he had successfully hidden away the New World from the Old for millennia, it was revealed at last by Columbus's discovery at the providential moment when Christian Europe had finally overcome the Muslim enemies of the Faith and was ready to assume its historical mission as the redeemer of America.[1]

As historians of colonial Spanish America such as Fernando Cervantes, Sabine MacCormack, and Carina Johnson have shown, it was by and large Acosta's demonological, rather than Columbus's and Las Casas's apologetic, reading of Native American spirituality that would prevail in the Catholic world by the end of the sixteenth century. And comparatist historian Jorge Cañizares-Esguerra has recently argued that demonology, as a sort of "colonial discourse," was also the dominant mode of reading Native spirituality for Protestant English writers about the New World—that, in this regard, "the English and the Spaniards were ultimately cultural twins."[2] Yet, as we will see, Protestants in general, and the English in particular, were not initially and uniformly predisposed toward reading Native American religions in Satanic terms. In order to understand the diverse European interpretations of Native American spirituality, it will be necessary to leave behind the notion that Satanism was merely an ideological armature of conquest, already available to Europeans and monolithically imposed upon the New World in order to rationalize imperial expansionism and the domination of colonial "others" (though it did, of course, frequently have the *effect* of providing such a rationalization). As historians of religion have recognized, the intense preoccupation with diabolism in sixteenth-century Europe was not a vestige of medievalism, but rather a distinctly modern phenomenon,[3] and it originated during the fifteenth and sixteenth centuries from a changing sense of the ontological reality of Satan's agency in the world. Whereas medieval theologians had by and large regarded the devil as impotent in the face of Christian ritual, early modern theologians came to regard the devil as an aggressively powerful agent, as a sort of counter-god whose kingdom existed independent from that of the Kingdom of the God.[4]

What caused this transformation in Western perceptions of the devil? Historians have usually traced its history in the context of the larger cultural schisms and socioeconomic transformations of early modern Europe—the challenges to the feudal social order by the rise of an aggressive mercantile class; the questioning of age-old scientific truths about the cosmos and man's place within it; the fusion of secular and ecclesiastic authorities with the emergence of nation-states, national churches, and inquisitions; and, most of all, of course, the rise of the Reformation and the Counter-Reformation, as well as the sectarian strife between them.[5] While all of these developments were clearly important factors, Heiko Oberman has also elucidated some of the philosophical and theological underpinnings in the debates of the "long fifteenth century"—in particular, the debate between the *Via Antigua* of Thomist Realism and the *Via Moderna* of Franciscan Nominalism. In essence, this fifteenth-century debate between Realists and Nominalists revolved around the relationship between human nature and God's saving grace as well as around the role of postlapsarian human reason within this relationship. Realists, following Thomas Aquinas, held on to the (essentially Platonic) notion that the conceptions of human natural reason were concordant with universal, objective truths: that natural reason was therefore a reliable guide in the human quest for knowledge of the true God, and that human nature was thus essentially continuous with (and even perfected by) salvation. Others, by contrast, following the "Nominalist" tradition of St. Augustine, Duns Scotus, and Wilhelm of Ockham, held that natural reason (and its linguistic conceptions) was vain, fallen, corrupt, and illusionary; that its triumph would inevitably lead to error and damnation; and that man's nature was therefore essentially discontinuous with (and even broken by) salvation.[6] Building on Oberman's account, Fernando Cervantes has pointed out the implications of this fifteenth-century dispute for the history of early modern perceptions of the devil during the sixteenth century, when the Nominalist *Via Moderna* increasingly preponderated over the Realist *Via Antigua*. "The nominalist tendency to separate nature and grace," he argues, "made the realm of the supernatural much less accessible to reason thereby enhancing the attributes of both the divine and the demonic in relation to the individual."[7] The consequences of this shift in balance were momentous not only for the understanding of the devil's agency in the world but also for the apprehension of the "pagan" religions Europeans encountered overseas, as all knowledge based on human natural reason and not assisted by divine revelation was understood to be perverted by the devil.[8]

If these accounts by Oberman, Cervantes, and (more recently) Stuart Clark have usefully shed light on the common root of demonology and other branches of early modern science in the age of "scientific revolution" by pointing to the late medieval philosophical crisis of the Realist assumption of a metaphysical concordance between the conceptions of human natural reason and the ontological reality of the universe, they have so far considered this religious transformation in a strictly European context. Even Cervantes, who was explicitly concerned with diabolism in the New World, told its history in terms of its European origins and its "impact" in New Spain (as well as the

Native American "response" to it). In this essay, I would therefore like to pose a slightly different question—not of how these developments in Europe "impacted" the perception of Native religions in America, but rather how colonial ethnography *participated* in this philosophical/theological debate and religious transformation during the sixteenth and seventeenth centuries. My examples here will be drawn primarily from the Protestant—Continental as well as English—ethnography of the New World. In the first section I focus on sixteenth-century English writings about the New World; next I examine the influential *America* series released by the Frankfurt publishing house of Theodor de Bry; and finally I will return to seventeenth-century British American intersections between demonology and colonial ethnography.

Pursuing the question of how the colonial ethnographic project participated in the philosophical debate that would lead to a Reformation/Counter-Reformation conception of human nature and human reason provides a glimpse of the larger role that Europe's colonial encounters played in the making of the modern subject during the sixteenth and seventeenth centuries. This period saw not only the expansion of Europeans on a global scale but also the rise of absolutist monarchies and modern nation-states, the emergence of mass culture, and the implementation of unprecedented instrumentalities of repression aimed at enforcing religious orthodoxy and conformity. The Spanish historian José Antonio Maravall has described this period of early modernity as the "culture of the Baroque," in which a profound sense of "crisis" manifested itself in art, literature, and even in political, moral, and scientific thought: "Many negative events struck the consciousness that the course of the previous epoch had awakened: the economic recession and poverty imposed at the end of the sixteenth century; the disorderliness and unrest created by repeated conflicts between states; the moral confusion deriving from the preceding epoch of expansion; and the unjustifiable conduct of the Church and the critiques it promoted, giving rise either to laxity or to pathological attitudes of exacerbated intolerance." This profound sense of crisis, Maravall shows, also led to a new quest for knowledge about the human being, "in the sense of an empirical knowing based on observation and directed toward [the] practical, operative end" of domination and manipulation of human conduct. The scientific discovery of "differential psychology" in this context promoted a belief in the diversity of individuals and peoples, reducing them to "types."[9]

It is in this historical context that a "new science" arose in which the early modern ethnographic project was an important component—a project that Father Acosta, lacking the modern word "ethnography," significantly called the "natural and moral history of the Indies." By treating the New World as an "experimental field" of philosophical inquiry, the colonial ethnographic projects of such Catholic authors as Acosta and such Protestant authors as the de Brys could lend powerful support to Reformation and Counter-Reformation theologians who, despite their obvious denominational differences, were in agreement that the path of human reason would lead natural man inevitably not to the ancient wisdom of a Plato, an Aristotle, or a Hermes Trismegistus, but rather to the savagery of the Tupinambá of Brazil and the demonic blood sacrifices of Aztecs of Mexico.[10] For Reformation and Counter-Reformation ethnographers, the New World was their "exhibit A," in their case against the ideas of Renaissance Humanists and Neo-Platonists that man retained, by virtue of his reason, a spark of divinity. "Idolatry" emerged as a point of emphasis in European ethnographic literature about the overseas world in this context as both a capitalist fetish and an ideological foil. Aiming to assuage the curiosity of maximum numbers of readers about the marvelous overseas world with lavishly illustrated books, these authors forged powerful connections linking paganism with savagery and (true) Christianity with civility. Whereas both Renaissance Humanists and (to a lesser degree) medieval Scholastics regarded the Ancients' wisdom, though pagan, as divinely inspired, and modern times as a degeneration from ancient civility, early modern ethnographies reinscribed paganism within a progressivist Christian teleology as incompatible with civility.

Early English Representations of Amerindian Religions

When we consider the history of English perceptions of Native American spirituality, it is important to remember that virtually all of the earliest English publications about the New World were translations of the writings of Continental explorers, conquerors, and cosmographers. While early English perceptions of the New World, of its inhabitants, and their religions were therefore invariably shaped by the lens of Continental, and especially Spanish, historiography of the New World, they were also indebted to the perspectives and agendas of the English translators such as Richard Eden (c. 1520–76), who recontextualized their source texts and gave them new and distinct meanings.[11] In these early publications about the New World, there is little evidence that the English initially perceived Native American religions in terms of diabolism. Indeed, to the extent that the Spanish and Latin sources translated into English offer demonological readings of Native American religions, the English translators seem to gloss over them, even resist them. For example, in Eden's 1555 English translation of Peter Martyr's *Decades* (1516–30), which were written in Latin in the form of letters addressed to various ecclesiastic dignitaries, the reader finds the Italian Humanist apparently ambivalent about the value of Native paganism. On the one hand, Martyr repeatedly describes Amerindians living in a utopian state without property, in a "golden world" that invokes Hesiod's idea of history as a degeneration from a primal Golden Age to a Silver and Bronze Age, and finally to the Iron present. On the other hand, Martyr associated Caribbean and Mesoamerican sacred images and figures, called Zemes, with diabolism. He writes (in Eden's translation) that,

> They make certeyne Images of gossampine cotton foulded or
> wrethed after theyr maner, and harde stopped within. These
> Images they make sytting, much lyke vnto the pictures of sprites
> [*sic*] and deuelles which owr paynters are accustomed to pain vppon
> waules. . . . These Images, th[e] inhabitants caule *Zemes:* wherof the
> leaste, made to the lykenes of younge devuels, they bind to theyr
> forheads when they goo to the warres ageynst their enemies. . . .
> For they thinke that these *Zemes* are the mediatours and messen-
> gers of the greate god, whom they acknowleage to be only one,
> eternall, withowte ende, omnipotent and inuisible.[12]

Martyr recounts an epic battle between two Indians, one of whom has adopted Christianity and the other who still adheres to his "*Zemes*," which are "the deuyll to whose similitude theyr Images are made . . . who immediately appeared in his lykenes about the younge man that stoode in the defence of Sathans kyngedome." But, as soon as the Christianized Native utters the Hail Mary, "there appeared a fayre virgin clothed in whyte, at whose presence the deuell vanguisshed immediately."[13]

Despite such demonological passages in Peter Martyr's text, in which the European conquest is framed as an epic battle between the forces of God and the forces of Satan, Richard Eden, in his "Preface to the Reader," offers an interpretation that is at odds with that of Martyr. He instead follows the earlier apologetic interpretations by Columbus and Las Casas of the Indians as spiritual "blank slates": "These simple gentiles lyuinge only after the lawe of nature," he writes, "may well bee likened to a smoothe and bare table vnpainted, or a white paper vnwritten, vpon the which yow may at the first paynte or wryte what yow lyste, as yow can not vppon talbes alredy paynted, vnless yow rase or lot owt the fyrste forms."[14]

While Eden's translations were prepared in the 1550s, under the Catholic reign of Queen Mary at the time she was about to marry Philip II of Spain, later Elizabethan and Protestant translators similarly resisted, and even suppressed, a demonological interpretation of Native religions. When Richard Hakluyt, for example, the most prolific Elizabethan collector of English travel literature, translated, in the 1598 edition of his *Principal Navigations*, parts of one of the most important texts in Spanish Counter-Reformation demonology and ethnography, José de Acosta's *Historia natural y moral*, he did not select a single passage that linked Native religions with diabolic perversions. Similarly, Sir Walter Raleigh, in his *Discovery of the Large, Rich, and Beautiful Empire of Guiana*, one of the most important and extensive texts of Elizabethan New World ethnographies, makes no mention of the devil. On the contrary, Raleigh reports showing a coin to the Natives of Guiana that displayed an engraved image of Elizabeth: "they so admired and honoured [it]," he writes, "as it had been easy to have brought them idolatrous thereof. The like and a more large discourse I made to the rest of the nations, both in my passing to *Guiana* and to those of the borders, so as in that part of the world her Majesty is very famous and admirable; whom they now call *Ezrabeta cassipuna aquerewana*, which is as much as 'Elizabeth, the Great Princess, or Greatest Commander.' "[15] Not unlike Christopher Columbus a hundred years before him, Raleigh here invokes an almost Las Casian notion of the Native impressionability. For Raleigh, it appears, "idolatry" was not a form of devil worship and a crime against God, but rather a more positive, useful, perhaps even Machiavellian tool in the affirmation of aristocratic power.

Similarly, in his *Briefe and True Report of the New Found Land of Virginia*, first published in 1588 as one of the most important Elizabethan ethnographic sources on Native Algonquian culture and religion in what today is North Carolina, Thomas Harriot provides a detailed description of Native religion, which, though flawed, had for him nothing to do with devil worship. "Some religion they haue alreadie," he writes, "which although it be farre from the truth, yet beyng as it is, there is hope it may bee the easier and sooner reformed."[16] By using the word "reformed," he suggests that Native religion may provide the foundation for the Indians' eventual conversion to the Protestant religion. His interpretation of Algonquian paganism parallels that of his contemporary Spanish/mestizo Humanist and Neoplatonist historian of Peru, "the Inca" Garcilaso de la Vega, who would argue, in his *Comentarios reales de los Incas* (1609), that the worship of the sun and of *huacas* (sacred places) that the Incas spread throughout the Andes prepared the New World for the coming of Christianity, just as pagan Rome had prepared Europe for the triumph of Christianity.[17] For Harriot, Algonquians were therefore not essentially different from Europeans before the advent of the Protestant (or Anglican) Reformation, when local saints were widely worshiped alongside God, except that the "Virginians" used different words. "They beleeue that there are many Gods which they call *Mantóac*," he wrote, "but of different sortes and degrees; one onely chiefe and great God, which hath bene from all eternitie. Who as they affirme when hee purposed to make the worlde, made first other goddes of a principall order to bee as meanes and instruments to bee vsed in the creation and gouernment to follow; and after the Sunne, Moone, and Starres, as pettie goddes and the instruments of the other order more principall."[18]

Moreover, he continued, like Christians, the Virginians already believe in "the immortalitie of the soule, that after this life as soone as the soule is departed from the bodie according to the workes it hath done, it is eyther carried to heauē the habitacle of gods, there to enioy perpetuall blisse and happiness, or els to a great pitte or hole, which they thinke to bee in the furthest partes of their part of the worlde towarde the sunne set, there to burne continually: the place they call *Popogusso*."[19] He explains some of the apparent errors and uncertainties in Native accounts of the creation of the world by referring to their lack of "letters nor other such meanes as we to keepe recordes of the particularities of times past, but onelie tradition from father to sonne," hereby echoing explanations some fifty years earlier by Las Casas and other Dominicans that Native religions are evidence of man's innate tendency of knowing the true God, a knowledge that has suffered somewhat in the New World due to a lack of writing, just as it had in Catholic Europe due to the Church's corruption of the Latin canon. What was most important for Harriot, as they were for Raleigh, were the positive social effects of religion more generally. "What subtilty soeuer be in the *Wiroances* and Priestes," he wrote "this opinion worketh so much in manie of the common and simple sort of people that it maketh them haue great respect to their Gouernours, and also great care what they do, to auoid torment after death, and to enjoy blisse; although nothwithstanding there is punishment ordained for malefactours,

as stealers, whoremoongers, and other sortes of wicked doers; some punished
with death, some with forfeitures, some with beating, according to the greatnes
of the factes."[20]

Thus, both Harriot's and Raleigh's ethnographies about the New World,
written at the very end of the sixteenth century, still manifest a Realist
understanding of paganism in general and of Native American religions in
particular. Native religions, despite their apparent imperfections, were in no
way seen as diabolic, but as evidence of a (however faint) memory of their true
creator, as evidence of man's universal strife to know the true God, and, thus,
not as idolatry that must be extirpated but rather a solid foundation on which
their reformation could be built. The resistance to a demonological interpretation of Amerindian religions in the early English historiography about the
New World is remarkable considering that, as Keith Thomas has argued, the
Protestant Reformation "did nothing to weaken" the belief in the devil; "indeed, it almost certainly strengthened it" in its conviction of human sin and
sense of powerless in the face of evil.[21] Indeed, in sixteenth-century England,
as on the Continent, radical Calvinist reformers such as William Perkins produced some of the most extensive and important treatises on demonology.

In part, the positive interpretation of Amerindian religions can be explained in terms of the promotional character of much early English writing
about the New World, which was intended to persuade adventurers to invest
in the colonial enterprise, despite the tenuous legal situation in which Elizabethan explorers operated in the New World. While English encroachments
into North American territory (such as Harriot's "Virginia") were justified by
Elizabethan lawyers by citing the first "discovery" of North America by John
Cabot in 1496–98 on behalf of the English Crown, North America still fell
within a part of the New World assigned to Spain's sphere of influence in
Alexander's *Inter caetera* bulls. England was, after all, still a Catholic country
under Henry VII when these bulls had been issued.[22] The justification of English encroachments was on even more tenuous footing in the case of South
America (such as Raleigh's "Guiana"), which not only fell (with the exception
of Brazil) to the Spanish sphere of influence (according to *Inter caetera*) but
had actually been first "discovered" by Christopher Columbus on behalf of
the Spanish Crown during his third voyage in 1498.

It was in this context that Elizabethan writers began to challenge the
justness of the Spanish rights of discovery on a number of grounds. On the
one hand, they claimed that the Spanish conquest had not been consistent
with an apostolic mission but was, in fact, motivated by avarice and perpe-

trated by cruelty. On the other hand, they challenged the notion that "mere discovery" (that is, without settlement) was sufficient ground for a claim to possession.[23] With regard to the first argument, they found a ready ally from within Spain herself—Bartolomé de Las Casas, whose *Brevíssima relación de la destrucción de las indias* was first translated into English in 1583 as *The Spanish colonie, or Briefe chronicle of the acts and gestes of the Spaniardes in the West Indies* and came to greatly promote the rise of the so-called "Black Legend" in the Protestant world, an anti-Spanish and anti-Catholic ideology that underwrote English and Dutch imperial expansionism in the New World.[24] Elizabethan writers such as Raleigh, Hakluyt, and Harriot eagerly seized on Las Casas's rhetorical model and added their own examples with the intent of proving that the English were the "protectors" of Native American victims of Spanish illegal usurpations and cruelties. Thus, Raleigh even argued that the English Reformers would restore the "legitimate" rule of the Native Inca elite, who had wrongly been deprived of their dominion by Spanish usurpers, writing that "by my Indian interpreter, which I carried out of *England*, I made them understand that I was the servant of a queen who was the great cacique of the north, and a virgin, and had more *caciqui* under her than there were trees in that island; that she was an enemy to the *Castellani* in respect of their tyranny and oppression, and that she delivered all such nations about her, as were by them oppressed; and having freed all the coast of the northern world from their servitude, had sent me to free them also, and withal to defend the country of *Guiana* from their invasion and conquest."[25]

Theodor de Bry's Baroque New World

Despite the generally positive view that Marian and Elizabethan English writers took on Native American religions and cultures in the early years of English overseas exploration, in Protestant Europe, too, an alternative perspective began to emerge—one that, though apparently echoing the Counter-Reformation historians of the New World, was nevertheless distinctive in the meaning it attached to allegations of Native American Satanism. In the Protestant world, the most consequential moment in the shaping of early modern ideas about the New World came in 1590, when a Calvinist engraver and book publisher from Liège working in Frankfurt, Theodor de Bry, launched his "Voyages," a lavishly illustrated collection of travel accounts about a century of European explorations, travels, and conquests in the overseas world that would become one of the most spectacularly successful publishing ventures of the early modern period. When the last volume was published by the de Bry publishing house in 1634, the series had swollen to a total of twenty-five volumes, the first thirteen of which dealt with the Americas (commonly called the "Great Voyages"), while the remaining twelve (the "Small Voyages") treated European travel to Africa and Asia.[26] In some respects, the de Bry Voyages were similar to the other great travel collections of the sixteenth century, such as the Italian Giovanni Battista Ramusio's *Navigationi et Viaggi* (1550–59) or the Englishman Richard Hakluyt's *Divers Voyages Touching the Discoverie of America* (1582) and *The Principal Navigations, Voiages, Traffiques and Discoueries of the English Nation* (1589–1600). More so than any other sixteenth-century travel collectors, however, de Bry, and later his sons, made maximal use of the possibilities of early modern print technology, including some six hundred lavish copper engravings that indelibly coined European ideas about the peoples inhabiting the overseas world in centuries to come. Also more so than any other travel collectors before them, the de Brys targeted an international and pan-European mass audience, releasing the first volume of the Great Voyages in Latin, German, French, and English, and each of the subsequent volumes in Latin and German.[27]

The story of the Voyages series begins in late 1584 or early 1585, when Theodor de Bry removed to London, after the city of his previous residency, Antwerp, had come under Spanish siege. Apparently, de Bry had already acquired a significant reputation as an artist by the time he arrived in London in 1584 or 1585, for he quickly became associated with prominent people at the Elizabethan court, including Raleigh, the heirs of Philip Sidney, and Anthony Ashley, the clerk of the Privy Council. When Ashley, in 1588, published his translation of Lucas Waghenaer's famous textbook, *The Mariners Mirror*, he commissioned de Bry to create the copper plate for the frontispiece. It was probably during his stay in London that de Bry had attained a copy of the 1588 edition of Harriot's text, as well as copies of the watercolors of John White, the painter who had served as an artist employed by Raleigh in order to take impressions of the Native peoples of Roanoke. Upon his return to the Continent, de Bry republished Harriot's text in 1590 in four languages, along with copperplate engravings prepared in his new shop in Frankfurt that were based on White's watercolors. The new section of engravings following Harriot's text also included a brief introduction by de Bry, his captions to the engravings, and some additional engravings, also based on watercolors by White, of the "ancient Picts" that inhabited the British Isles in ancient times and that were supposed to illustrate the cultural similarities between modern Virginians and ancient Britons.

As historians have widely noted, whereas White's watercolors and titles generally defamiliarize and decontextualize Native religious practices, emphasizing ethnic difference and exotic strangeness, de Bry recontextualizes and refamiliarizes ethnic elements by Europeanizing facial features in the stylistic convention of European Mannerist visual art and by including landscape settings.[28] Of particular interest for my purposes here is the representation of Amerindian religion in the de Bry volume, as it stands in marked contrast to that in Harriot's earlier English publication (without images) of 1588. Thus, in the engraving of an Algonquian shaman prepared by one of de Bry's engravers, Gijsbert van Veen, which was based on a watercolor that had been entitled "The Flyer" by White (Figure 3), the new caption reads, in the Latin edition, "Prestigiator;" in the English edition, "The Conjuror;" and in the German edition, "Der Schwarzkünster oder Zauberer," meaning "one adept in the black arts" or "a magician" (Figures 4 and 5).

In addition, the new caption reads "They haue comonlye coniurers or iuglers which vse strange gestures, and often cótrarie to nature in their enchantments: For they be verye familiar with deuils, of whome they enquier what their enemys doe, or other suche thinges."[29] This association of Native American shamanism and European devil worship and witchcraft is also invited by the iconography of de Bry's engravings depicting Algonquian religious rituals. Thus, in an engraving entitled "Their manner of prainge with Rattles abowt te fyer," de Bry organizes the image around a column of bellowing smoke that is reminiscent, as Michael Gaudio has shown, of an iconographic tradition of representing the Witches Sabbath, such as Hans Baldung's woodcut of that title.[30] The apparent similarities between Algonquian and Christian religious rites—which in Harriot's original 1588 text had still signified the Realist idea of pagans' faint memory of their true maker—imply in this new context of de Bry's publication diabolic imitations and perversions of Christian rites. Thus, his caption to de Bry's engraving of "Ther Idol Kivvasa" reads, "The people of this cuntrie haue an Idol, which they call KIWASA:. . . Thes poore soules haue none other knowledge of god although I think them verye Desirous to know the truthe. For when as wee kneeled downe on our knees to make our prayers vnto god, they went abowt to imitate vs, and when they saw we moued our lipps, they also dyd the like."[31]

Although de Bry goes on to express the hope "that they might easelye be brongt to the knowledge of the gospel," the overall demonological interpretation

Figure 3. John White, *The Flyer*. Courtesy of the British Museum.

The Coniuerer. XI.

Hey haue comonlye coniurers or iuglers which vfe ftrange geftures, and often cō-
trarie to nature in their enchantments: For they be verye familiar with deuils, of
whome they enquier what their enemys doe, or other fuche thinges. They fhaue
all their heads fauinge their crefte which they weare as other doe, and faften a fmall
black birde aboue one of their ears as a badge of their office. They weare nothinge
but a skinne which hangeth downe from their gyrdle, and coucreth their priuityes. They weare a
bagg by their fide as is expreffed in the figure. The Inhabitants giue great credit vnto their fpeeche, which oftentymes they finde
to bee true.

B 3

Figure 4. "The Coniuerer," Theodor de Bry, *America*, part 1, Frankfurt, 1590. Courtesy of the John Carter Brown Library at Brown University.

of Native shamanism here is in tension not only with Harriot's own earlier portrayal of Native paganism in the 1588 edition, but also with the connotation evoked by White's watercolors. Thus, the title of White's portrait of the Algonquian shaman, *The Flyer*, would have reminded the reader of the Greek god Hermes, European Classical paganism generally, and especially of the Renaissance Hermetic tradition that had been brought to Elizabethan England by Giordano Bruno during his visit to London from 1583 to 1585 and that was associated with the members of the Hermetic circle that had gathered around John Dee, Edward Kelly, Sir Walter Raleigh, and even Harriot himself.[32] That White may have had just such a learned, philosophical, or

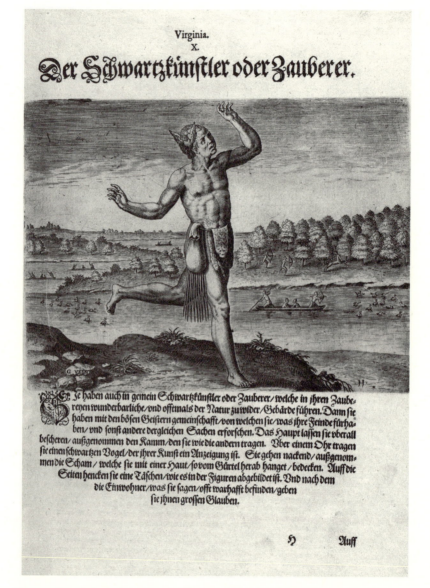

Figure 5. "Der Schwarzkünstler oder Zauberer," Theodor de Bry, *America*, part 1, Frankfurt, 1590. Courtesy of the Kraus Collection of Sir Francis Drake, Library of Congress.

Classical Hermes in mind when he portrayed the Algonquian shaman in his watercolor is suggested by the similarity that his "flyer" bears, in posture and expression, to the Hermes in Botticelli's *Primavera*, which depicts a "magical" Renaissance garden with many medicinal herbs and references to alchemical motifs (Figures 6 and 7).[33]

The new captions in the various editions of de Bry's volume, by contrast, strip the Native shaman of any connotation of a "learned" or "philosophical" Hermeticist in the Ficinian tradition of the Italian Renaissance. The subtly various connotations of these captions in the different languages are hereby instructive. The *prestigiator* in the Latin edition refers to someone who causes a *praestigium*, which, according to Isidore of Seville's *Etymolgia*, was the "'binding' of the pupil of the eye."[34] In other words, it involved visual deceptions primarily by the use of natural magic. As Stuart Clark observes, a prestige "might involve anything from high-class subtlety to low-class duping, provided the twin elements of artifice and imposture were present, but it was invariably a visual matter."[35] Modern English translations of *prestigiator* might thus include magician, trickster (one who practices deceit); juggler; impostor, cheat, deceiver. In the seventeenth century, Francis Bacon used the word in his *Novum organum* to denote the wit and dexterity of jugglers.

Whereas the Latin *prestigiator* could imply white or black magic, as well as learned or vulgar magic, the English "The Conjuror" has more limited connotations, invoking the European contexts of folk jugglers, witch doctors, and perhaps even diabolic "Catholic" superstitions, hereby foreshadowing an increasingly radical Protestant hermeneutics in which preternatural phenomena such as "flying" (or levitation) must no longer be associated with saints but only with witches.[36] Perhaps most unequivocal in this context is the German translation, *Schwarzkünster oder Zauberer*. Three years earlier, in 1587, de Bry's rival printer in Frankfurt, Johann Spies, had published the *Historia von D. Johann Fausten*, one of the first in a series of narratives that would grow, in the 1590s (and subsequent centuries), into the Faust legend—the famous story about the scholar and physician who signs a contract with the devil, selling his soul in exchange for magic powers in this world. The subtitle of Spies's publication was *dem weitbeschreyten Zauberer und Schwarzkünstler / wie er sich gegen dem Teuffel auff eine benandte Zeit verschrieben* (the notorious magician and adept in the black arts / how he enlisted himself with the devil for a named time) (Figure 8).

Spies's *Historia* was republished the following year, in 1588—two years before de Bry's publication of Harriot's account. Then, in 1593, a sequel to Spies's *Historia* was published anonymously about Faust's *famulus*, Christoff

Figure 6. Botticelli, *Primavera* (detail: Hermes).
Courtesy of Wikipaintings.org.

Figure 7. Botticelli, *Primavera* with Hermes (left). Courtesy of Wikipaintings.org.

Wagner, who, like his master makes a pact with the devil but only gets five years of power from the devil. Also, unlike his master, Wagner travels to Europe's "newly discovered world" (*neuu erfundene Welt*) of America.[37] On his ship passage, he encounters various exotic animals such as the "flying fish," which had been depicted in one of John White's watercolors and described in numerous natural histories of the New World. After the conventional ethnographic descriptions of stereotypically Amerindian customs—the use of tobacco and of poisoned arrows, and of going about naked—Wagner witnesses their religious practices, which clearly echo de Bry's depictions in his edition of Harriot's texts. "About their religion, it is like this. They pray to many and various gods, some are painted, some carved out of chalk or wood, or from gold and silver, [the are] strangely shaped, some have birds and other hideous animals, in the way we paint the devil, with craws' feet and long tails. . . . The devil deceives them often and in various form, and promises their priests something . . . So, he confuses the poor people, this deceptive, lying charlatan."[38]

In the context of this generic interference between demonology and ethnography in late sixteenth-century Germany, subsequent volumes in the de Bry collections became less and less ambiguous in their representation of Amerindian spirituality. Part Two, published in Latin and German in 1591, featured translations of Rene Goulaine De Laudonniere's account of

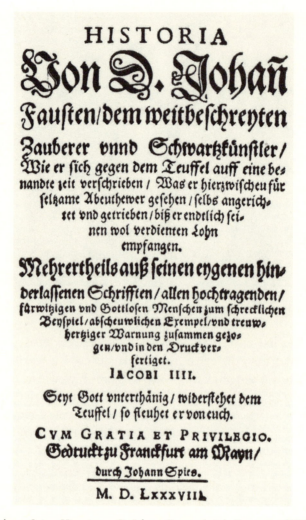

Figure 8. Johann Spies, *Historia von D. Johann Fausten* (1587). Courtesy of Wikimedia Commons.

Jean Ribault's French Huguenot colony in Florida, originally published in 1586 under the title *L'histoire notable de la Floride, contenant les trois voyages faits en icelles par des capitaines et pilotes français*, as well as engravings based on (mostly now lost) watercolors by the artist Jacques le Moyne. Although Laudonniere focused on the Native Floridians' idolatrous worship of sun and moon, while de Bry's engravings depicting them worshipping a column deco-

Figure 9. "Wie die Wilden in Florida die Seul vom Obersten in seiner ersten Schiffahrt aussgerichtet verehrt haben," Theodor de Bry, *America*, part 2, Frankfurt, 1591. Courtesy of the John Carter Brown Library at Brown University.

rated with the French royal coat of arms and garlands (Figure 9), overall his volume refrained from associating Amerindian religions with diabolism. This changed, however, with Parts Three (1593) and Four (1594), about Brazil and New Spain, respectively. The frontispiece to Part Three, which included his edition of the narratives of Hans Staden and Jean de Léry about their experiences among the Tupinambá of Brazil, displays several Tupis gorging themselves on human limbs (Figure 10).

Figure 10. Theodor de Bry, frontispiece, *America*, part 3, Frankfurt, 1593. Courtesy of the John Carter Brown Library at Brown University.

In the dedication to the Duke of Palatine Ferdinand IV, de Bry reflected on the remarkable diversity of the peoples, cultures, and religions of the New World: "It is important when reading these three descriptions of mine, of Virginia, Florida, and Brazil, to take note the great diversity (*ungleichheit*) among these nations with regard to clothes, weaponry and armory, customs of life." This is not surprising, he continued, as "these lands are not small but each one extends over several hundred German miles." He noted that apart from their various styles of dress and hair, these nations also differ greatly in religion. In Virginia, they believe in a god that created everything, "but they have no knowledge of him, with the exception that they believe in life after death." In

Florida, the Indians "have a different god, the sun and the moon. But these of which we are dealing with here [the Brazilians] believe in nothing else except in a great fruit that resembles the egg of an ostrich. This, they hold to be their god, as they are persuaded by their priests. Such is the great blindness of these poor people."[39] In his edition of Léry's narrative, de Bry includes a prefatory poem that offers an allegorical reading of the Tupi's "wildness" and that links the Tupi's savagery in America to Catholic cruelty in Europe, making it clear that he understands the significance of New World ethnographies such as Léry's to be a commentary on human nature more general:

> I only want to tell you that in our country, where art and science
> is abundant, there can be found people much more terrible and
> monstrous so that you can better believe what I write here. Even
> though they may have a horrific way of life, cooking, roasting and
> eating their enemies, they have more peace than France right now.
> Take me there [to Brazil], learned Léry, before it gets any worse in
> France. You hear of monstrous people and hear of adventures in the
> New World, of people who live naked in the outdoors. This is the
> guilt of old Adam, who so pathetically scorned the image of God,
> through his sin and crime. That even though they are born in a
> good country and are without crime, they will remain wild like a
> beast without being subjected to [Christian] instruction.[40]

The path of degeneration of humans who live without the assistance of the light of Christianity chronicled by de Bry's ethnographies comes to a nadir with Part Three of the America series, which presents translations (Latin and German in separate editions) of the first book of Girolamo Benzoni's *Historia del Mondo Nuovo*. The narrative provides a panoramic overview of the Spanish history of the discovery and conquest of the New World, beginning with Columbus's voyages and culminating with the conquests of Mexico and Peru. The frontispiece of de Bry's edition of Benzoni presents a winged and wholly demonic Aztec god Huitzilopochtli, with claws of a large cat and a giant toothed mouth in his chest, demanding blood sacrifices. Interestingly, however, in Part Nine of de Bry's America series, published after Theodor's death in 1601 by his son Johann Theodor, and which also deals with Mexico, Aztec religion and even Montezuma himself are painted in the brush of ancient Rome, bearing testimony to the lingering ambivalence in Continental European representations of Native American paganism (Figure 11).

Figure 11. Theodor de Bry, frontispiece, *America*, part 4, Frankfurt, 1594. Courtesy of the John Carter Brown Library at Brown University.

Demonology and Ethnography in Seventeenth-Century England and British America

The emergence of the Faust legend in print during the 1590s underlines a changing religious climate not only on the Continent but also in England, where English versions of the Faust book and of the Wagner book were published in 1592 and 1594, respectively, to become two of the most important sources for Christopher Marlowe's famous play about the diabolic magus.[41] Ironically, Harriot found himself, in this new climate, repeatedly accused of being an atheist and even a sorcerer, as were such associates as Walter Raleigh, John Dee, and Henry Percy, the Earl of Northumberland (known as the "Wizard Earl").[42] In England, the interest in diabolism intensified, especially among the elite in church and state, with the succession of the Stuart dynasty, as well as with the radicalization of the conflict between sectarians and an increasingly calcified orthodox Laudian church. Perhaps the most famous expression of this interest on the part of the political elite is the publication of James I's *Daemonologie*, already five years before his ascension to the throne of England in 1603. James's primary target was not malefic witchcraft, but rather magic. He therefore attempted to delineate the lawful sciences (such as astronomy) from unlawful magic (such as divinatory astrology), as well as from the art of conjuring spirits. Since God is all-powerful, there was nothing that the devil could do without God's permission. Instances of witchcraft were therefore to be interpreted as evidence of God's displeasure, which resulted in the withdrawal of his protection, thus allowing for malefic witchcraft. Witchcraft could therefore only be remedied by fasting and prayer, rather than, as in the Catholic context, through rituals of exorcism. It was for this reason that Protestant demonologists such as James deemed magic a crime worse than witchcraft itself, as the witch was an instrument of God's wrath, whereas the conjurer had "knowledge," but still attempted to resist or "trick" his way out of God's providence through his magic, which made his crime an offense against the Holy Spirit. The "first cause" in witchcraft is God, he wrote, "and the Devill as his instrument and second cause shootes at in all these actiones of the Deuil, (as Gods hang-man)."[43] To be sure, James's treatise, written in a Socratic dialogue between two allegorical figures, Philomates and Epistemon, is primarily an attempt to persuade his readers of these theological implications of conjuring from the point of view of the Reformation. Nevertheless, what had previously been primarily a *moral* question—an opposition between white magic and black magic (or malifice)—became in his text, as in many others in seventeenth-century Protestant England, primarily a question of "conscience," as Stuart Clarke has put it, when any sort of conjuring was increasingly seen as a crime against the sovereignty of God, Church, and State.[44]

It was in the context of this new intellectual climate that one of the greatest Counter-Reformation demonologies about the New World, José de Acosta's *Historia natural y moral,* saw its first complete translation into English in 1604 by Edward Grimstone.[45] The first Englishman who prominently picked up on Acosta's contention that Native American religions were diabolic in origin was the biblical scholar and millenarian Joseph Mede, who, in the 1620s, argued in his "A Conjecture Concerning Gog and Magogs in the Revelations," that "[T]he people of America are Colonies of the nation of Magog." Thus, Satan's army "shall come from those nations, which live in the Hemisphere opposite to us, whom the Best and most Great God in his secret judgment, for the most part shall not cherish with the light of his Gospel."[46] Whereas the Old World (what he calls the "universal Hemisphere" of old), is the "onely . . . partaker of the promised instauration, shall become the camp of the Saints, and the seat of this [God's] blessed kingdome . . . whatsoever nations are without this (in the places where the Ancients placed the seat of Hel) shall be reserved to the last triumph of Christ, to be destroyed by fire from heavn, by his just (though to us unknown) judgment." In other words, the New World will be redeemed from the devil only with the coming of the Apocalypse itself.[47]

Nevertheless, if Grimstone's translation of Acosta and Mede's millenarian speculations had set the stage for the interpretation of Native religions as diabolism by English writers, the ethnographic literature about British America during the first decades of the seventeenth century still reflected little of it. Even in Puritan New England, apologists for the English invasion of Native lands made at first little rhetorical recourse to the devil. Some of the prominent New English clergymen, such as John Cotton, asserted that the English Puritans were a type of new Israelites destined to drive out the Indians, a new type of Canaanites. The New Englanders therefore saw themselves as a people "set aside" from the worldly reign of Antichristian Catholic (and Anglican) Europe, and America was their "refuge."[48] For the English, land, rather than labor or souls, was the commodity they sought in the New World, despite some notable exceptions, such as the Puritan missionary John Eliot, who belatedly discovered the Puritans' apostolic mission during the 1640s.[49] Showing little interest in Native Americans as either an object of conversion or as a source of labor, the English colonists interpreted their removal into the New World through a typological exegesis of the book of Exodus, where the devil did not play a prominent role. Thus, in "God's Promise to His Plantations" (1630), Cotton admitted of "three ways" in which the Indian Canaanites might be deprived of their land: (1) "cast out" by "lawful war;" (2) "mak[ing] room . . . by way of purchase" or simply "courtesy;" and (3) by acting as a "void").[50] The stunning devastation that European diseases had wrought among the Indians after first contact with the Europeans was interpreted by the Puritan observer not as a sign of God's displeasure with the way Europeans had conducted themselves in the New World (as did Bartolomé de Las Casas), but rather as a confirmation that the Indians were indeed a type of Canaanites who were making room for God's people. Thus, John Winthrop, the first governor of the Puritan Massachusetts Bay colony, plausibly argued that "if God were not pleased with our inheriting these parts, why did he drive out the natives before us?"[51]

This interpretation of events, and of the meaning of the Indian, not only proved the typological progress of sacred history, but also conveniently provided the "answers" to certain "objections" voiced by enemies of the Puritan and Separatist colonial enterprises concerning the "warrant to enter upon that land which hath been so long possessed by others."[52] One such critic was the Separatist ethnographer Roger Williams, who argued that the English king had no right to grant Indian lands to Englishmen, as the Indians were the legitimate owners of these lands. He had therefore purchased the land for his colony of Rhode Island from the Indians (even though he later still sought a royal patent for the purchased land). In his ethnographic tract the *Key into the Language of America* (1643), he adopted a distinctly Realist, and even Neoplatonic, view on the origins of Algonquian culture and religion. "They have no *clothes*, *books*, nor *letters*, and conceive their *fathers* never had," he wrote, "and therefore they are easily persuaded that the *god* that made *English* men is a greater *god*: because He hath so richly endowed the *English* above *themselves*: But when they hear that about sixteen hundred years ago, *England* and the *Inhabitants* thereof were like unto *themselves*, and since have received from *God clothes*, *books*, &c. they are greatly affected with a secret hope concerning *themselves*."[53]

According to Williams, even though they were without letters, the Indians still retained a faint memory of the son of God, whom they called "Wetucks." Thus, they "have many strange relations of one *Wetucks*, a man that wrought great *miracles* amongst them, and *walking upon the waters*, &c. with some kind of broken resemblance to the *son of God*." He even suggested that, based on certain linguistic affinities between Algonquian and Greek, the Indians might be descendants of the Greeks, while he also acknowledged the theory, increasingly popular during the 1640s, after the publication of Thomas Thorowgood's *Jews in America*, that the Indians might be descended from the Ten Lost Tribes of Israel, a theory that harked back to Spanish theorists during the sixteenth century.[54]

Throughout British America, however, the demonological interpretation of Native religions and cultures did come into play more frequently in the aftermath of armed conflict that inevitably erupted as a result of the English hunger for land. In the literature about the first permanent English colony in America, Jamestown in Virginia, this moment arrived with the Powhatan confederacy's attack on the fledgling colony in 1622. Writing in 1625, and apparently remembering Acosta and Mede, the Anglican minister Samuel Purchas, Richard Hakluyt's successor as collector and historian of English overseas exploration and colonization, composed a short treatise entitled "Virginia's Verger," which offered an extended theoretical disquisition on what he called the "Law of Nature and Nations" and which was one of the most elaborate articulations yet in English of the justification of the English conquest. The English claim to the land had be established, he argued, by the rights of "first discovery, first actuall possession, prescription, gift, cession, and livery of seisin, sale for price natural Inheritance of the English their naturally borne, and the unnaturall outcries of many unnaturally murthered."[55] In order to preempt conceivable objections that the acts of violence committed by the Indians had been in legitimate self-defense, Purchas emphasized their allegedly natural savagery and the diabolic nature of their religion.[56] "[C]onsidering so good a Country, so bad people, [he wrote] having little of Humanitie but shape, ignorant of Civilitie, of Arts, or Religion; more brutish then the beasts they hunt, more wild and unmanly then that unmanned wild Countrey, which they range rather then inhabite; captivated also to Satans tyranny in foolish pieties, mad impieties, wicked idlenesse, busie and bloudy wickednesse: hence have wee fit objects of zeale and pitie, to deliver from the power of darknesse."[57]

Similarly, John Smith, in his work *The Generall Historie of Virginia* (1624), published two years after the massacre, portrayed the Powhattans' religion as Satanic spectacles about which he reported with what he claimed was the authority of an eyewitness captive. In his *Generall Historie* he reproduced de Bry's image from Harriot's account of "their idol Kiwasa," as well as de Bry/ Harriot's designation of a Native shaman as a conjurer (Figure 12). In Smith's account the conjuror (as well as the priest) appear as minions to an idol with clearly demonic characteristics. Thus, Smith reports that, during his captivity among the Powhattans, "they entertained him with most strange and fearefull Coniurations," and he concludes that the Powhattans' religion is essentially diabolic and entirely born of fear.

All things that are able to doe them hurt beyond their prevention, [he writes] they adore with their kinde of divine worship; as the

Figure 12. "A description of part of the adventures of Cap. Smith in Virginia," John Smith, *The Generall Historie of Virginia, New England, and the Summer Isles*, London, 1624. Courtesy of the John Carter Brown Library at Brown University.

fire, water, lightning, thunder, our Ordnance, peeces, horses, &c. But their chiefe God they worship is the Devill. Him they call Okee, and serue him more of feare then loue. They say they haue conference with him, and fashion themselues as neare to his shape as they can imagine. In their Temples they haue his image euill favouredly carved, and then painted and adorned with chaines of copper, and beads, and covered with a skin, in such manner as the deformitie may well suit with such a God.[58]

This Okee, continues Smith, demands yearly sacrifices of fifteen children, which "they they held to be so necessary, that if they should omit it, their Okee or Devill, and all their other . . . Gods, would let them haue no Deere, Turkies, Corne, nor fish, and yet besides, he would make a great slaughter amongst them." Although he also reports that the Indians held the English God as more powerful than theirs, given that he supplied them with weapons superior than theirs, they appear to be beyond salvation by human endeavors.

"In this lamentable ignorance doe these poore soules sacrifice themselues to the Devill," he concludes, "not knowing their Creator; and we had not language sufficient, so plainly to expresse it as make them vnderstand it; which God grant they may."[59] This interpretation is a long way from Harriot's earlier portrayal of the "Virginians'" religion, as their alleged diabolism puts them beyond the possibility of salvation. For Smith, as for the majority of Protestant ethnographers in the seventeenth century, it is not man's business to extirpate or exorcise witchcraft. Thus, Smith, enduring the afflictions of Powhattan's Satanic malefice, commends himself to God, who, miraculously, sends him a young Indian maiden, Powhattan's daughter Pocohontas, and Smith and Jamestown are restored to God's good protection.

In New England, a similar transformation in the perception of Native religions took hold in the second part of the seventeenth century, especially after King Philip's War. However, unlike the representations of Native religions of late sixteenth- and early seventeenth-century Spanish accounts of conquest (such as Bernal Díaz del Castillo's *Historia verdadera de la conquista de la Nueva España* or Gaspar de Villagrá's *Historia de la Nueva México*), the Puritan accounts of King Philip's War, such as William Hubbard's *A Narrative of the Troubles with the Indians,* Increase Mather's *A Relation of the Troubles with the Indians*, or Mary Rowlandson's *The Soveraignty and Goodness of God*, conceive of Native diabolism not as something to be extirpated but rather to be suffered. It is interpreted entirely within the Protestant understanding of witchcraft as a matter of "consciences," couched in the rhetorical structure of the Jeremiad, where Native Americans and their diabolic god prevail only temporarily when God's protection of his "new Jerusalem" in New England is temporarily lifted as the colony's collective punishment for some of its internal backsliders and degenerates. In Mary Rowlandson's *The Soveraignty and Goodness of God* (1682), for example, the interior "wilderness" of the colonial soul was projected upon an exterior "Indian wilderness"— upon irredeemable "black creatures in the night," as Rowlandson wrote, "which made the place [of her captivity] a lively resemblance of hell."[60]

Similarly, in *Wonders of the Invisible World*, his account of the Salem witch trials, Cotton Mather, the most prolific New English writer of the seventeenth century, synthesized Mede's notion of the hemisphere's Satanic past with the providentialist understanding of witchcraft as a case of conscience. One of the reasons, he argued, why New England was afflicted so severely by witchcraft in Salem and Andover in 1692 was the circumstance that New England was located in America, which once was "the *Devils* Territories" before the arrival of the Europeans. "When the Silver-Trumpets of the Lord Jesus were so sound in the other *Hemisphere* of our World," he wrote in his *Seasonable Discourses,* "the Devil got a forlorn Crue over hither into America, in hopes that the Gospel never would come at them here." One of the weapons that the devil employed in his retaliation against the New English Christian vanguard was his art of mimesis, or imitation of the Christian church and rituals, such as an organization "after the manner of Congregational Churches," the celebration of a baptism, and a supper, as well as "Officers among them, abominably Resembling those of our Lord." "'Tis very Remarkable to see," he wrote, "what an Impious & Imputent *Imitation* of Divine Things, is Apishly affected by the Devil, in several of those matters, whereof the Confessions of our Witches . . . have informed us." Clearly, Mather echoed here the demonology of José de Acosta almost a hundred years before, citing him in Grimstone's 1604 translation in one of the editions of *Wonders* printed by Benjamin Harris in 1693, which added to the previous editions of this work also a number of natural and preternatural "curiosities" concerning the phenomenon of witchcraft, which Mather recorded in the empiricist spirit, becoming of a member of the Royal Society of London. "[T]he Indians which came from far to settle about Mexico," Mather wrote, "were in their Progress to that Settlement, under a Conduct of the Devil, very strangely Emulating what the Blessed God gave to Israel in the Wilderness." Citing Acosta, Mather continues to relate the story of the Aztecs' migration to Mexico under the command of "the Devil" god Huitzilopochtli.[61]

Thus, for Mather, the witches of Salem perpetuated a long tradition of diabolism already begun by the Aztecs in Mexico. However, if the New World, both North and South America, was thus more dangerously exposed than its Old World counterpart to the machinations of a raging devil deprived of his last hideout, so well disguised by the Atlantic ocean for millennia, it was only because of the sins of New Englanders that he was able to inflict any harm. Thus, Mather writes,

> The first Planters of these Colonies were a *Chosen Generation* of
> men, who were first so *Pure,* as to disrelish many things which
> they thought wanted *Reformation* else where; and yet withal so
> *Peaceable,* that they Embraced a Voluntary Exile in a Squalid,
> horrid, *American* Desert, rather than to Live in Contentions with
> their Brethren. . . . But alas, the Children, and Servants of those
> Old planters, must needs afford many, *Degenerate Plants,* and there
> is now Risen up a Number of people, otherwise Inclined than our

Joshua's and the *Elders that outlived them*. . . . Hence tis, that the
Happiness of *New-England,* has been, *but for a Time,* as it was
foretold, and not for a *Long Time,* as ha's been desir'd for us. A
Variety of Calamity ha's long follow'd this Plantation; and we have
all the Reason imaginable to ascribe it unto the Rebuke of Heaven
upon us for our manifold *Apostasies;* we make no Right use of our
Disasters, if we do not, *Remember whence we are fallen, and Repent,
and Do the first works.* But yet our Afflictions may come under a
further Consideration with us: there is a further cause of our
Afflictions, whose *Due* must be *Given* him.[62]

Conclusion

European expansionism beyond the Pillars of Hercules had been inspired not
only by the intense religious messianism of the Middle Ages but also in part
by the great cultural syncretism of the fifteenth century, which fused, as
Anthony Grafton has written, a "kaleidoscopic variety" of Christian, Jewish,
Muslim, and pagan knowledge traditions into a coherent, if elastic, body of
Renaissance philosophy that attributed unprecedented agency, nobility, and
efficacy to human reason, technology, and magic, as evidenced by the writings of such fifteenth- and sixteenth-century philosophers as Marsilio Ficino,
Giovanni Pico della Mirandola, Cornelius Agrippa, and Paracelsus.[63] On the
other hand, the establishment of transoceanic colonial empires resulted in
the formation of unprecedented concentrations of state power in Europe,
with the rise of the early modern absolutist states that aimed to impose
unprecedented levels of religious unity and conformity upon the myriad, lo-
cally diverse forms of local saint worship (much of it with pagan origins) that
had characterized Christianity in Europe throughout the Middle Ages.[64]
While the forces of the Reformation and Counter-Reformation were battling
one another in sixteenth-century Europe (with conscript armies largely paid
for with American gold and silver), the nationalized churches, Protestant and
Catholic alike, launched an all-out ideological assault that sought to purify
Christianity not only of the "magical" aspects that had been an integral part
of Christian practice for hundreds of years, but also of the learned "new
paganism" of Renaissance Neoplatonists and Hermeticists such as Ficino
and Giordano Bruno.

Both Spanish and English writers increasingly came, in this context, to associate Native American religions not only with paganism but with Satanism in the course of their respective colonial encounters. By keeping a dual focus on Amerindian diabolism and savagery, colonial ethnography could provide rhetorically powerful arguments for Reformation and Counter-Reformation conceptions of human nature and natural reason, which, in turn, would provide proto-Hobbesian arguments rationalizing absolute monarchy and the baroque state. While the baroque state has usually been associated with the Spanish Habsburgs and the Counter-Reformation, Maravall has emphasized that the Habsburg state was only the first in Europe to implement a Counter-Reformation/Reformation ideology of human nature that had, as we have seen, its origins in the philosophical debates of the fifteenth century.[65] To this end, it employed mass communication in an attempt to indoctrinate the masses with full programmatic rigor. However, while the English writers appeared to be following here on the rhetorical and ideological coattails of the Spanish historians of the New World, the demonization of Native American religions took nevertheless distinct forms and served very different rhetorical purposes in the ethnographic literatures of each realm. In Spanish American Counter-Reformation ethnographies, such as Hernando Ruiz de Alarcón's *Tratado de las supersticiones y costumbres gentílicas que hoy viven entre los indios naturales de esta Nueva España*, Native religious rites are represented for the purpose of extirpation (or exorcism), as his entire text was written, the author explains, to serve as a guide to other missionaries in the detection of diabolism when they find themselves in its presence, though often without being able to tell the difference between Catholic sacraments and Native superstitions, whose forms had dangerously fused in the course of decades of missionary work.[66] In other instances, such as Pedro Sarmiento de Gamboa's *Historia Índica* or Bernal Díaz del Castillo's *Historia verdadera*, the demonization served plainly political ends in debunking any claims by the Native American elites and their clerical defenders that they were the true and only "natural lords" of the New World, that the Spanish conquest had been a cruel and unjust war, and that the Spanish conquerors were illegitimate usurpers. In British America, by contrast, conquest was predicated on the legal notion of terra nullius and the fiction that America was a "virgin land" or "wilderness" that could be lawfully settled by Englishmen, not, as in the Spanish conquest, on the model of the Reconquista—the subjugation and conversion of infidels, new American vassals whose labor could be exploited.

This fundamental difference had profound consequences for the encounter between Europeans and Native Americans, for the colonial societies that developed in each realm, and also for the role that "diabolism" played there. Thus, whereas Englishmen did, at times, see themselves as victimized by the devil and his New World minions, for Franciscans in New Spain (such as Motolinía or Jerónimo de Mendieta), the devil's victims who had to be redeemed were not primarily European settlers but rather the Native neophytes, who had to be liberated from his clutches through extirpation and exorcism. In predominantly Protestant British America, by contrast, diabolism continued to be interpreted as a "matter of conscience," as something that had to be suffered and endured as a sign of God's righteous displeasure, and therefore is most typically subsumed in the rhetorical structure of the American jeremiad. When considered comparatively, the histories of both Spanish and British American perceptions of Native American religions suggest the important role that the colonial encounter itself played in the shaping of Western Christianity in the religious transformations of the early modern period.

CHAPTER 3

Martín de Murúa, Felipe Guaman Poma de Ayala, and the Contested Uses of Saintly Models in Writing Colonial American History

DAVID A. BORUCHOFF

The provision of good examples has always played a key role in missionary endeavor, both to attract and instruct converts, and to memorialize the qualities of those who would assume this task. In the Christian tradition, the paragon in both domains is understandably the example set by Christ himself. There has nevertheless been little comparative study of this phenomenon in the early Americas due in part to differences between Catholics and Protestants on the issue of individual sanctity.[1] The Catholic Church endorsed the celebration of martyrs and other saintly persons as a means to incite its adherents "to the adoration and devotion of God, and to the cultivation of piety," as explained in the decree "On the Invocation and Veneration of Saints and Their Relics, and on Holy Images," issued at the Council of Trent in 1563.[2] In contrast, Protestants were pressed to follow the teachings of Martin Luther and Philipp Melanchthon, who, even as they approved paying honor to saints as examples of God's mercy, and thus as a spur "to the imitation, first of faith, and then of the other virtues that each person should imitate in the interest of his calling,"[3] were nevertheless careful to insist that no human being should be venerated. For indeed, they maintained, no man is himself holy; rather, it is the image of Christ and the power of God that are seen in and through him.

This stand against writings and works of art that might be seen to invest their subjects with *sanctitatis fama* (a reputation of holiness) soon proved problematic for many Protestants, especially those who wished to portray their newly founded churches as inheritors of the "true Church" of the Apostles by brandishing the example of those who gave up their lives to create or defend them. This was, after all, a time-honored practice of Christian historiography, dating back at least to Tertullian (ca. 160–220), who averred that the Church as we know it sprouted from the blood of Christian martyrs.[4] John Foxe likewise wrote in the preface to his *Actes and Martyrs* (1563) that when Eusebius of Caesarea (ca. 260–340) was asked what action he held to be most "expediēt or necessary for the state and commoditie of his Churche," his reply was simple: to memorialize "the names, sufferings and actes, of all such as suffered in al that time of persecution before [Constantine's conversion] for the testimonie and faith of Christ Iesus."[5]

In 1550, when the English Protestant, Christopher Hales, wrote to a colleague in Zurich to commission five or six portraits of Huldrych Zwingli and other leading reformers, he found himself obliged to justify his request due to the fear that by this means "a door shall hereafter be opened to idolatry."[6] In this, Hales also responded to the more basic belief that "portraits can nowise be painted with a safe conscience and a due regard to godliness."[7] This response is significant, for Hales not only noted that "images were forbidden in the sacred books for no other reason than that the people of God might not be drawn aside from the true worship of one true God to the vain worship of many false gods," but moreover said that the context in which any image appears determines its potential for good or evil.[8] Because Hales proposed to use the portraits at issue, not to "impair the glory and praise of God,"[9] nor to "do honour to individuals,"[10] but instead to set before his own eyes the values and character requisite to "a more complete reformation of our church,"[11] it was, he reasoned, wholly proper and beneficial to have them. The affinities of this supposedly Protestant explanation to the stand of the Catholic Church at the Council of Trent are striking, indeed.

In 1580, the French Calvinist Théodore de Bèze would make a similar defense of the advantage to Christian society of both verbal and engraved portraits of exemplary men. Based as he was in Geneva, the most austere center of Protestant theology, Bèze (Calvin's lieutenant and then successor as leader of the Reformed movement) was well aware that not a few of his fellow reformers would object to his publishing a collection of portraits, "lest this become an occasion for us to be falsely accused of idolatry by adversaries, whom we indict as idolaters." Yet, like Hales, Bèze maintained that portraiture itself should not be forbidden just because it has been used "recklessly and against God's instruction" by others. To the contrary, if images and accounts of "learned and pious men" are used devoutly to support true Religion, they can "rouse Christians to holy thoughts, as though [we] were beholding them face-to-face, with our own eyes, as they still teach, admonish and chide us."[12]

Though already breached in practice, the rift between the official stands of Protestants and Catholics would narrow in the seventeenth century due to a series of reforms instituted by Pope Urban VIII partly in reaction to the arguments of Protestant critics concerning the merits reserved for God alone, and thus wrongly attributed to those cast "not only as intercessors, but as propitiators or mediators of redemption."[13] Besides setting restrictions on the iconography by which one might represent the person or the actions of anyone reputed to be saintly after death, yet not canonized or beatified by the Holy See,[14] Urban ordered that all "books containing the deeds, miracles, or revelations" of such people must explicitly declare at the start that "praises of saintly or blessed people that fall simply on their persons are not to be admitted, [yet] those that fall on their habits and repute are allowed."[15]

Despite this rapprochement, Protestants would continue to censure not only the agency imputed to saints by Catholics, but also the means by which Catholics were wont to record the lives of saintly people. Catholics themselves invited this rebuke, in that Urban's prohibitions were duly respected in books about miracles and revelations that might lead to beatification or canonization,[16] but not in those treating saintly deeds and experiences more broadly. The issue of individual sanctity has therefore troubled not only recent historians, who as a result tend to ignore the hagiographic bent of certain Protestant writings, but moreover early reformers such as Hales, Bèze, and Foxe, and later Puritans such as Cotton Mather, who in 1702 lamented the deleterious effect that the refusal to honor the merits of exemplary people had on the piety of his contemporaries. He asserted in his *Magnalia Christi Americana; or, The Ecclesiastical History of New-England*:

> We are not so Wise, as the Miserable Papists! Among them, a
> Person of Merit shall, at his Death, be Celebrated and Canonized
> by all Men agreeing in it, as in their Common Interest, for to
> applaud his Life. Among us, let there be Dues paid unto the
> Memory of the most Meritorious Person after his Decease; many
> of the Survivers are offended, I had almost said enraged at it: They

seem to take it as a Reproach unto themselves . . . That so much
Good should be told of any Man. . . . This Folly is as Inexpressible
an Injury to us all; as it cannot but be an Advantage unto Mankind
in General for Interred Vertue to be Rewarded with a Statue.

   If ever I deserved well of my Country, it has been when I have
given to the World the Histories and Characters of Eminent Persons,
which have adorned it.[17]

Such sentiments are frequent in Mather's writings, and in those of other
Protestants on both sides of the Atlantic in the latter decades of the seventeenth century. With the Authorized or King James version of Paul's second
letter to the Corinthians as a paratext,[18] Mather would indeed use Protestantism's disapproval of the idea of individual sanctity as a starting point for his
own belief in the symbiosis of Christian living and Christian historiography.
He states:

I Solemnly Declare, That my Pen should not have been Employ'd
on this Occasion, if I had not been verily perswaded, That it would
be a thing *Acceptable* to the Glorious GOD, and *Serviceable* very
many ways unto the cause of PIETY, to Exhibit the *Conduct* of His
Providence in the *Life* of a *Good Man*, and the *Exemplary Methods*
taken by such a Man, to do *Good* in the World. THIS is the *Mark* I
would perpetually Aim at; And if it has been Determined, That the
Name of an *Historian* shall be, *Vertues Secretary*, I know not how
the *Pen* of an *Historian* can be better Employ'd, than in Reporting
the *Vertuous* Tempers and Actions of the Men that have therein
shown forth the Vertues of our Blessed REDEEMER, and been the
Epistles of CHRIST unto the rest of Mankind.[19]

By replacing the expected sobriquet "Apostles of Christ" with the more idiosyncratic "Epistles of Christ," Mather brings into focus the dualism of his
service to the cause of piety. For if it is his aspiration as a Christian "to exhibit
the conduct of [God's] providence" in his actions, it is his duty as a historian
to commemorate the example set in this regard by others.[20] He accordingly
suggests at the outset of *Magnalia Christi Americana* that "our Lord Jesus
Christ carried some Thousands of *Reformers* into the Retirements of an
American Desart, on purpose that . . . He might there, *To* them first, and
then *By* them, give a *Specimen* of many Good Things, which He would have

His Churches elsewhere aspire and arise unto."[21] This is a theme to which the text returns time and again, indeed with ever greater insistence, as in the following preface to Mather's account of the lives of several eminent ministers: "I will add, That *Examples* do strangely charm us into Imitation. When *Holiness* is pressed upon us, we are prone to think, that it is a Doctrine calculated for *Angels* and *Spirits*, whose *Dwelling* is not with *Flesh*. But when we read the Lives of them that excelled in *Holiness*, tho' they were Persons of like *Passions* with our selves, the Conviction is wonderful and powerful. *Reader*, Behold loud Calls to *Holiness*, from those who said, not *Ite illuc*, but *Venite huc*, when the Calls were uttered."[22]

This understanding of exemplarity as a thing to be learned, lived, and memorialized, so that, through repetition, Christ's example might become universal, is normally undervalued as a factor in the mentality of early Protestant America, despite its recommendation by canonical authors such as Isaac Barrow and John Foxe.[23] Indeed, the latter's *Actes and Monuments* were prefaced with the idea that, by reading about those who in the past suffered "for the testimonie and faith of Christ," his contemporaries "may learne to knowe: not onelye what in those dayes was done, but also what ought nowe to be followed."[24] Despite resistance and misgivings, this conjointly documentary, celebratory, and exhortatory intent was by no means ignored by other Protestants. And it was far less problematically embraced by Catholics, both ordained and lay.

Exemplarity and Historiography: Missionary Authors in New Spain

Franciscan missionaries, in particular, were concerned to provide in their conduct, and also in their writings, a testimony (to use Foxe's term) of Christian comportment that might, on one hand, be emulated by the peoples they wished to convert, and, on the other, move other members of their order to join in missionary endeavor. In both facets of this undertaking, Franciscans were asked to conform to a rule set down by Francis of Assisi himself, who wrote that "all brothers must strive to follow the humility and poverty of our Lord Jesus Christ."[25]

In 1523, as the military conquest of New Spain was drawing to an end, the Franciscan minister general, Francisco de los Ángeles, explained as follows the mission to be undertaken by Fray Martín de Valencia, its custodian or leader:

What our most blessed father Francis learned from Christ and his
disciples, he showed you as well in his work, not only by going out
himself to preach to diverse parts of the world, but also by sending
his friars to the unenlightened masses, so as to make known to us
the true and pure observance of his Apostolic and Evangelical
Rule. . . . And for that reason, I now, in the same way, send forth
twelve friars with a single prelate, as this was the number of the
disciples of Christ sent to convert the world, and the number of
companions sent by our most holy father Francis to announce the
Evangelical life.[26]

Similarly attentive to the importance of precedent, the first bishop of New
Spain, Fray Juan de Zumárraga, would, in 1533, call on other Mendicants of the
Franciscan and Dominican orders to join him in America with these words:

Dearest brothers: if it behooves all Christians to assume such pious
and holy work, we surely must more promptly take it up ourselves,
if we wish to resemble our patriarchs, Francis and Dominic, . . .
not only in dress and name, but also in life and habits. It is well-
known to you how much they labored, bearing so many hardships,
enduring thirst, hunger, cold, heat, injuries, and insults to enlarge
the kingdom of Christ. . . . Imitate Christ, who from infancy wan-
dered in Egypt and beyond the confines of his homeland, not even
having a place to rest his head. Imitate, indeed, the founders of our
orders, Francis and Dominic, who nearly never remained at home:
instead, the one, that is Francis, made his way as far as the kingdoms of the Sultan to enlighten with the fire of true faith those
who were blinded by the errors of Mohammed. And the other,
Dominic, inveighed so vehemently against the confusion of the
Albigensians, so as to obliterate their errors, that he seemed to wish
to be torn to pieces one limb at a time.[27]

Statements of a similar tenor abound in the endogenous milieu of missionary writing, appearing not only in letters of recruitment, like the above,
but also in the menologies, annual reports, and memoirs with which the
mendicant orders sought to document their adherence to Christ's example.
Indeed, when, beginning in the 1560s, Spanish authorities joined with secular
clergy in a campaign to rein in the missionary orders and the so-called In-

dian Church of New Spain mainly due to dissatisfaction with the imperfect faith and nonassimilation of indigenous communities, missionary authors retorted that their intent to spread Christianity, not through coercion, but by embodying the virtues that they would have the Indians learn and adopt, was the only way suited to the ideals of their faith. New England Puritans would make similar arguments approximately a century later, as the elders of their church began to die off and membership declined. For, despite differences in their missions, both communities sought to renew themselves by celebrating the lives of their founders.[28]

For a sense of how this complex scheme worked in practice, one might consider a few moments in the historiography of New Spain in which, when reflecting on the instrumentality of the example set by others, Franciscan missionaries reveal the similar effect that they hoped to produce with their own writings. This is what I have elsewhere dubbed "the self-conscious practice of missionary history."[29]

In the final years of the sixteenth century, Jerónimo de Mendieta wrote of how the first Franciscans were received by Hernán Cortés when they arrived in 1524 in the Mexican capital of Tenochtitlan. After recounting the long trek on bare feet from the coast, and how the natives "were stunned to see the Franciscans in such ragged attire, so different from the splendor and the gallantry that they had before seen in Spanish soldiers, for which they said to one another: 'What men are these poor folk? What manner of clothing is this that they wear? These are not like other Christians from Castile,'" Mendieta declares the following: "The governor [Cortés] went forth to receive the Franciscans, accompanied by all the Spanish noblemen and principal Indians, who had gathered for this purpose. And, kneeling on the ground, he set about kissing their hands, going from one to another until he had kissed them all, as did Pedro de Alvarado and the other Spanish captains and noblemen. Seeing this, the Indians began to follow them, also kissing the friars' hands in imitation of the Spaniards. So powerful is the example of the elders."[30]

If Mendieta's report is similar in substance to those of lay contemporaries,[31] in that all who wrote about the reception of the twelve Franciscans agreed that Cortés's example played a crucial role in converting the Indians of New Spain, this is by no means the only lesson that Mendieta had in mind. For, in addition to confirming the practical impact of Cortés's gesture by reporting that "there are paintings of this much celebrated act in many parts of this land of New Spain as an eternal memorial to such a memorable deed, . . . by means of which the Holy Spirit laid a solid foundation for his divine word," Mendieta insists on its value to Christians of every stripe, be they American or European, neophytes or old. He explains: "This deed was certainly the greatest of the many said to have been performed by Cortés; for, in the others, he came to master other people, whereas in this he became master of himself. By the doctrine of the saints and all wise men, this mastery is more enduring and powerful, and more difficult to attain, than that over other very mighty things of the world."[32] I will return to this conclusion at a later point to explain its origin and the explicitly Christian sense of Cortés's self-mastery.

In a similar vein, the "Prologue to the Christian Reader" in the last book of Mendieta's *Historia eclesiástica indiana* (Ecclesiastical History of the Indies) notes the importance given to exemplarity in biblical times, in order then to proclaim the comparable worth of the legacy left to modern readers by the missionaries who devoted themselves to the conversion of New Spain. Incanting the words *remember* and *memory*, *example* and *emulation*, Mendieta writes:

> Holy letters record . . . that once, when about to battle the enemies
> of God's people, the valorous captain of God's army, Judah
> Maccabaeus, seeing the vast number and strength of his opponents,
> said, so as to encourage and incite his troops: "Remember how . . .
> our fathers and forefathers saved themselves, how they struggled,
> how they fought like men against their foes and ours." These words
> deserve to be brought and applied to our own purpose, and we must
> remember them, for at every moment we fight a spiritual battle. . . .
> We must therefore call to memory and note how the blessed priests
> and friars, whose lives I here examine, saved their souls; how they
> fought with vigor against their spiritual enemies: the world, the
> devil, and the flesh. . . . Oh blessed fathers, servants of Our Lord,
> exemplars of all virtue, luminaries who shone in all the world like
> torches lit with the love of our Lord God and of our fellow men! . . .
> For, in emulation of Christ our Redeemer, these his servants . . .
> wished with the most fervent zeal to convert unbelievers to the
> faith of our Lord. They wished to win lost souls, and to return
> others who had strayed to the path of salvation, repenting of their
> offenses to God. And if these fathers had had a thousand lives, they
> would have given them all to save one sinful soul.[33]

In much the same way, almost a century later, Agustín de Vetancurt launched his *Chronica de la provincia del Santo Evangelio de Mexico* (Chronicle of the Province of the Holy Gospel of Mexico, 1697) by proclaiming that "the father of the Maccabees, wishing to persuade his sons to defend their Law, reminded them of the works done by their ancestors." This allusion to the role that good examples have always played in fomenting religious if not patriotic fervor leads Vetancurt to set forth the principles that he himself aspired to practice in the history to follow. He states:

The lives of the venerable fathers of this Province of the Holy Gospel ought rightly to be written, so that, by seeing their humility, poverty, and zeal in converting souls, the spirits of others be moved to imitate the works of such religious men. . . . It is not right that the chastisement that God gives to worldly men—that their glories end with their lives—be given by our neglect to so praiseworthy men of religion. For although *they* have the reward of being written in the book of life, and this is sufficient for them, *we* are in need of their virtues, which God wishes be written down in history as exemplars for our [religious] order, so that we might be what they were, and raise ourselves up to what they are.[34]

The insistence with which Franciscans such as Mendieta and Vetancurt endorsed both the provision, and the emulation, of an ideal of piety consciously patterned on the example of Christ is extreme, yet understandable, given the experience of their order in New Spain.[35] For, in the sixteenth century, the authority of Franciscans in this territory not only surpassed that of other missionary groups, but indeed was such that an apostolate like the primitive Church, and independent of the Spanish state, seemed entirely possible. In this, millenarianism also played an important role, insofar as the recommendation of a single model of Christian or Christlike comportment itself reflects the end to which both Catholic and Protestant millenarians aspired in the age of European expansion: that is, the conformity of all the world's peoples in a single Church. Despite the popularity in other milieux of a more diverse set of exemplars such as the Virgin Mary, or other martyrs and saints, among missionaries *imitatio Christi* was paramount, informing not only the value attached by the willing pursuit of privations and suffering in the texts with which Zumárraga, Mendieta, and Vetancurt sought to goad their brethren to action, but moreover the insistence put on humility, piety, self-control, and mercy, ideals to which all Christians can and should aspire, regardless of their status as ordained or lay members of the Church.[36] The remainder of my comments involve this second facet of *imitatio Christi*, so as to assess the broader impact of the missionary idea of exemplarity, that is, the impact that the ideal of Christlike saintliness had in communities far less successful and self-reflective than that of the Franciscan order in New Spain, and indeed among authors not usually seen to have drawn inspiration from religious teachings.

Exemplarity and Historiography: Martín de Murúa and Felipe Guaman Poma de Ayala

The Mercedarian Fray Martín de Murúa is today remembered primarily for his personal and professional interactions with Felipe Guaman Poma de Ayala, the native Andean artist and writer who created most of the illustrations included in Murúa's two interrelated works: the *Historia del origen y genealogía real de los reyes ingas del Piru* (History of the Origin and Royal Genealogy of the Inca Kings of Peru, finished in 1596 or a bit later) and the *Historia general del Piru* (General History of Peru, whose final revisions date to 1616). This focus on the at times conflictive collaboration of Murúa and Guaman Poma, particularly as reported or reflected in the latter's *El primer nueva corónica i buen gobierno* (The First New Chronicle and Good Government, 1615), has led critics to all but ignore the religious intent that guided both authors at key moments in their writings. And because the chapters on colonial society, polity, economics, law, and religion in Murúa's *Historia general* are far fewer than those dealing with Andean peoples in preconquest times, this text has normally been studied for the ethnographic interest shared by his earlier work on the Incas and Guaman Poma's *Nueva corónica*. In other words, it is commonly read as a record of what were then called *antigüedades* and *antiguallas* or "things of another time," as defined by Sebastián de Covarrubias in his *Tesoro de la lengua Castellana, o Española* (Thesaurus of the Castilian or Spanish Language, 1611).[37]

Although this may have been Murúa's original purpose, it is problematic to neglect the extensive reworking—or more properly reconceptualization—of the *Historia general del Piru* in anticipation of its publication, especially in light of the still effective royal order "that in no way is anyone at all [to be allowed] to write things that touch on the superstitions and manner of life that the Indians had in the past."[38] Given this prohibition, it is understandable that most of the ecclesiastical and bureaucratic approvals required by law for publication, and therefore included in the preliminary pages of Murúa's manuscript, take pains to stress the spiritual and political benefits of documenting indigenous customs. These aver, for example, that "knowing them will be of great advantage to priests who attend to Indians in this realm,"[39] and that, from the examples of "rites and gentilities" presented by Murúa, "one will be able to infer the great mercy that God has bestowed on this realm of Peru by the hand of the Catholic kings of Spain in sending his ecclesiastical and lay ministers here to preach the Gospel."[40] Such assertions in regard to the value of *antigüedades* were in fact common, as evinced by the prefaces of Diego Durán and Bernardino de Sahagún in New Spain, among others. However, Murúa intends not only to record native customs and traditions, so that others might "apply, as is proper, to each illness the contrary medicine," as Sahagún explained,[41] but moreover to frame his narrative in the teleology of Christian salvation. That is, Murúa does not merely recount the progress from barbarism to civilization featured in the histories of the Incas themselves, while divorcing this political and cultural achievement (made possible by Natural Law) from the divine knowledge required for salvation.[42] Instead, like José de Acosta before him,[43] he casts the Incas' progress as an inexorable march from chaos and superstition to harmony and truth, ideals that are to be fully realized in the Church triumphant.

It is here that the missionary notion of *imitatio Christi* is most perceptible in Murúa's work. By the time that Murúa began to write his *Historia general del Piru* in the first decade of the 1600s, the Mercedarian order was in steep decline, having lost its foundational mission of redeeming Christian captives from the Moors, and having played a relatively minor role in the spiritual conquest of New Spain and other major centers of native population. This is not to say that the Mercedarians' contributions were trivial, or that the exploits of certain friars—such as Bartolomé de Olmedo, chaplain to Cortés, and Francisco de Bobadilla, who arbitrated the disputes of Francisco Pizarro and Diego de Almagro—had gone unnoted, but instead that, because of their geographic dispersion, Mercedarians did not enjoy the repute of Franciscans and Dominicans, or even of Augustinians and newly founded Jesuits. An exception was their agency in the region of Cuzco; yet here, too, there were signs of trouble in the early 1600s, as *doctrinas de indios*—parishes for the indoctrination of indigenous peoples that were entrusted to regular clergy with the understanding that these temporary settlements would be taken over by secular clergy once the natives were deemed to have become sufficiently proficient in their new faith—came under attack because of their corruption and inefficiency, bringing increased ecclesiastical oversight and a vigorous campaign to extirpate idolatry, as in New Spain.[44]

To combat this tarnished image, the Mercedarian order began in the second decade of the seventeenth century to subsidize publications to celebrate its prior glories, most notably a general history of the order by its official chronicler, Fray Alonso Remón. As Rolena Adorno has noted, Murúa's effort to see his history into print was compromised, not only by the need to compete for funding with Remón's project, whose first volume was released in 1618,[45] but also by the priority logically given to other works more clearly beneficial both to the cause of the Mercedarian order, and to that of Spain's American conquests in general.[46] A case in point is Bernal Díaz del Castillo's *Historia Verdadera de la Conqvista de la Nueva España* (True History of the Conquest of New Spain), whose publication in 1632 was praised by Remón as an action "in honor of the pious services of my holy religion and . . . of the notable deeds and never imagined incidents that were seen in the first conquests of New Spain."[47] Similarly of greater advantage to the Mercedarian order were quasi-hagiographic texts such as the bluntly titled *Recuerdos históricos y políticos de los servicios que los generales y varones ilustres de la religión de Nuestra Señora de la Merced . . . han hecho a los Reyes de España en los dos mundos* (Historical and Political Memories of the Services that the Generals and Illustrious Men of the Religious Order of Our Lady of Mercy . . . Have Done for the Kings of Spain in Both Worlds, 1646), by Marcos Salmerón. A work focused, like Murúa's, on the traditions of peoples still not fully assimilated into the Spanish Church and state could apparently not hope to compete with these other histories for funding by the Mercedarian order.

This did not stop Murúa and his editor Remón from trying, however. In addition to the reorganization of Andean history into a chronological narrative leading up to the present,[48] the revised text of Murúa's work locates the culmination of this process, not in the rule of Spanish political authorities, but in that of the "very saintly shepherds" who have "attended only to the spiritual interest [of Indians], and the winning of their souls, oblivious to the temporal rewards of estates and riches."[49] Murúa reports that the Andeans were overcome by the "good example and saintly life of these men of religion, [who] always strived to preach more with works than with words," and so the Andeans "received the holy Gospel so truly that they directly flocked to the church with great fervor to hear the mass . . . and, noting the life that those saintly men led, they even decided to undertake many acts of discipline and other spiritual exercises, carried along by the [friars'] good example, which is the thing most apt to move the heart."[50] Passages of a similar sort abound in the chapters added to Murúa's history, in effect making the virtuous agency of the Mercedarians the linchpin in the transition from native to Spanish-Christian society. Thus, ignoring the problematic situation of the early 1600s, Murúa was able, on one hand, to argue the symbiosis of political and spiritual governance under Spanish rule, and, on the other, to honor his Mercedarian order.

In the first of these veins, he proclaims in the final paragraph of the section that, again, sets out the new teleology of his revised history:

> And thus, if in the time that their Incas and kings ruled and
> governed the Indians, they were sustained in peace, tranquility,
> and justice, and lived with safety and quiet, today, under the order
> and monarchy of the Catholic kings of Spain, they are more
> protected, defended, and sheltered, with a king so zealous of their
> well-being, and so merciful and Christian. . . . And thus, the state
> of the Indians of Peru is more felicitous and fortunate than in
> ancient times. They are set on the path of the salvation of their
> souls and, living under saintly and just laws, are governed by very
> loving fathers, for thus may be called the kings and prelates that
> they now have.[51]

While Murúa lauds the civil order achieved by the Incas, so, too, does he insist that Christianity brought an essential change, seen here in the contention that the king of Spain is both merciful and fatherly, concerned for the Indians' welfare in a way that the Incas were not.[52] Hence, the unmistakably Christian conclusion that the Indians are today "felicitous and fortunate." If this fiction is designed to flatter and coerce the crown to support the missionary cause, it is also of a piece with the various reports of conversion, indoctrination, admonition, and castigation with which Murúa documents the achievements of his fellow Mercedarians. For, in each and every case, he makes evident the political and civil benefits—and greater efficacy—of entrusting the spiritual governance of the Indians to the Mercedarian order. As a result, Murúa can argue the importance of the chapters added to his history in conceits akin to those used by Mendieta and Vetancurt:

It is not without mystery that I have set into this book of the
General History of Peru these . . . chapters, which to some it might
seem better to exclude. I myself would rather have excluded them,
had I not seen that, in reading the saintly life of the religious men
of this sacred order, and in seeing the benefit that the elders did in
all of Peru and in all its cities and villages, we in the present might
endeavor to do as much, moved by their good example and stirred
by the reward that God promises to those who fight on until the
end, like valorous soldiers in the defeat of infidels.[53]

The reiteration of such claims about Mercedarians in Peru invites one to
infer that they adhered assiduously to the evangelical ideals of Christ and his
apostles, and therefore, like the Franciscans in New Spain, saw the intervention of other ecclesiastical and political authorities at the time when Murúa
was writing to be not only unwelcome, but also improper and indeed subversive.
This conclusion is surely what Murúa intended, and various of the revisions
made to the manuscript by Remón additionally seek to make Murúa's tributes
to the positive effects of missionary zeal in general apply more particularly to the
Mercedarian order. So, too, did he erase most vestiges of Murúa's personal contacts and experience, so as to make his history an account of the benefits of
collective action.[54]

Quite otherwise is the picture of the Mercedarians painted by Guaman
Poma de Ayala. Citing their greed, impiety, wantonness, and cruelty, Guaman
Poma indeed singles out Murúa, his former collaborator, for special reproach,
addressing the reader directly as follows:

Look, Christian: what evil and harm has been done to me as a poor
man, and what will be done to other poor people who know nothing
and are poorer still and without favor. Afterward the fathers say:
"Oh, what bad doctrine [the Indians have]!" As we are not rich, all
these things occur. You'll say that the protectors sent at the king's
expense are put here to prevent this, but instead they steal and rob
and take counsel with the others, and there is no remedy. The same
is the wont here of the principal *curacas* and mayors and treasury
officials; for they all steal and are arrogant, enemies of the poor,
devotees of taking their estates, [and] far more so the mestizos,
mulattoes, and Spanish Creoles, who, in my presence, mistreat the
Indians. Look, Christian: all the aforesaid offenses and harm and

evils have been done to me; a mercenary friar named Morúa in the town of Yanaca even went so far as to want to take away my woman. And they do not wish to see educated Christian Indians speaking Spanish; it frightens them and they at once order me thrown out of the said towns; they maintain that we are all simpleton asses in order to end up taking away whatever one has: an estate, woman, and daughter.[55]

Guaman Poma continues in this vein for several pages, alternating between the first and third persons, between his own experience and that of other Indians in general. Amid all the lapses in grammar and diction, a few stand out as almost certainly intentional: for example, when he calls Murúa a *mercenario*, rather than *mercedario*, that is, a mercenary and not a Mercedarian. This barbed characterization is recurrent in the *Nueva corónica*, appearing as a caption on the drawing (Figure 13) that shows Murúa beating a native weaver to epitomize the conduct typical of his order: "MERCENARIAN FRIAR MORÚA. They are so angry and quick to punish and mistreat Indians and, with a stick, make [them] work in this realm in the *doctrinas*; there is no remedy."[56]

From this and similar remarks, it is evident that Guaman Poma was not only cognizant of the theological tenet turned missionary slogan *fides suadenda est, non imponenda* (faith has to be won by persuasion, and must not be imposed),[57] but, moreover, was determined to damn the neglect or, worse yet, repudiation of this ideal in common practice. In contrast to his generally uneven command of Spanish, Guaman Poma correctly uses a series of theological catchwords to expose the sinful practices of those who minister to Indians, pointedly offering the resulting account of things done and gone wrong as an admonishment to the Christian reader, so that he might go on to rectify them. If the intent of this is primarily to win more humane treatment for his fellow Indians, Guaman Poma is also quick to note that cruelty and disdain in fact obstruct the presumed interest of the Christian reader in the spiritual, political, and cultural assimilation of Indians. This informs the previous example of how natives who, like himself, are educated and able to speak Spanish are nevertheless shunned and abused by their religious and political "protectors." Such complaints about the failure to concede the rights, privileges, and honors of citizenship to converts and conquered or subject peoples have deep roots in both theology and political theory. These two strains converged in Spain at the turn of the seventeenth century in the debate on the status of the

Figure 13. "MERCENARIAN FRIAR MORÚA. They are so angry and quick to punish and mistreat Indians and, with a stick, make [them] work in this realm in the *doctrinas*; there is no remedy." Felipe Guaman Poma de Ayala, *El primer nveva coronica i buen gobierno*, 647 [661]. Reproduced by permission of the Danish Royal Library.

Moriscos (Christianized Moors), leading the eminent humanist Pedro de Valencia, for one, to note that if this minority "were to remain distinct and secluded, forever marked with infamy and disdain, and weighted down by special tributes, it will come to persist as servants [as a subject people] and not as true citizens, and it will carry forward its hatred and desire for the perdition of the republic."[58] It is therefore crucial to the health of the Spanish state, and to the salvation of all its citizens, old and new, to treat those who have been conquered in a Christian way. In this vein, Guaman Poma proclaims:

> Do not be annoyed in reading this book, Christian reader; read it very well and restrain yourself with it. . . . Good people will laugh at this book; the bad will be angered and afflicted by it, and they will desire to kill me. But I tell you, Christian readers, that you have never had a brother in this world who has so greatly desired the salvation of your souls and consciences, and who has freed you of [so many] travails and afflictions and sins, and has honored you so much. Take this book and read it *de verbo in verbo* [word for word], and you will agree and cry with all your spirit, and you will see what is evil, and what is not. And rid of [evil], you will speak freely with your lord and prelate, and you will be honored. And you will fit into the world with the small and the great—and you will deal with the pope and king, and they will keep you in their sight and spirit.[59]

Such calls for the reader to note, understand, and take to heart the examples found in the pages to follow, so that he might reform himself and others, run throughout the several introductions and prologues of the *Nueva corónica*, revealing its origin in the troubled reality of Peru, and its intent as a spiritual, political, and moral corrective.[60]

Although the disdain expressed by Guaman Poma for Mercedarians also extends to the Dominicans and Augustinians, it clearly does not to the Franciscans and Jesuits, whose "great obedience, humility, charity, and love of others" are said so greatly to impress the Indians that they not only hasten without fear to kiss their hands in obedience, but also wish to follow their "saintly and very Christian" example.[61] As we have seen, such claims are the stock-in-trade of missionary writing, used to defend both the sanctity and the benefits of kindness in converting others. Leaving aside the clearly political intent behind Guaman Poma's use of spiritual ideals to censure practices and policies that do not conform, I would note that palpably saintly actors appear at a number of key points in the *Nueva corónica* with a more particular, self-interested, and curious purpose.

Indeed, at the very start of the work, Guaman Poma sets forth "the history and life and Christianity" shown in the service of God, first by his father and then by his half brother, both of whom were named Martín de Ayala. Following on the heels of a prologue addressed to the Christian reader, in which Guaman Poma states that he endured the many years that it took to finish his work "by bearing in mind that it had to be of use to faithful Christians in amending their sins and evil lives and errors,"[62] the story of the two Martíns is clearly intended as more than a documentary exercise. Although it opens with Guaman Poma's noble, pious, and heroic father, who, we are told, "passed on his example, advice, and doctrine to his stepson Martín de Ayala, the saintly mestizo, and prodded and set him to serve God,"[63] it is soon evident that the real focus of interest is the stepson-turned-priest himself. In the two drawings that accompany the text, the first (Figure 14), captioned "how God ordained the said history or first chronicle," depicts the dove of the Holy Ghost descending to illuminate the young Martín, as his parents look on. In the second drawing (Figure 15), entitled "father Martín de Ayala, saint, beloved by God," Guaman Poma and his parents kneel with clasped hands before the adult priest Martín, devoutly awaiting his instruction or blessing. The lives of the two Martíns, father and son, are presented together, as a preface to the *Nueva corónica* proper, in order to infer the continuity of pre- and postconquest ethics—or, more precisely, the continuity of pre-Christian and Christian virtue—a key theme in this and other texts by indigenous and mestizo authors, particularly El Inca Garcilaso de la Vega in Peru and Fernando de Alva Ixtlilxóchitl in New Spain.[64] Guaman Poma repeatedly insists that where this continuity has been interrupted and the morality of his people has decayed, it is due to "bad fathers" (meaning *priests* in the first instance) and a lack of decent examples, as well as the "great damages and evils" done to Indians by an oppressive and confusing surfeit of "incas," that is, overlords.[65]

Even in this self-interested context, the terms in which Guaman Poma presents his half brother's devotion stand out prominently for the insinuation of saintliness. A third drawing (Figure 16) has a tonsured Martín flagellating himself in penitence before an image of Christ on the cross, even as he is crowned by an angel. In all of these illustrations, Martín's hair is wavy and his clothes are European, features not regularly found in Guaman Poma's

Figure 14. "How God Ordained the Said Histories [or] First Chronicle." The kneeling hermit Martín de Ayala is illuminated by the dove of the Holy Ghost as his mother and stepfather, Juana Curi Ocllo and Martín de Ayala, look on. Felipe Guaman Poma de Ayala, *El primer nveva coronica i buen gobierno*, 14. Reproduced by permission of the Danish Royal Library.

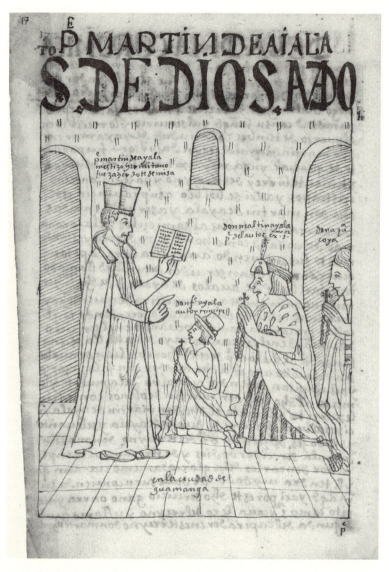

Figure 15. "Father Martín de Ayala, Saint, Beloved by God." The author Guaman Poma de Ayala and his parents, Juana and Martín de Ayala, kneel before Father Martín de Ayala to receive his blessing. Felipe Guaman Poma de Ayala, *El primer nveva coronica i buen gobierno*, 17. Reproduced by permission of the Danish Royal Library.

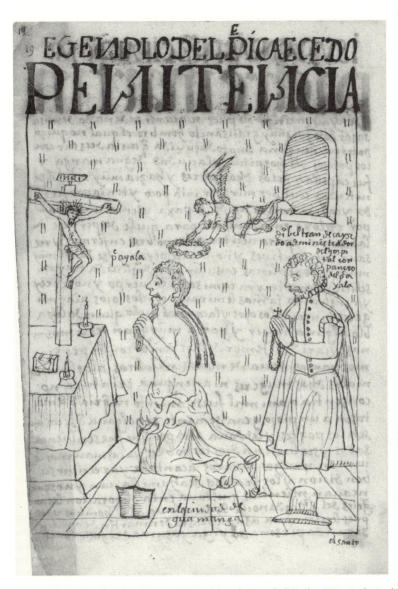

Figure 16. "Example of Father [Martín de Ayala] and Caicedo." Father Martín de Ayala is accompanied by Diego Beltrán de Caicedo, administrator of the hospital of Huamanga. Felipe Guaman Poma de Ayala, *El primer nveva coronica i buen gobierno*, 19. Reproduced by permission of the Danish Royal Library.

depiction of other mestizos.[66] It would therefore appear that Martín is acculturated, yet, in context, this acculturation is truly to a Christian, rather than
political or social, ideal.[67]

Guaman Poma's iconography is certainly heavy-handed, using devices
of the sort soon to be prohibited by Urban VIII, yet it pales in comparison to
the conceits that Guaman Poma uses to set forth the saintly life of Martín
as a priest:

> Father Martín de Ayala was a very highly saintly man who, after he
> had been ordained as a priest to say mass, did not want any *doctrina*,
> but instead had to be all his life with the poor of the hospital of the
> city of Huamanga; and he was chaplain of the said poor and did
> very many acts of penitence. He slept little and had as his blanket
> and mattress a mat woven from straw; and at the head of his bed he
> had as a clock a rooster to wake him for prayer and to visit the poor
> who were ill. And he prayed his matins, nones, and vespers, and
> inflicted many acts of discipline on his flesh. All his life he wore a
> cilice, and never a shirt against his body. And he did not laugh in all
> his life; he never looked with his eyes at women, and fixed his eyes
> and face on the ground whenever a woman spoke to him. And he
> gave very abundant alms as charity, for fear of God and for love of
> his fellow men. He never said bad words to men or to women or to
> any creature. He did not consent that any creature be killed, nor did
> he wish to kill even a louse. He was greatly pleased that the poor
> should marry, and gave them dowries so that they be well married
> and serve God. In the mornings, many birds would come to sing to
> him and to receive his benediction, and mice would bow down and
> not fidget while he was saying this prayer. Each night, the angels of
> the Lord would reveal [themselves] to this saintly man, and after-
> ward he would teach his stepfather don Martín de Ayala . . . and
> mother and brothers God's holy commandment[s] and holy Gospel,
> and good works of mercy, from which his stepfather don Martín de
> Ayala and his mother doña Juana came more strongly to believe
> and, together with all their brothers, they served God and had great
> competence and faith in God.[68]

This is no historical account, but instead a parable about the need for compassion for even the smallest and weakest of God's creatures, and thus for the

poor and lowly Indians of Peru. And needless to say, it is by means of this compassion that Indians will become good Christians.

Guaman Poma's account of his half brother's virtues draws heavily on the *vitae* or life stories of consecrated saints, notably those written about Francis of Assisi (d. 1226). Foremost among the latter for its enduring influence and popularity was Bonaventure's *Legenda maior* (Longer Compilation), which was declared to be the "only authentic and official" biography of Saint Francis in 1266. Like other *vitae*, the *Legenda maior* dwells on the humility, charity, piety, obedience, poverty, and care for all creatures embodied in Francis, and on the salutary effect that his lifestyle had on others around him. The chapter on his austerity begins with the following report: "When that worthy man of God, Francis, discerned that many were inspired by his example to carry the cross of Christ with fervent spirit, he himself, like a good leader of the army of Christ, was inspired as well to [gain the] palm of victory by attaining to the height of invincible virtue."[69] So, too, are we told of the awe caused by how, when Francis preached God's word, birds "suddenly fell silent, and did not move out of place until the whole sermon was brought to an end. Everyone who saw this, being filled with wonder, did therefore glorify God. News of this miracle, having spread in every direction, incited many to awe for the saint, and to devotion of the faith."[70] Clearly, Bonaventure's intent was not simply to celebrate the holiness of this one man, but instead to highlight the importance of his example.

This instructive aim is magnified in the popular literature based on the *Legenda maior*, especially given the homogenizing tendency of menologies, *sanctorales*, and other collections of *vitae* such as Jacobus de Voragine's *Legenda aurea* (The Golden Legend, ca. 1270) and its vernacular successors. One of the latter, Pedro de la Vega's *Flos sanctorum* (Flowering of the Saints), indeed makes explicit many lessons that Bonaventure deemed self-evident. Referring to Francis's refusal to kill insects and his "compassion for brute animals, who lack reason," it asks, rhetorically, "how great (one must believe) was the compassion that he had for men."[71] Such conclusions are precisely what Guaman Poma wished us to draw from his portrait of his half brother Martín. And, like Bonaventure, Guaman Poma also intended that Martín's saintly example inspire others to live in a more Christian manner, starting with the reader.

Given their origin in such statements, the hagiographic conventions used in the *vita* of Martín de Ayala understandably call into question the authenticity of his portrayal, if not also his status as "a very highly saintly man." Nevertheless, because his story is placed at the start of the *Nueva corónica*, it serves as a standard against which to measure the events that follow. Indeed, this is its explicit purpose in the long chapter, of more than one hundred pages, on the sins and abuses committed by priests in Peru. The title page of this chapter proclaims that "the first foundation . . . of Christian and holy fathers was Jesus Christ, the apostles Saint Peter and Saint Paul, and the saints,"[72] an idea also suggested on the following page by a drawing (Figure 17) of a "very Christian father" flanked by Saints Peter and Paul. As commentators of the work rightly note, the designation "very Christian father" clashes with the relentless vituperation of priests in the chapter itself. Nevertheless, the irony is intended not simply as ridicule, but as a means to instruct and reform. For whereas the title page explains that priests are to follow the example of Jesus Christ, his apostles, and other saints, the drawing suggests that this is not the case in Peru. Indeed, the priest's pristine vestments, rigid carriage, and oddly blank expression starkly contrast the humble, wise, and rumpled appearance of the barefoot Peter and Paul. In a work whose illustrations pay such careful and persistent attention to footwear, headgear, hair, clothing, and facial features as indications of ethnicity, social status, wealth, and perhaps more intimate or transcendent qualities—such as wisdom, sanctity, compassion, and goodness—it is hard to miss Guaman Poma's point.

The chapter goes on to give examples of the many ways that priests and other religious authorities in Peru spurn Christian ideals and obligations, notably by putting their own interest and comfort, as well as their frequently sinful desires, above the welfare of their flock. In each case, Guaman Poma insists, the result is ruinous:

> By this means, harm is done to Spaniards and even more to New Christians, that is, to Indians and blacks; [for] how can [a priest] with a dozen children give a good example to the Indians of this kingdom? As the fathers and curates of *doctrinas* are very readily moved to anger, and [are] absolute lords and arrogant, and carry great weight, the said Indians flee from fear. And the said priests do not remember that our Lord Jesus Christ made himself poor and humble in order to gather together and attract poor sinners, and bring them to his holy Church, and to carry them from there to his celestial kingdom.[73]

Within the frame of this remonstrative paradigm, Guaman Poma cites the contrasting example of his half brother Martín, pointedly addressing it first

Figure 17. "First Chapter of Father[s]." The central figure, labeled "very Christian father," is flanked by Saint Peter and Saint Paul. Felipe Guaman Poma de Ayala, *El primer nveva coronica i buen gobierno*, 561 [575]. Reproduced by permission of the Danish Royal Library.

to delinquent priests and then, through them, to the reader: "My fathers, see what God commands in the Gospel; see how the blessed saintly apostles, and other saintly martyrs, and confessors and virgins followed [it]. And in order that you might see [it], it is shown to you by this saintly man of God, father Martín de Ayala, who was mestizo, and the life of [Francis of Assisi by?] Saint John Bonaventure, [who was] black, and [the life] that these saints made."[74] Guaman Poma then recounts the greatly austere, pious, chaste, and compassionate ways of father Martín in much the same—if perhaps more blatantly hagiographic—terms as at the start of the *Nueva corónica*,[75] before insisting yet again that the sins of other men of religion in Peru "sully the honor and merit of being priests." The point of all this is patent. Nevertheless, Guaman Poma states in conclusion: "Good priests must submit themselves to God and leave behind all the riches and vanity of the world; they must drive the flesh and the devil out of themselves, and win souls to set before the eyes of the Holy Trinity. It is for this that he anointed and made himself Christ and a blessed apostle. You must be a martyr, rather than a confessor, to receive honor, like the saints of God."[76]

Exemplarity, Indoctrination, and Self-Mastery

If in the writings of Foxe, Mather, Mendieta, Vetancurt, and Murúa the example of Christ and his apostles intends to honor and inform the virtue of their brothers in religion, for Guaman Poma de Ayala it is instead a contrapositive reminder of the injustices to which he and his fellow Indians have been subject. In both cases, saintly models aspire to influence the transformation of religion in the early Americas by showing the benefit of conformity to evangelical ideals. It is nevertheless problematic to try to separate the reform of religion from the reform of society and politics more broadly. If one takes as an example Mendieta's conclusion that self-mastery was the greatest of Cortés's achievements, it becomes evident that this, too, was conceptualized as a Christian deed. Despite roots in the writings of Seneca, the phrase *vencerse a sí mismo* (to defeat or master oneself) was a touchstone of Spanish-Christian piety in the sixteenth century, mainly due to the intercession of Erasmus. Both in his anthology of moral advice from Seneca (*Flores Lvcii Annei Senecae Cordvbensis*, or Flowers of Lucius Annaeus Seneca of Córdoba, 1528), and in his own guide to the conduct befitting the soldiers of Christ (*Enchiridion militis Christiani*, or Manual of the Christian Soldier, 1503),

Erasmus constructed a context in which Stoic self-mastery does not lead simply to wisdom, as Seneca asserted,[77] but instead to the highest form of Christian bliss—beatitude and salvation—a thesis made still more explicit and emphatic in the Spanish translations of both works.[78]

If Mendieta therefore deployed an already Christianized understanding of self-mastery and self-knowledge, his point of reference was more particular and suggestive of his intent: he followed the lead of Fray Gualberto Fabricio de Vagad, whose prologue to an anonymous *Flos sanctorum* based on Voragine's *Legenda aurea* was repeatedly published in both Spanish and Portuguese between the 1490s and 1579.[79] Noting that he "has drawn one common expression and one accordant history" from the *vitae* of many saints,[80] Vagad sets forth the importance of their singular example of "good living and perfect life," using conceits, vocabulary, and syntax markedly similar to those of Mendieta:

> By God's special valor, shelter, light, and favor, these knights of
> God, his saints, were able so highly, virtuously, and marvelously to
> defeat, not only the world, the devil, and the flesh, but . . . even the
> highest princes of the kingdom of the spirit, which are [our] under
> standing and will. These are the most mighty princes and the most
> difficult of all others to defeat, because they are not only the origins
> and cause, but also wholly kings and sovereign lords, of all our free
> determinations. . . . Therefore, to defeat one's own understanding
> and will—not only to defeat, but even to subject and hold captive
> one's understanding with faith, and [likewise] one's will with the so
> steadfastly avowed and perpetually promised obedience of religion . . .
> —is a much greater deed than to defeat the world and hell, or even
> to subjugate their highest kings and most powerful princes. To this
> end, it is greatly helpful, and a very salutary thing, to have to
> recount and read the passion of . . . our redeemer Jesus Christ, and
> the lives, martyrdom, and miracles of the blessed saints, who have
> value, first because of the immortal memory and glory for which
> they will always shine, and, moreover, so that examples of their
> good living and perfect life might be a doctrine and teaching for us
> to live well.[81]

In sum, when Mendieta recounts Cortés's most memorable and most difficult achievement—his self-mastery, his submission to Christian ideals, and thus his restraint in the subjugation of others—it is with the same didactic and normative intent of hagiography, again set forth in the colophon of the *Flos sanctorum*: "This material is necessary and likewise useful to the soul, in that those who might read and hear the marvelous lives and holy works and virtuous practices of the saints will endeavor to follow and imitate them. In doing this, they will deserve to attain from our redeemer Jesus Christ the reward that the saints deserved in eternal glory."[82]

In the hands of both Catholic and Protestant authors, the history of religion in America intended to document and also to inspire, to use the past to shape the future. In this regard, the mastery of others at the core of missionary endeavor—the attempt to win over nonbelievers—was of a piece with the self-mastery of concern to all Christians, of both denominations, in the pursuit of faith, virtue, and finally salvation. In both cases, good examples were revered, not as an end, but as a means, and as a guide to the work that still remained to be done.

PART II

Crossings

CHAPTER 4

Transatlantic Passages

The Reformed Tradition and the Politics of Writing

DAVID D. HALL

"What must I know about seventeenth-century New England?" a doctoral student preparing his field exams in American religious history asked me a year ago. All too conscious of the tides that ceaselessly sweep in and out of "Puritan Studies," I hesitate. But the student is already alert to my proclivities: certain questions endure, as do attempts to answer them. Some of Perry Miller, therefore (certain essays and chapters), and Edmund S. Morgan. Something as well on doctrine that has the depth of E. Brooks Holifield's work on the sacraments; a reading on "declension" that avoids any oversimplifying dichotomy between religion and society, as Mark E. Peterson is able to do in *The Price of Redemption: The Spiritual Economy of Puritan New England* (1997); and something on the Mathers that takes them seriously as theologians—say, Richard Lovelace in *The American Pietism of Cotton Mather*.[1] And what would such a reading list be without the documents of the Antinomian controversy!

But my inquiring student wants more—as he gently suggests, less of the old and more of the new. Uncertain of what has become authoritative within the more recent scholarship on early New England and the Atlantic world, we both hesitate. The "new imperial history" that rearranges the customary story so that it is told from the standpoint of the regions being colonized? The missionary endeavor (Catholic and Protestant) viewed as much from the experience of those who accepted or resisted Christianity as from that of the missionaries themselves, and replacing "conversion" with a multifaceted description of encounters, exchanges, affiliations, and the destabilizing of identities? The process of "communication" that, from the vantage of some historians, was accelerating in the seventeenth century, with significant consequences for the politics of representation on both sides of the Atlantic, a good example being how the administrators of the nascent English empire viewed the colonists? Or should we seek out scholarship on "creolization" and the ways in which the mingling of races and peoples in the New World brought about cultural change?[2] Questions of this kind emerge from Alison Games's *The Web of Empire: English Cosmopolitans in an Age of Expansion 1560–1660* (2008) and Carla Gardina Pestana's *Protestant Empire: Religion and the Making of the British Atlantic World* (2009), as well as several of the essays that are part of this volume.

Meanwhile, my inquirer has been browsing in the classic literature on popular religion and popular culture in early modern Europe, a literature that anticipated the excitement within religious studies about re-imagining the very category of religion, the affiliations between cultural and religious history, and the interest in "lived religion."[3] These debates have rendered religion less totalizing or self-contained and, in its social consequences, less predictable. The "religious" seeps into social life, and vice versa; and, as studies of the "wonders" tradition in early modern England have demonstrated, narratives that ostensibly emphasize the doctrine of divine providence depend as much on "popular" literary genres for their blood and thunder motifs as they do on the reasoning of theologians.[4] How should these lines of work be incorporated into his exams?

What follows is a three-part response to these questions. I begin by re-emphasizing the merits of a traditional framework that, from my vantage, enables the historian to comprehend certain kinds of transformations: a framework foregrounding theological traditions, in this case the Reformed. Having proposed how such a framework can be helpful, I complicate it by looking at social practice, or what people actually did, with an emphasis on the sacrament of baptism. In the final part of the essay I rely on the concepts of Atlantic exchanges and mediations as a doorway into recovering the politics of texts written in seventeenth-century New England but finding their significant audience in Stuart England.

Like Caesar's Gaul, the Protestant Reformation of the sixteenth century found itself divided into three traditions or types: Lutheranism; the Reformed or, in more casual nomenclature, Calvinism; and the Anabaptist (Free Church).

As was also true of Lutheranism, the Reformed became a family of country- or region-specific churches—a strong presence in certain city-states of Switzer- land and in several German territories; in France, although as a much-embattled minority; in Scotland, where, after prospering as a semi-underground move- ment during the Regency of Mary of Guise, coming to power in 1560–61 and ensuring its dominance after forcing Mary Stuart to flee to England in 1567; and in the Netherlands after several provinces of the Low Countries revolted against Spanish Habsburg rule. In England, the situation was a good deal more confused. The Reformed "two-kingdom" understanding of church and state was unacceptable to Elizabeth I and her successors, who preferred the "Erastian" (after Thomas Erastus) principle of state over church. In worship, Elizabeth and her bishops insisted on preserving the Book of Common Prayer, more or less in the version of 1552 that others in England found unsatisfactory because of its "Catholic" aspects, or what John Calvin and the Reformed International had stigmatized as "idolatry" and "superstition." Then there was the Episcopal structure of the Church of England, which violated the Reformed premise of an equality of ministers. The "Puritan" wing of the church openly appealed to the Reformed model of ecclesiology and worship, as when the authors of the *Admonition to the Parliament* (1572) cited the "examples" of Scotland and the French.

The history of the Puritan movement is a superb example of evangelism acquiring ever greater force and effectiveness despite the obstacles of Episco- pacy, prayer book, and Erastian civil state. A handful of strongly Protestant (and Reformed) books abetted this evangelism. Without fanfare or agitation, the community of "Marian exiles" in Geneva had prepared a fresh transla- tion of the Bible into English (1560) that became the most widely used ver- sion until the publication of the Authorized (King James) version in 1611; and another book that owed much to the community of exiles and its sympathies, *The Whole Booke of Psalmes*, became the most widely used psalter, employed everywhere in English congregations (parishes) that adopted psalm singing in the Genevan manner. Local attempts at a "reformation of manners" were another instrument of Reformed preferences. So was foreign policy, for the English state could not ignore the perilous situation of the Reformed interna- tional in France, the Netherlands, and the Palatinate. Beginning with Eliza- beth I, thousands of English and Scottish troops served overseas on their behalf. By these several routes, elements of what might be described as a Re- formed culture took hold in England as they also did in Scotland, a culture that, in both countries, became instrumental in the fashioning of a protonationalist

understanding of past, present, and future: a past marked by decay and corruption; a present marked by renewal and, perhaps above all, a covenant (implicit if not explicit) to defend church and nation against "popery;" and a
future charged with expectations of the coming kingdom, provided that
the people and their leaders remained faithful to their covenant with God.
This protonationalism was also nurtured by cheap print in late sixteenth-
and seventeenth-century England, especially the many versions of the lore
of wonders.[5]

England as church and country was thus Reformed and something
else—possibly "Anglican," although no tradition of this kind had been consolidated before 1660. Always, however, the Reformed aspects of church and
culture were dogged by the hostility of the crown, the indifference of a large
swath of "the people," and the mixed allegiances of the political elite. Hence
the emergence of what have often been referred to as "dilemmas." The earliest
of these may have been nonconformity, the practice of flouting some of the
rules of the church (i.e., ignoring what the state church regarded as obligatory). Almost to a person, the ministers who came to New England had engaged in some version of nonconformity, as had many of their lay admirers
and advocates. Nonconformity may be likened to a liminal space just beyond
the reach of the authorities. By the early seventeenth century, this space had
become deeply rooted in local communities. A telling example is the Stour
River Valley in the county of Suffolk, where John Winthrop and gentry of
his persuasion "gadded" to parishes other than their own to listen to "godly"
clergy and supported such men politically and financially.[6] A second dilemma concerned the few and the many. Granted, a national church had to
encompass everyone. But what if the true church consisted of the "few" who
practiced a high level of faith in contrast to the dismal performance of most
others? The tiny groups of people who withdrew from the Church of England, a step that gained them the name of "Separatists," understood themselves as the faithful few even though it meant sacrificing the ideal of a national
church as a means of grace to everyone. In a weaker form, the tension between the few and the multitude spawned an idealization of fellowship that
Lady Brilliana Harley captured in a comment from the 1620s. "We must be
careful of our families," she wrote, "of our parents, of our kindred, if they be
of the household of faith . . . our delightest love must only be to the saints on
the Earth." In the same vein, when the prominent mid-century English minister Richard Baxter looked back on his childhood in a Shropshire village
where his father was scorned as a Puritan, he recalled having realized that

"godly people were the best, and those that despised them . . . were a malignant unhappy sort of People." A third dilemma arose out of the tension between loyalty to God and loyalty to the monarch. Strange as it may seem in retrospect, the Separatists tried to have it both ways; and the attempts of John Winthrop, John White, and John Cotton in 1630 to reassure the English government that the immigrants who were leaving for Massachusetts were utterly loyal represents another attempt at masking this dilemma.[7]

Given the politics of religion under Elizabeth and her immediate successors, the Reformed tradition in England had something of a "now you see it now you don't" character. Puritanism was even more quixotic or elusive. The turning point in modern British understandings of the movement was the scholarship of Patrick Collinson. His achievement was to overturn centuries of disdain on the part of Anglican historians for Puritanism, a disdain registered in the judgment that only a tiny fraction of English people participated in the movement. This too was a judgment that enabled hardline Anglicans to represent the movement as the sectarian fringe of an otherwise broadly inclusive and broadly endorsed state church. Collinson demonstrated exactly the opposite, recovering, for example, the sympathies of a Reform-minded group of Elizabethan bishops, several of whom, as Marian exiles, had gained direct knowledge of the Reformed model of churchmanship, and, recovering as well a point lost from view in the thickets of Anglican invective, that the moderate wing of the Puritan program was not sectarian (i.e., pitting the few against the many) but thoroughly magisterial, its goal nothing less than reforming a *national* church that would collaborate with the civil state. Well aware that a "moderate" style of Reform existed alongside the vehemence of the authors of the *Admonition to the Parliament*, and appreciative of the organizing genius of John Field, who helped bring into being informal networks of clergy and laypeople who, under his guidance, bombarded Parliament with petitions calling for action against incompetent clergy and Catholic recusants (and at times, for replacing the Book of Common Prayer), Collinson took the further step of arguing that much of what had been stigmatized as utterly opposed to the Church of England was in fact part of a broader consensus about good religion and good church order. Thus Collinson transposed Puritanism from the margins to the center, albeit a broadly imagined center, in his scholarship. He also urged his fellow historians to discard the narrative structure of denominational history, with its insistence on origins or founders and reifying such categories as "Presbyterian" and "Congregationalist." As he pointed out, no clear-cut categories of this kind existed in the Elizabethan period, an argument others have expanded to include the early seventeenth century.[8]

Collinson was well aware of certain tensions within the movement of the kind I have specified. In more recent scholarship, historians on both sides of the Atlantic have made several of these tensions visible and specific. From my vantage (which I share with historians such as Holifield and Stephen Foster),[9] any inquiry into "transformations" must begin with these tensions. They are our necessary point of departure if we want to understand the dynamics of a movement that was constantly in motion. With the exception of nonconformity, the tensions that become apparent in the 1570s were virtually the same as those that would bedevil the colonists in seventeenth-century New England. In this regard, the history of Reformed Protestantism in New England stands in remarkable continuity with the history of Reformed Protestantism in England. What follows is a fuller description of these continuities and their consequences.

The Church

As John Foxe and his collaborators were assembling their great collection of martyr stories, the *Acts and Monuments* that gained the official endorsement of the church, they found themselves telling two quite different stories. One was of Christianity's triumph in the fourth century C.E. after Constantine made it the official religion of the Roman Empire. Here, in this triumph, lay the source of the image and idea of England or, more expansively, of Europe, as a Christendom, a harmonious union of church and civil society acting in accordance with divine law. In keeping with this story, Foxe could salute the newly crowned Elizabeth I as another Constantine who had ensured the return of Protestantism to England and would serve as its protector.

Intermingled with this story, and, in the long run, possibly of more importance to Foxe and his cowriters, was another, the scenario sketched by John Bale in *The Image of Both Churches* (1547) of a tiny group of the faithful fleeing into the Wilderness as the rest of the church fell into apostasies of one kind or another—principally for Foxe as for Bale, those associated with the rise of the papacy. This scenario seemed especially telling to the earliest English Protestants for whom Henry VIII was as much a menace as he was a righteous king. It appealed anew to the Marian exiles who left England once Mary Tudor restored Catholicism as the state religion. For martyrologists such as Foxe, the execution of some three hundred fervent Protestants during her reign was a hopeful sign of things to come. After all, the story of the suffering few who became martyrs at the hands of the Antichrist was also a story of the coming kingdom when the "beast" would be overthrown and the saints restored to power.

Thus did the apocalyptic scenario described in Revelation impress itself upon Foxe and, more generally, upon the imagination of countless English Protestants, though especially, perhaps, upon the imagination of the "Puritans" who found themselves at odds with the English government and the Church of England. Ever malleable, the narrative of the two churches, the one all powerful, the other composed of the suffering few, found its way into William Bradford's "Of Plimmoth Plantation" (ca. 1630–46), with its story line— suspended after the opening chapters—of "the saints" suffering "bloody death and cruel torments" at the hands of the Antichrist (or Satan) as they await the moment when "the churches of God . . . recover their primitive order, liberty, and beauty." And, as Adrian Weimer has demonstrated in *Martyrs' Mirror; Persecution and Holiness in Early New England*, the more mainstream colonists of Massachusetts Bay were equally determined to align themselves with the suffering few.[10]

The two kinds of churches had two very different perceptions of what it was to be a true saint. As though they were anticipating Dietrich Bonhoeffer, the more radical Puritans recognized that the institution of the church and the spiritual economy of divine grace were rarely one and the same: the church as an institution inevitably partakes of the things of this world and is therefore incapable of barring those without any signs of being among the worthy from participating in the Lord's Supper or having their children baptized. The alternative was a church composed of fervent, well-informed, and righteous Christians who, in keeping with Paul's evocation of the church as Christ's body, were "living stones" suffused with the Holy Spirit. Within the Reformed tradition, the tension between these two possibilities was registered in John Calvin's churchmanship in Geneva. For him, the visible church had a role as means of grace (instruction) to everyone, a position grounded in part on the argument that here on earth no one could validly differentiate saint from reprobate. In the same breath, however, Calvin envisioned the visible church as always in motion as it approached the moment when the kingdom would be restored. The visible church was therefore a community constantly pursuing the goal of holiness or sanctification, using to this end the machinery of church discipline. Expecting that the "elders" within a Presbyterian system would vigorously employ the instrument of excommunication, Calvin also insisted that the church leaders scrutinize the fitness of everyone requesting to participate in the Lord's Supper and exclude those deemed unworthy. Within the Reformed model, therefore, some were more privileged (that is, more "worthy") than others.

The imperative of more effective discipline and of remaking a comprehensive, "national" church into a sanctified community reappears in *An Admonition to the Parliament*, and, as the British historian Peter Lake has pointed out, in Thomas Cartwright's programmatic statements of the 1570s.[11] In effect, the leaders of the Puritan movement connected ecclesiology and soteriology. That no such program could be accomplished within the Church of England was a reality that warranted separating from such a church or, once the migration to New England began, of creating "gathered" or selective congregations limited to "visible saints" who, by their behavior and other evidence, were deemed proper members of a sanctified community. A marvelous demonstration of this thinking occurred in February 1636 when a small group of men organized a congregation in Newtown (soon to be renamed Cambridge) under the leadership of Thomas Shepard. That he chose Ephesians 5:27 as the text for his sermon at this event is indicative of how fervently he wanted the new congregation to be "a glorious church . . . holy and without blemish," as Paul had counseled the Ephesians. Shepard's first act on the day the church was organized was to pray "with deepe Confession of sine," a process of self-cleansing in which the six or seven others who had been singled out as founders also participated. Nor was this process merely personal. As the "great Assembly" of people on hand to watch and learn would have recognized, the ceremony underscored the rupture between a corrupt Church of England and the purity of the Congregational Way: reordination for Shepard, a selective membership, no liturgy taken from the Book of Common Prayer.[12]

A sermon series on the parable of the ten virgins (Matthew 25:1–13) that Shepard began to preach in June 1636 is suffused with an idealization of the church as community or, as he remarked, the true "kingdom of heaven" on earth. Here in New England, he told the congregation, we have set up "pure, chaste, virgin churches, not polluted with the mixture of men's inventions, not defiled with the company of evil men." It was crucial, therefore, to keep careful watch on who was admitted; never should the church open the "doors to all comers" now that it knew the satisfaction of celebrating the Lord's Supper with the "saints alone." How different this was from their English experience when, in his words, godly people had grieved "when . . . profane persons" were admitted to the sacrament. With purity ensured, the saints would enjoy a fellowship akin to that of the saints in heaven. So he reminded them in the parable sermons, telling everyone in the congregation that they would know what it was like to "walk as men come down from heaven, and returning thither again; and that as it were already in heaven."[13]

Not only in Cambridge but also elsewhere, the principle of a selective or "gathered" membership became one of the major elements of the Congregational Way. In a formalized statement of this system, *A Platforme of Discipline Gathered out of the Word*, more familiarly known as the Cambridge Platform (completed in 1648; printed in 1649), the ministers extended this principle to the sacrament of baptism. In the early 1630s, the practice of baptism had emerged as an issue within the heterogeneous community of English exiles, soldiers, and merchants in the Netherlands, a community that encompassed a spectrum of practices and attitudes, from radical Separatism to mainstream Reformed. Now, with more radical nonconformists arriving from England after being deprived of their positions, men such as Thomas Hooker and John Davenport were telling the overseas congregations that offered them employment that they would baptize only those children whose parents could be questioned beforehand about their faith, the premise being that baptism required parents to meet some standard of adequacy. Within the Dutch Reformed, however, no such standard prevailed. Transposed to New England, where Hooker and Davenport went after leaving the Netherlands, their position found its way into the Cambridge Platform: no child could be baptized unless a parent was in church membership, that is, qualified to join a gathered congregation.

On the one hand this policy promised to preserve the kind of church Shepard was extolling: "pure chaste, virgin churches, not polluted with the mixture of men's inventions, not defiled with the company of evil men." On the other, it coexisted uneasily with the conception of baptism that prevailed among ministers and laypeople alike. In and of itself this conception was a hybrid forged out of two divergent possibilities: that baptism was merely a "sign" of grace already present or implied, or that baptism was a significant vehicle or means of grace that offered distinct benefits—in particular, the benefit of being brought within the scope of the church "covenant." As Holifield has demonstrated, this mixture of assumptions, both of them inherited from the Reformed tradition, invested the practice of baptism with what can justly be described as ambivalence: what the ministers denied with the one hand, they offered with the other. To wit, baptism provided distinctive benefits within the economy of grace, although not yet (as with the doctrine of election) benefits certain to endure.

The tensions inherent in this ambivalence had become evident as early as 1634 when John Cotton floated the possibility that a *grandparent's* church membership would allow a grandchild to be baptized, and became more pressing once the children of the immigrants began having children of their own. In 1657 the Connecticut General Assembly asked a group of ministers to ponder the alternatives, and, in 1662, a larger group in Massachusetts resumed these deliberations. One possibility was to inform all the "adult children" of local congregations—adults who, as infants, had been baptized on the basis of their parents' membership—that, if they failed to meet the criterion of a "work of grace" by a certain point, their membership would lapse or somehow become attenuated. Another was to take advantage of a distinction between the covenant as "external" (but nonetheless real) and "internal" (*very* real, because linked with grace). As is well known, the majority ruled that, on the basis of the external covenant, adult children were legitimately members of the church and could bring their own children to be baptized. Having undercut the Cambridge Platform in this regard, the synod of 1662 hastened to defend the purity of the Lord's Supper, which only "full" members (those asterisked as participating in the covenant of grace) could enjoy. An enduring contradiction between comprehensiveness and selectivity was thus brought into local congregations in the form of two quite discrete possibilities for participation.

Church, State, and Godly Rule

From Luther and Calvin onward, the Reformers sought to strip their churches of secular authority of the kind that, from their point of view, had ruined Catholicism. The solution was to describe the church as having an authority different in kind from that of civil rulers: "spiritual" as contrasted with "temporal." This much decided, the Reformed firmly rejected the Free Church position that the Christian community should abandon all connections with the civil state. Drawing on Romans 13, the Reformed leadership insisted that civil magistrates were commissioned by God to protect the church and uphold righteousness. Church and state were "nursing twins" differentiated from each other in certain fundamental ways but nonetheless closely linked. To us, this "two kingdom" theory may seem extraordinarily conservative or reactionary, but in the England of Elizabeth I and the Scotland of James VI it was a daring alternative to what James and Elizabeth insisted upon, that *they* were rightfully the rulers of both church and state, albeit limited by their obedience to Christ and divine law. The Separatists who informed Elizabeth I that she could be excommunicated by the congregation to which she belonged were being faithful to the principles of the two kingdom theory, which assigned the work of "discipline" solely to the church. But to the Queen this was rank sedition.

The two kingdom theory had rough sledding in England and Scotland, with the Long Parliament reluctant to endorse what it took to be the clericalism of this theory. Only in the orthodox New England colonies (Massachusetts, Connecticut, New Haven, Plymouth) was it fully enacted, although not without scuffling and confusion.[14] It is easy to oversimplify or, worse, overlook the colonists' achievement, real though it was within the context of the Reformed international. On both sides of the Atlantic, a deeper issue emerged during the period of the English Revolution: would church and civil state collaborate on bringing about "godly rule," a program consisting not only of purified churches and the semi-separation of church and state but, more grandly, of employing the Bible to install righteousness as the goal of social and political policies, and shifting political and social power to the saints in keeping with Daniel's vision (Daniel 7:27) that "the saints of the Most High shall receive the kingdom and reign forever"? Within the framework of godly rule, the question became whether church *and commonwealth* would be remodeled so that Christ was truly "king," and all policies, practices, and structures were aligned with his commands. As one of the colonists in Massachusetts who favored such a move would say in 1637, a society ruled by Christ was one in which "whatsoever is done in word or deed, in church or common-wealth, must be done in the name of the Lord Jesus Christ."[15]

Here, the tensions may seem all too obvious, as they were to many in England and to some of the colonists. If power fell into the hands of the saints, how would these people be identified? And what kinds of power would they have? The first of these questions had already divided the Puritan movement. The second was essentially political given that the political class in both England and the colonies did not look with favor on a redistribution of offices and political privilege. For these reasons as well as the enduring tension between the church as persecuted few and as comprehensive many, godly rule came to naught, its most spectacular (or amusing) failure being the ineptitude of the "Barebones Parliament" that Oliver Cromwell called into being and quickly dissolved in 1653.[16] Experiments were tried, experiments were unsuccessful or compromised: in the longer history of the Reformed tradition, this pattern had already been established by the end of the sixteenth century. What happened in mid-seventeenth-century England and New England was of a piece with that longer history. The program of state-enforced righteousness is an ideal case in point. Godly rule seemed to require that adultery become a capital crime. So it was voted in Massachusetts in 1638 and in England in 1650 by the Rump Parliament, a Puritanized subset of the Long Parliament. But in neither place did courts enforce the law. The price of doing so would have been a fractured social peace and, as the history of law enforcement in Stuart England and Puritan New England demonstrates, social peace usually trumped moral rigor.[17]

The Practical Divinity

By the beginning of the seventeenth century, minister-theologians in England and Scotland had fashioned a "practical divinity," or, to borrow a phrase from Peter Lake, an "experimental predestinarianism." Singular within the Reformed tradition and, in the course of time, widely influential on the Continent, the practical divinity was a proto-pietist soteriology that foregrounded the experience of being transformed by saving grace through the instrumentalities of preaching, counsel, and godly reading.[18] For Americanists who begin with Perry Miller's *The New England Mind: The Seventeenth Century* (1939) or essays like his "'Preparation for Salvation' in Seventeenth-Century New England" (1943), the question that hovers over the practical divinity is whether the colonists were compromising the authentic theology of John Calvin, a question Miller answered with a muted yes. This question continues to animate one branch of scholarship on "Calvinism" in Europe and New England, with the answers steadily becoming more emphatic and more nuanced at one and the same time: there was no betrayal of Calvin, but rather a deploying of new strategies for doing theology. To cite a specific example, it has become clear that the language of covenant, which, for Miller, became the opening wedge of a quasi-Arminian adaptation of Calvin's system, was conventionally orthodox.[19]

Within studies of the practical divinity, the focus has shifted to assurance of salvation and, implicitly or explicitly, to the burdens this framework of self-understanding may have created for ordinary people, including the

great difficulty of being certain of one's state of grace. At this point, it is helpful to look sideways at practice or behavior and what it tells us of everyday
piety. As soon as we do so, we begin to discern expectations and practices
that mute the impact of the practical divinity. The most obvious of these is
the much greater appeal of church membership to women than to men, even
when church membership and the practical divinity were closely linked, as
they were in early New England: women joined congregations in greater
numbers than men, and if they were married, did so before their husbands.
Doing so (joining the church) enabled these women to claim the sacrament
of baptism for their children. That is, it enabled these women to construct a
singular legacy within the household, not a legacy of material goods (although this too interested them), but a religious legacy that, within popular
religion, would ensure the spiritual health and therefore the social well-being
of children for generations to come. The sacrament of baptism thus became
invested with meanings that, strictly speaking, had nothing to do with Calvin or his successors but a great deal to do with the nexus between family and
everyday religion. To bring this point home, when date of birth and baptism
are correlated for children born in a Massachusetts county in the early eighteenth century, we learn that 60 percent of those children were baptized
within ten days of birth—striking evidence of high expectations for a Protestant sacrament that no longer carried the Catholic promise of saving grace.[20]

Thus do unexpected possibilities emerge within a religious system that,
from the standpoint of intellectual history, seems so tightly constructed. And
there is more to the story, for church records demonstrate inconsistencies that
seem almost unimaginable: families postponing baptism until something
pushes them to want it for their children, whereupon four or five are baptized
at once; children who go unbaptized; children who, as already indicated, are
rushed to the meetinghouse at the earliest possible moment; and, if we play
out the timeline, children who, as adults, sometimes ignore and sometimes
take seriously their baptismal covenant or—by the mid-eighteenth century,
find in spasms of evangelical fervor a means of accommodating the religious
and the social. A history of lived or popular religion is never the same, therefore, as what we might expect from reading sermons and the like; and certainly not what we expect if, as historians, we overlook the tensions that were
sustained within the Reformed tradition.

But let me attempt a different perspective on early New England, one that
builds upon several decades of bibliographical and "history of the book"

scholarship on the workings of two interrelated ways of writing and publishing in the seventeenth-century Atlantic world: the more traditional mode of scribal publication—that is, the production and distribution of handwritten texts—and the mode that figures in most histories of publishing and authorship—the more public and commercial process of printing. In recent years both trajectories of scholarship have successfully challenged the premise that authors controlled their texts. According to the new wisdom, writing (or authorship) was inevitably "social" in specific respects. Handwritten texts were usually the doing of copyists who rarely compared their work to a putative original, thus generating a stream of variations and, for printers, several different copy texts. Printed books were just as unstable, thanks to printing shop practices (for example, the altering of sheets as these were being passed through the press) and the willingness of booksellers to add prefaces, forewords, and other matter that authors may never have seen or sanctioned. Or it may be that a printer's copy text had been reviewed and reworked by an intermediary.[21] As for printed sermons, a substantial portion were based on an auditor's notes but not, as we so easily presume, on a fully written-out manuscript provided by the preacher. Hence the dismay of the New England minister John Cotton when someone in the late summer of 1642 showed him a newly arrived book that had his name on the title page. According to John Winthrop, Cotton learned for the first time that John Humfrey, a former member of his Boston congregation, had arranged for sermons he had preached in Boston to be printed in London. And printed, Cotton realized, using sermon notes taken as he was preaching. An entry in John Winthrop's journal records Cotton's reaction: "Now came over a book of Mr. Cotton's sermons upon the seven vials. J. Humfrey had gotten the notes from some who had took them by characters, and printed them in London, he had 300 copies for it, which was a great wrong to Mr. Cotton, and he was much grieved at it, for it had been fit he should have perused and corrected the copy before it had been printed." In truth, Cotton was overreacting, for what happened in this instance had already occurred with other texts of his, and as he surely knew, was a well-entrenched practice within the book trades.[22]

   Here, in the transmission of manuscripts and the making of books, lie endless possibilities for expanding our awareness of the politics arising out of the structures of the first imperial system. Taking for granted the instability of texts, what does that instability tell us about the exchanges between center and periphery and the complexities of the colonial situation itself? Taking for granted, too, Philip H. Round's argument that the colonists were obliged to participate in a "civil conversation" centered in the metropolis of London, we can ask, as he does, how "the very existence of first-generation New England texts" manifests the consequences of that participation.[23] In what follows, I limit myself to three examples, each of them previously described in my *Ways of Writing: The Practice and Politics of Text-Making in Seventeenth-Century New England* (2008), but worth returning to in this context. Books suit any inquiry about transformation and interchange because of their mobility. Passing out of one interpretive community into others, reworked in their materiality, and reinvented by those who participate in a process of cultural and social translation, books become ever more complex emblems of the Atlantic world.[24] They do so in even more ways than the ones on which I linger—for example, arising within a diasporic community, as is the case with the texts Pier M. Larson describes in *Oceans of Letters: Language and Creolization in an Indian Ocean Diaspora*, a description of literacy and text-making in the Indian Ocean, with particular reference to Madagascar, a description echoed in studies of eighteenth-century evangelical networks that linked Scotland, England, Ulster, and the American colonies.[25]

I find this language of travel, exchange, and hybridity useful in understanding the multitude of texts written by the New England colonists in the 1630s and 1640s defending their experiment in church order, texts that cannot be understood apart from English-based texts written in response, and all of them reflecting deep-seated anxieties about the politico-religious situation in Civil War England. The total number of texts arising out of this give-and-take was substantial—according to one recent survey, more than a hundred, and the quantity would be even greater if manuscripts were included.[26] Nor can a comprehensive reckoning with these texts overlook the role of tale-bearers such as Roger Williams who, once he reached London in 1643, rattled on to the Scottish Presbyterian Robert Baillie (ideologically his opposite) about people and policies in New England, and in doing so providing tidbits that Baillie, no fan of New England, passed on to the embittered Thomas Edwards, who used one or two of them in *Gangraena: Or a Catalogue and Discovery of many of the Errours, Heresies, Blasphemies and Pernicious Practices of the Sectaries of this Time* (1646), directed in particular against the English "Independents" and their New England allies.[27]

To go straight to a hot moment in these transatlantic exchanges, I turn—as Round has done before me—to the publishing history of *A Short Story of the Rise, Reigne, and Ruine of the Late Antinomians, Familists and Libertines* (1644), a book Baillie plundered for information that would enable him to discredit John Cotton. The *Short Story* contains four key texts of the Antinomian controversy that broke out in Massachusetts in late 1636 and ended with the expulsion of Anne Hutchinson, John Wheelwright, and others. One of these texts concerns a dispute about the merits of a law regulating who could be received in New England. Another was the report of a special "synod" that met in September 1637 to resolve certain theological questions in the hope of effecting a reconciliation between Cotton and his colleagues. A third described a "monster birth" exhumed in early 1638 and attributed to the "Antinomian" Mary Dyer, a text almost certainly written by John Winthrop, who may also have written the first text in this list. The best known in the series is the fourth, which summarized a session of the Massachusetts General Court (November 1637) during which the court questioned some of the signers of a petition and "examined" Anne Hutchinson. Two of these texts, the report of the Synod and the summary of the court session of November, were probably created by John Higginson, a university-educated youth who was hired to make a written record of the synod's conclusions; I have speculated elsewhere that he also prepared the fourth. No author's name appeared on the title page of the *Short Story*. Given its eclectic contents, it should be considered an authorless book. However, it begins with a preface and concludes with something like an afterword written by Thomas Weld, a former minister in the Church of England who moved to New England in 1632 and, at the behest of the leadership of Massachusetts, returned to England in 1641 in order to represent the interests of the colony. His was intrinsically a political task and, as Weld immediately understood, the *Short Story* was a political document.

The story of its politics begins with the making of the book itself *in New England*. Realizing that, via letters and the traffic of people back and forth across the Atlantic, word was reaching the Puritan community in England of disputes among the ministers—disputes that had already led to the banishing of Roger Williams in December 1635—the ministers and magistrates who triumphed in the controversy pondered the benefits of sending an official account to their friends in England in order to forestall rumor and false information. To this end, Higginson took up his pen in September 1637, and almost certainly it was to the same end that he or others packaged the four texts together, knowing as they did so that it was not a coherent "book." Meanwhile, the political and religious leadership was becoming indecisive about these materials. Would making them public benefit the reputation of the colonists? The right answer was yes, or so Thomas Hooker of Hartford argued in April 1637 in a letter to Thomas Shepard in Cambridge. Though Hooker feared the damage being done in England by word of mouth, he was realistic about any efforts to preserve secrecy. Would "naked" publication serve the colonists better and be more convincing than rumor, he wondered? "My present thoughts run thus," he wrote Shepard, "That such conclusions which are most extra, most erroneous, and cross to the common current,[28] send them over to the godly learned to judge in our own country, and return their apprehensions. I suppose the issue will be more uncontroulable. If any should suggest this was the way to make the clamour too great and loud, and to bring a prejudice upon the plantations, I should soon answer, there is nothing done in corners here but it is openly there related and in such notorious cases, which cannot be kept secret, the most plain and naked relation ever causeth the truth most to appear."[29] Who acted on this advice cannot be determined, but someone did, for copies of a few of the more theological documents were in English hands by the end of 1637.[30]

Within two or three years, however, agreement had been reached that the documentary record created by Higginson should *not* be sent to England. He handed in his pile of manuscript to the Massachusetts General Court in May 1639. What happened after he did so is critical to an understanding of the political history of these documents. In Higginson's words, the court "ordered that the Ministers should have the viewing of it: and then that it should be printed and that I should have the benefit of the printing of it for my paines It being then conceived it would amount to about a hundred pounds[.] And so it was returned to me again by the Court with a charge that I should so order it that it should be faithfullie printed[.]" This was an extraordinary bargain—extraordinary to the point of being fantastic, for it was absurd to assume in 1639 that the Cambridge, Massachusetts, printer, then just barely under way, could have sold enough copies to earn Higginson one hundred pounds, and no less absurd to suppose that a London bookseller would have risked this amount on the documents. That there was more at work than simply a commercial transaction was indicated, however, in the stipulation (as reported by Higginson) "that no damage might arise from it either to the cause or the Countrey, and then that I should have the profit of it."

For what happened thereafter, we depend on a letter he wrote the court in 1643 in a final attempt to be reimbursed for his labors. The dunning letter of 1643 suggests the sequel—no printed book, no payment as yet to the clerk who had spent so much time preparing the text, and the reason for inaction: "being thus ordered by the Court I left it for a time in the hands of the ministers who had the viewing of it &c. After which I had the occasion to understand the Judgment of divers concerning the publication of it, and I found that so some were for it, yet others were against it conceiving it might possibly be an occasion of further disputes and differences both in this Country and other parts of the world; whereupon I found a Scruple arises in my spirit so that I durst not have a hand in the publishing of it, fearing what might be the consequence of it." All this transpired by May 1641, when Higginson first petitioned the court to release him of responsibility for the manuscript and pay him something. But debate was not yet ended. "It was then considered of mutually by the Magistrates and Ministers, and it was resolved (upon the grounds before mentioned) that it should not be printed."[31]

Interred in New England, the documents compiled by Higginson were resurrected in early 1640s England. Who carried one of Higginson's several copies across the Atlantic remains unknown, but cross the Atlantic a copy did, whereupon it came into the hands of a printer/bookseller who published it in January 1644. This printing lacked Weld's preface and afterword. As he remarked in the preface he added to a fresh printing a few months later, he realized that the documents themselves provided no context or narrative framework for identifying the villains of the affair or adequately dramatizing the success of the magistrates' riposte to "Antinomianism." All this he provided, the main point being, from his perspective, to refocus the dispute on the figure of Anne Hutchinson. She was the source of all the difficulties in Massachusetts—not John Cotton or Henry Vane, Jr., whose names he never mentioned, although each had been a crucial player. At once, therefore, the *Short Story* becomes an unstable text both in its materiality and in the writer's voice: the pedestrian resume of the Synod of 1637's eighty-two errors juxtaposed with a (relatively) matter-of-fact transcription of the "examination" of Anne Hutchinson (that is, if we stop short of Weld's gloss on the text) and the heated rhetoric of the "monster birth" story. Multiple authors, divergent voices, some of which are named in the different documents—a book, in short, that lent itself to being reshaped and reappropriated.

The *Short Story* arrived in England at a critical moment in the making of the English Revolution: the rupture that had emerged between factions within the Westminster Assembly and, beyond the Assembly, within the circles of Puritan-minded religious reformers. Passing by the details of this rupture, which crippled the attempts of moderate Puritans to take over and manage the Church of England and prompted Scottish Presbyterians to ally themselves with Charles I, what is of interest is its literary context, the campaign against the Independents undertaken by a coalition of Scottish and English ministers. To this campaign we owe Edwards's *Gangraena* and Robert Baillie's *A Dissuasive from the Errours of the Time* (1645), a freewheeling attack upon the colonists and especially John Cotton, as well as a host of other texts, some of them by ministers in New England attempting to set the record straight, others by English Independents, and still others linked to Baillie and Edwards and their coterie. The noise was terrific, the fray intense. Given this context, it should not surprise us that the colonists who participated in it were always a bit obtuse and a little behind, not quite understanding how to intervene or what the stakes really were. And it should not surprise us that the documents assembled in the *Short Story* would pass out of the colonists' control and assume a life of their own.[32]

The person whose literary career was most deeply affected by this struggle was John Cotton. Anne Hutchinson was utterly unknown to the English reading public, but Cotton had begun to publish before he immigrated and had been the much-consulted rector of a major town church. He had already lent his pen to the Massachusetts Bay Company as part of its campaign to defuse rumors that the company was "Separatist" in its outlook, to this end writing a letter to the two ministers in Salem once he learned (in 1630) of their refusing to admit Winthrop and others to the sacrament of the Lord's Supper, a Separatist-like gesture. The letter did in fact reach Salem, but its intended audience was the Puritan community in England, which came to know it via multiple handwritten copies. Then, once in New England, Cotton began to expound on the "Congregational Way," initially in a manuscript that, when it was printed in England without his knowledge in 1645, carried the title, *The Way of the Churches of Christ in New England.* He had *already repudiated* some aspects of this text in a book that appeared in 1644, *The Keyes of the Kingdome*, and the embarrassment of *The Way* prompted him to write a third account, *The Way of the Churches . . . Cleared* (1648), not so much because of events in New England but because of what he was learning of the turmoil in England.

It is fascinating to listen in on the two men who arranged to have *The Way* of 1645 published, for they began the book by acknowledging what any reader who compared this text closely with the *Keyes* of 1644 would realize, that Cotton was moderating a few of the arguments he had been making in the 1630s, especially his enthusiasm for lay rule of local congregations. To indicate their own position, the two editors inserted asterisks next to passages they did "not yet fully close with." The editors also had to explain why, in light of the already printed *Keyes* and without being asked to do so by Cotton, they had arranged for publication despite "Diverse Objections . . . laid against the Printing of this Book (to the saddening of the Authour)." The best they could say in their own defense was that the manuscript had come into the hands of Presbyterian critics and that "others" were "conscientiously and candidly cry[ing] out for information" on New England practices.[33] A process of metropolitan reworking and reappropriation thus marked every aspect of Cotton's attempts to elucidate the Congregational Way.

Nor were another group of well-known texts exempt from the heated politics of Civil War England: the "Eliot Tracts," in which the missionary project in Massachusetts and on Martha's Vineyard was described and celebrated. The de facto editor and crucial intermediary for several of these texts was Edward Winslow. Like Weld before him, he returned from New England, where he had resided since the beginning of the 1620s, to represent the interests of the orthodox colonies. He did so at a moment when a newly constituted Parliamentary Committee on Plantations, chaired by the Earl of Warwick, an aristocrat of moderate sympathies, was hearing accusations that the founders of Massachusetts Bay had trespassed on other land claims and that the colony was disregarding English law and the everyday rights of Englishmen. The committee had already agreed to Roger Williams's request that it grant a charter to "Rhode Island and Providence Plantations," a decision that ensured that colony's place at the table in high-stakes negotiations with its neighbors about boundaries.[34] Winslow's task was to create counternarratives to the stories being told of arbitrary governance and the colonists' indifference to the task of Christianizing the local Indians. He undertook the first of these in *Hypocrisie Unmasked* (1646), which he dedicated to the Earl of Warwick, and *New Englands Salamander* (1647), a response to another London-printed text, John Child's *New Englands Jonas Cast Up* (1647). It is telling of Winslow's alertness to the riptides of revolutionary politics that he arranged a second printing of *Hypocrisy Unmasked* in 1649, this time shorn of the dedication to Warwick, whose politics had cost him his post, and now retitled as *The Danger of Tolerating Levellers In a Civill State*, in order to link the colonists' gestures of repression with the anxieties of the political class in England about Leveller-style demands. The same astuteness marks the Eliot tracts he assembled in England out of the letters of John Eliot and Thomas Mayhew and others; lacking the originals, we cannot discern the details of his editorial work, but it seems certain that he recommended inserting a description in *The Clear Sun-Shine of the Gospel* of how William Laud as

Archbishop under Charles I had persecuted some of the colonists, a means of repositioning them as victims to counteract the reputation they were gaining as persecutors.

For the rest of the century, narratives of Indian-colonist relations remained deeply political, as did narratives touching on religious and social orthodoxy. The one difference between the texts of the 1640s and the texts arising out of King Philip's War (1675–76) is that, with the passage of time, the colonists themselves began to contest the proper policies to adopt and the legitimacy of certain actions—for example, the brutality unleashed on the "Christian Indians" during King Philip's War—in the context of ever-increasing pressure from the English government to acknowledge its imperial authority. Hence the contradictions that mark so many of the texts that postdate the Restoration of Charles II in 1660, one of them a translation of the Bible into Algonquian.[35] The two Cambridge printers, Samuel Green and Marmaduke Johnson, issued the New Testament in 1661, and, two years later, the Old, whereupon the two parts were bound together. The thousand or so copies of *Mamusse Wunneet-upanatamwe Up-Biblum God* would mainly find their way into the hands of the Christian Indians in New England. John Eliot, who supervised the project of translation, used others as gifts to reward the agencies and individuals in England who had financed the project and supported his missionary outreach. His instructions in hand, together with a shipment of two dozen or so Bibles, the English corporation known as the New England Company (officially, The Corporation for Propagation of the Gospel) voted in March 1664 that "5 of the Bibles sent from N. England . . . bee Disposed according to Mr. Eliotes request," he having specified "Sion College, Jesus College Cambridge, one each to the universities of Oxford and Cambridge, and a fifth Lady Armin." The agreement authorized the head of the corporation to present other copies to "such persons" as he "shall think fitt." Robert Boyle, who held this post, had just the person in mind, the king. He personally handed Charles II a copy, reporting in a letter to Eliot and the Commissioners that the king had "very gratiously" accepted the book.[36]

Three years earlier, in September 1661, the question before the Commissioners of the United Colonies, the group that oversaw the dispersing of funds sent by the New England Company, was to whom to dedicate the New Testament. It debated this question at a moment when all English corporations had been dissolved by Charles II. This bad news came with a dose of good, for the company officer who wrote to tell them of the dissolution intimated that the king might allow the company to be rechartered. Finger to the wind, the commissioners voted to "present his Majesty with the New Testament" and to include in the two presentation copies (of twenty printed in a larger format and "very well bound") a dedication to him, worded, after some debate, as an address to their "Dread Sovereign" and, in carefully chosen language, acknowledging "the Favour and Grant of Your Royal Father and Grandfather of Famous Memory," an allusion to the charter of 1629. The irony of doing so was compounded by the final sentence of the dedication: "Sir, The shines of Your Royal Favour upon these Undertakings, will make these tender Plants to flourish, notwithstanding any malevolent Agent from those that bear evil will to this Sion, and render your Majesty more Illustrious and glorious to after Generations." (Another irony is that other copies destined for England were dedicated to Robert Boyle.) Here, the unspecified "malevolent Agent" encompassed the many in Charles II's entourage who had good reason to be hostile to Puritan-style nonconformity.[37] Copies destined for the Indians themselves had neither the English title nor dedication of those sent to England.[38]

As these few examples begin to indicate, the truism within book history that texts are unstable acquires a distinctive significance within the politics of religion I have been sketching. This was a transatlantic politics. So, of course, was the Reformed tradition, and although I began by emphasizing the continuities that bound together all of the regions or movements that collectively comprised the Reformed international, those continuities were overlaid with elements of transformation, some arising out of political circumstances, some of the uncertain logic of theological ideas, and others out of the cultural and social fields in which religious practice inevitably unfolds.

CHAPTER 5

Dying for Christ

Martyrdom in New Spain

ASUNCIÓN LAVRIN

> He, who loves God the most, offers what he loves the most (which
> is his life) for His love and service. For this reason, it is well to
> conclude that martyrdom is the greatest gift of love to God, and it
> is a most perfect act, and the greatest service we can render God.[1]

The theme of martyrdom in Spanish America signified a revival of the experience of Christianity contending with pagans and nonbelievers that had previously played out in Europe as a saga that pitted Catholic manhood against diabolic forces and that promised the highest reward for its efforts. Thus, when Fray Jerónimo de Mendieta, a Franciscan who spent his life at the service of his order in sixteenth century New Spain, wrote a history of the Franciscan endeavors there, he dedicated a special section of his book to the martyrs. Addressing the Christian readers, he defined the meaning of "martyr" in the context of the New World. In his words, the life of any Christian who followed the Evangel was in itself a "cross and martyrdom," especially those who "suffer willingly for Christ; those who keep His commandments; those who go naked and discalced for Christ; those who go hungry or eating lowly food simply to sustain nature rather than to satisfy hunger." However, "those with whom we deal in the final part of this book were martyrs in the aforementioned ways, but added to their exemplary and apostolic lives that which exceeds everything else, which is to have offered their lives, and received death witnessing and extolling the name of our Savior Jesus Christ and His holy faith. They deserve more fully so, the title of martyrs."[2] Chronicler Fray Juan de Torquemada, who "borrowed" much information from Mendieta, describes his own take on martyrdom in a prologue to the lives of Franciscan martyrs. He explained the conditions of martyrdom as threefold: the first was to receive torture (*tormento*), which meant that the martyr's body suffered a violent attack and that he should die as a result; the second condition was that such death must have been caused for the love of Christ or in the defense of any moral virtue based on Christ's words; the third was that martyrdom must be voluntary. All those requirements were clearly met by the Franciscan friars whose lives he wrote about.[3] Although recalling the early Christian tradition of martyrdom, these and other chroniclers opened the eyes of the reader to a physical world that had little in common with antiquity, Europe, or the Far East. The New Spain martyrs stepped into that world and met people who were unlike any other, and who became one of the most difficult adversaries Christianity had ever met.

Spain's vast expansion in the American continent and the Orient offered two distinct non-European scenarios for conversion and martyrdom. In the New World the Spaniards found well-organized urban societies in two large areas of Central and South America, but also a significant number of tribal peoples at the edges of the core of politically sophisticated states. They were seminomadic tribes without strong political organizations, in constant warfare with one another, and lacking writing systems or the use of metals as tools or arms. Contrariwise, in the Orient, the missionaries found organized kingdoms, deeply rooted ancient religions, and well-organized armies. The Far East was too far for any effective penetration and it remained resilient to any massive European incursion.[4] The New World was vulnerable, and eventually it was overruled and occupied.

Despite the successful territorial occupation, the religious conversion agenda in New Spain was a long and not always satisfactory experience. Despite their cultural, technical, and political disparities, the seminomadic tribes beyond the central areas created enormous difficulties for conquerors and settlers. The contact between indigenous nations and friars left a trail of European men who perished in the process of trying to convert reluctant neophytes and led to the creation of new martyr prototypes. Missionaries were not killed by powerful lords who imprisoned them and ordered their public execution, as in the more iconic narratives of early Christian martyrs and those killed in the Far East. Nor were they martyred by believers in a different interpretation of Christian practice, as was happening in sixteenth-century Europe. The Amerindians who killed the missionaries were not even in agreement with each other or believed in the same gods. Martyrdom in New Spain was a unique experience that, while retaining some features of its European signification, acquired features of its own. Since the differences were not simply an issue of dealing with a different terrain or different people, could the traditional features of martyrdom be reconciled to the realities of the New World? It was the task of the chroniclers and biographers to do so.

Background and Context for Martyrdom in the New World

The meaning of martyrdom in New Spain is better understood by briefly reviewing the historical context of martyrs. Most of them were of Spanish ancestry, and had traveled to the New World infused with sixteenth-century spirituality and seeking the conversion of the indigenous peoples as part of a larger plan of salvation for all humanity. Between the arrival of the Franciscans in Mexico in 1524 and the end of the sixteenth century, the unfolding of Protestantism in central Europe and England yielded a significant number of martyrs to all sides of the religious split. As more friars arrived in New Spain, the knowledge and memory of those events shaped their attitude as missionaries and guided their activities in the viceroyalty. Tribal opponents differed greatly from "heretics" in Europe, but awareness of a weakened and harassed Roman Catholicism in the European scenario kindled the enthusiasm of Catholic missionaries.

In addition, early sixteenth-century Spaniards could recall their own relatively recent memory of martyrdom under Islamic rule and were engaged in the evangelization of a significant number of Muslims still living in their midst. The martyrs included two members of the Roman militia, Emeterio and Celedonio, who refused to worship pagan gods and were martyred in the city of Calahorra at the end of the fourth century.[5] Under Islam and beginning in the eighth century A.D., local resistance resulted in the death of several secular men and women. St. Eurosia (Orosia) was martyred at Jaca in the Pyrenees in 714. She was followed by Valentine and Engratia, martyred at Sepúlveda (Castile) in 715. However, the center of martyrdom under Islam was Córdoba in the ninth century. Between 835 and 864, forty-seven men and women, some of them nuns, were martyred in that city. All were later elevated to sainthood.[6] The ultimate defeat of the Muslims in the peninsula in 1492 did not diminish the passion that had been spent in the reconquest of the territory. Islam thrived across the Mediterranean on African shores, and some members of the church dreamed of the possibility of venturing into the African territory to reignite conversion.[7] Franciscan Fray Martín de Valencia, one of the original twelve missionaries arriving in Mexico in 1524, had first wished to go to Africa to preach. In his old age he still hoped he could travel to China to continue the work he had initiated in New Spain.[8] Spain also had firsthand experience in the Christianization of tribal peoples in the Canary Islands, conquered and annexed during the fifteenth century. The aboriginals fiercely resisted settlers and Christianity. San Diego de Alcalá (1389–1463), canonized in 1588, was among the Franciscans who established convents in the islands. Diego sought martyrdom in Gran Canaria, asking to be sent ashore while on his way to the island of Fuerteventura. The captain denied him permission. For the rest of his life Diego regretted the fact that this opportunity had been denied to him.[9] By the mid-1520s there was, however, a wider scenario in which to play out the dream of Christianization. Exploration and settlement in other parts of the world expanded the number of potential conversions to astronomical figures. The incorporation of China, Japan, and the Philippines to the religious map inflamed the imagination of sixteenth-century Spanish and other European evangelizers and took its place side by side with the conversion of the neophytes in the New World. As John Phelan suggests, in those days ardent Christians saw a teleological march of Christianity after the fall of Constantinople, moving from Europe to the West in a swift and unstoppable progression. Mexico was a middle station to reach the Far East.[10]

The march of Christianity was, however, severely handicapped by its own internal breakdown. New interpretations challenged Roman Catholicism's claims as guardian of the "true" word of Christ. In sixteenth- and seventeenth-century Europe, Protestants and Catholics both argued that theirs was the only true Christianity according either to the New Testament or the word of the early Christians. Willing to die for their faith, martyrs reinvigorated the concept of martyrdom. However, in the early modern period this sought-after fate was heavily tinted with state politics and was no longer the same process its apologists claimed it to be.[11] Sixteenth- and seventeenth-century martyrdom in Europe was embedded in the struggle to control and subject entire populations to a king's or a prince's religion, and it was manipulated to benefit their status and power in the concert of emerging states. Thus, martyrdom became an issue of treason to the ruler's will as well as of faith.

In his pithy survey of European martyrdom, Brad Gregory distinguishes between the early Catholic martyrs under Henry VIII, of which the best known were Thomas More and a group of Carthusian monks, and Elizabethan and post-Tridentine martyrs caught up in a widespread religious struggle highlighted by the effort of Catholic recusants. Spain was more involved in the second phase than in the first.[12] During the short reign of Mary Tudor, Protestants were the victims of religious persecution, but after Elizabeth I's consolidation of the throne of England, Catholics were vulnerable and on the defense again. Between the late sixteenth century and the mid-seventeenth century, a host of brilliant intellectual minds reinforced efforts to restore Catholicism, and martyrdom reached its apogee in England as well as the Netherlands, where Spain was battling a very strong Protestant bastion in the northern provinces.[13] In England, Protestants were divided into several denominations, but they found a powerful and charismatic voice in John Foxe, who evolved from being a Catholic in his early youth to a Puritan in spirit in his late years. Having had to leave England during the reign of Mary Tudor, he returned in 1558 after her death. In 1563 he published the first edition of the *Acts and Monuments of These Latter and Perilous Days*, later to be known as the *Book of Martyrs*. This work was revised and enlarged in several editions and enjoyed great popularity through the seventeenth century.[14] A veritable battle of writings in favor of one cause or the other was waged from the 1560s onward.

Of particular interest to Spain was the translation into Spanish of the history of the so-called "English schism" written by Jesuit Robert Personius (Persons), a work that exposed the persecutions of Catholics in England and answered the charges raised by Foxe.[15] This translation was openly a work of propaganda and came on the heels of the defeat of the Spanish Armada. It definitely contributed to creating an atmosphere of hatred toward Protestants and to kindling missionary and pro-martyrdom feelings.[16] Martyrdom was a living and heartfelt reality in Spain, even though it was not experienced *in situ*. The literature of the Golden Age and the historiography of the period reflected a keen interest in saints and martyrs. The audience for stories on martyrdom was expanded through the theater. Some of the most respected Spanish playwrights of the early seventeenth century, such as Lope de Vega and Pedro Calderón de la Barca, wrote works based on saints and martyrs.[17] Spain, as well as other Catholic European countries, also had a powerful tool in the visual arts to convey its messages on martyrdom, which were largely confined to classic martyrs, until the incidents of martyrdom in the Far East and the New World provided fresh images to venerate. Strict Protestant iconoclastic culture had to resort to imprints, while Catholicism used religious paintings and sculptures to nurture its followers in their beliefs.

With the spirit of Catholic Reform taking root after the Council of Trent (1545–63), Spain, as Europe's champion of Catholicism, did not lack volunteers to the missionary enterprise in the New World and the Far East. While there were never enough missionaries to serve in the missions, there were still plenty of men willing to travel to the frontiers of "civilization" to preach Christianity and maybe have a shot at dying for its cause. Although the three Mendicant orders engaged in evangelization in New Spain, Franciscans suffered the largest number of losses to martyrdom, with the Jesuits following in the second place.

Mexico as Scenario for Martyrdom

As the first large-scale evangelizing agenda developed, martyrdom was soon a part of that experience. Mexico was a "mission" land in itself and also the bridge to the islands of the Pacific and Mainland China, which became the target for conversion work for a select group of dedicated individuals. From the mid-sixteenth century onward, Catholic missionaries reached India, Japan, China, and the Philippines, and most of them departed from Mexico.[18] The evangelizing dream that mesmerized many men is described in Jerónimo de Mendieta's history of the Franciscan Order in Mexico.[19] Such dreams are also described by the Dominican Order's Fray Luis Gandullo, who arrived in Manila in 1588.[20]

Could New Spain rival the missionary and martyrdom mirage of the Far East and become a promised land for willing friars? The New World was halfway across the planet, and because it had yielded to European conquest it made the evangelizing task appear relatively easier in comparison to that of the Far East. However, although the Mendicant orders began to see more clearly the evangelizing promise of New Spain by the mid-sixteenth century, some of their members continued to use Mexico as a stepping-stone for the dreamed of Far East. In a unique way, the history of martyrdom in Mexico and the Far East converged in the figure of Felipe de Jesús, a Mexican-born martyr who was beatified in the seventeenth century and thus fulfilled the dream so many others failed to accomplish, a story I will touch on later. The image of Mexico as a missionary site with martyrdom potential was unclear until the 1540s, when the politically sophisticated central regions of New Spain were conquered and explorers and settlers began pushing north. The exploration and eventual conquest of the province of New Galicia opened the eyes of the advancing Spaniards. The land became less hospitable and the inhabitants more challenging. They were nomadic or seminomadic tribes that bore no resemblance whatsoever to the highly developed kingdoms of the areas west and south of Tenochtitlan. They spoke multiple languages not related to those of the central areas, waged war among themselves, and, above all, opposed the newcomers and their indigenous allies. The mountains of the Western Sierra Madre, and the Sierra Gorda northeast of Querétaro, gave shelter to a variety of tribal people whose main objective was to keep settlers out, and as the first religious martyrs met their death in the 1550s, the Mendicant orders became aware that martyrdom and its glory could be achieved in New Spain.[21]

The first martyrs of Mexico, ironically, were not the friars seeking the conversion of the Natives. They were three indigenous children who were killed by their own parents for having become Christians. Their story was repeated by several Spanish authors who sought the value of an "edifying" preamble to the history of conversion, but it did not have much purchase in colonial historiography.[22] The memory of martyrdom of the Mendicants, on the other hand, had a special appeal to the religious orders because the charisma and piety of the fallen men reflected well on their evangelizing endeavors and their brothers in religion. Martyred friars connected the Mendicants with the European Christian tradition, the memory of the martyrs in Muslim Spain, and the more contemporaneous sixteenth- and seventeenth-century Catholic martyrs in Europe and Japan. In addition, the story of New World martyrs was more than welcomed in the peninsula itself, as it strengthened the spiritual cause of Counter-Reformation Catholicism as well as fired up the imagination of common folk. Take, for example, the story of Dominican Fray Sebastian Montaño, who died in a rebellion of the Tepehuanes in November 1616. Fray Alonso Franco, historian of the order, who had known Fray Sebastian personally as a conventual brother, not only extolled his martyrdom but preceded the account of his life with the numerous citations that his blessed death had received in Spain, Portugal, and Rome.[23] The remarkable dispersion of the news about martyrdom in a remote area of New Spain is evidence of the avidity with which religious orders and Catholic believers followed the deeds and sacrifices of their own abroad.

The scenario for martyrdom in Mexico had no resemblance to those of Europe or Asia, and this was part of its appeal. There were no urban centers where one could stage a spectacle for hundreds to witness. There were no events such as parading the would-be martyrs in chains, or roped to each other and dragged to burn at the stakes, or to be decapitated at the chopping block. There were no crosses on which to die, imitating the death of Christ, as in Japan.[24] In New Spain, martyrdom took place in small, sometimes makeshift churches in remote missions, or in the vast and empty landscape traveled by foot by the missionaries. In the North, early European cities like Zacatecas, Durango, and Guadalajara were separated by large expanses of threatened territory. The land in-between was the domain of tribal indigenous peoples, whose presence was a challenge to the settlers as well as the missionaries, and for whom the newcomers were intruders who always meant the loss of their ancient habitat and their personal freedom.

For the missionary friars, access to their neophytes in the provinces of Zacatecas, Sinaloa, New Mexico, New Santander, New Biscay, and Texas meant defiance of a harsh environment that limited the possibilities of success. Extraordinarily rich silver mines were the magnet for Spanish penetration, which, to some extent, helped pave the way for the evangelization process, although settlers and friars were not always in agreement on how to deal with the indigenous population. In some areas, water sources were unreliable and food was scarce. Friars and settlers had difficulty accessing the seminomadic tribes living in *rancherías*, small settlements perched on rough mountainous terrain that could be moved with ease and where few dared to go. Most of the northern tribes were hunters, unwilling to settle down as agriculturalists. Roaming for food, Native peoples spent little time within the reach of the friars and Christianity itself; they decided when to approach the Spaniards and not the other way around. Defense of the missionary posts became a key issue for the civil authorities, who, since the mid-sixteenth century, began a combined effort of settlement with assimilated Indians, civilians, soldiers, and evangelizers.[25]

Martyrs were the casualties of the persistent resistance of Natives who fought against secular Spanish entries in their territory and the imposed labor they demanded. Tribal groups rejecting the invasion of their territories experienced different fates. The successful resistance of some allowed them to remain free of Spanish dominance for as long as two centuries, while others were defeated, punished, and enslaved. Enslavement as a result of "just war" was practiced through the eighteenth century. Tribal groups that offered no resistance and welcomed settlers and missionaries (*indios de paz*) were absorbed as free subjects and became members of *reducciones*, towns inhabited exclusively by the indigenous under ecclesiastic supervision, where they were taught all the trappings of European culture, such as agriculture, crafts, and Roman Catholic rituals and devotions. In time, they were recruited to work in mines and agricultural estates.

Missionary Expansion and Indigenous Disaffection

The struggle for the Native souls in peripheral areas that offered consistent resistance to Spanish penetration was a long chapter in the story of evangelization. It helped define the missionaries as warriors for Christ engaged in relentless struggle against defiant tribes and the demonic forces that in their view kept the indigenous population in darkness and resistance to Christianity. Every life spent in the catechization of the indigenous was an offer to God, but those lost to their arrows and *macanas* were especially relevant in keeping the evangelization drive alive. Missionaries were successful in establishing dozens of missions in the North, but every missionary's death signified a failure. From the outset, European Christian images and values made the missionizing friars the protagonists of a drama of male heroism clothed in virtue, selflessness, and utter dedication to the salvation of the souls of peoples about whom they had the greatest doubts. The purpose of evangelization was not martyrdom, even if some friars hoped for it, but when martyrdom occurred it was used to buttress the evangelization campaign and bring material and military support to the missions.[26]

The missionary frontier began moving north in the 1540s, following a general motion largely north-northwest from the central basin of Mexico. Inland from the western Sierra Madre and on its coastal flanks lived a diversity of ethnic groups the Spaniards hardly comprehended, as they were so different from the central and southern nations, and to whom they applied the generic term *Chichimecs*. The penetration was slow and punctuated by concomitant rebellions and a practical state of war in which the missionaries saw themselves as playing a key role.[27] For the Jesuits and Mendicants, who renounced the use of arms, the cross was their main tool of persuasion as they raised it when they preached. The support of troops and the presence of soldiers was a necessity in the eyes of the Spanish government and, eventually, the missionaries had to acknowledge the need for it in critical areas. However, they remained adamant about first entering the new territories by themselves, relying on the help of God.

Whereas the mountain tribes of New Galicia were the first scene in the history of martyrdom, the discovery of the mines of Zacatecas in 1548 and Guanajuato in 1552 opened the gates to the central north and to raids of the Chichimecs, such as the Xiximes, Acaxees, Zacatecos, Guachichiles, Pames, and other ethnic groups. The Mixton rebellion in the province of Jalisco in 1540–41 was the first great sixteenth-century rebellion. After it, the potential of rebellion increased with every mile of territory gained.[28] Between 1601 and 1603, the Acaxees rebelled in the Sierra de Topia [Durango], inspired by a leader who called himself "bishop" and imitated the episcopal functions of the Catholic hierarchy. Susan Deeds regards this first rebellion as a first-generation "pattern" that was copied throughout the century by other rebels.[29] Rebellions cascaded throughout the seventeenth century, with little relief in between. In 1616, when the Tepehuanes orchestrated a massive rebellion in Nueva Vizcaya, ten missionaries lost their lives: eight Jesuits, one Franciscan, and one Dominican, and more than two hundred settlers lost theirs too.[30] The attack was aimed at the Spanish presence, and the missionaries were casualties because they were part of the system. However, the intent to desecrate, humiliate, and reject Christianity was very clear. The missionaries were killed and the churches and icons broken or scarred in a clear message of contempt. The Tepehuan revolt was under control by early 1619 at the cost of the loss of thousands of men for the rebels. The remnant splinter groups retreated into the mountains, where the seeds of resistance remained ready for further action.[31]

In the aftermath of this rebellion Franciscans aimed at the northern frontiers, leaving the western Sierras to the Jesuits. They built up missions in Atotonilco (Durango) and San Francisco de los Conchos (Chihuahua) and were able to proceed to New Mexico, where they had a toehold since the 1610s. Under the care of dedicated custodians, the missions in New Mexico thrived in the 1630s. The volunteer missionaries of this period were Spanish-born and willing to see wonders and riches, both spiritual as well as material. In the remote North, Fray Estevan Perea and Fray Alonso de Benavides became the torchbearers of these "golden" decades. The latter wrote a memorial to the king, carefully assessing the nature of the indigenous tribes and the rapid spread of the faith among some of them.[32] "Our Lord has wrought so many wonders and miracles," wrote Commissary Juan de Santander, imbued with enthusiastic faith in the future. By mid-century the Franciscans had established a string of missions among the Pueblo Indians, but they had also collected more martyrs. Two friars were killed by the Jemez and Taos by 1640.[33] Civil and religious authorities did not seem to get along together and the structure sustaining the extensive missionary network began to crumble. The apparently peaceful coexistence of mission Indians and friars was easy to upset, especially as shamans revived the belief in the ancient religion and the common people became restless under heavy labor and goods taxation largely imposed by settlers and by the missionaries themselves. Tribes that had been "friendly," and some that had never accepted Christianity, engaged in constant plots that maintained a general mistrust and tense preparation for attack. A carefully planned New Mexico revolt exploded in 1680. Twenty-one Franciscan missionaries were killed, increasing the ranks of martyrdom exponentially. Among the many possible causes cited for this revolt are famine produced by droughts, forced labor, disrespect for indigenous culture, tribal divisions, the collapse of Indian-Spanish relationships that had hinged on half-baked acculturation, and the lack of appeal of Christianity.[34] Above all, the revolt meant the lack of acceptance of Roman Catholicism, despite decades of catechization, and the desire of indigenous peoples to get rid of the Spaniards and their religion.[35] It took the Spaniards ten years to return, and not until 1693 could they claim a secure settlement. Nevertheless, another revolt took place in 1696, which cost the lives of four more Franciscans. By the end of the century, forty-nine of them had died as martyrs.

Rebellion and repudiation of Christianity persisted through the eighteenth century, especially in the northwestern part of New Spain, the remote areas of the Colorado and Gila rivers, and the more recent missionary territory of Texas. As an answer to the seventeenth-century revolts, the Franciscan order introduced the Colegios de Propaganda Fide in the early 1680s. They were missionary training centers that began to direct some of their members to the Seris and Yumas of the Sinaloan province and further north.[36] The *colegios* lived under strict observance and depended on periodical recruitment of peninsular volunteers.[37] In the northeastern part of New Spain, Franciscans reached present-day Texas by the mid-eighteenth century. Their contact with the Apaches and their tribal enemies in the remote Texan frontier in the late eighteenth century was the last and not very auspicious chapter of the Franciscan experience. By that time, the indigenous population of the North and far North had suffered enormous demographic losses and, while some had been assimilated as labor, they remained a marginal social element, "unreduced" or half-Christianized, since the Franciscan missions had no resources to sustain them in a permanent manner and could only interact with a small number of the indigenous population. It is against this background of hostility, defiance, warfare, surrender, enslavement, or eventual assimilation of some indigenous peoples, that the martyrs loom large in the history of the Jesuits and the Franciscans.[38] Missionaries had a message to deliver and a mission to accomplish. For that they needed an interlocutor, the object of their spiritual engagement to validate their endeavors. The Native Americans were the "other" to whom they addressed their message. How they defined the indigenous "other" and their ability to become Christians was an essential element in the construction of their own saga. What mattered to the evangelizers, and what may explain their success or lack thereof, was not the Indians themselves, but how they were perceived by their self-appointed saviors.

The Prospective Christians

At all times missionaries faced a fundamental issue: the nature of the people they sought to Christianize. Those Natives who accepted Christianity were regarded differently from those who refused it. The rejection of Christianity was personified in individuals who became the prototype of evil tendencies in human nature and were under the spell of demonic forces. The reality was that North and far North hunters and gatherers responsible for killing missionaries were not accustomed or willing to living in towns or *reducciones*, which for them meant renouncing to their customary ambulatory life and their traditional way of worship. Due to their refusal to accept Christianity by the third quarter of the sixteenth century, the northern provinces of New Spain became islands of Christian and "civilized" population surrounded by non-Christian indigenous peoples, who were regarded as "barbarians." The degree of sacrifice the missionaries were willing to face was tied to the adversarial behavior of the potential neophytes: the more difficult the possibility of catechizing and converting, the more worthy the effort to convert them; the fiercer the enemy, the sweeter the potential victory over their state of "darkness." Throughout two centuries, these adamantly independent people were the object of the unrequited desire of friars inflamed by evangelism to make them Christians, more European and less "Native."[39]

Fray Jerónimo de Mendieta, who lived a very long time in New Spain, thought it was mandatory to describe the indigenous "enemy" for his readers to underline the nature of the war sustained by the friars for Catholicism. In the sixteenth century, the Chichimecs comprised people who were both brave and wild, and lived a "bestial life."

> They know not of wealth or delights, or contracts, or social order (*policía*). Although they go around naked and sleep on the ground, even swamps, they remain healthy. They suffer bitter cold, snow, heat, hunger and thirst, but they never show any sadness on account of them or other things. They eat venison, cattle, mules, horses, vipers and other poisonous animals, at best half washed and half raw, tearing the flesh with nails and teeth like dogs. They differ from peaceful Christian Indians in language, customs, strength, ferocity and body shape, perhaps as a result of a bad star or the bestial manner in which they are raised.[40]

He characterized them as nervous, lacking beards, and so different from other men that in some way they could be regarded as monsters of nature— alike to animals (*brutos*) in their abilities (*ingenio*). Mendieta judged the Chichimecs by standards of European "civility" like dressing, eating properly cooked foods, showing emotions understandable to the Europeans, and having an organized religion, features that the indigenous groups in central Mexico displayed. As long as the Chichimecs would not surrender to "*policía*," that is, social order expressed in urban life, legislation, and a social ranking based on political categories, they remained "barbarians," the designation for all indigenous peoples that rejected Spanish acculturation. Yet, he and others recognized that the Chichimecs had qualities Spaniards could respect, like their perseverance, strength, dexterity in handling arms, and temerity in battle when they chose to fight. In fact, many Spaniards remained afraid of them, having hundreds of their own perish at their hands. However, Mendieta thanked divine providence for having intervened on behalf of the Spaniards, the peaceful Indians, and Christianity. One of the Chichimecs' weaknesses was their engagement in constant internecine territorial wars, which they had carried on for generations over hunting and gathering territories. Indigenous peoples fought with each other as a matter of survival in harsh environments, and ultimately their fragmentation worked in favor of the European invaders. Mendieta realized that Christians had succeeded more on account of such wars than because of their own efforts. "If the chichimecs had agreed to unite to wage war together, they would not have met any resistance among the Indians of this New Spain."[41] Other Spanish writers of the seventeenth and early eighteenth centuries also compared the indigenous to their own culture and found them lacking. For example, Fray Alonso de Benavides, in a 1626 report on the nations of New Mexico, characterized some of them as "very fierce and barbarous . . . they go completely naked without having a house or cultivated field." Like Mendieta, he noted how they warred against each other over hunting grounds.[42] For the most part, religious and secular Spaniards regarded hunters as barbarians, even when they were friendly, and wondered how they could survive living "so remote from the customs and common life of all men."[43] Fray Joseph Arlegui, who claimed to appreciate the dexterity of indigenous peoples in hunting and knowledge of medicinal and venomous herbs, was horrified by their habit of eating human flesh, the bartering of wives, and some incest and homosexual practices. He despaired of their misguided beliefs, which he described in detail. To him, they were under the power of the devil.[44] Reports from Propaganda Fide's missionaries in New Mexico in 1696 also decried the lack of interest of the majority of the indigenous there in converting to Christianity and their "rebellious and contumacious" character that led them to relapse to apostasy.[45] Propaganda Fide's chronicler, Fray Isidro Felix de Espinosa, a missionary among the Texans in the early 1700s, admired the indigenous for many reasons, although not for their beliefs. He headed one of the early four missions and thought the indigenous were "pleasant, happy, good looking and very friendly towards the Spaniards." He considered the Assinais of coastal Texas (now known as Caddos) to be perspicacious, friendly, but haughty, and although always ready for warring, he felt they had good hearts. In general, he opined, the Lord had endowed them with a good clear intelligence (*entendimiento*), and since they were clever to deal with material things, "it would be easy that, on learning, they will raise their thoughts to the eternal."[46] As agriculturalists, they gained his sympathy because land cultivation was a sign of civilization, but he remained skeptical about the possibilities of redeeming the negative features of other indigenous groups.

Some of the Franciscans of Propaganda Fide showed a moderate appreciation of the indigenous as people, especially toward the end of the eighteenth century. They understood the politics of Native tribal interaction and were level headed about the limitations of their conversion campaigns.[47] However, when facing some groups they found intractable they still displayed despair and harsh judgment. Fray Juan Domingo Arricivita cited letters from missionaries to the Yumas (today's Arizona) that described the Natives as "too stupid to be attracted to spiritual things." These friars did not expect many baptisms.[48] The negative comments beg the question of why did the missionaries persisted in their intentions. Their motivation as bearers of the word of Christ was deeply embedded in their training. They were committed by their vows and by their faith, and the latter did not exclude the possibility of conversion as well as martyrdom. The latter cannot be eliminated as a factor in the dedication of their lives to a task otherwise considered so difficult to attain. The palm of martyrdom was the most precious symbol of dedication to God as well as the most rewarding prize for a man of the cloth *if* it were to occur. It was a risk they understood.

Essential Martyrdom

The eulogies of martyrs set down in the chronicles of the Mendicant orders offer a glimpse of the mind-set of the period and the actors. Direct testimonies from martyrs prior to their personal sacrifices are hard to come by, since most of the friars had no time to write anything but letters and reports to their superiors, and hardly any of them ever engaged in personal accounts of their own spiritual lives. Further, martyrdom was not preceded by imprisonment or a waiting period that could have allowed such correspondence. Martyrdom was sudden and fast. Biographers and chroniclers struggled to rescue letters and statements of the evangelizers, including some rare ones from men who later became martyrs. Among the latter, we have a letter from Fray Joseph Matías Moreno, a peninsular recruit who was killed in the Colorado River, which offers a glimpse of his burning desire to attain the palm of martyrdom. On explaining to his sister the reasons for having left Spain and his family behind, he cited "the zeal (*celo*) of the faith, the desire of the conversion of the souls, and the desire (*ansias*) of martyrdom." Those elements had moved him to put off all personal considerations. As he put it: "Work, hunger, thirst, unbearable heat and roads are all true, but what are they compared to the cost of souls to Christ? If some of us would not undertake His spiritual conquest, many souls would ineluctably fall in the snares of Satan. I owe Him many benefices."[49]

Moreno's view reflected the personal and institutional expectations of those who tried to make their vows a live experience in their own flesh. Another testimony of the expectations of those traveling to the New World was recorded by Thomas Gage. Having disembarked in the Caribbean island of

Guadalupe, some of the traveling missionaries were carried away by the prospects of converting the islanders. In the ensuing discussion, some were of the opinion that it was temerity to disembark and stay in the island and expose their lives among such people who were more like wild animals than rational men. Gage records that the exalted would-be missionaries answered that perishing by the hand of the savages was among the reasons they had left the motherland—to be martyrs.[50] Whatever the chroniclers said about the martyrs was part of their own thoughts and sentiments, and should be understood to be similar to what was in the minds of those who became martyrs. The "burning zeal" to indoctrinate sustained their willingness to suffer pain, sickness, calamities, and poverty, as Fray Juan Domingo Arricivita explained: "It was not leisure, rest, security or comfort in life the missionaries searched among those barbarous nations, but the travails, dangers, and all that belonged to Jesus Christ and his greater glory, the exaltation of the Faith through the evangel and the salvation of the souls."[51]

In reality, most missionaries did not expect to be martyrs and most did not want to become martyrs, but they were cognizant of the possibility that this could happen. Most of those who became martyrs—with some important exceptions—were born in Spain and came to the New World seeking specific conditions not available in the peninsula or even in Protestant Europe: a new flock and the challenge of non-European civilizations, those exotic peoples about whom they knew only that they were fierce and difficult to convert.

The martyrdom of sixteenth-century evangelizers is not very different from those who died in the eighteenth century. The geographical scenario changed, but the risks were similar and the results invariably the same. The progress of martyrdom's history had its beginnings in New Galicia in the early 1530s, when the Franciscan Fray Juan Calero, a lay brother, volunteered to go into the Tecuila, a mountain post of rebellious Indians. Although, according to Mendieta, they heard him preach in peace, he was killed by another band of Indians on his way back to his convent in Ezatlan. Three of his companions, newly converted Indians, were also killed.[52] The lure of "the beyond" pushed the Franciscans hundreds of leagues into the open spaces since the 1530s, and they never stopped. Welcoming towns did not necessarily mean true and lasting conversion. "Treacherous" rebels could spring from the rugged Sierras any time and assault the traveling friars on their many peregrinations. Retaliations by Spanish and Christianized indigenous forces simply reinforced the antagonistic feelings of the communities under attack. Friars who asked to be sent to the far North beyond Zacatecas knew that the area known as Nueva Vizcaya (New Biscay) was dangerous, but it was precisely that danger that triggered their desire to serve their order and fulfill their missionary commitment.

Friars were great trekkers. In the sixteenth century they had sworn to follow apostolic example and travel on foot and while this was not the case for many in the late seventeenth and eighteenth centuries, the fact remains that many still traveled alone or with a small retinue to earn the trust of their potential converts.[53] In imitation of historical hermits and saints, the early missionaries never took food along and lived on berries and nuts or what "divine providence" would provide. They were defenseless and open to attack, but their choice was guided by the need to seek the good will of the reluctant "gentiles."

Since the end of the sixteenth century the areas close to Zacatecas were held to be "safe." This was more assumption than reality, and friars who continued to travel north probably hoped to succeed in their endeavor without losing their lives, although they did not intentionally evade danger. By the 1730s, when Arlegui was writing his Franciscan chronicle, he claimed that the Indians had become acquainted with the Franciscan presence. They knew that the friars traveled in pairs or alone and without arms. These facts had earned them a "pardon" during some attacks, or a safe passage to their destination. Having learned this, some members of other orders and even laymen put on Franciscan habits when they went north in the hope that if attacked they would escape with their life. Arlegui mentioned several other occasions in which the Indians attacked the civilians and let the friars go, but friars feared such occasions. He said as much. All the friars in Zacatecas, Nuevo León, and Nueva Vizcaya lived in continuous apprehension (*susto*), surrounded by untamed indigenous, and regretting the death of numberless secular settlers. The respect shown by some attackers (not all) to the Franciscans could cause some strange incidents, as when one unnamed provincial vicar, carrying out the obligatory visit to his province, was attacked three leagues from the city of Durango. The vicar and his accompanying friars were spared, but their secular companions were killed. After this, the Indians approached the friars with gestures of friendship and asked them to place their hands over their heads. Having been "blessed," they took the clothes off of the dead corpses and left the friars alone in the midst of "that bloody spectacle." The provincial's secretary was so affected by the circumstances that he lost his mind and died shortly thereafter. Fray Marcos de Mezquia suffered a similar fate, who, having escaped with his life during an attack, also lost his mind. He had been a scholar and preacher, but after the attack he could hardly remember his name. The "fright" also affected Fray Joseph de Rentería, of the convent of San Juan del Rio, who was returning from confessing some sick people when he was attacked.[54]

Reporting from New Mexico in 1696, Fray Francisco de Vargas also acknowledged fear among the missionaries.[55] Such candid acknowledgement belies earlier sixteenth- and seventeenth-century chronicles, even Arlegui's own, in which martyrs were presented facing death without fear. Friars who escaped with their lives, said Arlegui, were simply lucky, and they lived with such an intense memory of their experiences that they were traumatized for the rest of their lives. "I have noted that those who fall in their hands never recover well of their fright. The memory of the Indian's naked bodies, of their screams and voices, and the sight of the harm they do, pulling the entrails and the heart of the corpses, leave them [the survivors] pale and withered."[56] Even when their lives were spared, the friars could be subjected to taunting, beatings, and threats before let go. The uncertainty about attacks or, worse, doubts of the loyalty of Christian converts, kept the friars in suspense about their own fate and that of their church.[57]

The north remained a land of rebellions and martyrs though the end of the eighteenth century. Some father provincials seemed to be determined to try the limits of their men, and some friars knew no limits to their zeal; they volunteered for the task. In the sixteenth century, Fray Pedro de Espinareda, head of the Franciscan convent of Zacatecas, sent twelve men to their deaths by urging them to missionize in Sonora.[58] They still retained what Mendieta had described as "the desire to obtain abundant fruit from such thorns and thistles of infidelity."[59] The vow of obedience to their superiors bound the evangelizers and later martyrs to proceed further north, but their method of approaching the indigenous was in some instances infelicitous, and resulted in their own demise. Mendieta and Arlegui, over one century apart, described how Franciscans approached new groups, exhorting them to conversion, smashing their "idols" if feasible, and telling them how wrong they were in their beliefs. In 1555, Bernardo Cossin, one of the early missionaries, became a martyr as a result of a frontal confrontation with the mountain Chichimecs tribes, who, running out of patience with his exhortations, interrupted him with a shower of arrows and killed him instantly.[60]

One wonders how effective the speeches were, since not all missionaries could speak the variety of languages of so many dispersed groups. In many instances, but not always, the preachers were accompanied by Christianized indigenous who, presumably, could speak several languages and translate their exhortations about Christianity for the friars, but it is not always clear that this was a fact. No words were necessary, however, when a stranger smashed their gods. Such actions incited the honor and loyalty of the indigenous to their ancestral beliefs, a fact that the friars seemed to ignore or simply not conceive at all. On one occasion, two friars, whose names have been lost to history, so astonished a group of Topia Natives (in Durango) with their preaching, that they stood speechless for a while until the speaking friar finished delivering his message. When they seemed to have recovered their composure, they killed the preachers on the spot.[61]

Those writing on martyrdom saw the martyr as their guiding light and inspiration to persevere in their determination to go to the dangerous frontiers of Christendom.[62] Addressing the act of dying, the chroniclers underscored the drama of the innocent martyred hero in contrast to the evil of the murderers. Since in some cases there were witnesses who escaped the debacle of an attack, the reports written by ecclesiastical authorities were taken as a basis for the chronicles and furnish details that suggest the pathos of the events. Death by martyrdom entailed a code of expected "gestures" that recalled images of religious rituals and excited the empathy of the readers. Most of the missionaries eulogized by Arlegui died preaching aloud. The sound of voices that would not stop was compared by Arlegui to the last song of a swan.[63] Preaching to the last breath was a common gesture among the martyred. Falling to their knees, holding a crucifix, or simply yielding to the attackers without resistance were others. If possible, the friars would confess each other, pray, and give each other words of hope and consolation.[64] Mendieta painted a vivid scene of one time when Fray Francisco Lorenzo and his companions came very close to death—which they escaped when the attacking tribe desisted from its apparent agenda. It is a description written to move the readers' hearts:

> That night they made the best preparations possible to receive their death for Jesus Christ. Fray Miguel confessed to his Guardian, and the Guardian lay on the floor, with many tears, begging mercy from God for all his transgressions, and having set up a crucifix on the ground, they knelt before it; they prayed at times and they consoled and encouraged each other to have hope; that all would be right because they had not undertaken that journey or peregrination in search of gold, silver, or any temporal goods, but only to find lost souls that had been redeemed by the Passion and blood of the son of God.[65]

Some writers did not spare details, albeit in a direct narrative without adjectives. For example, Bernardo de Lizana, in his history of Yucatan, tersely states how the Mayas of Taiza made pieces of Fray Diego Delgado, and impaled, removed the heart, and cut the head off of Fray Juan Enríquez and several soldiers. Enríquez was tied to a pole while the soldiers were killed and he continued to preach aloud until his turn came.[66]

The hagiography sometimes presents the martyr either as predestined to die or willing to die. There is probably no hyperbole on the issue of willingness, suspicious as it may look to contemporary eyes. The sense of mission as a duty to spread the Evangels was sincere among those who made a voluntary decision to meet the risks involved. Brad Gregory makes a strong case for accepting the reasons given by the martyrs and their contemporaries based on the spirituality of the late fourteenth century (*devotio moderna*) that infused the writings and behavior of the regular orders through the end of the sixteenth century and even beyond. The imitation of Christ, coupled with the meditation on his passion and death translated into a desire to meet a similar death.[67] In creating a frame for martyrdom, the hagiographies refer to premonitions that are humbly and willingly accepted. Dominican Fray Alonso Franco narrates the martyrdom of Fray Sebastian Montaño, implying that, since his years as a novice, he had presaged his demise at the hands of people bearing arrows, like his namesake Saint Sebastian. He arrived in Mexico City at age twelve in 1603, accompanying his father, who was a member of the retinue of the viceroy marquis of Montesclaros. After becoming a Dominican in 1615, he asked to be sent to the convent of Zacatecas, where he arrived in 1616. Once there, he asked to be sent to the hinterland (*tierra adentro*) to collect alms for the convent. Despite his youth and his lack of knowledge of the land, he was given the assignment, a fact that was interpreted as God's will, but also suggests that the ecclesiastical authorities were probably banking on the vigor and idealism of some of the younger members of the order. Following what was possibly the routine of the times under the circumstances, Fray Sebastian made a general confession, bid his brothers farewell, and set to travel in "mission" land. His first stop was in a Jesuit convent in the mission of Zape. Hospitality was extended to any brother in religion in those remote areas. There he begged confession from a Jesuit named Juan del Valle, whom he convinced to do likewise, since he felt that both would soon die. In letters written to his superior in Zacatecas, which were retrieved from his body, Montaño wrote about his possible death and set the accounts of the alms he had so far gathered to ensure they would be carried out. This detail speaks of the inner resolve of these men, a factor that idealistic missionaries obviously possessed. He and his Jesuit companion were walking into a large rebellion staged by the Tepehuan nation in 1616.[68] Neither of them returned alive to their convents.

Contrasted with the soldiering activities of other men, the *mansedumbre*, or meekness, of the friar in accepting his death was among the most appealing aspects of their martyrdom. Being humble, they did not avoid danger. Martyrdom was a manly choice precisely because of the strength necessary to face death without shaking. That was, at least, the hagiographer's message. Even if there was fear, the martyr did not stop from willingly moving on with his task. By spiritualizing the struggle, the hagiographer and his readers understood that willingness to die was appropriately masculine. It was essential that religious manhood was not associated with physical aggressiveness, but with a sense of dignity and full consciousness of the meaning of the undertaking. A rational, if effective, choice was made when the friar decided to seek the salvation of the infidels. He could volunteer for that task, or obey orders to travel to their territory. In either case, his guiding light was the imitation of Christ, both in preaching and in dying. Warned about his more than probable death, Fray Francisco Lorenzo, preaching in the northwest of Guadalajara in the sixteenth century, counterargued that Christ had known about his forthcoming death and did not stop preaching. If Christ had died for him, it would not be too much for him to die for Christ at the hands of the "barbarians."[69]

If there was humility in accepting death, there was also a spirit of defiant soldiering in the activities leading to martyrdom. Albeit spiritual, the process of conversion was regarded as a military operation, carried out for the glory of gaining souls and, although biographers and chroniclers endeavored to put martyrdom within a religious framework, they did not disguise the fact that there were military connotations in the actions of martyrs and in their own writing. Chroniclers often used martial metaphors to describe how friars protected themselves with the "shield of the faith" and "presented open battle to Hell." Friars "hoisted" the crucifix when preaching to the Indians, who were expected to "surrender" their hearts to their words.[70] The Indian gods had to be "exterminated." Fleeing Indians left "the field of victory" for the friars. Arlegui does not hesitate to call them "heroes." The "defeat" of the enemy simply meant the destruction of their attachment to paganism, but it was at the same time a victory for their souls, as the missionaries envisioned it. In theory, there was an open war against paganism, albeit not necessarily against the pagan or gentile. In practice, missionary activities were backed by military protection and involved battles, resulting in deaths and imprisonment and enslavement of the Natives. Those who met death by martyrdom were always involved in skirmishes or violent attacks from rebellious tribes. Even though wrapped in religious meanings, as long as the missionary was at risk of his life, the use of military metaphors by chroniclers and biographers injected virility into this spiritual endeavor. There was also a clear political implication in martyrdom. As long as there was no tolerance for any other belief or religion, the missionary was assuming a political—that is, manly—role on behalf of the state. The occupation of an alien territory in the name of God and Christianity, and the exercise of military power to back up the spread of the faith were actions with long-lasting political consequences. Even though the martyred friars traveled largely alone or lived in quarters separate from the presidios, they were accompanied or followed by soldiers, presidios, and the foundation of towns. As such, they were actors in the imperialistic designs of the crown to annex the non-Christians to their political system. They signified a militant church that demanded a fighting spirit until the final victory that, even though understood as a matter of faith, implied the hegemony of a single religion and Spanish institutions.

The fiery example of the soldiers of Christ had a final pious reward, not only in their expected prize in heaven, but in the signs that they left behind as proof of God's favor. The hagiographic halo was put on the heads of martyrs in writings since Mendieta's time. Readers and writers expected miraculous events to reiterate the blessedness of their deaths. The bodies of the martyrs were often left in the open fields or, otherwise, amidst the ruins of a ravaged mission. The murderers of Fray Juan de Tapia in 1557 stated having seen shining shadows following them. The bones of Fray Juan del Rio, who had been martyred in the 1580s, were rediscovered one hundred years later, and were reported as being red and sweet smelling. The Native who killed Fray Esteban Benítez close to San Juan del Río could not move from away from the victim's body and, having been found there with the stone he had used to murder the friar, he was eventually hanged. The bodies of three friars knifed by apostates in their cells appeared all together as if they had been confessing each other. Dismembered or heavily damaged, some of those bodies remained "fresh" and supple for days or even weeks. Some remains escaped destruction from wild animals. Such was the fate of Fray Pablo de Acevedo's body, which was found intact but shrunken to the size of a child. God, stated Arlegui, wished to equate the innocence of this martyr to the innocence of a child.[71] "Prodigies" punctuate Arlegui's narratives, which are mostly absent from Mendieta's.[72] The hagiographical intent, already developing in Mendieta's works, strengthened throughout the seventeenth century. This was in no small way helped by the story of Felipe de Jesús.

Martyrdom Connections with the Far East: Saint Felipe de Jesús

Martyrdom in New Spain must be related to the feedback it received from the Orient. News of friars killed during the performance of their evangelical duties in the Far East enhanced the cause of those confronting local circumstances in New Spain.[73] The strongest link between the two geographical areas was the first beatified martyr, Felipe de Jesús, who was Mexican by birth and a novice in the Franciscan Order when was killed in Nagasaki in 1597. He and his companions were beatified in 1627. His fast elevation to beatitude caused great pride to the Mexican church, which had been trying very hard to have the distinction of a "saint" born in its territory. After his beatification, Felipe de Jesús gained some popularity throughout that century, and although his name declined in public devotion thereafter, the cause for his elevation to sainthood remained active in Rome until the end of the colonial period. He achieved sainthood in 1867.[74]

Felipe de Jesús lived and died at a time when missionaries believed that China and Japan were the highest prize in the universal acceptance of Christianity. Several of Felipe's biographies tried to reshape the meager information on his short life to fit the image of a man of God with a will to ascend to the glory promised to martyrs, but his path to martyrdom was rather sinuous and it was probably not his choice. Born in Mexico City, he was the son of "noble" parents, which meant they possessed civic and personal virtue rather than real aristocratic roots.[75] His father, Juan de las Casas, was a well-to-do merchant dealing with the Philippines. He was also a *familiar* (distinguished supporting member) of the Holy Office. Felipe was the oldest of ten children. Two of his brothers entered the Augustinian Order after his death. Francisco de las Casas professed in 1609 and Juan de las Casas in 1607. He was killed in the Philippines in 1607.

Little is known of Felipe's younger years, but his biographers acknowledged that he was more interested in youthful merriment than in holy pursuits. He was supposed to have been a novice at the convent of Santa Barbara in Puebla.

Presumably, his novitiate was very short and he dropped his intentions. What is known is that he was sent by his father to Manila in charge of some of his merchandise in the hope that he would gain in maturity and experience. According to one of his biographers, Fray Baltasar de Medina, he dressed as a soldier, and bore arms while in Manila. However, this author also indicates that it was the custom of many young men who dealt in merchandise to dress as soldiers to attract less attention to their real purpose. Bearing arms and "soldiering" was an acceptable practice for a young man in those days. Medina also hints that he engaged in all the expected activities of a "green youth" with ardor and a purse to support them.

Yet, after time spent as a so-called merchant in the Philippines, he entered the Franciscan Order in the convent of Santa María de los Ángeles in Manila in 1594.[76] His biographers agree in underlining his great virtues as a novice. He may or may have not been as perfect as he is painted but the bottom line is that there was no reason to believe that he was less sincere than other novices, and this was sufficient in the mind of the biographers to present him as a model man. However, to be fully ordained, Felipe had to return to New Spain because there were no bishops in Manila to perform the ceremony. Having obtained permission to do so, Felipe set on his way to New Spain. He boarded the "San Felipe" on 12 July 1596. Apparently, during the voyage he gained a reputation for "sanctity" owing to his modest and devout behavior. Severe storms and the loss of the rudder and sails obliged the ship to land in the Japanese island of Toza several months later. The local lord ordered them to stay—the ship was loaded with merchandise and it is possible that he had his eyes set on it—and argued they needed a permit of the emperor to continue their voyage. As the religious lore would have it, they all saw a cross in the sky that changed colors from white to red, a presage of the fate of the friars who traveled in the ship. The captain of the San Felipe sent gifts to the emperor with three of his men and three friars, an Augustinian (Juan Tamayo), a Franciscan lay brother (Juan Pobre), and the novice Felipe de Jesús. His role as an ambassador, not as a local missionary, should have protected him from his fate, as argued by his biographers. The story of how the reprisal against the Christian missionaries developed as a result of this visit to the emperor is quite muddled, but it appears that Emperor Taycozama, who had already signed an expulsion of Christians in 1587, must have been at the end of his patience with Christian proselytizers, and he might have also been interested in a share of the merchandise. Be that as it may, according to the chroniclers, the fate of the Christian missionaries was sealed

The Japanese emperor's changing mood about Christians made the missionary enterprise in Japan different from others elsewhere in Europe, but the intense feelings nurtured by the missionaries was very much like their brothers in Mexico and Europe. The missionaries were accused of "treason," and they were rounded up and put under guard on 9 December 1596. By the end of the month, all the religious were taken to a public jail, a step in the process of a death penalty. As another biographer, Pedro de Ribadeneira, narrates, once the Franciscans sensed that martyrdom was certain, Felipe de Jesús accepted the will of God and conveyed this sentiment to a secular Spaniard who talked to him during his forced travel to Nagasaki.[77] Twenty-six men were martyred on 5 February 1597. Among them were a Jesuit and six Franciscan friars. The rest were Japanese laymen, including a young boy. Felipe de Jesús was the first to die, having been attached to a cross with metal rings and lanced twice from the side of the body through the shoulders, the usual mode of execution at the time. Their martyrdom was well documented by many secular and religious witnesses.

Felipe de Jesús was not the only native of Mexico to die in Japan. The other Mexican martyr had little chance to compete with the beatified Felipe de Jesús. He was the Augustinian friar Bartolomé Gutierrez, who was born in Mexico City in 1580 and professed in 1597.[78] In 1606 he joined a contingent of Augustinians on their way to the Philippines. It was not until 1612 that he left for Japan, which still appeared a greater attraction than the Philippines. Banned from Japan along with other regulars, he returned with other friars, who dressed up as Japanese to elude the authorities. For fifteen years he survived in Nagasaki, tending to his ministry and taking great risks He ran out of luck in 1629 and was apprehended by a "tyrant," Tacanaga, who became famous for the persecution of Christians. Along with several other Augustinians and a Japanese Jesuit, he was in prison for two years. After suffering torments for one month, they were condemned to be burned. Their ashes were scattered in the sea to avoid having any relics.

The ties with the Far East became important to the regular orders as evidence of their apostolic role in the global process of Christianization. Augustinian Fray Joseph Sicardo, peninsular by birth, but with a long career in Mexico, espoused the cause of the martyrs of the three Mendicant orders and laymen and laywomen in an attempt to promote their canonization and to prove the universal embrace of Roman Catholicism. Martyrs were missionaries first and martyrs only as a result of adverse circumstances. Their deaths were used to strengthen the piety of those already converted, but it took more than their sacrifice to root Christianity in the New World and the Far East axis.

Ultimately, what did the blood of the martyrs buy? Franciscan Commissary General Fray Manuel de Monzabal wrote to his missionaries in New Mexico in 1696 that "With the blood of your five religious, with the shedding of this blood in the continuation of martyrs, the religion will be multiplied and extended throughout the entire world. And in New Mexico, although the blood that was shed with the constancy and valor by twenty-one of our brothers is not yet dry, it has been a seed that has borne fruit in the garden of God."[79]

The "fruit in the garden of God" were the missionaries themselves, certainly not the evidence of widespread conversions. The history of missionary struggle and Native Americans' resistance for over two centuries gave the civil authorities overseeing the administration of the northern territories pause to ponder over the nature of their indigenous subjects and the role of the missionaries as reliable trustees of the Spanish Crown and the Catholic faith. As chronicled by Arricivita, in June 1769, Joseph de Gálvez, who oversaw a process or administrative reform in the far north (Coahuila and Texas), decided to turn over the missions to the Franciscan Order, thus continuing to rely on religion and its ministers for winning half of the battle to conquer the land. Franciscan missionaries remained skeptical of their trustees, the inhabitants of the Pimería Alta. Fray Mariano Buena, Franciscan president of the missions, argued that they were improvident; they would not cultivate the land or look after the animals as expected in missionary towns. He complained, "They do not plan for future needs." When they had plenty, they wasted it. Once all was consumed they would retreat to their *rancherías*. The indigenous needed the missionaries "to avoid the inconvenience of their irrational self-government." Arricivita eulogized his brothers' persistence and dedication but granted that the success of the missions was owed to the military support and the presidios, which held the reins over the "inconstancy of the barbarians."[80]

The blood of the martyrs had purchased their own personal salvation and merit for their order, as well as the political expansion of the Spanish government, but certainly not the conversion of the Natives, who had no desire for it. Christian martyrdom made sense only to the Western minds that had forged it, and who saw honor and salvation in the immolation. For the indigenous it was due punishment for those who had the audacity of trespassing their "habitus." Was there evil in the act of taking a life and goodness in offering it? Were the martyrs of New Spain men of God, or intruders?

The answers to these questions depend on who is answering them. Indigenistas will never cease to deplore the replacement of Native beliefs and customs with a half-baked Christianity. Native people's resistance expressed resentment, and today speaks of the futility of the forced nature of the process of conversion and the great effort it has taken for Native peoples to reconstruct their own original vision of the cosmos. Only in recent times have students of religion and religious culture begun to appreciate the challenge of understanding the idiosyncratic acculturation and the violence implied in this process of conversion. The violence we call martyrdom remained intact insofar as it was almost a "canonical" aspect of Christianity, but its reenactment in the north of Mexico brought new peoples and circumstances to its repertoire. The exoticism of the indigenous became the "demonic" force antagonizing the "good" message of Christianity while giving the regular orders an opportunity to construct an extension of a "Western and European" experience in the Americas. That was the lasting contribution of the martyrs and their religious chroniclers to the history of Mexico who, at the end of the eighteenth century, felt entitled to remember "so many heroes who have offered their lives for the propagation of our holy faith over the ruins of idolatry."[81]

PART III

Missions

CHAPTER 6

Believing in Piety

Spiritual Transformation Across Cultures
in Early New England

MATT COHEN

Piety has a central place in the study of colonial New England—and by extension, in the successive schools of thought about the origins of the United States and U.S. exceptionalism. It is part of broad arguments like Max Weber's, for explaining the deeply felt emotional drive of a certain kind of capitalism. It plays a role for those who argue that the New England Puritan Way transformed into a secular republic with a patriotism deeply structured by piety. It is crucial for arguments about the transformations of religious feeling that ebbed and flowed through a series of religious revivals in northeastern North America.[1]

But with the meaning of "piety" upon which that series of debates depends in mind, can we speak of *indigenous piety* in the early period? It might be argued that the most extensive religious transformation of the early settlement period in New England resulted from the death and displacement of a massive number of indigenous people. There is disagreement about the effects of the epidemics on the spirituality of the woodlands. Some scholars say Native beliefs persisted; others that they transformed superficially but stayed structurally intact; still others that they were changed sufficiently by that mortality and subsequent colonization that we cannot be sure they share anything deeply significant with the precontact period. We know that the objects

associated with what anthropologists and archaeologists interpret to be indigenous spiritual acts changed, and had done so at various times and to
various degrees many times before contact. Certainly the religious forms of
the Europeans who settled northeastern North America changed, some say
radically, within just the first century of their residence there. Some scholars
insist that the changes had to do with a shifting global economy, a capitalist
inclination powered in part by the very religious beliefs that tended to be
held by the settlers. For others, internal dynamics of the New England Way
forced changes—Creole believers did not have the same motivation that the
original settlers had, while theological disagreements among dissenting factions mapped onto evolving social conflicts.[2] The "Christianization" of Native populations has until very recently been an adjunct to the story of the
shift toward worldliness and the decreasing authority of New England's ministers, rather than being understood as part of that shift's engine. What if
what appears to be the trend toward worldliness and the decreasing location
of authority in New England's ministers was viewed as part of a longer, local
spiritual history—that is, what if the settlers were becoming more like Indians were becoming, with respect to religious feeling? Slightly differently put,
what if a Western modernity were not the eschaton of our analysis, but an at
least partly Indian future, as yet not quite visible to us?

Without trying fully to explore that question, this essay will suggest that
one of the advantages of such a reframing is that it highlights stumbling
blocks to thinking interculturally about religion in early colonial New England. Though focused on that region and time, my account is designed less
as a historical argument and more as a disciplinary and philological discussion. Two key terms have tended to divide Native American and Puritan studies, *piety* and *reciprocity*, limning a tension that is ultimately about conceptions
of history, both in the academic disciplinary realm and more broadly between groups of people today. Showing my belief in, if not piety, the importance of the early colonial period in our thinking about it, I analyze two scenes
of early colonial cohabitation that might offer a way of shifting our imaginations, and perhaps our vocabularies, of piety and reciprocity. These episodes
call for us to problematize not just piety as we know it, but piety as a sectarian,
or even cultural, boundary marker. To do so helps us see the consequences of
the relationship between the history of piety and piety's historiography.

To talk about how we might change the way we tell stories about religious
change in colonial North America, I invoke Michel Serres's philosophical
model of the parasite, which encourages understanding human culture as a set

of permeable boundaries, and an endless, turbulent activity of taking and of giving, hosting and guesting. Serres's insights are rooted in a longstanding rift between science and religion—an evolving construction of difference that obscures a complex and sustained back-and-forth transmission of ideas, desires, and practices.[3] Structurally similar practices are at work in the study of early America. Epistemes that seem to be oppositional also dog the discussion of the effect of European and indigenous beliefs on each other: orality and writing, "religion" and "spirituality," linear history and circular time, interiority and performance. Each of these epistemes is revelatory, telling us stories about sacred experience and social power that we would not otherwise have imagined. They give us new notions about indigenous beliefs, even as they disagree about what should serve as evidence or how we should read that evidence. But these are not just descriptions. The contests between these epistemes, historically, are a product of colonial encounter and settlement, and of ongoing attempts to contain indigenous power or presence (as well as that of other savage "others," from slaves to women to the poor). I begin, then, with an account of current approaches to telling the story of early New England's religious landscape interculturally. Given the centrality of the linked notions of reciprocity and piety in those approaches, I offer an account of the careers of those terms across disciplines. Finally, turning to the capillary relations between the material and supernatural worlds of early colonial New England, I examine two objects and their environments, points of conjunction for visible and invisible worlds, but also for existing and emergent ways of speaking about the past.

Faith and Culture

In their collection of essays *Native Americans, Christianity, and the Reshaping of the American Religious Landscape*, editors Joel Martin and Mark Nicholas situate their approach as informed both by religious historians who focus on lived practice and popular religion and by Latin American historians interested in the relations between political movements and popular religion in indigenous context. Such a strategy, they argue, "enables scholars of contact and colonialism to demonstrate how Native American individuals and communities could appropriate Christianity without necessarily agreeing with what missionaries and other professional Christians said about Christianity." Indeed, this approach has been key to telling stories long hidden, and it would be hard to find a better example than David Silverman's study of the

Wampanoag of Martha's Vineyard and their complex relationship with Christianity, *Faith and Boundaries*.[4] Silverman uses the term "religious translation" to describe the colonial religious transformations of Martha's Vineyard, borrowing from, but in some ways setting aside the arsenal of terms precipitated from the past few decades of anthropological and cultural studies, from assimilation through syncretism to interculturality. Religious translation in this context, Silverman argues, moved in two directions: the Mayhew family, lords of Martha's Vineyard, used Wampanoag concepts to convey Christian ones to their converts, while Indian listeners adopted and pushed back according to the needs of their community.

Silverman's analysis is sensitive to the ways in which Christian and Wampanoag traditional beliefs shared conceptual common ground in key points. This is a fact that Nancy Shoemaker has also emphasized in questions of gender, governance, and the body, and that Jill Lepore has influentially argued in the case of war.[5] But in other applications of it, this guiding idea for a religious studies methodology can promote a more or less similar understanding of any given colonial religious situation, wherever it might be, with respect to the agency of the colonized. "Resistance" or "co-optation" might, in other words, become the new "authenticity."

There is a multilayered politics here, weaving together the concerns of Native groups struggling for federal recognition or simply creating tools for survival, and a larger, longstanding debate about culture and agency in the humanities. Nicholas Thomas, in *Colonialism's Culture*, argues against a reading of colonial narratives as "elements of a code" and more as "signifying practices."[6] Certainly his larger point seems salutary: Colonialism (including the Bureau of Indian Affairs's rubric for recognition, which demands a narrative of distinctiveness) works against the perception of similarity—and, implicitly, multiplies codes that obstruct bonding, rather than linking people. What is fascinating about early New England, though, is precisely the tension between a code-driven theology and a set of signifying practices that only together can explain both the efflorescence of religious orientations (including Native Christian practices) and legal and violent domination of Indians by settlers. And the recent rise to power of the Pequot and Mohegan tribes, through both federal recognition and successful gaming investment, may well rest upon a long history of code-switching and cultural adaptiveness. Colonial forms of domination have found their strength in flexibility too; the bureaucracies or deadly logics of European colonial ventures or nationalism cannot be reduced to codes per se. But even ordinary folks took codes seriously in the colonial era, and believed in their efficacy, or in the efficacy of replacing one sort of code with another—a kind of spiritual and political "hacking," as we will see in the objects discussed below—even as their symbolic practices sometimes mixed them unconsciously.

Moreover, though Martin and Nicholas avow that the essays in their collection move beyond "authenticity" or cultural reification, one gets a sense from time to time that cultural particularity is not so much displaced by hybridity or practice-based appropriation in the book, as that it has moved somewhere else. This is evidenced in, for example, Daniel Mandell's description of Massachusetts Natives' "distinctive regional subculture"; the conceptual tension inherent in Douglas Winiarski's claim that Native Americans had "their own hybrid folklore traditions"; or Joanna Brooks's identification of northeastern Indians' "distinctive rituals."[7] Inside a shared resistance to describing cultural boundaries as clear (either at the historical moment under analysis or today) or fixed, disagreements gestate about how to locate or describe particularity.

We stand in relation to the religious transformations of the past as both inheritors and others. Can we expand the imagination of piety in New England overall to bridge cultures but also to give specific interest to Indian audiences today who are reimagining, reviving, or even creating new forms of piety? And can we at the same time suggest a more complex understanding of "culture" itself? More is at stake here than the description of vernacular theology or an interrogation of the role of codes in the evidentiary regime by which piety was inculcated, asserted, and evaluated. Involved is how we imagine the relationship between a feeling self and the world—what might be called *agency*, or more properly, what we, informed by the sometimes repulsive historical specificities of past pieties, might be able to understand as agency in a world unfamiliar to us.

Reciprocity and Piety

That relationship among agencies present and past might be described as a sort of historical reciprocity. But *reciprocity* has an important presence in Native American studies that is worth closer attention. On the one hand, it seems to be the key to bridging the notion of piety to Indian country. On the other, it emerges from a Western context and fails to capture sufficiently the complex sacred economies of the early colonial period. The *Oxford English*

Dictionary records the first use of this form of the word in 1753, but there are instances of it earlier. In the eighteenth century, *reciprocity* was often used in reference to treaties or other agreements, and began to take on a conceptual or theoretical dimension as well. In treaties or trade agreements (in the nineteenth century often known as Reciprocity Treaties, and today still sometimes referred to as reciprocity agreements), the term made reference to specific, parallel rights that would be allowed to each party by the other—for example, nations might agree to permit each others' ships access to ports or to trade in specific goods. Reciprocity here is *in kind*: that is to say, the objects or privileges or punishments on either side are agreed upon in advance, and have a one-to-one relation. (In the nineteenth century, scientific uses of this term in mathematics and physics would follow this economic logic as well; this likely reflects the original use of the term *reciprocate* within the field of logic, where it signals transposability or reversibility of definitions, dating at least to the early sixteenth century.)

Robert Keohane suggests a difference between this kind of relation, which he calls *specific reciprocity*, and *diffuse reciprocity*, in which an agreement gestures to a broader basis of trust and equality of exchange.[8] The distinction helps describe the evolution of the term *reciprocity* and its entry into writing about Indian-European relations, because the diffuse version of reciprocity was linked to a philosophical or theoretical discussion of the term. In his *Rights of Man* (1791), Thomas Paine exemplified in a key phrase the philosophical bent to which the word could be put: "A Declaration of Rights is, by reciprocity," Paine wrote, "a Declaration of Duties also." Reciprocity is an important concept in the work of Immanuel Kant, as well, but in a different way, emerging as it does from the more basic, universal condition, as he argues it, of coexisting entities; but in both Kant and Paine, the term describes the basis for an ethical community.[9]

The term *reciprocity* has made its way into the mainstream of Native American studies, where it is now commonly used by theorists, literary scholars, historians, anthropologists, and ethnohistorians. This use of the term emerged out of twentieth-century anthropology. Reciprocity—a much younger word than piety, anywhere but in the realms of mathematics or natural philosophy—rose to prominence in anthropology in the twentieth century largely outside of the American context. It was important in Bronislaw Malinowski's writing about the Kula ring, for example, and was perhaps most influentially elaborated in Karl Polanyi's *The Great Transformation*, which was particularly influential in economic anthropology, and proposed a tripartite scheme of societies based on reciprocity, redistribution, and capitalism. Among the early influential uses of reciprocity by a North Americanist was David Aberle's 1966 study, *The Peyote Religion Among the Navaho*; and it has also been used to describe frameworks for gifting practices, as in Marcel Mauss's work, and the northwestern potlatch ritual.[10] From these specialized uses, scholars began using reciprocity to describe foundationalist, pan-Indian claims about the basic ethics of indigenous North American societies, often to distinguish Indian beliefs from those of European settlers and their descendants. Barre Toelken made the term the axis of an essay in an important early collection on Indian religion, *Seeing with a Native Eye* (1976).[11] Kenneth Lincoln used the term in his influential book *Native American Renaissance*, referring to Toelken as its source.[12] In recent scholarship, there seems to be disagreement about the term. Some scholars, such as David Silverman, use *reciprocity* cautiously, in reference to the ethics of a specific Indian group—in Silverman's case the Wampanoag of Martha's Vineyard, for whom he finds kinship to be a more crucial framework for understanding both individual commitments and broader historical transformations in the group. Lisa Brooks, in her study *The Common Pot*, uses it several times, most often in its nineteenth-century political sense, of equal obligations between nations. But in her essay "Digging at the Roots," which directly tackles the question of what an ethical Nativist criticism might look like, she leans harder on the term *relationality* (which has several meanings that Brooks weaves together) and does not use *reciprocity*.[13]

In all of these applications of the term *reciprocity*, equality of exchange is key. There is a fantasy lurking behind even the most technical uses of the word, that the moment or condition of exchange somehow will not, or ideally will not, affect the value of the thing being exchanged. Here the diffuse notion of reciprocity is key, because it seems to allow one to compensate for that inevitable difference: the Sioux refuse payment for the loss of the Black Hills, for good reason—the United States cannot seem to afford to return the Black Hills, and therefore a monetary exchange falls short. Such an exchange would be out of tune with history and the land as the Sioux, or at least the Sioux involved in such decisions, regard them. But we might wonder if, in intercultural exchanges, equivalence is ever possible. What is more, the deal well sealed is never independent of an imagination of the future. Reciprocity gestures, conceptually, to an ongoing state of imbalance, however slight, and however (one hopes) brief.

And then there is the more difficult question of altruism. Reciprocity is imagined to produce well-being and harmony, but it is seldom imagined as a creative force—that is, as a key to startling excesses of beauty or good for a society. A potlatch song and gift are given, fully in the expectation of another song and gift; creative energy channels the wind or the sun or the truth of relations in song, but it is always an energy that can be sung in return. Much of the time, in Indian country as in the West, complete gifting is reserved for the supernatural creators or originators. Nature itself is locked in the reciprocity cycle, in most visions of American Indian spirituality. If you do not give to nature, she will take. Vine Deloria, Jr., reflecting after twenty years on the influence of his book *God Is Red*, lamented that his predictions about the religious roots of global conflict had come true: "Nor," he writes with chagrin, "do I look forward to paying the penalties that Mother Earth must now levy against us in order for Her to survive."[14]

In *God Is Red*, however, Deloria does not use the word *reciprocity*. Like N. Scott Momaday, he tended to use the words *responsibility* or *relationship* in talking about the spiritual obligations entailed by the connections among people and between people and the rest of the world, visible and invisible, in Indian country.[15] Deloria talks about having "as a structure a set of relationships in which all entities participate" and "a recognition of the sacredness of places."[16] These are more open-ended forms of relation than reciprocity, and less subject to objectifying or superficial interpretation. For Deloria, the devil is in the details—which is to say (to paraphrase Hyman Rickover), so is salvation.

Not only is the term *reciprocity* in its various forms absent from Deloria's frequently reprinted and updated *God Is Red*, but the terms *pious* and *piety* are associated with (usually acerbic) accounts of Western religious practice. The same, for both terms, is true of his influential book *Custer Died for Your Sins*.[17] Though he is sensitive to variations among American Indian religious practices, in *God Is Red* Deloria is searching for differences between Western and American indigenous religious foundations, in order to teach a lesson about Western failings. His use of piety, then, reinforces its identification of culture with a certain form of religious feeling—even in a book expressly designed to help bridge cultures of the sacred. The suggestion here is that piety ill fits Indian notions of a sacred relationship among a person, a people, and the supernatural; or that it is too laden with the history of justifications of Indian genocide and cultural conversion to function in a positive way. This is worth pondering as we shape our vocabularies for studying early America— our desire to use terms with sensitivity to their living meanings at their historical moments notwithstanding.

Rooted in the Latin *pietas*, piety has a long, vexed history. The early modern period saw a split in the English meanings of the word *piety* into "piety" and "pity." The former came to have the connotations we associate with it today: positive ones, on one hand, about deep personal religious devotion, and negative ones, in which that same sort of devotion becomes bigotry or uncritical worship of an unworthy object. Its function in describing personal spiritual experience has become significant in contradistinction to the way one imagines a relation to state or family. The term *pity* has largely retained its constellation of meanings related to compassion, derived from vernacular uses of the term *piety* (synonymous with the meaning of the Latin *misericordia*) in various languages of Latin descent from the early Christian era through the sixteenth century.

In the classical tradition, exemplified by Vergil's depiction of Aeneas, *pietas* implied a devotion to the gods, to one's family, *and* to one's country. It described an attitude or relation—and it was tied to "an unmistakably Roman ideal of principled conquest," in James Garrison's words, "that confers the blessings of order exemplified by the devotion of sons to fathers."[18] In Vergil, it is the occasion not for a formulaic set of actions, but rather for depicting complex, tension-ridden decision making by Aeneas as he attempts to manage the different demands of kinship, the civic, and the divine. *Pietas* thus reached across arenas that increasingly became stratified after the seventeenth century. As David Hall's chapter in this collection suggests, Puritan controversies over how government and church might interrelate under a pious commitment to God's rule may have kept alive, through the seventeenth century, the more complex notion of *piety* as a term to describe the navigation of a matrix of duties both supernatural and earthly. But others, including John Dryden, questioned the decline of the broader sense of the word *piety*. "Piety alone," Dryden wrote, "comprehends the whole Duty of Man towards the Gods; towards his Country, and towards his Relations."[19] Dryden offers this reminder in the preface to his translation of Vergil's *Aeneid* (*Aeneis*, London, 1697), published in the same year that Cotton Mather's *Pietas in Patriam* was first issued in London, a text deeply invested in bringing the notions of piety as service to God and piety as service to the state into relation.[20] Still, it seems that by the eighteenth century, as today, it was unusual to speak of one's devotion to family or to the state as "pious."

It has been argued that piety's decline as a broad cultural ideal was a function of its slipping solely into the domain of personal religious transformations, an Augustinian subjection only to God: "For piety," writes Augustine, "is the true cult of the true God."[21] The pre-Christian colonial connotations of the term would seem to have disappeared with this transition. But it could be argued that colonization and religion's enormous role in it throughout the sixteenth and seventeenth centuries was integral to both the specialization of the term and the decline in its ability to speak to a form of commitment that would reach across kin, state, and the supernatural. Certainly some seventeenth- and eighteenth-century critics of the role of piety in colonialism implied that a more complex grappling with the relationship of personal to national commitments might render at least a different sort of colonialism. Consider the Leiden Separatist pastor John Robinson's reaction to news of the Pilgrims' killing of Wituwamat and his Algonquian co-conspirators in 1622—"How happy a thing had it been," he wrote, "if you had converted some, before you had killed any"[22]—or the well-known passage from Swift's *Gulliver's Travels*: "Here commences a new Dominion acquired with a Title by *Divine Right*. Ships are sent with the first Opportunity: the Natives driven out or destroyed . . . a free License given to all Acts of Inhumanity and Lust . . . And this execrable Crew of Butchers employed in so pious an Expedition, is a *modern Colony* sent to convert and civilize an idolatrous and barbarous People."[23] The Black Legend resonates here, to be sure, but piety and colony are linked in a way that makes a critique cutting across national boundaries.

The imagination of affiliation offered by the term *piety* has long had implications for the establishment of cultural boundaries, then, even as its precise meanings varied. One of the reasons for this may be that, ever since at least Plato's dialogue *Euthyphro*, there has been a tendency to define piety in ways that transcend space and time, which can direct attention away from the ways the term divides groups of people. For Perry Miller, avatar of American Puritan studies, piety exhibited itself in intricate ways, including through social frameworks, "a recurrent spiritual answer to interrogations eternally posed by human existence," but its appearance was almost biologically encoded. "Puritanism was," Miller wrote, "yet another manifestation of a piety to which some men are probably always inclined and which in certain conjunctions appeals irresistibly to large numbers of exceptionally vigorous spirits." This definition of the "exceptional" is not limited to America—indeed, is implicitly non-Western. Yet for Miller, the point of studying New England's piety is to describe a broader Western orientation toward the divine, because he saw the American Puritans as "spokesmen for what we call the Renaissance."[24] This is a transatlantic intellectual history, with a touch of universalism in its definition of piety, but it is about some people and not others, constitutively; Walter Mignolo's "darker side of the Renaissance" is missing from Miller's formulation.[25] While Janice Knight has elucidated the multiple pieties within the mainstream American Puritan world, and while Matt Brown has pointed out the irony that the archive on which Miller's argument was built was in part printed by Indians and also in many cases directed at an Indian audience, in effect these arguments continue to posit cultural difference as fundamental to understanding piety. As Jordan Stein and Justine Murison put it, "reading these studies, it becomes difficult to imagine what 'religion' could mean, besides something like 'culture.'"[26]

According to the *OED*, piety's meanings in English have come to be "godliness," or, in Calvin's formulation, "fervent attachment to the service of God and to the duties and practices of religion." But compare this to the use of the term in Saba Mahmood's influential book *Politics of Piety*, a feminist analysis of Islam in contemporary North Africa: the Arabic equivalents of "piety," such as *taqwa*, involve fear no less than duty. Mahmood's analysis respects the particular instantiation of fear—both a display and a feeling— that characterizes the women of the Egyptian mosque movement.[27] The Quran here is not the source of a timeless definition of piety, but a plank for historically specific interpretations and behaviors. For early modern English print culture historian Tessa Watt, piety functions at a lower stratum than theologically underwritten emotion. There was a "popular piety" that consisted of Christian emblems and widely agreed-upon tenets, which could be used to exercise more particular kinds of beliefs.[28] Certainly ethnohistorians have suggested that a set of broadly held beliefs about people's relation to the supernatural existed among Algonquians of the northeastern woodlands; that there were popular or everyday practices among New England-area Indians as well as more formal rituals and enactments of a particular community's spiritual commitments. If the ontologies of religious feeling may differ, so too may the disciplinary uses of the term *piety*, which develop an analytical patina that might obscure alternative histories, or that might simply make it hard for us to imagine another phenomenon as the axis of analysis of a time and place like early colonial New England.

In his book *The Pilgrim and the Bee*, Matt Brown builds on the work of both Watt and David Hall. He modifies previous accounts of New English piety by situating it within what he terms the "multicultural setting" of early America—yet ultimately, indigenous culture remains largely that for Brown: a setting, an environment. This happens in part through a careful management of the cultural boundaries of piety. Brown describes seventeenth-century New English piety as a devotional style—a set of gestures and habits rooted in a consuming obsession with the relationship between the fallen world and the eternal one. The piety of which he writes is a matter of English interiority, mediated by book technology and social performance. "English readers are defined against the Amerindian's superstitious naïveté," for the most part. But this was not the case for all English readers—such as, for example, the man "worthy of Credit" that Matthew Mayhew reported having visited a *powwow* for assistance in the late seventeenth century.[29] Nor was it the case during the entirety of the seventeenth century, which saw the expansion of literacy and Christianity among eastern Natives. Indian believers showed the dangers of a piety dependent on performance, particularly in the wake of King Philip's War, when hundreds of Praying Indians were detained and many died as a result of English fears of insurrection. But that is different from definition by difference alone—Praying Indians were interned because they were *both* Indians and Christians. The dynamic whereby Indian politics or beliefs suggest the shaky foundations of Western ones is still at work today, inasmuch as Indian politics are often organized on logics and protocols distinct not just from mainstream "American" ideals, but from the legal organization of the United States. The matrix of legal relations between English political entities and Native ones played a role in the changing place of piety in intercultural interactions and anxieties.[30]

Brown's revision of our understanding of the intellectual and physical underpinnings of Puritan piety is compelling. But its real power, I think, will be felt when its techniques are used to interrogate *piety* itself as an organizing force in the study of early New England. When, during King Philip's War, an Algonquian warrior cut open Goodman Wright's body and stuffed a Bible into him, was it an act of piety? Of reciprocity? Or both? What we call piety and reciprocity, it would seem, could be applied equally to a discussion of both Indian and European settler communities. In the general sense, Puritans had forms of reciprocity deeply rooted in both social form and senses of tradition. Social historians have argued that the reciprocity of English activities such as trading labor and goods in practices of bookkeeping-based barter extending over many years are evidence of the priority of communal commitments over market values. Walter Woodward, in a recent book on John Winthrop, Jr., shows how Winthrop's embrace of alchemy (whose logic was based on reciprocities among substances, or "sympathetic correspondences") and, by extension, various other sorts of pansophic reform, helped him engage more sensitively with local Indians in Connecticut, in particular with Robin Cassacinamon's group of Pequots, in part by sharing medicines.[31] Winthrop frequently corresponded with Roger Williams, whose intense relationship with the Narragansett is well known, and whose book *A Key Into the Language of America* is still a major source for both ethnohistorical evidence and Indian efforts to reconstruct the region's Algonquian dialects.

Piety connotes a mode of religious faith and spiritual intensity; but it is linked to reciprocity through a social relationship, with the individual in a subservient position before an inscrutable, hierarchical God, who arbitrarily bestows grace on that individual and thereby raises his status now and in the hereafter. In communion, Congregationalists enjoyed the fellowship of saints—a reciprocal bonding much theorized by spiritual leaders, but also by laypeople—even as they are distanced from the larger body of the unregenerate. The utopianism of the Puritans' pious vision was enacted in the drive of early churches to enforce this reciprocity, to bring every inhabitant of a town within the fold. If this is what we mean by piety, then Indians were no less pious; the Narragansetts were famed for their commitment to sacred observances, which neighboring tribes believed protected them from the plagues and which may have been a factor in their maintaining a number of festivals down to the present day.[32] The Wampanoags of Martha's Vineyard practiced a Christian piety of a different sort, but one that David Silverman shows is inexplicable without reference to the group's traditional practices. There were different pieties—both imaginations of a service to God and social manifestations of that commitment—in different communities: Rhode Island was different from Plymouth, Pequot different from Narragansett.[33]

Analyzing two sets of objects, I consider available interpretations of their significance or function using the histories of reciprocity and piety I've just outlined as cautions. Using these objects' alienness to our time's economies of cultural exchange as a cue to speaking differently about their meaning, I try to imagine ways of interpreting them at the nexus of disciplinary concerns now and of visible and invisible worlds then. These sites for rethinking the language of cultural exchange are chosen not as representative but as provocative. They hint at a different archive for thinking about piety than the devotional steady seller or Native writings in English. Implicitly, the readings that follow also suggest a different or more specific economy of reciprocity than outlined above. This archive emphasizes the holes in the holy, made up of holey as much as holy texts, the interpretability of its objects dependent upon their interlacings with other things. The two sets of objects are a Pequot burial bundle and a pair of English poppets found embedded in a wall in a late seventeenth- or early eighteenth-century house on Long Island.

Kevin McBride, an archaeologist and ethnohistorian, was working for the Mashantucket Pequots on their reservation inside Connecticut when he found a burial of a young Algonquian, probably Pequot, girl, which contained a ritual bundle. The bundle included a bear's left paw and a fragment of finely woven cloth with a piece of a page of a small-format Dutch-printed Bible in it, featuring part of the text of Psalm 98. The date of the burial is conjectured at between 1660 and 1720. This object has attracted interdisciplinary attention: both McBride and Hugh Amory, a Harvard book historian and bibliographer, have written about the bundle. Amory emphasizes that the small-format Bible is a "hand piety" object, to use Matt Brown's term. Such books were personal copies whose format and structure aided the "religious socialization of readers" through habitual consultation of a sacred text and a performance of godly inclinations.[34] But Amory suggests that the Bible from which the fragment in the Pequot bundle was taken might have been a war prize.[35]

I would add another possibility: that it may have been given as a gift or token, or stolen, from a household in which a Pequot slave worked. Many such "servants" allocated to English settlers in the wake of the Pequot War of 1637 eventually ran away from their masters. A group of Pequots led by Robin Cassacinamon cohabited with John Winthrop, Jr.'s settlers at Nameaug, a plantation Winthrop established in 1645 and that would come to be known as New London.[36] As for the use of an English-language Bible among Pequots (and setting aside the possibility of a fully English-literate Pequot, which some translators probably were), Amory suggests that "both cultures recognized its decorative, talismanic function . . . On some level, it matters little whether we describe small-format Bibles as European medicine bundles, or this medicine bundle as an Indian Bible. The two are culturally congruent, in their respective cultures." Amory's assertion that there is "cultural congruency" to guide us seems to posit isomorphic pieties, but can we be sure? This statement echoes older anthropological arguments about the universality of pious rituals in an assertion of boundaries—"respective cultures." We have here what Nicholas Thomas calls "entangled objects," for sure, but do we have "entangled pieties"?[37]

Kevin McBride disagrees about congruency, even as he relies on an assertion of definite cultural boundaries structurally similar to Amory's. "The inclusion of the page in the bundle," McBride argues, "transforms the symbolic system of the printed word to another communicative system—that of the

Pequot mortuary ritual." "In the context of the mortuary ritual," he continues, "Native and European objects represented links with the community,
the individual, and the afterlife and were considered highly symbolic of
Pequot beliefs and practices in the physical and spiritual worlds."[38] Certainly
this is true, but it is equally so of the Puritan mortuary rituals that are an
important focus of Brown's analysis. Of course, were we to speak of English
practices more broadly, we would find differences in the ritual, and in what
people were willing to bury with the dead, by locale, time, and sect, as Erik
Seeman shows in his book *Death in the New World*. Those differences often
spoke to different ideas about the afterlife and the person being interred,
whether political or theological (say, in the case of traitors, or of Quakers
unlucky enough to be put to death in Massachusetts). The Pequots appear a
unified group in these analyses—but we know that they were and are one of
the most spectacularly contentious groups in New England, woven by kinship relations into the fabric of both surrounding and distant communities.[39]

Rather than insist upon the unity of Pequot piety, we might speculate
more aggressively across the conceptions of the supernatural in a New England both shared and divided. The concepts of "community mortuary ritual" and of "piety," as linking the worlds of human, other-than-human, and
the supernatural, are both useful in some ways. They can, however, impede
more flexible ways of thinking about a shared past and future, keeping us
from certain interpretive insights. The bear paw, for example, McBride tells
us, is unusual in sites like this. The bear was considered "capable of transi-
tioning between the physical and spiritual realms of the sky and the terrestrial world and between the terrestrial and underwater worlds." The paw,
though, reminds us of the bear's power to deal shredding, mortal blows; its
presence in conjunction with a page torn from a Bible might suggest a less
rosy interpretation of the kind of power being sent along with this child to
Cautantowwit's house. Moreover, among the bear's distinctive behavioral
properties is hibernation: a state between life and death, a survival habit
based on renewal and reemergence. Finally, if it is true that, as McBride argues, "children were perceived to be in a state of liminality, existing on the
threshold or boundary between the physical and spiritual worlds," the same
might be said of Puritan children.[40] The Salem witch trials serve as an excellent example of that—and seeing across the rituals and pieties of these two
groups reminds us that children were also importantly, and troublingly, on the
threshold between the Native and English worlds as denizens of the region
imagined their futures.

The in-between use of the page might be understood structurally as significant because it is parasitical. That is, the Bible buried represents a means of opening a path or window to another world, a cosmos from which power might be drawn. But as is often the case with real parasites, there is more than one potential host—more than one cosmology from which a practice might draw power: Bear, Algonquian traditions, Pequot kinship, English piety, European technology, and earth are all potentially contributing domains in this instance. The burial and its objects constitute a technology of mediation between the visible and the invisible, but simultaneously between the long-standing and the newcomers. Amory was probably wrong, too, to say that the function of the Bible is the same—the formal context matters, here, and not least because of the well-documented foundational significance of spatial orientation in indigenous North American ways. So I turn to a different object, from English traditions, to suggest an environment saturated with attempts to open otherworldly connections that do not quite fit what we have taken to be either Indian or Puritan standard forms of supernatural mediation.

Behind the original walls of Benjamin Horton's Long Island house, first erected in 1649, were found three cloth poppets, with stick legs, held now at the restored "Old House" in Cutchogue (Figure 18). In an article describing the restoration of the house in 1940, Frank Brown speculates that the poppets were preserved by chance, dragged into the walls by rats. Robert St. George, perhaps doubtful of Brown's interpretation owing to the comparatively undamaged quality of the poppets, suggests that these may be similar to poppets found in 1685 when the Salem house where Bridget Bishop lived was torn down—found "w'th headles pins in Them, w'th the points out ward."[41] Magic and counter-magic items were buried in and around Puritan houses, as a means of circumventing the powerful pull of providence. Such practices were, as David Hall has shown, constitutive of the vernacular world of spirituality, which drew upon both magic and Christian worship.[42] As St. George shows, houses were contested spaces, both between men and women and between earthly needs and divine authority. But the categories of the public and the private, too, shaped the power of magical mediations like those offered by poppets; buried in the wall of the house like a gifted termite, an invisible third power could lurk, contending with that of man and God. Given Puritan ideas about predestination, it is not just that spatial propriety was being transgressed with such objects, but time that was being mastered, in the old, magical mode, against the logics of divine temporality of Calvinism. For St. George, such practices indicate a syncretism *within* Puritanism—but Indians are, in his

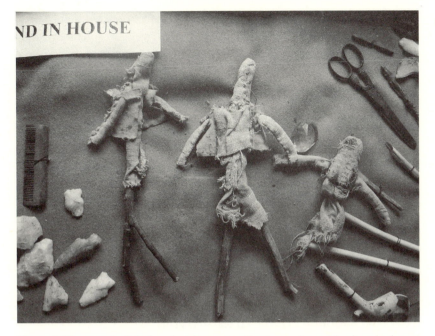

Figure 18. Photograph of cloth and stick poppets, Cutchogue, Long Island, and other items discovered in the mid-twentieth-century renovation of a seventeenth-century house now known as "The Old House." Photograph by Dorothea Jordan, courtesy of the Cutchogue-New Suffolk Historical Council.

analysis, mere projections. The Puritans' denial of Indian subjectivity, for St. George, robs real Natives of cultural agency. This is a pity, not least because we know from both ethnohistorical and archaeological evidence that lodgings, in their construction, orientation, size, allocation of interior space to individuals, and decoration, were also sacred mediators for Indians of the region. Still, perhaps it is true that these poppets owe less to the presence of Native American modes of communication than to the traditional magical world Keith Thomas describes; or that they, as Brown suggests, were unbidden gifts to the house's furry parasites, the rats. But then again—these poppets were found in a house in Cutchogue, just across the Long Island Sound from Pequot territory (indeed, a number of Horton relatives had come from Connecticut) and near one of the prime wampum-manufacturing areas that the tribe controlled on the eve of the Pequot War.[43] And in the settlers' understandings, the degenerate sons of Adam roaming the wilderness did not lack for magical power. So the imagination of agency that attached to the risky practice of trying to work around divine providence might have been enhanced by the presence of people across cultures accessing alternative supernatural powers.[44]

Neither the poppets nor the bundle clearly indicates "piety," broadly speaking, as we tend to understand them today, either for American Congregationalists or Algonquians. Either could be supernaturally additive, or syncretic, or simply traditional (in the sense of pronouncing, "I have taken the other's spiritual power and carried it with me to the invisible world"). Neither quite *proves* a synthesis of beliefs, either. These are parasitical objects: they are placed in-between, both materially (between the earth world and the human world, in the Pequot case; the public and the private in the Puritan one) and supernaturally, as mediators. Structurally, these practices unite Puritans and Pequots; cohabitation seems in this case to be a mode of transformation. Contextually, these practices acknowledge and draw power from difference. Amory and McBride's differences boil down to classic epistemological schemes that are products in part of colonial activity: a prioritization of the universal for Amory, a prioritization of difference for McBride. Perhaps beyond this is a diachronic parasitism—in the critical act, experimenting with a different concept of time and evidence that might make a virtue of the unknown by embracing the unknowable in an act of intuition or imagination.

The experience of North America for many of its denizens has been, Joanna Brooks observes, "a story of catastrophe, chance, and radical disruption." A narrative of personal revelation, of a path to wholeness outside of dominant discourse and under the eye of God, addressed this experience, Brooks claims. It "worked for so many Americans in the eighteenth century, and . . . might work as the conceptual engine for one new way of telling of American religious-literary history: it is a narrative formula that summons meaning from randomness and disaster and uses this meaning as the basis for new, if temporary, forms of intimacy and relationship."[45] This is an elegant reformulation of the story of American religion, on a more inclusive basis than many previous narratives, routing it through seeming discontinuities and surprising personalities, such as Samson Occom, John Marrant, and James Baldwin. And I do not want to deprecate the importance of healing, or intimacy, or of reliable relationships. But that same deeply felt experience underwrote some of the more violent instantiations and narrations of piety—heterodox and orthodox—whose relationships were built on exclusion, not extension, and were comforting precisely for that reason.

Different conceptions of subjectivity might help us write about early colonial religious transformations. Postulating these could hold transformative possibilities for us today as well, at a time when what is often referred to as the modern liberal or neoliberal subject is under debate across the humanities. Vincent Brown, in his study of death in eighteenth-century Jamaica, offers a provocative model. Widespread mortality, high rates of immigration and slave importation (from disparate regions of Africa), and other factors "confounded efforts to find common modes of communication and forced the population to achieve considerable dexterity in negotiating intercultural complexity," Brown demonstrates. "Caribbean peoples," he concludes, "developed 'plural personas, command of multiple communicative registers, and mobile social forms' to navigate their heterogeneous societies."[46] Crucially here, piety can function not in a holistic way, but as the pillar of personal modes, while reciprocity can function in some realms and not others, depending on local and instantaneous configurations of power. This helps us address the risk that Brooks identifies, one Elizabeth Maddock Dillon describes as the problem that, with a conception of piety rooted in cosmological repletion, "religion (and the secular) are not simply moments to be identified within a historical narrative, but rather modes of understanding the world that determine what constitutes history itself."[47] We might, then, recognize the quality of cross-cultural or transtemporal appeal in the term *piety* as something that itself can both build and help us criticize or reformulate cultural boundaries.

The objects discussed above and the trickiness of piety call attention to the difficult position scholars are in, writing across time and parasiting evidence to try to shape our futures. "Historical knowledge," Carlo Ginzburg writes, "is indirect, presumptive, conjectural."[48] The logic of spirituality in a colonial condition is multiple, transformative, emergent, and even resurgent (as our current great religious awakening suggests), and Brooks is right in saying that it calls out for a different sort of narrative about history. Making poppets or the bear paw and Bible-page bundle and then removing them from human circulation may be regarded as attempts to master time, to refold it according to the desires of the individual or small groups that crafted and buried these things. These uncanonical objects and their users' attempts to disrupt the temporalities of their moment hold a lesson for our narratives, about the knowable and the unknowable, and about the persistence of the not-modern or the already presentness of the future, as we attempt to change the asymmetries of power in the present.[49]

CHAPTER 7

Return as a Religious Mission

The Voyage to Dahomey Made by the Brazilian Mulatto Catholic Priests Cipriano Pires Sardinha and Vicente Ferreira Pires (1796–98)

JÚNIA FERREIRA FURTADO

This chapter analyzes the mission to Dahomey undertaken by the Brazilian Catholic priests Cipriano Pires Sardinha and Vicente Ferreira Pires between 1796 and 1798.[1] My aim is to raise provocative considerations about various aspects of the voyage, but I shall limit my discussion to the religious aspect of the mission to convert the king of Dahomey, Agonglo or Adanruzâ VIII (1789–97)[2] and his subjects to the Catholic faith. This essay will explore what Robin Law terms the "combination of missionary with commercial enterprise," assuming that, ever since the fifteenth century, as Europeans spread their power to Asia, Africa, and America, there had existed "a complementarity of interest between the two; wealth from trade would strengthen Catholic Christianity; and the conversion of Africans to Christianity would make them better trading partners."[3] This voyage represented a new moment in the series of attempts at converting Northwest African kingdoms—the Slave Coast—to Christianity. From the fifteenth century to the early eighteenth century, missionaries had been sent to Allada or to Whydah by the Portuguese, Spanish, and French in order to try to convert their subjects to Catholicism, but all had failed.[4] Those missionaries came from various orders, in particular the Jesuit, Capuchin, and Dominican.[5]

The new target was the Kingdom of Dahomey, later to be known as Benin. Dahomey was expanding and held a new strategic importance, fulfilling the need for slaves in Portuguese America. Dahomey conquered Allada in 1724, Whydah in 1727, and was expanding northward.[6] The need to strengthen the connection with this kingdom thus became manifest to the Portuguese authorities, and they adhered to the notion that religion once again would be a powerful weapon. New to this situation were the renewed forms of connection that now existed between state and church in the Portuguese Empire. After 1759, with the expulsion of the Jesuit Order and the rise of Jansenism, new alliances were forged in Portugal between the state and the Catholic Church, the latter put under the control of the former. Missions to turn pagans to Christians were now a matter of state and were performed by secular clergy within their jurisdiction. In light of these new factors, I aim to analyze some of the strategies employed by the missionaries in Dahomey and to compare them to those adopted by the Portuguese in Africa from the fifteenth century onward, given that, within the Congo and Angola in particular, Catholicism had been presented to tribal chiefs and kings as something that could strengthen their power.[7]

It was no coincidence that the two priests chosen for the mission to Dahomey had Brazilian origins, and their backgrounds, as we shall see, were crucial to both the impetus behind the mission as well as to its outcome. Thus, a study of their role in the mission to Dahomey allows for the writing of the history of the Luso-African-Brazilian Empire from an Atlantic perspective[8] as we connect the three continents through the methodological tool of "connected histories."[9] The ocean becomes a site not only for the exchange of goods but also for the exchange of culture and of religious spirituality. Another important aspect of the priests' role in the mission to Dahomey concerns the dyad of tolerance-intolerance as I examine how the missionaries represented the African continent in their text. This latter point is particularly relevant when we consider that of the two secular priests at least one of them was known to be descended from African slaves, while it is possible that the other could have been classified as mulatto. In addition, both had resided in towns and cities—Tejuco and Salvador—that were deeply influenced by strong Afro-descendent populations. The citizens of these towns lived their lives surrounded by the African culture brought to the colony by recently arrived slaves and were no strangers to African drums, rituals, and ceremonies.[10] How did generations of mestizo Brazilians like the two priests deal, on one hand, with their black heritage, largely maternal in origin, and, on the other, with the white Western Christian tradition that stood as their sole platform to social insertion and advancement in Luso-Brazilian society?

This story begins on 26 May 1795, in Salvador da Bahia, in northeastern Brazil, when a diplomatic mission sent by King Agonglo arrived from Dahomey.[11] The ambassadors came to propose that the Portuguese slave trade out of the Benin Gulf operate exclusively from the Portuguese port of São João Baptista de Ajudá, in Whydah on the Dahomean coast, and to protest the progressively diminishing weight of the tobacco rolls they were receiving as payment for slaves.[12] This proposal was symptomatic of the intra-African disputes over the lucrative transoceanic slave trade, which gave the tribal elite access to Brazilian and European merchandise, particularly tobacco from Bahia and *cachaça* (rumlike cane spirit), which had become quite a hit among the local nobility.[13] This was the second ambassadorial visit sent to Salvador from Dahomey for precisely these ends, the first having been made in 1750.[14]

At the beginning of the eighteenth century, Whydah had become the most important slavery export center in Benin Gulf, in the northwest of Africa. It is estimated that until 1725, 40 percent of all slaves—around four hundred thousand—who had endured the Middle Passage across the Atlantic Ocean had embarked from this port.[15] Salvador da Bahia was an important destination port for the slave trade, and for this reason both ambassadorial visits came to this city.[16] However, unlike the first trip, the two ambassadors insisted on delivering their petitions to Portugal to Queen Maria I and to the heir of the throne, the Prince Dom João, regent at that time since his mother had been officially declared insane. The ambassadors arrived in Portugal on 21 October 1795.[17] Neither the Portuguese authorities nor the traders in Bahia had any interest in running the slave trade exclusively from Dahomey. In fact, the concession of such a monopoly to any single African port could have had disastrous effects, not only on prices, but also on the very conditions of the trade. So, once the ambassadors were in Lisbon, the Prince Regent D. João had no option but to deny their request, though he did think it opportune to send a diplomatic mission to Dahomey with orders to catechize the kingdom.[18]

Religious and Economic Interests

Catholicism and European economic interests had been closely linked since the beginning of the early modern period. Portugal, in particular, during its period of overseas expansion in America, Africa, and Asia, coupled religion and politics to sustain their conquests. Since the first half of the seventeenth century, Portugal had witnessed the decline of its presence in West Africa, a region that stretched from Guinea-Bissau, through the so-called Costa da Mina or Slave Coast, down to Equatorial Guinea (to combine Portuguese toponomy with African geography). During this period, the Dutch trade companies started a series of military campaigns against the Portuguese fortress in order to break its monopoly, and, in 1630, they took control of the slave trade in West Africa.[19] In fact, they were able to capture several Portuguese forts where the trade was carried out, including the highly important fort of São Jorge da Mina. After that, the Luso-Brazilian slave traders had to negotiate with and pay the Dutch in order to complete their slave shipments.

The 1721 establishment of the Portuguese fort of São João Baptista de Ajudá in the port of Whydah confirmed the important role that the Kingdom of Dahomey now assumed for supplying the Brazilian slave system. Since the end of the previous century, in 1699, according to law, Brazilian traders had petitioned the king of Portugal to establish a fortified post in Whydah. Not by chance, their arguments suggested "that this would confer religious as well as commercial advantage" as it would prevent the slave cargos from being captured by Protestants (the Dutch in particular), thus saving them from paganism or Protestantism. At that point, however, the Overseas Council rejected the suggestion, concluding instead that a religious mission would be more effective for the cause of Christianity, although they failed to organize one at this juncture.[20]

By the end of the 1800s, it was now the French and English merchants who were in competition with the Portuguese in the port of Whydah for access to the local slave trade. The French reestablished the Fort of Saint Louis de Grégoy (1703) and the English founded Fort Williams.[21] It was said, moreover, that during this period the Portuguese fort was partly abandoned and in ruins.[22] The commander-in-chief complained that there were few slaves to embark, and that the French and English were bringing tobacco from Lisbon to exchange for slaves, thus competing with the Bahian merchants.[23] To make things worse for the Luso-Portuguese economic interests, Whydah suffered several attacks after 1793 from French pirates bringing disorder to the local slave trade.[24]

Unlike what had occurred in Congo and Angola, where the Portuguese started the Catholic process of converting the African population in the fifteenth century, Dahomey still presented a barrier to Portuguese commercial and religious interests. Portuguese missions had been established in the nearby kingdom of Allada after 1472, but after the 1630s, "when the Dutch entered the trade there in competition with [them]", the Portuguese ceased to send missionaries there.[25] Since the rule of Dom João II (1477–95) in Congo and Angola,[26] the missionary policy had been commonly coordinated by both the state and the Catholic Church. In the years to come, both Dom Manuel I (1495–1521) and Dom João III (1521–57) reinforced this connection, guaranteeing the economic interests of the Portuguese, who had in the slave trade their principal local resource. Dom João III was responsible for permitting the Jesuits to gain a foothold in Portugal and had started the process of building missions to convert the Indians in America and in Africa. In both the kingdoms of Angola and Congo, religion was used as an instrument of the Portuguese state and to promote the interests of the slave trade in Africa. Since that time, the Portuguese Crown had succeeded in maintaining peaceful collaboration with the local African kings and protecting this longstanding trade exchange without the need for military campaigns. As a strategy of conversion, the Portuguese priests presented Catholicism as a way for the local king to strengthen his power,[27] and converting the monarch led to the conversion of his subjects.[28] In the ports, there were even priests to baptize the slaves before they embarked on the Middle Passage.

In eighteenth-century Dahomey, on the contrary, the Portuguese were restricted to the Fort of São João Baptista of Ajudá in the port of Whydah, where the slave trade was performed and its residents were all members of the military. Although it was expected that a local priest would help to introduce Catholicism in the African kingdom as a priest's "responsibilities would include the provision of summary instruction and baptism of slaves prior to embarkation, . . . it proved difficult however, to find the required personnel, and the missionary project once again lapsed."[29] The European presence, Portuguese included, was very limited. Few Portuguese civilians lived in Dahomey, most of whom were involved in trade, but they submitted to the local king and had no protection from Portugal.[30] The mission of the priests to convert Dahomey would involve recreating the colonization strategies that were used in Congo and Angola in favor of Portugal's local trade interests, but with new ingredients.

Since the Enlightened reforms carried out by the Marquis of Pombal during Dom José I's reign (1755–77), the process of laicization of the state and secularization of the Portuguese Church was accelerated. The Jesuits were expelled in 1759, and the Inquisition and the Brazilian Indian missions were put under the control of the state, the so-called *Diretório dos Índios*. Jansenism, characterized in Portugal by the defense of unrestricted regalism and the submission of the church to royal ecclesiastical power, as well as a more spiritualized religiosity, became the basis of the religious reforms made by that time.[31] Evergton Sales Souza distinguishes between French and Portuguese Jansenism in the following terms: "In contrast with French Jansenism, which had a history profoundly marked by conflicts with royal power, Portuguese Jansenism had developed under the auspices of royal power."[32,33] Thus there would be no surprise when Prince Dom João decided to send two secular priests as diplomatic representatives of the state, entrusting them with the mission to convert Dahomey to Catholicism in order to reinforce the crown's economic projects.

The Priests Chosen to Accomplish the Mission

Those chosen for the mission were the priests Cipriano Pires Sardinha and Vicente Ferreira Pires, both from the Americas, but at that time living in Lisbon. The first was born in Tejuco village, in the captaincy of Minas Gerais, in the southwest of Brazil, and the latter came from Bahia, in the Northeast. Tejuco was in the center of the diamond production area and Salvador was a major port for exporting sugarcane and importing slaves from the Northwest of Africa. Cipriano was a mulatto, son of a black slave woman and her master, and Vicente was an *exposto*, that is, someone who was abandoned just after birth in the streets, considered an orphan, and raised by someone else or in a public institution at the expense of the Municipal Chamber. There were suspicions that he also was a mulatto. It has never been known for certain if he was white or mulatto. It was common for the authorities to refer to "low birth" in the case of mestizos. His birth certificate states that his parents were unknown, and he was abandoned and raised in the house of a white person. *Expostos* were often baptized as whites, but studies show that this was commonly employed as a strategy to give white status to a mulatto child.[34]

The priests were granted the title of Apostolic Envoys of His Most Royal Highness, Prince Dom João, and charged primarily with the goal of converting the king of Dahomey and his subjects to Catholicism, but also to record scientific observations of the lands they visited.[35] Here we see the importance not only of religion but also of science in order to facilitate the production of knowledge that would further "enlighten" imperial economic projects of the

Portuguese Crown. Since 1779, the newly created Royal Academy of Sciences of Lisbon was in charge of coordinating several scientific missions that would study natural resources of the different parts of the empire to be explored in the name of its expansion. Cipriano Pires Sardinha certainly owed the honor of this appointment to his intellectual capacity and to the influence he held in Lisbon, where he constantly rubbed shoulders with the intellectual elite of the Royal Academy of Sciences of Lisbon, which gathered around the figures of its founder and president, the Duke of Lafões, the Overseas Minister Dom Rodrigo de Souza Coutinho, and the Prince Regent Dom João.[36]

In Lisbon, Cipriano Pires Sardinha was responsible for baptizing one of the African ambassadors, the uncle of the Dahomean king, who was given the Christian name of Dom Manuel Constantino Carlos Luiz.[37] It was common for African ambassadors to be baptized and become Christians upon arriving in Europe, a protocol that exhibited their submission to the customs of the Christian kingdoms they were visiting.[38] In 1658, for example, the Allada ambassador in Spain was "instructed in the Christian faith and baptized [as Don Phelipe Zapata],"[39] the same name as King Phillip IV. Unable to acclimatize to the European weather, Dom Manuel died before he was able to return home. The other ambassador was baptized with the name D. João Carlos de Bragança, the same as the Prince Regent. It was also suggested that the latter's name was chosen because of his godfather, the second Duke of Lafões, Dom João Carlos de Bragança de Sousa e Ligne.[40] Both suggestions are plausible. We can therefore presume some involvement on the part of members of the Royal Academy of Sciences of Lisbon in the baptism of the ambassadors from Dahomey, in the decision to use the visit to collect information about the region *in locu*, and in the choice of Cipriano for the task.

The party, consisting of the remaining ambassador, his secretary/interpreter, and the two priests, left Lisbon in April of 1796 and arrived in Salvador in May, exactly a year after the ambassadors' departure from that city. From there, on 29 December of that same year, only the ambassador and the two priests set sail for Dahomey.[41] Cipriano arrived with nothing but a trunk containing his few clothes and instruments for observation and annotation, as well as fifty thousand *réis* given him by Prince Dom João (the future Dom João VI) to cover his costs and as payment for recording his observations.[42]

Cipriano would never return from Africa, falling victim to a virulent case of malaria.[43] Only the priest Vicente Ferreira Pires returned to Bahia, where he arrived on 5 February 1798. He was very ill, stricken too by the malaria he contracted in Africa. Throughout the year to come, he would ask for several posts in the Catholic Church as reward for all the suffering he endured in the mission, but he was not to succeed.[44]

The orders the two priests received on how they were to conduct the mission to Dahomey specified that Cipriano Pires Sardinha had "various observations to make on that coast, as recommended in person by His Royal Highness, Our Lord the Prince [Dom João], as well as . . . the baptism" of infidels wherever he passed.[45] As attested to by the Archbishop of Bahia, Fray Antônio Correa, in a missive sent to Dom Rodrigo de Sousa Coutinho, Cipriano had the necessary background and preparation to fulfill the task. In the cleric's words, "Sardinha . . . in addition to vast experience, possesses great erudition."[46] During his youth in the captaincy of Minas Gerais, he had studied Latin with the parish priest of Tejuco, the village of his birth, and went on to attend the Boa Morte Seminary in the city of Mariana, the seat of the bishopric, where he trained for the local clergy. He received an excellent religious education at the seminary. He graduated from the seminary after the Jesuits were expelled from the Captaincy of Minas Gerais on 31 January 1758. Following the expulsion, the Bishop Dom Frei Manuel da Cruz ordered all members of the Society to Rio de Janeiro. Thus Cipriano's education bears the hallmarks of Jansenism.[47] He also had some training in medical surgery, being able to conduct bleedings.[48] Unusually for a mulatto, he attended the University of Coimbra, where he studied canon law for two years.

Unlike Cipriano, there are countless references in the documentation to Father Vicente Ferreira Pires's intellectual limitations. The archbishop of Bahia, Antônio Correa, remarked that he was "reputedly ignorant even of Latin grammar." He goes on to say that, in Salvador, before embarking for the kingdom, Father Vicente was a mere sacristan, an office in which he had always proved deficient. In fact, we are told that such was his unsuitability that he was "expelled from the post" for "deflowering a white maiden." It is also related that Father Cipriano had a similar opinion of his companion and that, in Bahia, he had "publically lamented having a dullard for a partner in that enterprise."[49] The governor of Bahia, Dom José de Portugal, stated that he shared the opinion expressed by the archbishop, by Cipriano, and by the commander of the Whydah fort, Manoel de Bastos Varella, in regard to Vicente. According to Bastos Varella, the governor remarked, "Father Vicente Ferreira Pires was a shambolic clergyman, entirely destitute of learning and inept for the task entrusted to him by royal decree of catechizing the king of Dahomey."[50]

The Account of the Voyage to Dahomey

An important aspect to be considered in the selection of both priests for the mission was their ability to communicate with the locals. To be able to communicate both in Portuguese and in *fongbe*, the local language, was a vital element in the selection process that would please both the king and the Portuguese authorities. There were very few Portuguese people living in Dahomey and some of them (usually sailors) were held captive by the kings to serve as interpreters (*línguas*—literally "tongues").[51] Agonglo and the other Dahomean kings had to use the *línguas* to express their demands in writing to the Portuguese kings. One of the letters that the Dahomean ambassadors brought to Bahia in 1795 was written by Francisco Xavier Alvarez do Amaral, lieutenant of the Portuguese fort in Whydah, and who served as secretary to Agonglo. The interpreter that the ambassadors brought with them to Salvador was a mulatto slave of Francisco Antônio da Fonseca Aragão, commander of the fort, who had escaped and asked for Agonglo's protection.[52] The lieutenant and this former slave were enemies of the commander of the Portuguese fort, and the use of these men as *línguas* was thus not beneficial to Portuguese interests.

In one of his letters, Agonglo asked Prince Dom João to send "a man who knows how to read and write well to stay with us,"[53] and in another, brought back with Vicente Ferreira Pires after his return to Salvador, he asked the governor of Bahia to send an inkwell. On 4 September 1799, in the context of a dispute with the new commandant of the Portuguese fort in Whydah, the new king, Adandozan, sent "a sack of letters to be delivered to the governor of Bahia."[54] The African kings' use of writing shows how the African oral system of communication was subjugated to European written culture as the kings sought to deliver their demands to the authorities in Portugal, the latter imposing their cultural signs on the Africans.

Cipriano was the man who could fulfill all the requirements for this mission, owing both to his education and to the close relationship he maintained with several members of the Royal Academy of Sciences of Lisbon. Dom João expected the mission would stay at least two years in Dahomey, and during this period Cipriano would have to employ his written skills several times to write a scientific report, letters bearing the demands of the African authorities, and religious texts necessary for the performing of his religious mission.

In 1800, just a few years after his return to Salvador, Vicente Ferreira Pires presented the Prince Regent with a manuscript containing an account entitled *Viagem de África em o Reino de Dahomé* (African Journey in the Kingdom of Dahomey).[55] The original is preserved in the Ajuda Library in Lisbon,[56] and the work was published in Brazil in 1957 by Clado Ribeiro de Lessa, constituting volume 287 of the Coleção Brasiliana.[57] Early in the narrative, on page 5 to be precise, it is Vicente Ferreira Pires, and not Cipriano Pires Sardinha, who claims authorship of the account. This claim, the authenticity of which has been questioned by me who is more inclined to attribute authorship to Cipriano, will not be discussed here. My aim is to draw upon the account in order to reconstruct the impressions these priests formed about their catechetic mission and the African world they were able to observe throughout. I will not be discussing this claim here, but am questioning its authenticity in my current book project where I attribute authorship to Cipriano.

Early on in the text, the reader's attention is drawn to the near-incredible misfortunes that beset the priestly pair in Dahomey, now transformed into narrative: "These [my writings], in part, shall move one almost to the point of the shipwrecked Sepúlveda, or that hapless, wretched Araguai; also in part, they shall spur one to even heartier laughter than an Alfarraxe, a Saint-Étienne or, finally, a Quixote, that wandering knight."[58]

To begin with, this passage makes reference to the poem *O Araguai [sic]* (*Uraguai* or *Uruguai*), written by the Minas Gerais poet José Basílio da Gama (1740–95), first published in 1769. In an epic tone, the poem narrates the destruction of the Jesuit missions in the Brazilian south after the expulsion of the Jesuit Order in 1757 by the Marquis de Pombal. The mention in the *Voyage to Dahomey* represents no idle reference, but rather one that displayed familiarity with a monumental work, connected to the anti-Jesuit propaganda circulated among the new elite influenced by Jansenism, the Enlightenment and science. The reference thus situates the author within the erudite, Enlightenment-minded circle gathered around the Royal Academy of Sciences of Lisbon. It is also interesting to note that the epic poem's author, Basílio da Gama, was born in the same captaincy as Cipriano and was his acquaintance. This reference to a countryman[59] also accentuated the importance that Brazil and its local elite had acquired thanks to the transformations underway in the Portuguese Empire, many of which were driven by reforms proposed by members of the Royal Academy of Science of Lisbon. It is not impossible that the two Brazilians had met in Lisbon, as both lived there during the 1790s (Basílio died there in 1795), and they certainly belonged to the same intellectual and social circles. The author follows this with references to two Spanish comic novels from the late sixteenth/early seventeenth century: *Guzmán de Alfar-ache*, by Mateo Alemán (1599 to 1620), and *Don Quixote* (1605) by Miguel de Cervantes. *Vida del pícaro Guzmán de Alfarache*, based on the two years the author spent in prison in Seville for not paying his debts, portrayed the underworld of criminality and roguery of the society of the day. This two-volume work was enormously popular, the burlesque novel par excellence, laced with adventures that revealed a world of violence and disorder, but which was nonetheless interlaced with counsel of an edifying nature. *Don Quixote* was classical reading, available in various erudite libraries at the time, even in Tejuco, where Cipriano could easily have had his first contact with the work. A scathing critique of the notion of chivalry still prevalent at the time of its writing, the rowdy adventures of Don Quixote and his loyal sidekick, Sancho Panza, also stand out for their tragicomic moral edge.

The story of Sepúlveda was set down in the famous *História trágico-marítima* (Tragic Maritime History), a collection of accounts of doomed Por-tuguese expeditions in pursuit of overseas expansion. Basically, the book was a history of shipwrecks and of lives and goods lost to the depths over the long course of Portuguese adventures on the high seas. Written by Bernardo Gomes de Brito in 1735, this compendium of tales of sunken ships was the flipside of the uplifting *épopée* of the discoveries summed up so famously in Camões's *Lusíadas*, which glorified the role of the Portuguese in opening the oceans to the European world. Manoel de Sousa Sepúlveda was the commander of a galley that set sail from Cochim, India, but ran aground off the coast of Na-tal, Brazil, in 1552, killing the commander, his family, and much of his crew. Making mention of such figures from books not only indicates that the au-thor was a man of some learning, whose varied reading habits went beyond texts of a religious nature, but also that he was addressing a cultivated reader-ship he knew would be capable of picking up on those literary references. By choosing these references, the author also aligned his narrative with certain literary styles, heavy on adventure, forays into the unknown, and encounters with the tragic. While he paradoxically appeals to laughter, the burlesque, and the tragicomic, his account also presents a morally edifying slant. Lastly, the reference to Saint-Étienne—Saint Stephen—adds a dose of martyrdom and mortification, underscoring the expedition's main goal as an evangeliz-ing mission. Saint Stephen was the first Christian martyr, murdered in Jerusa-lem, whose sacrifice signaled the onset of the persecution that drove the followers of Christ from the region. The priests, especially Cipriano, were prepared to offer their martyrdom in exchange for Dahomey conversion.

The passion of Christ became a pillar of identity and acquired an exemplary and pedagogical meaning that was often repeated by the apostles, early Christians like Saint Stephen, and by Christians all throughout history.[60] Yet it was the Jesuit preachers of the early modern era who made most masterly use of the paradigm of martyrdom, the holy death, as a form of Christian teaching.[61] However, in the case of the Dahomey account, the martyrdom of Saint Stephen, allied with a veiled reference to the expulsion of the Jesuits, underscored the fact that the Portuguese Crown, through the secular clergy as opposed to the primary orders, had taken the missionary task of converting the African peoples into its own hands.

In Portugal and its overseas domains, the prevailing law was the so-called *Padroado*, according to which the appointment and sustenance of parish priests fell to the state, which, through the Tribunal of Conscience and the Orders, in Lisbon, was coresponsible, alongside the Vatican, for the secular clergy—brethren not belonging to the regular or primary orders, like Jesuits, Franciscans, and so on. As such, church and state were united in the evangelizing cause, with the latter under the tutelage of the former. This unification constituted recognition of the importance of religion to the consolidation of imperial Portuguese colonization, but at the same time it was an indication of how the Vatican was losing some of its power and had to submit itself to the interference of the crown.

As for the evangelization of the New World, the primary orders, especially the Jesuits, had assumed a preponderant role.[62] It was during the reign of Dom João III (1521–57) that the Society of Jesus, founded by Ignatius of Loyola in 1534 and approved by papal bull in 1540, established itself in Portugal. Dom João III "believed that Portuguese colonization in the New World would only take firm hold and reach completion with the conversion of its peoples to Catholicism,"[63] thus expanding the founding mission of the Portuguese Crown, and in this endeavor he found an ideal partner in the Jesuits. In 1541, Francisco Xavier set sail for India, where he arrived in 1549. That same year, accompanying the entourage of the first governor, Tomé de Souza, the Jesuits disembarked in Brazil. Many primary orders followed in their wake, such as the Franciscans, the Carmelites, and the Benedictines, but these had a structure that was independent of the state and even of the Vatican, which meant that, though recognized as important and viewed as partners, they were also feared because they were hard to control.

The secular clergy, however, had always served as an important instrument of evangelization in Portuguese expansion.[64] In the Congo, for example, in 1491, following the expedition that initiated the kingdom's conversion to Catholicism, four priests stayed behind armed with the necessary objects to perform the mass and with only an interpreter to facilitate communication with the local population.[65] At the end of the eighteenth century, Fathers Cipriano and Vicente, following in the steps of their predecessors, were entrusted with teaching the Catholic dogmas to the Dahomey elites and with performing their religion's main rituals there, in the hopes of spreading their religion to the local population.

Portuguese Catholicism adhered to the principles of the Council of Trent. Held between 1545 and 1563, the council established the bases with which to fight Protestantism and to spread Catholicism overseas. The secular clergy was prepared under its tenets and, in the case of Brazil, the *Constituições Primeiras do Arcebispado da Bahia*, first published in 1719, adapted its commandments to the religious needs of local communities.[66] In this text, there is a great preoccupation with the conversion of slaves and with the promotion of the martyrdom and pain of the saints as great examples of Catholic virtues.[67] Bishop Sebastião Monteiro de Vide, the author of the *Constituições Primeiras,* also published a *Catechism to the Slaves*; a *History of Mother Vitória da Encarnação*, an example of virtue and suffering; and a *Chronology of the Life of Saint Ignatius of Loyola*.[68] Adapted to the conditions of the New World, the *Constituições Primeiras* were applied in all the Brazilian bishoprics, not only in Bahia, and even in Angola.[69] The text received support from the Jesuits who were responsible in their colleges and seminaries all over Brazil for the education of the secular clergy and of the local elite.

In Minas Gerais, the Jesuit Order, although forbidden to settle in the city beginning in 1720, had wielded an enormous influence on the elite as well as on the mentality of the secular clergy. The Boa Morte Seminary, founded in 1749, was the only local institution for training the clergy. Founded by Bishop Manuel da Cruz, the seminary was first directed by Jesuits, who were responsible for establishing its religious teaching bases.[70] At the Boa Morte Seminary, Cipriano Pires Sardinha received the part of his religious training that was marked by the promotion of virtue and pain proclaimed both by the Jesuits and by the *Constituições Primeiras do Arcebispado da Bahia*. Cipriano's education also stressed, however, the principles of secular priesthood influenced by Jansenism: the importance of service to the crown and loyalty to the state, as well as a purer sense of religiosity.[71]

The Sermonist Issue

Before discussing the missionary character of the two priests' undertaking, it is important to highlight that the expedition was, in fact, also a scientific mission. This fact wielded influence over the way the two men recorded the African reality they observed, as well as the manner in which the travel account was written, thus also molding the religious discourse contained therein. One important feature of the narrative is the overriding tone of empirical observation, even if, as the author himself recognizes, the observed may seem to beggar belief. In this respect, the text sounds like it has flowed from the quill of a naturalist, someone who has carefully observed the reality, both of nature and of man and his customs, so as to set it forth for the benefit of the reader. A curiosity to learn is clearly what drives the writing. Curiosity—as the thirst for knowledge—is continuously evoked as the sentiment of reference, and it orders the observation of what is seen throughout the voyage and subsequently registered in the chronicle. Our author's approach is aligned with the empirical tone required by the Royal Academy of Sciences of Lisbon, founded some time later, during the reign of Queen Maria (1799). The new academy, dedicated to the Enlightenment, intended to impose the dominion of the empirical in the observation of reality, under the auspices of the nascent natural sciences, for the benefit and development of the Portuguese Empire.

No matter how hard the travel account tried to observe the requirements of science, however, we cannot forget that an important reason for the mission was the conversion of the Kingdom of Dahomey to Catholicism, which is why two priests were chosen as ambassadors instead of a pair of career bureaucrats. It was not the first time the crown had employed clerics on diplomatic missions,[72] as they "had certain advantages over laymen; as holy men they were granted easy access to royal palaces, while as confessors, they knew how to keep a secret."[73] Just as important was their facility in carrying out the apostolic mission in which the Portuguese Crown had been engaged since the first waves of the struggle against the Moors on the Iberian Peninsula and the beginning of overseas expansion.[74]

It can also be noted that the narrative is impregnated with a clear sermonic discourse, which required full mastery of the rhetoric that was typical of the Jesuits, such as was taught at the Boa Morte Seminary, where Cipriano Pires Sardinha had trained. When the seminary was founded, two Jesuit priests were entrusted with organizing the curriculum.[75] The Jesuits were masters of the sermon and of rhetoric, and, prior to their expulsion, effectively dominated all the educational institutions of the Portuguese Empire. Even after their expulsion from the Portuguese Empire in 1759, the Jesuit pedagogic influence lingered for quite some time.

If, as the bishop of Bahia had affirmed, Cipriano was indeed erudite, then mastery of rhetoric, the key to a good sermon, that bastion of Catholic preaching, would certainly have ranked among his qualities. The practice of rhetoric demanded that the sermon be tripartite: first, the orator should convince the congregation that the normal order had been breached, and that the world was in chaos, causing suffering and bewilderment; second, the listener should be persuaded to repent; which leads to the third and final part, a divine invocation to restore the lost order. The first part, which Valéria Maria Pena Ferreira calls the "rhetoric of tears,"[76] can be readily identified in the Dahomey account, bringing the discourse of travel in contact with a sermonic discourse. As such, the reader is informed from the start that the voyage "to the Promised Land [Dahomey], like other Israelites, [is marked] by distance, labor and the discomforts of travel."[77] The overseas voyage, the crossing of the vast ocean, is here both comparable to and symbolic of the flight out of Egypt toward the Promised Land, and signals the rupture between the civilized world—of Europe and the Americas—and the rough, wild world of Africa.

The Mission as Martyrdom

According to Inácio Felizardo Fortes (1818),[78] the sermonist had to possess three qualities: "I – Goodness, II – Science, III – Legitimizing Mission."[79] Cipriano had put forth all these discernible qualities in the account of the journey to Dahomey. He led an exemplary life, the apex of which was his personal delivery, having given up all that was familiar to him in order to become a missionary in unknown pagan African lands; secondly, he had a training in science (there were mathematics and geometry classes in Boa Morte Seminary)[80] and possessed knowledge of "Philosophy, Rhetoric, the Holy Scripture [the soul of sacred oratory], Dogmatic and Moral Theology."[81] This knowledge was accumulated at the institutions where he had studied and was not only attested to by all who knew him, but readily perceptible from a reading of the account. Finally, he had undertaken an apostolic voyage as narrated in the manuscript itself.

The apostolic model—after all, the voyage was a mission to convert the Natives to the Catholic faith, particularly the king of Dahomey—demanded a decent dose of martyrdom and suffering: "To the hardships to which the body of the missionary is submitted over the course of his journey one can add the level of sacrifice required for the perfect fulfillment of the evangelizing task."[82] As a pilgrimage, the author of the account tells us, the journey to Dahomey "is a medley of pain, scorn, pity and laughter."[83] The roads are only traversed with great effort, "the monsters and beasts are immense," even the fruits are unpleasant to taste.[84] The entire journey is one of sufferings that mortify the traveler's body, even where relief and comfort is expected. As such, exhausted after the crossing, having sailed along the coast to the Whydah fort and continued to the seat of the kingdom, in Abome, the author recounts that the first night was one of vigil, saying: "[as] the houses are open in a ring, such was the wind that blew upon us that we were mortified and discomforted . . . we lay awake, receiving visits from sundry vermin, among them lizards, geckos, small snakes, frogs and other critters of the like, not to mention the choir of wolves that howled through the night around our hut."[85]

It is upon the body of the missionary that true mortification is most perfectly visited, where the "rhetoric of tears"—that first of the sermon's three parts, and the one that the author demonstrates mastery of throughout most of the account—finds fulfillment. In this manner, soon after arriving in Abome, the two missionaries, having endured a wide variety of discomforts, are finally beset by fever, as if to complete the ordeal of body and soul, and which the author describes in the following terms: "a cruel molestation that attacked us so that I was left with but part of my reason free to function, which made my sentiment all the greater."[86] The arduous physical journey across the wilderness of the Atlantic New World became an allegory for the journey of the soul.[87]

If the "rhetoric of tears" marks the opening chapter of a sermon, it is followed by an exhortation to conversion and repentance that can only be achieved under divine inspiration. This type of rhetoric also features in the narrative, thus demonstrating the author's mastery of the style. This exhortation coincides with the moment when the reader is told of the king of Dahomey's willingness to convert to Catholicism. Physical suffering then gives way to rejoicing of the soul, the sublimation of pain through the conversion of a Native heathen. The author says: "Satisfied with that response [the king's decision to convert to Catholicism], which filled our hearts and souls with such joy, so little did our past hardships mean to us now, much less those that still lay before us; as what greater adventure might we have had than to see that barbarous king reduced to our Holy Faith, a man so powerful that most of his people and neighbors would also choose the same true and righteous path, we having been the secondary movers who opened the road to salvation for so many souls?"[88]

However, the true show of faith with its final martyrdom was yet to come: the total surrendering of the missionary's body, the mirror of the most profound conversion, the journey of which, with its daily mortifications, is but the first stage in the mission.[89] On many occasions throughout the text, the author affirms that the two missionaries were willing to make the ulti- mate sacrifice. Narrating the apprehension felt after the assassination of the king by his own brother, eager to prevent him from converting, the author relates that the terrified pair "Returned to that hut, or rather that place of martyrdom, where, reconciled to our fate and pressing the image of Jesus Christ to our breasts, we waited for the final instant that would sever the thread of our lives. We offered up this event in the memory of the most pre- cious blood of Jesus, for the forgiveness of our sins."[90]

This importance given to the issue of martyrdom in the text reveals that the author bore the influence of the secular clergy's ideology shaped by the values of suffering and virtue the Jesuits inculcated in their students and by the *Constituições Primeiras do Arcebispado da Bahia* taught in the Seminary of Boa Morte. The Jesuits introduced "new elements into the cartography of Eu- ropean martyrdom . . . and martyrs were restored to the foreground of Chris- tian history."[91] On its missionary forays overseas, the Society of Jesus supplied hundreds of new sacrificial victims who died in imitation of the example of Christ. These new martyrs were fundamental to the expansion of Catholi- cism in the wildernesses of the New World, but they also fulfilled an indis- pensable educational role, as, in embodying a narrative geared toward the newly Christianized peoples, they served as an example of the Christian life.[92] The Jesuits resurrected the martyrdom,[93] and the *Voyage to Dahomey* makes full use of the rhetoric of sacrifice preached by the order, with "the blood of martyrs consecrating the land"[94] to be conquered by the cross and by the sword. The ceiling of the sacristy at the Jesuit College in Salvador, certainly known to Vicente Ferreira Pires, "richly adorned with images of martyrs from the Company who had died in Portuguese America and be- yond"[95] must have served as guiding inspiration not only for the conduct of the two priests on their mission in Dahomey, but also for the rhetoric of the account they wrote. This rhetoric was marked by the martyrdom of the two missionaries, now no longer within the scope of the company, but under the auspices of the Portuguese monarchy as expressed in the figure of the Prince Regent Dom João, to whom the text was addressed.

This total delivery, the exchange of one's own body for the conversion of infidels, was the ultimate goal of all missionaries.[96] This apotheosis of faith was only to be experienced in the flesh by Cipriano Pires Sardinha, who, at the end of the journey, was attacked by *carneirada*, as malaria was then called, and died on or around 20 August that same year. Back in Whydah, "with gasps and sighs, that body bid his soul farewell."[97] Only Vicente Ferreira Pires returned to Salvador Bahia, severely sickened by malaria himself.

Cipriano Pires Sardinha's death prevented him from completing the task entrusted to him, that of presenting the prince regent with an account of his voyage. It strengthens the argument, however, that up until the passage quoted above, he had been the author of the text, as from this point on, the narrative stands out for its starkly contrasting discursive weakness. This supreme sacrifice, the aspiration of any evangelizing missionary, is not used to exalt faith or missionary endeavor in the manner one would expect of a sermonist trained in the art of rhetoric. Contrary to all that went before, the passages after his death reveal no such discursive mastery. In this part of the account, the (new) author—now certainly Vicente Ferreira Pires—begins to express his fear of his own impending end, revealing that he found himself in a "veritable state of inaction and apathy,"[98] but, in order to keep up appearances and despite his gloom, knowing that there were many who wanted to convert to Catholicism, he set about conducting baptisms as they were required.

Return as a Mission

The rhetoric employed in the account of the voyage to Dahomey is also marked by a sense of intolerance toward the African world that reveals itself over the course of the expedition. The selection of both priests for the mission had to do, it is important to note, with their Afro-Brazilian origin, which provided them a familiarity with African language and costumes. Cipriano's mother came from the Slave Coast, as did the mothers of his two half-brothers. The three women, who had all been slaves of a certain Manoel Pires Sardinha, remained close even after they were freed.[99] Given the massive contingent of Africans not only among slaves, but among freedmen in Brazil as a whole, and in Tejuco and Salvador in particular, vestiges of African cultures were embedded in the practices of daily life. In 1806, for example, when the Bahian doctor Luís Antônio de Oliveira Mendes presented a memoir describing Dahomey to the Royal Academy of Sciences of Lisbon, he based it in part on the "memories of his childhood, what he had been told by the fons slaves and from information he had collected from a certain Francisco Leite, a native of Dahomey," when he lived in Salvador, the city where he was born.[100]

African culture, of course, underwent a permanent transformation in Brazil as people from different regions of Africa mixed and cohabitated in the slave quarters and as it was further molded and constrained by the imposition of Portuguese culture and Catholicism.[101] There are numerous accounts of the sharing of African traditions and customs amongst Africans in towns and cities, even if their countless cultural assimilations meant they were no longer a simple reflection of the original practices. Every year, for example, a King Congo and Queen Ginga were chosen in Brazilian cities for the Rosary Brotherhood celebrations in a clear throwback to the political organization of the African tribes and kingdoms. As Jose Ramos Tinhorão writes: "The kings of Congo coronations were, in reality, a symbolic projection of the missionary policy created in Africa by the Portuguese crown and the Catholic Church . . . to guarantee the State's economic enterprise in Africa, of which the slave trade was the key part."[102] The festivals of the Rosary Brotherhood exemplify how Catholicism was embellished through this African encounter, thus impacting religiosity in Brazil. The African slave population used the perpetuation of African dress and political organization to empower their conversion to Christianity and to accept both Catholicism and their enslaved status.

The Rosary festivities "always involved dances, music, processions, pageants, [liberal] consumption of food and drink."[103] Another characteristic of these festivals was the use of instruments, particularly drums that conjured up the sounds of African musicality that was not confined only to feast days. Throughout the Minas Gerais captaincy, "at night the blacks danced while clapping and stamping on the ground with their feet,"[104] accompanied by the "clatter of log-drums, tambourines, rattles, jars and castanets."[105] As Ramos Tinhorão points out in his book about the music produced by black slaves in Brazil, Africans performed anytime and everywhere. They chanted their music during work and in their spare time, frequently accompanied by drums. Some of the dances that were very popular in colonial Brazil, such as *lundu* and *fofa*, clearly had African origins.[106] Thus, it would be impossible that our two priests, Cipriano and Vicente, would have been hearing such music for the first time in Africa. Both the village of Tejuco in Minas Gerais[107] and Salvador da Bahia had large black populations from Africa who had brought their customs with them to Brazil. Despite this familiarity, the priests' description of what they heard and saw in Africa bore the mark of prejudice.

As Marina Mello e Souza writes, the "affinities cemented within colonial society, like neighborhoods, the workplace and even within families"[108] not only forged new forms of sociability between Africans from various regions of origin and their descendants, but also allowed for exchange and the discovery of shared cultural values. In the particular case of Cipriano, we can see that the bonds of sociability woven between his mother, Francisca Pires, and two former slave companions, Francisca da Silva—Chica da Silva[109]— and Maria Gomes, endured throughout their lifetimes, even as freed women. These three women (all Creole, but only Chica was a mulatta) acted as godmothers to each other's children, demonstrating how bonds of god parentage consolidated and strengthened the relationships they had established with one another during their slave days. Through this close contact, begun in the slave quarters, the three would certainly have shared values inherited from their forebears, adding to those they witnessed on the streets of Tejuco, and thus drawing a mantle of African culture about themselves and their offspring, as was the case with Cipriano.

We can be fairly sure that at least one of the two men possessed the ability to communicate with the Africans in their own language. Several reasons substantiate this belief. First, the African interpreter who had accompanied Agonglo's ambassadors to Salvador had not returned to Dahomey with them since he broke his leg on the eve of the trip. However, no efforts seemed to have been made to locate another interpreter to accompany the two Brazilian priests that could be easily have been found among the Bahian slaves and freedmen. Second, in the *Voyage to Dahomey*, we find several references to how the priests "spoke with people from that land,"[110] making no reference to the use of an interpreter. The only exception to this is during their official reception by Agonglo, but here it seems the presence of the interpreter indicates a desire to provide security for the king rather than to facilitate communication. On this occasion, the king relied upon one of his subjects, one Leguedé, and the priests used the ambassador Dom João Carlos de Bragança.[111] The Leguedés were trustful bilingual eunuchs who served the king and who were obliged to accompany his ambassadors on their missions in order to certify that the ambassadors only relayed the king's specific wishes. This custom verifies that ambassadors and Europeans were always received in the presence of a Leguedé who would then report everything that was said to the king.[112] In further support of the theory that one of the priests spoke an African language, one can also consider how, shortly after their arrival, the two priests were separated from the African ambassadors. This notwithstanding, the two men were able to talk and put together a lot of information about the kingdom. They also mention that they gleaned most of their information from the "people from the land that we talked with" and of course mulattos and black American Christians, that is from Brazilians, and some shipwrecked people.[113]

However, despite the significant presence of traces of African culture in Brazil, and in Tejuco or Salvador in particular, alterity and intolerance still mark the relationship between the author and the Africa of his forefathers. He writes: "so we began to observe the extravagant difference there was between our customs and those of the barbarians, and the savage ways of that unhappy race."[114] This line, like a great deal of the rest of the text, reveals the priests' heavily negative vision of the continent, laced with intolerance toward the local habits and customs, which he refers to always in terms of a lack of civilization.

Whenever some vestige of civilization is found, the narrator always assumes it pertains to the legacy of European contact. As such, the tribal king, who lived in the vicinity of the São Jorge da Mina fort, and whom the author describes as "old and blind in one eye," presented himself "seated on a large high-backed chair, old and antique, covered in floral satin drapery of similar age, with a gilded silver crown atop his head, apparently given to him by a governor of the Portuguese castle when this was still under the control of Portugal."[115] Marina de Mello e Souza notes how it was customary for the African courts to dress in European styles, associating such finery with the symbols from which they derived their power.[116] The manner in which this custom is depicted by the author, however, makes a caricature of the royal figure, which seems reduced by Cipriano's account to something more akin to the fake kings chosen to lead the carnival processions of the black brotherhoods back in Brazil. While, on one hand, the kings wore objects from European culture generally associated with royalty, they were all as old and worn as the tribal kings themselves. For the narrator, the same objects that had attained their true significance within European culture became in the hands of the African kings a pale, vague, and almost pathetic reminder of the symbolism they embodied.

The Strategy of the King's Conversion

After visiting several places along the Slave Coast, "finally in April, 8th, 1797," the priests declared that, after great suffering, they had "arrived to the Promised Land, like the other Israelites, because of the great distances and misfortunes of the trip."[117] When they arrived at the fort of São João Baptist, they made their religious intentions clear. On Easter Sunday, they celebrated a mass and began to baptize both Portuguese and French children. These baptisms numbered more than one hundred, according to their calculations, since more than ten years had passed without the presence of a Catholic church in Whydah. Cipriano announced there was no time to baptize the adults and that, moreover, they were not authorized to do so and could not offer the catechism.[118] Although no references can be found in *Voyage to Dahomey* regarding the baptism of Africans, after his return, Vicente Ferreira Pires maintained that, armed with the king's order, they baptized more than three hundred savages, both children and adults.[119]

When the two men, finally, were officially received by the king in the city of Canamina, where his court was settled, they declared that they had been sent by the prince of Portugal to "baptize him, and to make him convert to Catholicism if he wants to live and die in the true law of God." The priests must surely have been surprised when the king, "full of contentment, responded to them that yes, that was exactly what he wanted and desired a long time, and so he would like to be baptized immediately."[120] But the priests declared that Agonglo must first see if the law of the whites pleased him as well as learning the principles of Catholicism. The king asked them to write these religious principles down in Portuguese, as he had interpreters to read it for him. The priests were very happy, thinking that their task would be much easier than they had initially believed and that in a short time all his subjects and those of the nearby kingdoms, following his example, would embrace Catholicism.[121]

The texts the priests produced for the king's conversion were not unique. In 1658, Philip IV of Spain sent a mission of twelve Capuchins to Allada in order to convert a few young men who could then be ordained as priests in Spain and subsequently return to Africa to spread Catholicism. A certain Father Joseph de Naxara penned a religious text specifically for this purpose. But we find certain key differences between this Spanish work and the text Cipriano and Vicente wrote in Dahomey. The earlier Spanish text, entitled

Doctrina Christiana, was printed in Spain and was the first book to be printed in an African language. Naxara was the ambassador the African king had sent to Spain as a translator along with a former slave who had lived there for forty-four years.[122] In the text Fathers Vicente and Cipriano produced for the king in Africa they summed up the tenets they thought were essential for him in his conversion to the Catholic faith. On the day they completed their book they put on their religious garb and set off to see the king. They were not allowed to deliver it in person to him, but were soon informed that the king was pleased with what he read and had decided to be baptized. Thus the two priests began to prepare the baptism ceremony.[123] But before it could take place, the king was murdered, and everything changed. But that is a story for another time.

The Religious Discourse

In order to understand why the king decided so rapidly to convert to Catholicism, as well as to better comprehend the religious foundation of the author of the *Voyage to Dahomey*, we must situate Cipriano's account within the overriding theme he himself gave it. His is a religious tale of the moralizing, edifying sort, mixed with objective observations fresh from the quill of an empirical naturalist. From the very beginning of the colonial period, especially during the Jesuit missions, the church observed a certain model, namely that, as Marina de Mello e Souza describes, "masters and slaves, whites and blacks, had to be, first and foremost, Christians. . . . In this model, there would be no truck with practices of African origin, which were seen as demonizing."[124] It was his subscription to this model that made Cipriano condemn and attribute to the devil almost everything he observed in Africa, despite his capacity to see the objective reality before his eyes, both in terms of the customs and society of the peoples with whom he made contact as well as with the nature, animals, and vegetation that surrounded him. His account reflects the struggle between Native paganism and the Catholic faith the missionaries were sworn to defend.

Yet, the decision of the king to be baptized was not as spontaneous as the *Voyage to Dahomey* describes. Two important moments—one preceding the priests' arrival and the other following—were crucial in the monarch's decision. The two passages in which the author recounts what happened are also very important to the religious discourse present in the report. They are good illustrations of this struggle between paganism and Catholicism, described as two edifying stories to the reader. In the first, a mulatto woman, spouse of the secretary/interpreter who was retained in Salvador with the broken leg, was responsible for stopping a great thunder storm by intoning the Hail Mary, "and such was the faith with which she prayed that the thunder soon calmed, making so great an impression on [King] Adarunzá VIII that he was forced to declare that the real magic belonged to the whites."[125] In the second story, the king asks the two priests just after their arrival to pray for victory in the war he was about to wage against an enemy tribe to capture slaves. When this war was eventually won, the priests fully expected the king was able to "believe in the Catholic faith" and, in fact, they received the news of his decision to be baptized only a few days later.[126]

On one hand, in both cases, we can see the tried and tested conversion strategy that the Portuguese had been employing in Africa since the fifteenth century, especially in the Congo and in Angola, where Catholicism was offered as an elixir capable of strengthening a ruler's power.[127] Catholicism, it is important to point out, was exported by European nations with muskets and powder. The latter gave the African kings who possessed it a significant advantage over enemy kingdoms in the African internal slave wars. The *Voyage to Dahomey* tells us that Agonglo was able to muster thirty thousand men with muskets to fight in his wars, which only the Dahomean kings possessed because of their contacts with the European nations. These muskets, the reader is told, intimidated his enemies, who must fight only with bows, darts, and swords.[128] For this reason, Agonglo and his successor, Adanruzá, were keen to maintain written communication with the Portuguese kings and displayed concern over finding a literate translator able to relay their requests to Prince Dom João and Queen Maria I for guns and powder. In one letter, Agonglo demands "40 strong cannons made of bronze and iron."[129] Adanruzâ, for his part, asks for two hundred to three hundred barrels of powder and gunshot "that which your soldiers use in your wars."[130]

On the other hand, we can see that in these cases, when turned into tales directed toward a Portuguese readership, of which the prince regent was the most illustrious member, the aim of the *Voyage to Dahomey* was to celebrate the victory of Catholicism over pagan idolatry. Prince Dom João, we must remember, was "an appreciator of the genre, [and] that he contributed a great deal to the development of the place and importance that the sermonists" enjoyed during his reign.[131] In this sense, the *Voyage to Dahomey* was not only a report of what happened in the mission but it also offered religious instruction to its princely reader through the example of piety and martyrdom. Religious spirituality thus took on a narrative form. The text furnished the discourse of a true conversion to Catholicism and the prince was no normal reader. If he was to be moved by the account and the message it hoped to convey, the author had to be—and indeed was—a deft hand in the art of rhetoric. In this battle between good and evil, the text reflects the clash in which Cipriano Pires Sardinha and Vicente Ferreira Pires found themselves embroiled, just like the generations of Brazilian Creoles upon whom the suspicion of African descent had fallen. The authors were caught between their African cultural heritage on the one hand, generally of maternal origin, and, on the other, a largely paternal Western Christian tradition, which constituted their sole platform for social insertion and ascent in that society.

CHAPTER 8

Jesuit Missionary Work in the Imperial Frontier

Mapping the Amazon in Seventeenth-Century Quito

CARMEN FERNÁNDEZ-SALVADOR

Geography as a scientific practice developed in the early modern period in connection with the emergence of the new European empires.[1] Chorography, a branch of geography devoted to the study of individual places—their inhabitants, climate, and vegetation—assured the specificity of knowledge required to support imperial power over a distant territory, varied and extensive. In Spanish America, too, scientific geography was closely linked to the spiritual and material conquest of indigenous peoples. The inextricability between apostolic work and imperial possession is particularly evident in maps and accounts of the Amazon Basin produced in seventeenth-century Quito by Jesuit authors. Both are concerned with underscoring the uniqueness of the individual parts that comprised the vast domain, thus creating an image of the region as differentiated space. If cartography pointed to the precise location of places in relation to each other and the whole, written accounts highlighted, through ethnographic and topographic description, human and natural diversity. The mapping impulse, along with the actions of spatial differentiation and ordering, also materialized an anxiety regarding the need to define the boundaries of the Spanish Empire in the Amazon in order to protect the region from potential invaders, whether they were Dutch corsairs or Portuguese soldiers.

The relationship between scientific geography and imperial possession was first present in the minds of Jesuit authors from Quito who wrote about the exploration of the Amazon Basin in the first half of the seventeenth century. This chapter analyses two of these accounts, written in the late years of the 1630s. The first of them, by an anonymous author (although references within the text suggest that he was a Jesuit, Alonso de Rojas, according to Marcos Jiménez de la Espada) is the *Relación del descubrimiento del Río de las Amazonas y San Francisco del Quito, y declaración del mapa donde está pintado*, a report addressed to the king of Spain in 1639, describing the findings of the Portuguese expedition that, leaving Pará in 1637 and following the course of the Amazon, had arrived in Quito a year later. The second account is the *Nuevo descubrimiento del Gran Río de las Amazonas*, written in 1639 by Cristóbal de Acuña, and published in 1641.

Both have in common a concern regarding the vulnerability of the Amazonian frontier. In both, too, the authors point to the paramount role played by Quito, and by the Jesuit Order, in the nascent conquest of the Amazon. While the former account refers to the testimonies of Portuguese soldiers that formed part of the expedition, as well as to the information contained in a map drawn by the expedition pilot major, the latter is a travel narrative with precise observations of what its author had witnessed when traveling from Quito to the Atlantic. Precisely because of this, it is in Cristóbal de Acuña's account that chorography and ethnographic description are first employed as tools in territorial reconnaissance and definition.

Written descriptions and maps of the Amazon portray the region as the ultimate frontier, a territory on the margins of empire that escaped civil and Christian order. In the early modern period, the Amazon Basin was also marked by the permeability and porosity of its boundaries. As revealed by contemporary accounts, it was a space of contact and encounter, of conflict and struggle, between missionaries, soldiers, and Natives, as well as between the Spanish and the Portuguese. Studying the complex interactions that took place in the region during the colonial period is thus fruitful, in the sense that it expands academic inquiry beyond the limits imposed by national and singular imperial projects.[2]

Stressing the predominant role played by Quito in the seventeenth-century exploration and colonization of the Amazon, I also here question traditional definitions of modern global geography in terms of a fixed opposition between center and periphery, between metropolis and colonies or provinces. Resting on Wallerstein's theory of the mercantile world system in the early modern period, as well as on the dependency theory of the 1960s and 1970s, the center-periphery dichotomy has often been employed to define asymmetrical power relations between complex political and economic structures in the core, and weak or nonexisting states in the margins. More recently, Amy Bushnell and Jack Greene have released these terms from an otherwise stable template, emphasizing their usefulness for the study of colonial experiences in the Americas.[3] Identifying multiple centers in the Spanish American territory as well as the network connecting them to their corresponding peripheries, they contend, allows recognition of internal regional differentiation as well as the development of local agencies.

In this chapter, I show that the center-periphery opposition takes on multiple dimensions. The main concern of the two early accounts I discuss here is territorial definition and recognition. That is, both authors, with differing levels of success due in part to where they were writing, attempted to transform an otherwise unknown and empty space into something that could be conceived in more real and tangible terms. In this respect, this chapter adds a new dimension to the center-periphery dichotomy, relocating the production of knowledge in the encounter between religious men from Quito and the Amazon.

As noted by Jorge Cañizares-Esguerra, most of the academic literature dealing with Iberian science in the colonial period has focused on advancements that took place in Spanish America during the sixteenth and eighteenth centuries—that is, during the highpoint of the imperial building project and during the reign of the Bourbons.[4] In the case of Quito, science has traditionally been viewed as an eighteenth-century occurrence, owing its emergence to enlightened ideas that arrived with French and Spanish scientists and circulated in books that interested the city's intellectual élite.[5] By contrast, this chapter presents Spanish American science in the seventeenth century in terms of historical continuity with respect to former developments. More important, it underscores its local particularities and nature, rather than its debt to European culture.

In the latter decades of the sixteenth century, Iberian science emerged in response to imperial needs for territorial recognition. The expedition led by the Spanish physician Francisco Hernández in the sixteenth century, as well as the *Relaciones geográficas de Indias*, a questionnaire that was sent out by Philip II to officers throughout the empire, demonstrated an early interest in botany, cartography, chorography, and geography, setting the stage for future scientific developments. As I will discuss, the *Relaciones geográficas* in particular had an effect on accounts of the Amazon Basin written in the first half of the seventeenth century, most notably Cristóbal de Acuña's text. The influence of the *Relaciones geográficas* is clearly manifested here in the dialogue between the specific and the general, between chorography and geography, as well as in the concern for ethnographic description and natural history.

Writing about the Amazon Basin in seventeenth-century Quito, however, was not just a gesture of compliance with imperial needs for territorial reconnaissance, but had to do as well with local preoccupations. Following Steven Harris's argument regarding the development of Jesuit science in connection to missionary work, this chapter emphasizes the role played by Jesuits as agents of imperial expansion but also rescues the links between apostolic and scientific work and the rise of a Creole identity in Quito.[6] It is true that in the latter years of the seventeenth century many of the Jesuit missionaries working in the Amazon were from Germany and Eastern Europe, with merely bureaucratic links to the College of Quito. Up to 1685, however, a good number of authors and evangelizers were either Creoles or, when born in Spain, had spent most of their lives in Spanish America. This is the case, for example, of Cristóbal de Acuña, who was born in Burgos but traveled to South America when he was still very young. In 1634 he was assigned to the Jesuit Province of New Grenade and Quito, where he founded the College of Cuenca. Alonso de Rojas, to whom the 1639 *Relación del descubrimiento* has been traditionally attributed, was born in Loja, in the Real Audiencia de Quito, according to eighteenth-century Jesuit historian Juan de Velasco.[7]

In Quito during the seventeenth century, stories about the death of Jesuit martyrs in Japan and other distant places circulated in printed form and in sermons, and entered into a dialogue with written and painted narratives that praised the deeds of missionaries in the Amazon. The identity of the Jesuit Order took shape at the intersection of such narratives, and was thus negotiated between the local and the global.

In the second half of the seventeenth century, Pedro de Mercado wrote an account of the Jesuit College in Quito, which included a biographical compendium of virtuous members of the order. Many of them had served as missionaries in the Amazon and had died as martyrs. In the corridors of the college, writes Mercado, paintings depicting their martyrdom served as exemplars of apostolic zeal for future missionaries.[8] Stories of missionary work and martyrdom in the Amazon also circulated among a wider audience. Thus, for example, Jacinto Morán de Butrón, biographer of the saintly Mariana de Jesús, wrote at the end of the seventeenth century about the sermons recounting the martyrdom of missionaries in the eastern lowlands, which had deeply moved the woman's religious zeal.[9] The lives of Jesuit missionaries and martyrs became intertwined with local history. Accordingly, in Mercado's narrative as well as in other contemporary texts, biographies of exemplary men and women overlap with other stories about contemporary secular and nonsecular events. These men and women were transformed into local heroes, and their exemplary virtue was instrumental in the construction of a local identity. Their martyrdom also served to justify Quito's, and the Jesuits', jurisdictional rights over the Amazon. Exploration of the Amazon certainly influenced the way in which the city imagined itself during the seventeenth century. Indeed, much of the literature from the period—both geographic and ethnographic descriptions of the eastern lowlands, as well narratives of Jesuit missionary work in the region—emphasizes the greatness and glory of Quito in connection to this apostolic enterprise.

As I will discuss, authors speaking about the exploration of the Amazon portray Quito as the capital of God's empire. In the second half of the seventeenth century, when missionary work was well on its way, Quito was also depicted as a new Rome, spreading civility to the margins and leading the spiritual conquest of its own periphery. A clear example of this is provided by Manuel Rodríguez in his history of the Jesuit Order in Quito and of its Amazonian missions. In *El descubrimiento del Marañón*, Rodríguez describes the arrival in Quito, in the mid-seventeenth century, of Father Raimundo de Santacruz, escorted by forty Natives from Mainas, in the eastern lowlands, a region that had been recently converted to Christianity. Rodríguez portrays the arrival of Santacruz in Quito as a triumphal entrance, similar to those offered to Roman soldiers after a victorious military campaign.[10] Writing in the early 1680s, Rodríguez's account borrows information from texts written in previous decades, and the patriotic tone that infuses his narrative is also found in the work of earlier authors.

At the very beginning of the seventeenth century, Rafael Ferrer, a Spaniard from the Jesuit College in Quito, was the first to engage in missionary work among the peoples in the Amazon. After his death, which took place sometime after 1612, the order stopped all apostolic work in the region, which was then taken over by the Franciscans. The ethnographic and geographic literature produced by Jesuit authors in the first half of the seventeenth century, which I discuss here, prepares the road for the renewed missionary enterprise that acquired significant strength after 1650. Beyond the scientific and political interest in territorial definition and recognition, these texts spoke of the possibility of spiritual conquest and redemption.

Down and Up the Amazon River: First Exploration Narratives

The first description of the Amazon Basin was written by Gaspar de Carvajal, a Dominican friar who accompanied Francisco de Orellana on the expedition that, departing from Quito in 1542, led to the discovery of the famed river.[11] This account is indebted to earlier exploration narratives, such as Columbus's diaries, as well as to medieval travel literature. The story finds legitimization on the narrator's voice as eyewitness to the events. Structured as an itinerary following the writer's movement along the river, time and space are closely intertwined. As in earlier works, however, Carvajal's testimony is faulted by his inability to recognize difference, both in nature and in culture. What the author encounters along the way is explained either in terms of comparison with the author's previous experience (the fertility of the land, for example, is described as being similar to Spain's) or is interpreted in terms of wonder (in this case, the myth of the Amazons).[12] Although Carvajal continually refers to the rituals that accompanied the taking of possession of the newly discovered territories, his account fails to provide useful information for the imperial administration.

Although a number of explorers attempted to repeat Orellana's feat, most notably, Pedro de Orsúa and Lope de Aguirre, it took almost a century for a second expedition to be successful. In 1636, Fray Domingo de Brieva and Fray Andrés de Toledo, two Franciscan missionaries from Quito, made a trip along the Amazon accompanied by six Spanish soldiers.[13] They arrived in Pará in 1637, at a time when the Spanish and Portuguese crowns were united. In San Luis de Marañón, the Portuguese authorities decided that a second expedition, formed by Portuguese soldiers commanded by Pedro de Texeira and under the guidance of Domingo de Brieva, should travel up the river and back to Quito, where they arrived in 1638.

Details regarding the journey of the Franciscans to Pará, and of the Portuguese expedition to Quito, are collected in a number of contemporary texts, particularly in the anonymous *Relación del descubrimiento del río de las Amazonas y San Francisco del Quito y declaración del mapa donde está pintado.*[14] The voice of the narrator, removed from the places he describes, presents a bird's-eye view of the Amazon Basin. The stereotypical information provided by the writer gives shape to an image of the region as uniform and undifferentiated, both in terms of its geography and of its population. Thus, in very general terms, the anonymous author alludes to the great variety of trees growing on the river shores, to the possibility of introducing European species and plants, to important local crops, such as cocoa and tobacco, and to the existence of ore mines. Likewise, he stresses the bellicose character of Amazonian peoples, their idolatry and cannibalism, as well as the large population of the region.[15]

More specific information is provided with respect to Portuguese settlements, such as Conmutá, San Luis de Marañón, and Pará. The writer also procures careful descriptions of two different indigenous groups that lived in the Amazon Basin, the Omaguas and the Estrapajosos. This owes, in part, to the uneven quality and precision of the testimonies provided by his informants, Benito de Acosta, pilot major of the Portuguese expedition, and one of the Spanish soldiers who had traveled with the Franciscan missionaries, whom the writer credits on certain occasions.

Surprised by the relative ease with which the Franciscan missionaries and, later on, the Portuguese Army had traveled down and up the Amazon, the author shows his concern regarding the protection of the imperial territories. He thus cites Acosta's informed testimony in order to stress the vulnerability of the imperial territory; having measured distances along the way, the pilot major assured that the journey between Pará and Quito could be made in only two months.[16]

Throughout the text, too, great attention is given to the description of fortress buildings and defensive walls. With regard to Gran Pará, the author writes that it has for "defense a castle built on top of a rocky hill, to the mouth of the river facing the sea, and in front a cove in the shape of a horseshoe." He continues to speak about the fort, which, he says, "has parapets falling to the river and to the cove, covered with roof-tile . . . for the defense of gun carriages where twenty pieces of artillery are encaved . . . and in the *plaza de armas*, albeit small, a residence house for the captain and another, separate house for ammunitions, built of stone. The fort has rampart-terrace walls on foundations of hewn stones and a moat, and there is no gate on the drawbridge but has a stronghold of two doors with embrasures."[17] A similar description is provided for the Fort of Conmutá, except that here the author adds that "to this castle has many times arrived the Dutch enemy." Portuguese soldiers, he writes, had often attacked Dutch fortresses built on the north bank. On one occasion, they had captured more than 1,600 Dutch-men, along with a large canoe with twenty pieces of artillery.[18]

Dutch corsairs had not remained in Portuguese territory along the river delta, however, but had penetrated deep inland through the river mouth. The enormous depth and width of the river, which allowed effortless navigation of large ships, only exposed its vulnerability. In fact, the author states that the enemy had already made attempts to navigate its waters.[19] Evidence of this was found by the expedition of Franciscan missionaries and Spanish soldiers. When they arrived in the province of the people known by the Portuguese as Trapajosos, they had been invited to visit a large settlement built on the shores of one of the Amazon tributaries. Here they found skulls, arcabuces, pistols, and linen shirts. The Portuguese later on explained that Dutch corsairs had reached this region but had been killed by the Natives.[20]

The author stresses the need to build a fortress on the main strait of the river in order to impede the navigation of enemy armies. Located at a distance of three hundred leagues from its mouth, in only a few days the fort could be warned of potential enemy attacks by small boats traveling up from the delta.[21] Citing once again the pilot major's authority, he states that "since navigation is easy, the river is quiet, supplies are abundant, and Natives little bellicose, it would be easy for the enemy to navigate this river and take advantage of the wealth and fruits of the land."[22] Presenting the military and spiritual conquest of the Amazon Basin as two complementary enterprises, he finally argues that while God had sent his ministers for the spiritual protection of the Amazon, the fortress would serve as a material shield for the region.[23]

The 1639 *Relación*, however, is not only concerned with stressing the need to safeguard the imperial territories, but also in demonstrating the importance of Quito in the spiritual and material conquest of the Amazon. Employing a vocabulary charged with patriotic sentiment typical of the Creole spirit of the seventeenth and eighteenth centuries, the author presents an edifying image of the city as a center for the diffusion of Christian and civil mores.

In the introductory paragraphs, the anonymous author argues that God himself had chosen the city of Quito as a "metropolis of a vast empire." Because of this, it had surpassed many famous cities from antiquity. He thus writes that "Babylon may found glory on its walls, Nineveh on its greatness,

Athens on its letters, Constantinople on its empire, but Quito vanquishes them all as key to Christianity and conqueror of the world."[24] In a similar vein, the Amazon is described as "the largest and most famous river of the globe," superior to the Ganges, the Euphrates, and the Nile.[25] Most important, the writer builds a juridical argument regarding Quito's possession rights over the Amazon, on the basis of historical precedence and geographic jurisdiction.

On the one hand, regarding the notion of historical justification, the author states that even though many parties had tried to explore the Amazon Basin, it was only the expedition formed by Franciscan missionaries from the monastery in Quito that, accompanied by Spanish soldiers, had sailed down the river from beginning to end. If previous expeditions had been moved by the desire for gold, he adds, the success of the latter was the result of the apostolic zeal of its members.[26] With respect to geographic jurisdiction, he affirms that although some people believed that the river originated in Cuzco, and others that it was born close to Potosí, it was also true that soon after it diverted its course toward the "kingdom of Quito," and then proceeded to the ocean along the equator. Quito's rights over the Amazon, however, were mainly legitimized by the close proximity between the city and the river. The writer argues that "running the great river of the Amazons more than 2,500 leagues, no city in the Indies gets so close to it, for [the river] could kiss its walls [of Quito] if the rugged mountains were not an impediment." He then adds that "the main port of the river is eight days away from Quito, a short distance in such extended regions."[27]

Notions of territorial jurisdiction and defense are also present in a map printed in 1880, which allegedly reproduces the original painting that accompanied the manuscript version of the *Relación* (see Figure 19).[28] A close inspection of both the map and the anonymous account suggests that they were meant to be consulted simultaneously and complementarily. In fact, the author of the *Relación* often conducts the reader's attention to the visual information that is explicitly shown in the cartographic depiction. For example, if, as we have noted, the text talks about the proximity between the river and the equator, so too, in the map, the equatorial line is clearly defined in red. Likewise, in the painting the islands in the river are depicted as "green Os," as it is described in the text.[29] More specific details are also shown, such as "the numbers written between the equator and the river" that indicate the latitude degrees that separate one from the other, as well as the relative

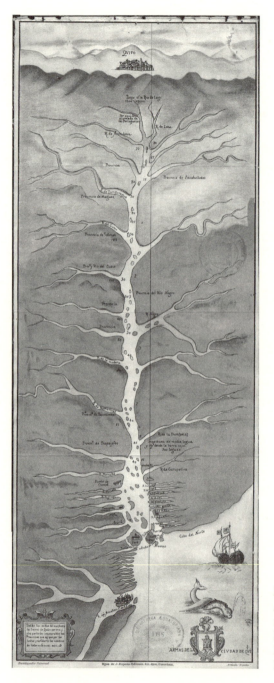
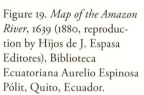

Figure 19. *Map of the Amazon River*, 1639 (1880, reproduction by Hijos de J. Espasa Editores), Biblioteca Ecuatoriana Aurelio Espinosa Pólit, Quito, Ecuador.

depth of the Amazon, identified "by the numbers that are noted inside the river."[30]

The map was probably based not only on the testimonies of firsthand witnesses, but also on a map that was drawn by Benito de Acosta, one of the anonymous author's witnesses, who, as pilot major of Texeira's expedition was in charge of measuring distances along the way. In fact, the Franciscan Laureano de la Cruz, who wrote an account of the missionary work of the order in the Amazon Basin in 1651, states that in compliance with a request made by the authorities from Quito, Acosta had drawn a map of the river "as a person who had marked it and [*tanteado*] had gotten to know it well, . . . which was very much appreciated by all who saw it."[31]

In contrast to modern cartography, the map shows the east at the top and the west at the bottom; the vertical format limits our perception of the geographic space, restraining it to the river course that runs parallel to the equator. On the one hand, the map contains extraordinary details, such as the text that identifies the province of Quijos, next to the eastern range of the Andes, and the distance, of 1,600 leagues, from there to the mouth of the river. The main tributaries are also identified, and, as noted previously, its relative depth and distance from the equator.

On the river delta are depictions of Portuguese settlements, such as Pará and San Luis de Marañón. On the top, crowning the Andes, Quito occupies a privileged position as indisputable head of the Amazon. This is further stressed by the fact that its coat of arms is portrayed in the Atlantic, by the mouth of the river. As if replicating the text, too, the city is shown so close to the Amazon that indeed it appears as if both could touch each other if it weren't for the mountains.

In the *Relación*, the author describes the Amazon Basin as overpopulated and overcrowded. In fact, citing Acosta, he states that "if a needle was ever dropped from the air, it would fall on the head of one of the Natives and not on the ground."[32] By contrast, the map presents the Amazon Basin as an empty space, save for a few inscriptions that identify the location of salient peoples and places. The economy in the representation of geography creates an image of the region as continuous and uninterrupted space, the borders between the Spanish and Portuguese empires blurred. While this underscores Quito's sovereignty over a large territory, however, it also stresses the vulnerability of the Amazon Basin. Needless to say, too, the unexpected arrival of Texeira and his army in Quito had alerted local authorities regarding the city's own defenselessness.

Cristóbal de Acuña: Chorography, Ethnography, and Spatial Differentiation

After the surprising arrival of Pedro de Texeira and the Portuguese troops in Quito, Spanish authorities decided to obtain more precise information regarding the geography and population of the Amazon Basin. It was accorded that on his trip back to Marañón, Texeira was to be accompanied by the Jesuits Cristóbal de Acuña and Andrés de Artieda. As a result of this trip, Acuña wrote the *Nuevo descubrimiento del Gran Río del Amazonas*, the first systematic description of the Amazon, published in 1641 in Madrid.[33]

Just as in the anonymous *Relación* of 1639, Acuña's narrative is infused with patriotic sentiment. Early on in his own account, he celebrates Quito as one of the most famous cities of the New World. The city is head of a province, the most fertile and abundant in the viceroyalty of Peru, he writes. He also praises the moral standing of Quiteños, their civility, good education, and Christian virtue.[34] From the earlier *Relación* Acuña also borrows the comparison between the Amazon and all of the great rivers from antiquity, portraying the eastern lowlands as a new Paradise.[35] More important, he also makes an argument regarding the jurisdictional rights of Quito over the Amazon. He states that since the origins of the river had remained unknown until recently, both the viceroyalty of Peru as well as New Grenade had claimed possession rights of the river on the basis of its alleged, although mistaken, proximity. In reality, the author states, the river was born only eight leagues away from Quito, on a lagoon located right underneath the equator.[36]

Instead of the distant descriptions of the 1639 *Relación*, Acuña's narrative contains precise, eyewitness information regarding distances, tributaries of the Amazon, natural resources, and the peoples that inhabited the basin, in terms of their social organization, customs, and so forth. It is precisely because of this precision that scientific maps, such as that produced by Nicolas Sanson d'Abbeville in 1657, are able to draw on the data provided by this account for the first accurate depiction of the Amazon Basin (see Figure 20). In contrast to the bird's-eye view presented by the anonymous *Relación* of 1639, Acuña's interest in chorography, that is, in specificity and in the local, gives form to an image of the Amazon as a highly differentiated space. Despite the absence of a map in this publication, the weight placed on ethnographic description allows the reader to imagine the different parts that constitute the imperial territory.

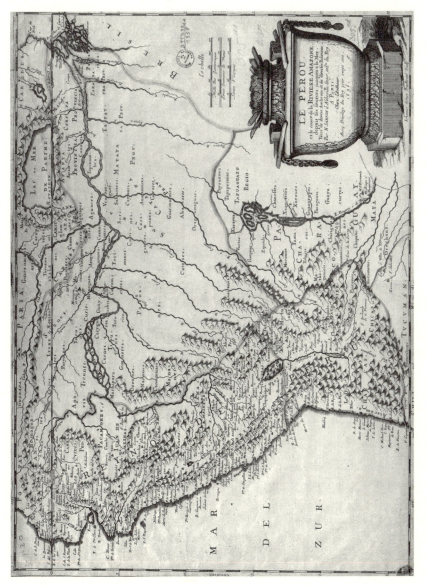

Figure 20. Nicolas Sanson d'Abbeville, *Le Perou: Cours de la rivière Amazone*, 1656, Fundação Biblioteca Nacional, Rio de Janeiro, Brazil.

In a way, Acuña remains indebted to the medieval tradition, just as Gaspar de Carvajal before him. Thus, he too searches for wondrous and fantastic creatures, similar to the monstrous races that, according to Pliny and other classical authors, inhabited the margins of the known world.[37] According to the Jesuit author, for example, on the margins of the Cuchiguará River, in the province of the Yoriman, lived the Curiguerés, who were "giants of sixteen palms of height, very brave, they go around naked, wear large ornaments [*patenas*] of gold on ears and noses."[38] In a similar way, he argues that close to the Tupinambá, on the south bank, "live, among others, two other nations, one of dwarfs, small as infants, called Guayazís, and the other of a people that have their feet turned backwards, so that if anyone who didn't know about this wanted to follow their footprints, he would always walk opposite to them, they are called Mutayus."[39]

In contrast to Carvajal, however, Acuña critically analyzes the validity of his information based on the legitimacy of his sources. With respect to the description of the Mutayus, for example, the author states that his informants had been the Tumpinambá, whom he portrays as "people of greater reason." Also with regard to the Tupinambá, he underscores the possibility of intercultural communication. He thus points out that they speak a "general tongue" that had been learnt by the Portuguese, "for they had been born and raised in those coasts."[40] Even with regard to the Amazons, Acuña relies on the large number of witnesses that validate the myth. He thus states, regarding their alleged practice of murdering their sons, that it "seems to be truer because it has been told by more people." He concludes with a skeptical remark arguing that "only time will uncover the truth, and if these are the famed Amazons of historians, their territory hides treasures enough to make the world rich."[41]

More often, Acuña provides accurate information based on his careful observation of nature. Early on in his account, for example, he speaks in general terms about the main natural products from the region that, if properly cultivated, could bring important financial revenues for the Spanish Crown. The first of these products was wood, so plentiful that it could never reach exhaustion. The second and third crops were cocoa and tobacco, which grew abundantly on the river banks. Finally, sugar would bring even more commercial benefits because it was found all along the river.[42]

Leaving aside his initial impulse at generalization, however, Acuña speaks later on about the potential of specific sites. Close to where the Aguas (or Omaguas) live, he writes, is a large plateau of cold climate where wheat could be cultivated.[43] Likewise, the lands of the Curuzirari, he writes, "are quite elevated, with beautiful prairies, and grass for cattle, forests not excessively enclosed, abundant lakes and promising many and good comforts for those who populated it."[44] The richest land was found on the banks of the Río Negro, he states, "the largest and most beautiful" of the tributaries to the Amazon, with raised fields for the cultivation of a wide variety of crops, prairies for the raising of cattle, abundant game and fish.[45] Gold was found in Yquiari, at only a three-day walk from the Yurupazi River.[46]

The interplay between the general and the specific is also found in Acuña's description of the different peoples that inhabited the Amazon Basin. On the first pages of his account, the author speaks about idolatry, which he considers was practiced without significant variation by different ethnic groups. He writes, for example, that "the rites of these gentiles are mostly the same; they worship idols, which they manufacture with their hands, attributing to some power over the water . . . others are chosen as lords of sowing fields, and others as patrons of their battles."[47] At the same time, Acuña shows his concern for understanding cultural difference. In a gesture that could be portrayed as early ethnographic practice, he attempts to explain local culture through comparison with European and Christian practices. Thus, if he describes shamans as sorcerers that, enslaved by superstition, spoke to the devil, he also compares their bones, revered by the faithful after their death, to the relics of Christian saints. He states that "with some kind of veneration, as if they were the relics of saints, they collect the bones of sorcerers that die, which they hang from mid-air, in the same hammocks where they slept when they were alive." He adds that sorcerers are "their masters, their preachers, their advisors, and their guides."[48]

Acuña's preoccupation with specificity is found in his description of the different peoples from the Amazon. In contrast to Carvajal, in fact, from the very beginning he recognizes the existence of a number of nations "of which I can certify, naming them by their names, and pointing to their places, some because I have seen them, others from information of all of the Natives that have been in them, they are more than one hundred and fifty, all speaking different tongues."[49]

At times, he focuses on the material culture of different nations as indicative of difference. With regard to the Caripunás and the Zurinas, for example, the author praises the artistry with which they manufacture different wooden objects. He describes the unique craftsmanship of benches carved in the shape of different animals, so that "neither comfort nor ingenuity could have imagined them better."[50] He also admires the exquisiteness of their spears, and, most of all, of a small idol crafted with so much naturalism that, he argues, "many of our sculptors could learn [from these artists]."[51]

More often, the author directs the reader's attention to the Natives' bodies. His detailed descriptions, while accentuating the exoticism and barbarism of indigenous peoples, also unveil his concern in representing diversity. Bodies artificially deformed, ornamented with paint, jewelry, and clothing, are portrayed as cultural objects, markers of ethnic differentiation. It is the physical and markedly visual distinction between nations that endows Acuña's itinerary along the Amazon with a sense of difference.

Acuña arrives first to the nation of the Encabellados, where some of the Portuguese soldiers awaited the return of Texeira and his army. He states that the first explorers had thus named this nation because both its men and women wore long hair, even below the knees.[52] However scant this reference is, the author's descriptions soon become more detailed and vivid, his painterly language fixing the reader's imagination on the portrayed bodies.

Next on the route, the explorers arrived in the province of the Omaguas, which Acuña argues are the "people with greater reason and better government along the river."[53] His remark had to do, partly, with the Omaguas' use of clothing, indicative of *policía*, or civility. The women manufactured cotton fabrics that were traded for other goods with neighboring nations. The author praises the beauty of these textiles, "not only woven with different colors, but painted with them, so subtly that one cannot be distinguished from the other."[54] He also marvels at the artificial deformation of their heads. "They all have flattened heads," he says, "which causes ugliness in men, although women can better hide this with their abundant hair." Interested in the art of skull deformation, he writes that "since infants are born, they are placed in a press, holding them from the forehead with a small wooden tablet, which serving as cradle receives all the body of the newborn, who lying on it on the back and tightened with the other, is left with the brain and the forehead as flat as the palm of the hand." He concludes by saying that deformed skulls looked more "like an ill-formed bishop's miter than the head of a person."[55]

In contrast to the Omaguas, the banks of the Río del Oro were populated by savages who went about naked. Their only attire was the adornment of ears and noses, "most of them with holes, deforming so much the ears that . . . the fist can fit in the hole that they have in the lower part, from where earrings usually hang, and which they normally fill with a mallet of tightened leaves, that they use for great adornment."[56]

Acuña's interest in local specificity follows the innovative preoccupations of the *Relaciones geográficas de Indias*, questionnaires sent to officers throughout the Spanish Empire in the 1570s and 1580s, in order to collect detailed information regarding the topography and population of all the territories belonging to the crown. The questions addressed a varied number of issues of interest to the royal administration, such as population and demography, government, history, and natural history, as well as subjects of economic concern. As noted by Barbara Mundy, the use of the *Relaciones geográficas* was not an isolated occurrence, but was closely tied to Philip II's preoccupation with efficient territorial administration and, in connection to this, to his role as patron of geographical projects, particularly with regard to mapping.[57] According to Mundy, the project eventually failed because of a lack of interest on the part of the Spanish American bureaucracy in complying with requests regarding geographical representation. With regard to Mexico, which is the region of her concern, she argues that officers did not value maps for their accuracy in geographic representation. Images were associated with Native manuscripts and writing, and were therefore considered inferior to texts.

Notwithstanding this apparent failure, particularly with regard to cartography, Mundy does acknowledge the innovative character of the *Relaciones geográficas*, which, in my own view, prepared the way for a new way of conceiving and defining space. As Mundy notes, some questions demanded their informants to recognize specificity, and difference, I may add, by requesting chorographic description and portrayal. Other questions, in turn, addressed the issue of distance between different places (in leagues), which led to imagining the imperial territory as lived space. In recognizing diversity and heterogeneity, the questionnaire used both chorography and geography as instruments of the imperial bureaucracy. More important, the *Relaciones geográficas* admitted the strong connection between scientific knowledge and efficient administrative control.

As in the *Relaciones geográficas*, Acuña's interest in human and natural scientific description was not an innocent gesture. Rather, geographical knowledge was soon revealed as the foundation for imperial domination over the Amazon Basin. Although Acuña recognizes previous expeditions along the Amazon, he is also quick to invalidate them because they failed to secure imperial power over the newly discovered lands. In fact, he repeatedly portrays the Amazon Basin as a new world, still waiting to be discovered.[58] With respect to Francisco de Orellana's trip, described by Gaspar de Carvajal, he states that the expedition had failed to follow the course of the river from beginning to end, reaching not the Amazon mouth but the coast of Caracas instead, thus frustrating the taking of possession of territories that rightfully belonged to the Spanish Crown. In a similar way, Lope de Aguirre's trip, completed after he had murdered Pedro de Orsúa, lacked legitimacy because, first, the expedition had unwittingly arrived at a site across from the island of Trinidad (instead of at the main river mouth) and, second, because Aguirre himself did not have the moral character needed to duly fulfill a service for the Spanish king.[59] Although Acuña describes the trip made by two Franciscan friars accompanied by Spanish soldiers as the fulfillment of a divine prophecy, he also argues that the two friars had not been successful in collecting useful information about the region. Thus, he writes, reports procured by members of this expedition revealed that their sole preoccupation was to "escape every day from the hands of death" and that all that they could say once they had reached San Luis de Marañón was that they came from Peru and that they had seen "many Indians" along the way.[60] In contrast to the failure of previous expeditions, Acuña's trip along the Amazon River had a clear purpose from the beginning, which was to take "sufficient information, and as clear as possible, of the nations that live in it, of the rivers that join it, and of everything else that is needed by the Royal Council of the Indies in order to have complete knowledge of this enterprise."[61]

Just as the anonymous author of the 1639 *Relación* had done, Acuña also shows his concern with regard to the frailty of the imperial frontier. He, too, is interested in identifying sites for the construction of military fortresses that could prevent the enemy from advancing into "this new world," as in the case of the Río Negro, one of the tributaries of the Amazon.[62] As I will discuss, Acuña, too, demands the presence of Spanish control in the region in order to assure protection of the Amazon Basin from the multiple enemies that threatened its territorial integrity.

The unification of the Spanish and Portuguese Crowns in 1580 had granted Philip II dominion over all Portuguese territories. In the long run, however, this would bring negative consequences for the Spanish Empire. By 1620, for example, Iberian authorities had grown concerned with regard to illicit activities of the Portuguese in the Amazon Basin, such as smuggling, and particularly the illegal traffic of silver from the Potosí mines to the Atlantic. Another source of concern was the defenselessness of the Brazilian coast, especially after the attack of Salvador de Bahia in 1624 by Dutch corsairs.[63] After the separation of the two crowns in 1640, Portuguese expansionism would become the main threat to Spanish dominion in the Amazon. Acuña's account is the product of this anxiety, an apprehension that emerges fully blown in an accompanying report written precisely in 1640 and addressed to the Council of the Indies.

In his report, Acuña argues that effective control of the Amazon could weaken the threat of corsairs and impede the traffic of metals from Peru to the Atlantic. He also foresees the future dangers for Spain posed by Portuguese colonizers from Brazil. Traveling from Quito to Marañón, Texeira had taken possession in the name of the Portuguese Crown of the territories south of a milestone that he had placed somewhere along the Amazon, the Cuchivara River according to some, a gesture that acquired new significance after 1640.[64] In this respect, the Jesuit author writes that "if the Portuguese who are in the mouth of the river (of whom anything can be presumed, because of their weak Christianity, and even less, loyalty) would ever want, with the help of some of the bellicose nations that they have subjected, penetrate up through [the river] and arrive at populated centers of Peru or New Grenade, although it is certain that in some places they will encounter resistance, in many others there will be very little, because they will reach towns lacking in inhabitants, and in the end it is these vassals who are disloyal to Your Majesty that will set foot on those lands."[65]

Acuña views the work of Jesuit missionaries from Quito both as apostles of the Christian faith and as agents of penetration for the Spanish Empire. He states that even though Spanish dominion over the Amazon Basin found legitimization on the principle of dynastic legacy, the ruler was also responsible for effectively exercising his authority over these lands. The establishment of Jesuit missions, he writes, would be instrumental in guaranteeing Spanish control over this vast territory. Only then would the Spanish monarch be able to enjoy what he had rightfully inherited from Charles V.[66]

Concluding Remarks: Beyond Cristóbal de Acuña

Acuña's interest in scientific geography was continued in the latter decades of the seventeenth century and well into the eighteenth century by fellow members of the Jesuit Order. Most notable among them was Samuel Fritz, a Bohemian who, after arriving in Quito in 1684, had spent most of his life as a missionary in the upper Amazon. Fritz's knowledge of cartography is evidenced in his map of the Amazon, drawn on ink in 1691, and engraved by Juan de Narváez in 1707 (see Figure 21).[67] The map shows the location of

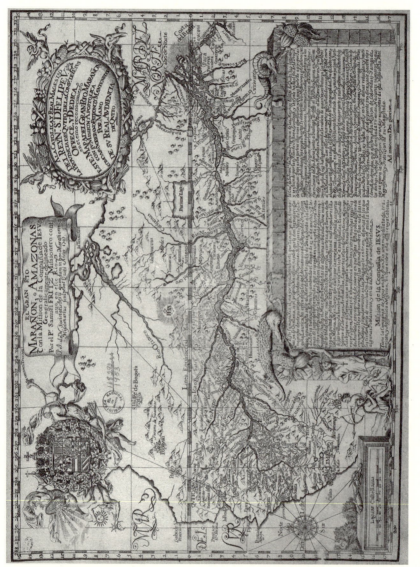

Figure 21. Samuel Fritz, *El Gran Río Marañón o Amazonas con las misiones de la Compañía de Jesús*, 1707, Fundação Biblioteca Nacional, Rio de Janeiro, Brazil.

important cities and towns, of Jesuit missions, and of different indigenous ethnic groups. Using a grid of longitude and latitude, Fritz is also interested in specifying the relative distances between sites, using leagues as units of measurement.

As with Cristóbal de Acuña, Fritz's preoccupation with scientific representation was moved by his concern with protecting Spanish territories in the Amazon Basin from Portuguese expansionism, while safeguarding, at the same time, the work performed by Jesuit missionaries from Quito. Indeed, in his diaries he insists on the need to define the borders that separated the Spanish and Portuguese Empires in South America. During his stay in Lima, where he had traveled in order to gain the viceroy's support for the Jesuit missions in the Amazon, he wrote a short historical essay regarding the demarcation lines between Portuguese and Spanish territories in the Amazon Basin.[68] The printed version of the map, on the other hand, shows the sites where Jesuit missionaries had been martyred, a gesture that symbolically claimed the Amazon for his order.

In 1740, a second scientific map of the region was produced by Juan Magnin, a Swiss Jesuit from the college in Quito (see Figure 22). In contrast to Fritz's attention to detail, Magnin's depiction of the Amazon Basin provides scant information regarding specific places, except for labels that identify different locations and peoples. This map, however, is accompanied by an extensive and detailed written account that has to be consulted concurrently.[69] As in Acuña's text, Magnin recognizes some general traits in different nations, such as painting their faces, teeth, feet, and hands. However, he also admits that "in particular, each one is different in costumes, kinds, offices, and maintenance."[70] It is through ethnographic description, and particularly through his attention to the body as cultural object and marker of difference that the reader can recognize the specificity of nations marked on the map:

The Yameos insert in their earlobes a round piece of wood that sometimes has four fingers of diameter and more than one of thickness. The flesh then grows in such an extraordinary way that when removing this plug they raise the lower part of the ear to hang it from the top. . . .

Placing another round stick, as half a coin, on the top lip is typical of the Yurimaguas, who also used to gash their ears . . . . The Iquitos or Coronados shave the top of their heads, deform their skulls, and paint them red.[71]

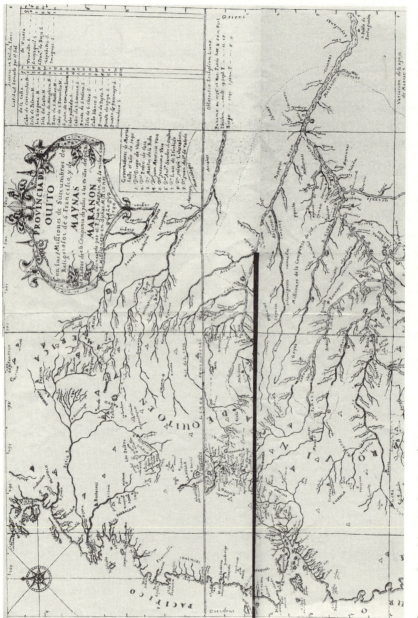

Figure 22. Juan Magnin, *Provincia de Quito con sus misiones de Sucumbíos de Religiosos de San Francisco y de Maynas de Padres de la Compañía de Jesús a orillas del gran río Marañón*, 1740, Biblioteca Ecuatoriana Aurelio Espinosa Pólit, Quito, Ecuador.

Inscriptions on the margins of the map identify salient locations in the region, both on the coast and in the highlands. A list of the governors of Maynas, where the Jesuits had their missions, is also presented. On the bottom left, a cartouche provides the key for different signs marked on the map: cities, villages, towns, missions, martyrs of missions (*muertes de misiones*), and roads. More important, as noted in the title of the map, Magnin is also concerned with the definition of boundaries within the Amazon Basin between Jesuit missions in Maynas, and Franciscan missions in Sucumbíos. The religious orders appear as colonizers of the Amazon, true agents of imperial expansionism.

Jesuit missionaries have often been praised for their interest in scientific knowledge, and particularly for their concern in understanding the culture of the peoples they were attempting to convert to Christianity. Jesuit accounts from the Amazon indeed suggest preoccupations similar to those of modern ethnographers. These narratives, however, also hint at less than innocent worries. In the Amazon Basin, understanding difference was not just a tool in the work of evangelization, but also an instrument for securing imperial dominion.

PART IV

Legacies

CHAPTER 9

"Reader . . . Behold One Raised by God"

Religious Transformations in Cotton Mather's
*Pietas in Patriam: The Life of His Excellency
Sir William Phips, Knt.*

TERESA A. TOULOUSE

Sir William Phips was a Maine-born ship's carpenter, treasure seeker, and entrepreneur, who discovered a vast cache of sunken Spanish silver off the coast of Hispaniola in 1687. He was knighted by King James II, adulated in London and Boston, and later, by dint of his transatlantic fame and his military exploits in Canada, nominated by prominent New English minister Increase Mather as the first royal governor under a much-contested royal charter negotiated by Mather with William and Mary in the wake of England's "Glorious Revolution" of 1688. As governor of Massachusetts from 1692 to 1695, Phips became embroiled in the Salem witchcraft trials, massive colonial debt accrued from his own 1690 failure to take Quebec, Indian wars, and unrelenting squabbling over the terms of the new charter, in which the governor and council were appointed, rather than elected. Entering into embarrassing quarrels with political opposition in New England as well as with British customs officials (one of whom he publicly caned), Phips was called to London to defend himself, and unexpectedly died there in 1695, to the great consternation of many in the New English religious hierarchy, who had supported him. Cotton Mather, Increase Mather's son, himself an important third-generation New English minister, wrote a defensive biography of the embattled governor, which was published in London in 1697 and then incorporated into his massive history of New England, the *Magnalia Christi Americana* of 1702.[1]

Given its focus on changes in governance in New England, Cotton Mather's *Pietas in Patriam: The Life of His Excellency Sir William Phips, Knt.*, has often been interpreted in its local and in its international dimensions as broadly expressing the process of the subordination of religious beliefs to secular beliefs that has traditionally been understood as "secularization." In the case of Phips, as in many others, the process has often been demonstrated in the ways religious beliefs become separated from understandings of governance.[2]

Political historians, for example, have used the Phips biography to show what they read as not only Phips's, but also Increase and Cotton Mather's, failed understanding of leadership after 1688, and to chart what T. H. Breen called the evolution in New England from a focus on piety in political life to a focus on property. Such an evolution is not distinct to New England, of course, but parallels broader changes in the traditional relations of religion to politics occurring in England and other English colonies in the aftermath of the Glorious Revolution.[3]

Many literary scholars have read the biography's rhetorical attempts under the new charter to link New English understandings of religious conversion to patriotic service, *pietas in patriam*, as paradoxically resulting in a similar subsuming and erasure of features of New English religious belief in the rhetoric of public service. Mather's treatment of Salem witchcraft, in which Phips early intervened, has also been used to indicate, more generally, the shift from a religious to a secular social order in provincial New England, as older Puritan beliefs in a community of visible saints become replaced by a recognition that a civil society in which religious toleration is politically required must be composed of citizens whose external behaviors manifest not shared religious beliefs, but shared acquiescence to agreed-upon laws.

While some critics, interested in the text's discussion of witchcraft, have discussed the ways in which Cotton Mather's images and rhetoric inescapably reveal his own inability to ground a Phips separate from the "spectrality" of writing itself, others offer historical reasons for why this might be the case. Features of the biography's descriptions of an "invisible world" have been recently read in their analogy to colonial ambivalence about engagement in a worldwide commercial system dependent on the spectral and invisible reality of credit. In each instance, whether *Pietas in Patriam* reveals a movement toward secularization, or, as in the latter instance, expresses a variant of secularization *avant la lettre*, literary critics share with historians the assumption that the life of Phips expresses a larger secularization process in which religious modes of understanding become separated from, erased, or subsumed into new secular political structures.[4]

The following reading of Mather's biography challenges assumptions about the text's relation to and expression of the secularization process so described. Drawing on the work of sociologist Bruno Latour, it suggests that the interplay of two larger rhetorical patterns in the text, the rhetoric of providence and the rhetoric of contract, demonstrates how this process should be read as incomplete in Cotton Mather's text. It further suggests how, by virtue of the biography's developing association of providential rhetoric with a third rhetoric of moral projecting, *Pietas in Patriam* points toward an alternative shaping of the secularization process for New England. Earnestly attempting to address the change in colonial politics embodied in the new royal charter and mandated by the new English imperial order abroad, Cotton Mather variously depicts and defends such political change in its relation to traditional colonial religious beliefs for English and New English audiences alike. In the twists and turns of his different rhetorics, Mather reveals an understanding of social change that is clearly affected by a secularizing process, but does not so much capitulate to this process as respond to it, become shaped by it, and in turn attempts to shape a New English interpretation of social change. In Mather's text, in short, colonial religious beliefs are not so much relinquished, or subsumed into transatlantic secularism through a process of secularization, but rather such beliefs are themselves transformed.

Commentators in a wide variety of fields have recently begun to suggest that a focus on the complex ways in which the Western secularization process is addressed globally by different colonial actors at different historical moments will perhaps prove more significant in the diverse responses and effects so located, than a focus on sweeping causes or ends of the process itself.[5] It is with the goal of tracing some of the different ways that understandings of social change become mediated in an important Anglo-colonial minister's biography of the first provincial New English governor that these preliminary comments are directed.

Rhetoric as Social Reassembling

Features of the thinking of sociologist Bruno Latour are useful for reconsidering the ways Mather's *Pietas in Patriam* describes the relation of religion to politics at the end of the seventeenth century in New England. Latour implicitly addresses assumptions about social change unexamined in certain general definitions of the secularization process, and also offers a different method of conceiving and tracing social change in its relation to secularization.

Latour has famously contended that certain sociologists, assuming a monolithic entity called "the social" that is affected as a whole by external "causes," have failed to understand the ways in which the social should instead be reconceived as an ongoing process of "assemblage," and "reassemblage" in which various disciplinary modes of understanding social relations come provisionally together. For Latour, the social is not a "thing" but a continually transforming process. Change happens within social assemblages not because of any single external cause, but because of continuously shifting relationships among different disciplinary modes of organizing social relations.[6]

While Latour's interests involve tracing the associations among different disciplinary practices, whether legal, scientific, religious, and so forth, the analysis here is more narrowly, yet analogously, concerned with examining the associations, dissociations, and reassociations of three rhetorics used within Cotton Mather's *Pietas in Patriam*. Still, Latour's broad conception of "the social" as a moving network of associations that is perpetually and minutely changing as disciplinary relations alter offers a compelling way of reconsidering Mather's rhetorical practices in their relation to a secularization process that Mather attempts to rewrite less as religious subordination than as religious transformation.

Balancing the Rhetorics of Providence and Contract

Pietas in Patriam is a narrative composed of twenty-one sections of varying length, each dealing with a major event in the life of Sir William Phips and the Massachusetts colony. As Stephen Carl Arch has usefully suggested, the narrative can be read as falling into three broader parts, with Sections 1 to 7 dealing with the rise of Phips, Sections 8 to 14 dealing with his "progress," and Sections 15 to 21 dealing with his failure.[7] In the interest of both space and focus, the ten sections examined in the following comments (Sections 6, 8, 9, 10, 11, 14, 15, 16, 18, 19) will be used to show how the biography's narrative events are in fact used by Cotton Mather to create a series of associations, dissociations, or reassociations among the three larger rhetorical patterns he employs throughout the text. While the text as narrative thus moves forward in time, it simultaneously figures a series of implicit and sometimes explicit rhetorical exchanges both within and between its numerically demarcated sections.

Arguably, the most famous event in the life of William Phips is his 1687 discovery of a fortune in sunken Spanish silver off the coast of Hispaniola. In *Pietas in Patriam*, Cotton Mather's description of the discovery is presented in Section 6. As would be apparent to New English readers, Mather's account makes general use of the language and the structure of the New English Puritan conversion narrative, the pattern whereby believers made public to ministers and fellow congregants the workings of God in their internal and external lives that led them to profess their humble belief that God had chosen them as one of his "visible" elect.[8] Even though, at this early point in the biography, Captain William Phips is not, in fact, converted, details of his men's and his own behavior are depicted by Cotton Mather in their relation to a providentially ordained conversionary design that Phips himself has yet to recognize.

As Mather tells it, for example, Phips's men's "despondence for their ill successes" in locating the wreck, is "at once" turned into "assurances," as a lone diver, seemingly by chance, spots the guns marking the location of the sunken ship. This pattern of despondence followed by assurance, a move characteristic of conversion narratives, continues as Phips's crew hide knowledge of the discovery from their captain. His crew relents when "hearing him still express his resolution to wait still patiently upon the providence of God under these disappointments," they reveal to Phips a "sow" of silver they have hidden under a table. Employing the language of a repentant sinner who first feels the workings of grace, Mather describes how Phips "cried out with some agony, Why! What is this? Whence came this?" Assured by his men of their find, Phips famously exclaims, "Thanks be to God! We are made."[9]

That Mather presents Phips's most famous economic exploit in these terms clearly serves rhetorically to enmesh the captain's financial success in a wider New English discourse of providence, that, as many scholars have pointed out, is both personal and communal in a very particular way. Phips alone is not successful; as he is "made," so are his men. The description of his victory in these specific terms marks the sea-going and entrepreneurial Phips as grounded in New England, literally by his Maine birth, and culturally, through the rhetoric of providence, even as Phips is depicted as not yet understanding how providence is working within him.

At the same time, however, the story of the rich discovery as Mather narrates it is also shot through with a rhetoric other than the overtly providential. No sooner has the silver been loaded then Phips's once-playful crew threatens to mutiny. Mather has presented this possibility several pages earlier, as Phips is shown forcefully warding off not only his rebelling men from an earlier voyage, but also his own possible temptation to join them and turn pirate. The rebuffed mutineers claim "they never had any thing against him, except only his unwillingness to go away with the King's ship upon the South-sea design" (170). In this second, more famous instance, rather than meeting the threat of mutiny with violence, Mather shows Phips taking two related steps: first, he makes religious vows to "serve" God and his "people," most particularly those in New England if he makes it to London safely with the treasure, and secondly, he makes promises to his men to boost their shares in the voyage out of his own share if his English investors refuse to do so. While his vows to God invoke the New English religious practice of making individual and group covenants, his promises to his men suggest Phips's equal awareness that such covenanting must be accompanied by his making of practical contracts.

Mather's narrating of Phips's honorable discharging of his financial promises to his crew upon his arrival in England is juxtaposed with a description of English detractors, largely envious courtiers, who attempt to argue that the captain has defrauded his English investors and the king of their contractually agreed-upon portion. As Mather tells it, the king himself, knowing of Phips's "character as an honest man," dispels such slander by claiming that "he should not want his countenance." Accordingly, James II unexpectedly grants William Phips a knighthood. Underscoring the providential nature of the king's act, Mather concludes the entire section by exclaiming, "Reader, . . . behold one raised by God" (174).

This scene thus makes use of two rhetorical patterns to depict Phips's financial success, the one providential, the other contractual, both of which become reframed within the providential raising of Phips at the end of the section. Phips is particularly distinguished here not only by his relation to New England, but also by his "honest" relation to England. Scholars who have also remarked on Mather's conversionary rhetoric have neglected the use of the contractual in his account of the discovery and its aftermath, thus missing out on Mather's rhetorical efforts, extending through the body of his text, to demonstrate to a wide range of readers the ways in which the peripatetic Phips associates English as well as New English religious, political, and economic interests within a larger providential frame.

That such a balance is Mather's rhetorical aim at this point in *Pietas in Patriam* is clearly shown in Section 8 in which he juxtaposes Captain Phips's behavior to that of Sir Edmond Andros, the last royally appointed English-born governor under the Dominion of New England.[10] When William Phips is threatened with mutiny, his leadership skills have been shown to be such that he can avert it whether through measured force or through renegotiating contract. Mather presents Andros, in contrast, as a bad leader on several fronts. "Giving out that the [first] charter's being lost," Andros and his Anglo-Catholic, English-born, French-sympathizing minions abrogate the legal, political, and property rights of the New English "people." Mather describes them as "furious wolves under the names of shepherds" (177). Detailing their trampling on colonials' shared English rights in terms drawn from his own earlier writing on the subject, and repeating rumors about their compliance with French Catholic aims to invade New England, Mather presents their political downfall not as resulting from the acts of mutinous colonials, but like the "Glorious Revolution" that precedes their removal, from a justified revolution against Stuart political and implicitly, religious, despotism.[11] Andros's inability to balance colonial and English imperial interests would seem to show to Mather's English as well as New English readers not only the urgent need to negotiate a new political contract, a new Massachusetts charter, but also the concomitant need for a leader who can address *both* colonial and royal interests.

Whereas the rhetoric of patents, contracts, and charters, whether absent, broken, or in dangerous need of political renewal, pervades the section on Andros, providential rhetoric almost immediately informs the section following it, Section 9, in which Mather specifically describes Sir William Phips as undergoing a now conscious conversion to New England Congregationalism. The conversion narrative, ostensibly written by Phips himself, is introduced by Mather's careful explanation of the practices of a New English "church-state" for English readers:

It has been the custom, in the churches of New-England, still to expect such persons as they admitted unto constant communion

with them, that they do not only publickly and solemnly declare
their consent unto the "Covenant of grace," and particularly to
those duties of it, wherein a particular church-state is more immediately concerned, but also first relate unto the pastors, and by
them unto the brethren, the special impressions which the grace of
God has made upon their souls in bringing them to this consent.
(180–81)

Phips's narrative, accordingly, following the now explicit pattern of the
conversion narrative, details the moment when he first became sensible of his
"miserable condition" as a sinner after hearing Increase Mather preach about
the religious duties of civil magistrates; how he put off pursuing his soul's
welfare, and how he met with providences "both merciful and afflictive" that
moved him to "acknowledge God in all my ways." Having perceived God's
gracious presence in saving his life and "smiling" on his affairs, Phips is described as repeating vows very similar to those he had earlier made on his
treasure ship: "That I would set my self to serve his people and churches here
unto the utmost capacity." While such a rhetoric indicates Mather's important
attempts, as many critics have suggested, to link Phips's grace experience to
his *pietas in patriam*, his religiously inflected patriotism toward New England,
it should also be more specifically read in its relation to the failed political and
economic contractualism represented in the case of Andros that just precedes
it. Andros's failures as leader point the route to Phips's political rise: his adherence to God's plan in its relation to earthly contractual obligations.

In the section following his conversion, Section 10, Mather presents a
Phips who is as good as his converted word. Balancing the interests of "King
William and Queen Mary" with those of New England, and even quoting
Paradise Lost to cement shared political and religious aims vis-à-vis the Indians, Mather describes how William Phips offers "his own person and estate
for the service of the publick" against the French and "Frenchified pagans"
attacking New England's eastern borders (183). Chosen captain of an expedition to Canada, Phips takes possession of Port Royal "for the English Crown,"
and also returns home as a freshly elected *New* English magistrate. Notably,
there is not a hint of mutiny against his authority rumored in this section.
Phips is rhetorically presented as effortlessly interweaving a commitment to
New England, already suggested in his conversion narrative and "election" to
New English government, and a commitment to the legitimacy of English
imperial political authority in colonial affairs.

From this point on, *Pietas in Patriam* moves to address Sir William Phips's more specific political role in the shift from an older to a newer Massachusetts charter. In Section 14, while Mather finally presents Phips as the figure in whom New English providentialism and English contractualism can meet, Mather's rhetorical capacity to associate providential and contractual rhetorics in the same ways become increasingly strained.

Contractual rhetoric of the political sort pervades the largest part of Section 14, as, moving readers' attention away from Phips in New England, Mather shifts to events in London to assert his father, Increase Mather's, loyalty both to the first New England charter and to the postrevolutionary sovereigns. Having argued for the first charter's restoration with the now fallen James II, Increase Mather is shown making the same pleas to William and Mary. Carefully supporting the legitimacy of the English king's right to negotiate such matters, no matter who holds the throne, Increase Mather "still prayed for no less a favour to New-England, than the full restoration of their charter-privileges" (197).

No sooner have his father's "Sisyphean labours" on behalf of the colony's traditional political organization been described, however, than Cotton Mather turns to the reasons why the first charter cannot and should not be restored to Massachusetts. Instead of focusing on the interrelation of the old charter and New English church organization, an interrelation in which only converted freemen elected their own governor and deputies, Cotton details specific structural problems with the first charter. He notes, for example, how the old charter lacks a house of deputies or an assembly of representatives who can legitimately levy taxes or form admiralty courts to manage trade relations (200). Specifically addressing propertied interests, Cotton also highlights the old charter's lack of status in legitimating land claims not only in Massachusetts, but in Maine and New Hampshire as well.

This rhetorical move to argue for new and apparently more secular ways to legitimate colonial governance through a different political structure seems straightforward initially. But Mather himself intermittently complicates it by qualifying the rhetoric he uses to argue for the new charter's value. At one point he notes, for example, "why should all this good be refused or despised because of somewhat not so good attending it?" (201). At another he admits that "Mr. Mather brought with him a charter . . . in divers points lacking what both he and they had wished for" (202). At moments like these, Mather addresses the much-disputed change in the status of New English freemen, particularly their former right, as converted church members, to participate in the election of their own governor. The traditional rhetoric of providence in its specific relation to the structure of Massachusetts governance is invoked in these instances by its absence.[12]

It is only at this fraught moment in the section that Cotton Mather rhetorically returns to London to usher in Sir William Phips, who has yet again crossed the Atlantic to be of service to New England in England: "Sir William Phips who had made so many addresses for the restoration of the old charter, under which he had seen his country many years flourishing, will be excused by all the world from any thing of a fault, in a most unexpected passage of his life, which is now to be related" (201). In his own capacity as a visible New English "saint," manifesting his justification through his sanctified behavior— here, the public service of Massachusetts—Phips is clearly described as representing crucial religious features of the old charter. As Increase Mather's nominee for the appointed governorship under the new charter, Phips is depicted as containing in his own person features of New England's just past political structure, in which personal experience of God's providential hand in one's own life fitted one, indeed sanctified one, for public political office. At the same time, neither Mather denies that Sir William Phips also represents the new royal charter. He is not an elected governor. As the shakily legitimated English king's own appointee in the terms of a new political contract, Phips must politically support English imperial interests in colonial affairs. At this point, it seems clear how the narrative of Phips's life has been rhetorically structured by Cotton Mather all along to demonstrate to his varying readers William Phips's capacity for balancing these interests.[13]

Underscoring Phips's capacity to engage New English and English aims within a changed political structure, Mather makes convoluted claims like the following: "I do not know a person in the world that would have been proposed more acceptable of the body of the people throughout New England, and on that score more likely and able to serve the King's interests among the people there, under the changes in some things unacceptable, now brought upon them" (201–2). In the next section (15), he specifically highlights why Governor Phips is so successful. He "studied nothing more than to observe such a temper in all things as to extinguish what others have gone to distinguish—even the pernicious notion of a separate interest" (203). As he had done earlier in his discussion of Phips's "raising" to a knighthood, so here Mather turns to an image drawn from the rhetoric of providence to express how the new governor rises above divergent political interests: "But

New England had now, besides the guardian-angel who more invisibly intended its welfare, a governour that became wonderfully agreeable thereunto, by his own imitation of such a guardian-angel" (204). Once a surprised recipient of the favors of divine providence, Governor William Phips here is revealed as its overarching agent to New England as a whole.[14]

The image of Phips imitating New England's "guardian-angel" works two ways. If it points back to the ways in which his loyal participation in charter making has enacted God's providential intentions, it also pivots forward to his role as a good "angel" in the witchcraft controversy, Mather's extended description of which immediately follows this section.

Splitting the Rhetorics of Providence and Contract

Given Cotton Mather's admission of "divers things" lacking in the "patent" supported by him and his father, the witchcraft episode (Section 16) presented a rich rhetorical opportunity for him to demonstrate the allegiance of the new Phips government to a New England providentialism no longer specifically formalized in the new royal charter's structure. In viscerally staging the real drama at stake in the colony as religious in nature, a focus on dissensions among divergent political interests could at once be diverted and contained in a shared cultural frame. Accordingly, the section begins with a dramatic depiction of a demonic enemy who pinches, pricks, poisons, burns, binds, drops, and bribes its colonial victims and otherwise manifests the palpable presence of the spiritual world in the world of men.[15]

As the section moves on to discuss the phenomenon of spectral evidence, in which the evidence of witchcraft provided by tormenting demons is replaced by the tormenting "specters" of living people, however, the providential clarity and meanings of the witch outbreak's attempt to mutinously wrest power from legitimate religious authority become drawn into doubt. The sight of specters, visible only to the afflicted, is used to accuse an increasing number of people, including, significantly, Mrs. Phips and Cotton Mather. This turn of events leads, in Cotton Mather's specific description of it in *Pietas in Patriam*, to a debate among "wise men" over different views of divine providence itself in which Mather moves from his own earlier claims about the manifest clarity of divine intentions, especially in their relation to the new royal charter, to a quite different description of providence in its relation to specific political structures.

On the one hand, as Mather stages it, stand those who believe God's providence would not allow the devil to take the shape of innocent people. In this view, God's providential intentions are viewed as directly available to human understanding. The seeing of "specters" by afflicted victims truly proves that those whom the specters represent are indeed witches and, in the view of this group, accordingly calls for explicit government action—whether courts, condemnation, or the possible execution of those so accused in order to defend and maintain good social order. Admits Mather, "it is while this opinion was yet prevailing in the minds of the judges and juries" that "diverse were condemned" solely on the basis of "spectral exhibitions" (209).

While Mather expresses some sympathy for this position, noting that specters do seem to disappear after the confessions of those accused of possessing them, he also offers another view of providence, one he depicts as drawn largely from his father's analysis. This view disputes the assumption that divine intention necessarily operates in a way immediately available or clear to human understanding or human judgment. This group argues, for example, that "spectral evidence," while sometimes pointing to true witches, could also be used by Satan to condemn the innocent. What is the meaning, these "wise men" ask, of the fact that so many people of good reputation are being accused through the use of such evidence? This group contends that specters could be a manifestation of the devil's wiles, sometimes true, sometimes false, rather than signs of providential clarity. They warn that if "spectral evidence" is demonstrated to be false and innocent people are hung or punished as a result of it, the community as a whole could lose its faith in providence altogether! Finally, and relatedly, in the light of this text's concern with governance, they contend that the social effects of accepting spectral evidence, "if suffered to be common, could subvert government and disband and ruin humane society" (210). Offering a very different reading of God's role in this phenomenon, this group suggests that "God sometimes may suffer such things to evene, that we may know thereby how much we are beholden to him for that restraint which he lays upon the infernal spirits, who would else reduce the world unto a chaos" (210).

In this understanding of providential intention, God's specific purposes are presented as not always available to human actors with any immediacy. What is evident is rather his sovereignty in at once allowing and restraining "infernal spirits" whose mutinous acts of competition with His own authority and power, He alone ultimately confutes and transcends. Providence, in this depiction of it, does not conform to expectations by easily resolving human confusions, but by instead using confusion itself to exhibit how humans in whatever form of government they find themselves are still beholden to God, not to their own efforts, to restrain the devil from breaking down the human social order. In this view of the providential design, solving questions of human guilt or innocence vis-à-vis a specifically religious phenomenon like spectral evidence in merely human terms is moot. Most strikingly, in this instance, the institution of government, while certainly still dependent on God's providence to sustain or work through it, is not presented as chosen by God as the explicit *formal* expression of a divine plan.

Cotton Mather's rendering of the sovereignty of providence as manifested in both God's allowance of the devil's lies in the world of human affairs and His restraint on such lies, highlights human dependence on God's power over *all* forms of government. Later ranging from New England to episodes in Sweden and in England itself to show how similar and worldwide confusions have been increasingly sewn by the devil, he argues that, in each instance, it is God, not human leaders, who ultimately keeps "humane society" from collapse. God's providence as such remains—but human governance, in this instance, seems reduced by Cotton Mather to far more contingent ways of organizing social relations.

William Phips, long absent from Mather's discussion in this section, enters as the "machin of heaven" in the Salem crisis in that he is directly described as acknowledging the separation of features of God's wider providential intentions from merely human structures. Even though the real Phips called the initial court of Oyer and Terminer into being in terms of one understanding of providence in its relation to governance, the Phips of *Pietas in Patriam* is praised for his heroic role in abolishing the second court because of its manifest inability to locate a cause for the spectral confusions seizing the accused, their accusers, and the people as a whole. Rather than solving the question of innocence or guilt in this arena, Mather argues that Phips's task, as he elsewhere demonstrates in his narrative, is to preserve the greater well-being of the entire community as such.

This notion of preservation is expressed in two classical images of leadership. As the people's captain, Phips, like Odysseus sailing away from the illusions of Circe's isle, steers the vessel of New England out of the *mare mortuum* of witchcraft. As the people's heroic defender, Phips, like Alexander the Great, cuts the "knot of witchcraft," rather than attempting to unravel it. Having earlier presented Phips as he who can best balance New England providentialism and English contractualism, Mather now presents William Phips as piously and humbly defending and enacting God's providential will precisely by *removing* God's larger providential plan from the local political structure within which Phips himself serves as governor![16] Phips's duty as governor is to "preserve" his people, not, ultimately, to embroil them in unsolvable spiritual conflicts and confusions that can lead to political breakdown and demonically driven social chaos.

Reassembling the Rhetoric of Providence

What does this description of these two rhetorics, as they intersect and divide, reveal about Cotton Mather's understanding of the transformations in Massachusetts governance he has described up to this point? While, as we have seen, *Pietas in Patriam* periodically separates the rhetoric of providence and the rhetoric of contract as Mather moves through his account of Phips's rise and fall, the text usually contrives to balance or reconcile them. By the end of his account of the witchcraft controversy, this is no longer case. The question becomes how Cotton Mather himself rhetorically accounts to readers for this separation.

Secularization theorists might suggest that this separation of providence from a form of governance indicates the Phips biography's final expression of a secularization process precisely defined by such separations. But is there not another way of interpreting the situation? Does the separation of the rhetoric of providence from the rhetoric of contract mean that the former simply disappears from a text so concerned with foregrounding the inner and outer workings of providence in the life of Phips? Here, the answer is no. Rather, as Mather presents it, the rhetoric of providence itself undergoes a transformation. Already implicit as that which returns to frame Mather's different acts of balancing throughout the biography, this providence, even as it remains free to intervene within human affairs and to use natural or supernatural instruments, operates on a plane above and beyond specific political forms of organizing "humane society." While political forms can serve as providential instruments, that is, they are not to be read as its instantiation.

Mather has in fact clearly employed this understanding of providential activity in his detailed depiction of William Phips's most signal failure: his aborted attempt to take the city of Quebec described in Section 11. As Mather presents it, in spite of Phips's courage and planning, in spite of the best efforts of his army, the preemptive attack of 1690 miserably fails, and casts the colony into self-doubt and immense financial debt. In Mather's detailed rendering of the debacle, the plan fails not only because of human errors by its notably English as well New English participants, but crucially because of "an evident hand of heaven sending one unavoidable disaster after another" (189). Once again attempting to convince his English as well as New English readers that his claims have a wider resonance beyond events in New England alone, Mather darkly notes that the "general disaster which hath attended almost every attempt of the European colonies in America to make any considerable encroachment upon their neighbours, is a matter of some close reflection" (190). At the end of Section 11, Mather depicts Phips commenting on the Canadian failure in terms very similar to those he will use to describe the governor's view of spectral evidence: "That the things which had befallen him in this expedition, were too deep to be dived into" (190).

Given the fact that a providence variously presented as transcending or according with human political aims pervades *Pietas in Patriam*, the issue at the end of Mather's account of witchcraft becomes not the disappearance of the rhetoric of providence as such, but the reasons for its reappearance in this particular form at this particular moment in his narrative. On the one hand, this rendering of the inexplicable ways of providence could be viewed as a brilliant self-defensive move on Cotton Mather's part. The problem of spectral evidence, as he depicts it in Section 14, provides a justification for the removal of specific religious features from the new charter, while at the same time indicating the broader cultural necessity for an ongoing trust in the beneficent plan of a providence whose aims will always trump the merely political. Unable to make this specific argument in the section narrating and defending the details of the charter itself, Mather now turns to the debate over providence's ambiguous role in spectral evidence to suggest the separation of an explicit providential design from the new structure of governance defined in the second charter.

On the other hand, given Cotton Mather's interest in retaining a clear providential role in the arena of "venefick witchcraft" more broadly, if not in the particularly unclear arena of "spectral evidence," must we then assume that this rhetorical move toward the end of the text should be read merely as a gesture of self-interest, geared solely toward defending himself, his father, and the acts of the increasingly discredited Phips's governorship? Far from being unusual, Cotton Mather's separation of ways of politically organizing the human world from the sovereign will of providence could also be construed as his recourse, not merely rhetorically, but also theologically, to the traditional Puritan view of general providence itself. While God's will at times appears to be revealed in special signs, as scripture, history, nature, and individual experience attest, at other times, His larger plan is ultimately mysterious, far from being immediately or clearly available to fallen human reason.[17] Read in this manner, the separation of specific locatable providential intentions from a particular political structure, could, as in the case of John Milton's later work, be used by Cotton Mather less to persuade certain readers on both sides of the Atlantic to capitulate to secularization as such, than to urge them to an act of characteristic and deeply difficult Puritan humility in the face of an emerging divine drama larger and different than their own specific political desires.[18]

It is in terms of this traditional understanding of providence in its relation to governance that Sections 18 and 19 of *Pietas in Patriam* turn from Mather's brief discussion of Phips's characteristically unwearied external activities to treat with or defend against duplicitous and more concretely "devilish" Indians, to a detailed portrait of the governor's own character under the conditions of his governorship. In Section 18, while admitting Phips's well-known faults, his impatience and quick anger, Mather's focus falls not on his "heroick virtue" alone, as it had earlier done, but on his "incomparable generosity," his "wonderfully forgiving spirit," his "long-suffering" under extreme "mortifications," his "humble and modest carriage," his religious tolerance coupled with his commendable hatred of "prophaneness," his respect for ministers of the standing order, the moral model he presents as a humble, yet industrious "rising man," and above all, his driving desire to direct his industriousness to the economic and political good of his "people" and of "England"! While some of this language replicates Mather's earlier description of the governor's ability to balance religious and political, and New English and English interests, the emphasis here falls less on Phips's outer activities and successes than on the inner ways in which he meets with calumny and criticism, but still retains his "unaccountable impulse" for serving the larger public. However moral the character that drives Phips's "unwearied" actions, however strong his *pietas in patriam*, this "Phippius Maximus," like the heroic Roman he emulates and as a Christian transcends, remains inexplicably unappreciated and reviled both by his countrymen, who are "under the epidemical vexations of the age," and by that "little party of men" who jealously seek at home and abroad to cause his fall from power (224).[19]

While this scenario strikingly replicates in a New English arena features of Mather's earlier story of the intrigues of English courtiers against the honest Phips, it importantly lacks the moment of vindication by an earthly king and Mather's claim of providence's definitive role in the governor's political ascension. Instead, uncleared in life of the charges against him, Phips abruptly dies of a "malignant feaver" caught in London, whence he had sailed to defend himself against his detractors. Quoting the biblical prophets Haggai and Zechariah, Cotton Mather sighs, "Man's breath goeth forth, he returns to his earth; in the very day his thoughts perish." The parallel with the beginning of the biography holds only briefly, divine providence here acting in a markedly different manner (227).

A similar, more explicit rendering of the mysterious ways of providence occurs in the section just preceding these comments, where Mather describes a younger Phips's encounter with an English astrologer, who had predicted his continuing rise. Here, contrasting the views of the New English minister and the English astrologer, Mather warns against the evils of "judicial astrology," using language drawn from his own discussion of spectral evidence: "albeit Almighty God may permit the devils to predict, and perhaps to perform very many particular things to men . . . yet the devils which foretell many true things, do commonly foretell some that are false, and it may be, propose by the things that are true to betray men into some fatal misbelief and miscarriage about those that are false" (223). As in the case of spectral apparitions, astrological predictions about the future can be jugglings of the devil permitted by God for His own larger ends. Rather than searching the current moment for God's intentions, as Mather has so strenuously done throughout the text, he suggests in his ending depiction of Phips's "interior" that the maligned governor's role, like those he serves, is rather to manifest scripturally sanctioned feelings and behaviors—forgiving one's detractors or enemies, doing good for the community, diligently following one's calling, and so forth—even as he cannot or should not assume that any of his ends will be met or that his community will respond gratefully.[20]

While such rhetoric can again be seen as defending not only Phips's actions, but also Cotton Mather's own tendency to predict a great future for him, this rhetoric too can be viewed in its larger theological dimension. Specifically, Mather's focus on doing good for the wider community as well as for oneself without hope of gratitude or reward is presented as structurally similar to the appropriate stance one is to inhabit before a larger providential will. Relying on the promises of scripture, one must feel as well as act as best one can, in the midst of confusion and mystery. In demonstrating what he presents as Phips's moral activity in the world and his equally spiritual passivity before God's will, Mather once again highlights the governor's own ongoing status as what amounts to a "visible saint," in spite of the removal of visible sainthood as a political requirement under the new charter. At the same time, as Phips's bad treatment by his people and certain party interests suggests, even those who prepare themselves in scripturally prescribed ways to serve God's interests cannot invariably predict how or when providential intervention will bless their activities.

In spite of a lack of human understanding in the present, however, Cotton Mather still argues that some knowledge of God's larger plan will eventually emerge. Whereas he counsels against reading forward in too definitive a way, Mather nonetheless makes a strong case here for reading backward, that is, retroactively, from events, once God's larger intention seems fulfilled. There are two marked instances of this latter kind of reading used in *Pietas in Patriam* in its specific association with politics. In the first, Mather comments in respect to Phips: "that as the eye sees not those objects which are applied close unto it, and even lye upon it; but when the objects are to some distance removed, it clearly discernes them: so we have little sense of the good which we have in our enjoyments, until God, by the removal thereof, teach us better to prize what we once enjoyed" (223). Reading retroactively, those who have scorned and demeaned the dead governor will come to realize his value. In this instance, the divine plan revealed to them is future economic and political loss for both New England and the "English nation." In Section 11, however, what Mather depicts are the circuitous ways in which providence will always ultimately work to the larger good. In the midst of ascribing the failure of Phips's attack on Quebec to providential design, Mather turns to an extended description, drawn from the work of Thomas Bradwardine, about how even the most apparent failures eventually come to fulfill the beneficent ends of providence.

In this rendering, a hermit tormented by doubts about providence is led to witness a series of alarming events in which an angel, acting on God's commands, steals and murders two people, one of them the child of a "godly man." The hermit, "understandably offended" by such acts, wishes to flee his angelic guide, but is taught by the latter how, in each instance, what had happened served actually to the benefit of those so afflicted. "Understand now," warns the angel, "the secret judgements of God!" (189–90). Clearly, the difficult lesson to be learned from both the death of Phips and the failures in Canada is that one must wait, albeit in a patient and faithfully prepared state, till the end of a given sequence of events in order to grasp their full meaning and function within a larger providential order, whose final ends cannot be glimpsed in a single fleeting moment.

Reassembling the Social: The Rhetorics of Providence and Projecting

The point of these concluding sections is not that the removal of religious features from the structure of the new royal charter unequivocally means that *Pietas in Patriam* points to, expresses, or gives in to the "secularization process." In Mather's own terms, he seems to rather signal a transformation in the association of the rhetoric of providence to the rhetoric of political contract. In the turns and twists of Mather's rhetoric, God's providential will, whether manifested in larger events or in personal conversion, increasingly appears unconstrained by any necessary association with a given institutionalized mode of organizing New English political life. Sovereign providence freely enacts its ends in a whole variety of new social and even material associations whose ultimate meanings will be known only in the fullness of God's time.

This freedom of providential action becomes discernible throughout *Pietas in Patriam* not merely at the fraught moment of the witch trials, but also at moments when the rhetoric of providence becomes associated with William Phips's "projecting" on behalf of the public as well as himself. Whereas Mather's tales of Phips's economic projecting, whether to locate sunken gold or to seize Canada's vast natural resources for the "whole English nation," often intersect with the rhetoric of contract, projecting in *Pietas in Patriam* is also always distinctively linked to the unseen workings of providence. In instances such as the story of Phips's massively successful treasure hunt, for example, providence is seen to have favored the enterprise, but not until the very end; in cases like the failure of the project to take Canada and control its trade and resources, providence is presented as momentarily hiding its larger aims. In these scenes, and indeed, up to the moment of his death, William Phips is depicted to readers as inhabiting a stance of determined, prepared, and extraordinarily patient waiting in the face of projects whose final providential meaning may only become manifest after the fact. Allied at times with Phips's activities before the governorship as well as with his unremitting

plans for the colony as governor, the rhetoric of projecting also offers the possibility of a relation with the rhetoric of providence different than the rhetoric
of political contract.

Whereas associating projecting with providence allows the ends of providence to be construed as more open, less institutionally fixed, what does its
connection with the rhetoric of providence do for the rhetoric of projecting?
As Mark Valeri has recently suggested with respect to New English commercial activity more broadly, the changed association of projecting with providence underscores the larger moral, even evangelical, aims that new economic
activities can serve when interpreted by certain religious, rather than secular,
leaders.[21] William Phips's projects, as Cotton Mather presents them, demonstrate not only Phips's spiritual, but also his material preparedness for whatever eventuates, and his equal belief in the moral and communal ends to
which individual projecting should be directed, whether it succeeds or not.
God alone can determine the success of a project; the role of the converted
projector is to create his projects, and to be prepared, spiritually as well as
practically, to patiently ask for and to acknowledge God's providential hand
at work in whatever occurs.[22]

As projecting on behalf of the "whole English nation" takes on a moral
cast in *Pietas in Patriam* through its association with providential rhetoric,
features of Mather's theology of doing good, a theology of religious experience that has already come to pervade a multitude of more explicitly evangelical texts surrounding the life of Phips, become momentarily visible in a
rhetoric of moral projecting.[23] Moral projecting, while it is often connected
to Phips's political rise, can also be dissociated from any distinct local party
interest. The contemporaneity of *Pietas in Patriam* with Mather's burgeoning
concern with Atlantic Pietism suggests his increasing focus on the providential role to be played by converted commercial as well as political actors in
furthering broadly Protestant evangelical and even millennial ends in what
both Cotton Mather and his father interpret as the coming "last days." But
one need not go outside *Pietas in Patriam* itself to also encounter Cotton
Mather's growing anger about, as well as his sense of alienation from, local
New English politics.[24] One need only look at the shifting relationships of
his different rhetorics.

As we trace the ways a rhetoric of moral projecting can become associated with a material and spiritual preparedness open to providential aims
unfixed from a local political structure, features of a transformation become momentarily visible in the New English "social assemblage" as *Pietas*

in Patriam has depicted it. In the life of Phips, as we have seen, the separation of institutional politics from institutional religion that is considered the hallmark of the secularization process is both acknowledged and then reinscribed within a colonial discourse of providence that is itself becoming transformed by its own new association with a rhetoric of projecting. While the secularization process expressed in and in part driven by the Glorious Revolution in England occurs in provincial Massachusetts, Cotton Mather's *Pietas in Patriam* thus demonstrates aspects of its curious incompleteness in this sphere. The association of broadly Protestant religious aims with economic projecting that is intimated in Mather's biography suggests moreover the possibilities for a new, powerful, and overtly international rhetoric within whose terms different colonial religious leaders could variously support, confront, or compete with the secular power of the new Massachusetts political structure that Cotton Mather himself helped to create. But that is a subject for another essay.

CHAPTER 10

Between Cicero and Augustine

Religion and Republicanism
in the Americas and Beyond

SANDRA M. GUSTAFSON

Historical studies of the emergence of the modern republic focus on the Anglo-American world, and much of the scholarship proceeds on the assumption that the modern republic was the creation of Protestants, particularly dissenting ones. This assumption informs J. G. A. Pocock's monumental *The Machiavellian Moment: Florentine Political Thought and the Atlantic Republican Tradition* (1975), which moves from Renaissance Florence to the English Civil War to the American Revolution, and portrays James Harrington as providing an important linkage between republican revival and dissenting Protestantism. It is likewise visible in J. H. Elliott's masterful comparative study, *Empires of the Atlantic World: Britain and Spain in America 1492–1830* (2006), which portrays American republicanism as an overwhelmingly British North American phenomenon. In contrast to the success of the federal republic in the North, Elliott writes, in the newly independent southern states, a fatal gap emerged between the Creole patriotism associated with "the interests of privileged elites" who wielded power and the "republican constitutions" of those same states, which "spoke the contemporary language of universal rights and gave at least nominal representation to social and ethnic groups traditionally regarded as inferior." The gap between constitutional ideals and social realities posed an enduring problem. Lacking established legislative institutions and experience with self-government, the new republics of the South struggled to fill the power vacuum left by Spain.[1]

Yet despite this lack of practical experience with republican civic practices, which contributed to halting postimperial transitions, the language and ideals of republicanism had a long history in Spanish America. As Sabine MacCormack has shown in her works on colonial Peru, republicanism was among the very first concepts that Spanish authors employed to describe indigenous American societies. The authors who wrote histories of the conquest of the Incas routinely compared Inca history to the history of the Roman Republic. Peruvian historians analogized Inca towns to ancient republics and evaluated the consequences of Spanish conquest by reference to republican ideals. This approach to indigenous America was likewise a common practice in colonial Mexico and elsewhere. The Spanish American version of a classical republican heritage later fed into the colonial independence movements of the South, alongside the models offered by the United States and France.[2]

The confluence of republicanisms in the Americas offers a parallel to the commonalities that Jorge Cañizares-Esguerra has identified in a demonological discourse shared by English Puritan and Spanish Catholic colonialist ideologies. In *Puritan Conquistadors: Iberianizing the Atlantic, 1550–1700* (2006), Cañizares-Esguerra describes a hemispheric imperial ideology built on the demonization of indigenous Americans and traces its spread by means of the circulation of Spanish colonialist texts in the English-speaking world. The formulation of modern republican thought in the Americas is tied up with the iconoclastic practices that he describes, which were directed both at the non-Christian beliefs espoused by indigenous societies and toward Christian opponents in the ongoing violence of European religious warfare. The competition between Spain and England for dominance in the New World is closely bound up with religious rivalries at home. My comparative study of republican rhetoric, imagery, and beliefs offers a related approach to developments in the Americas, as well as connecting this history to a contemporary global issue that has important historiographical dimensions: the relationship between religion and the modern republic.[3]

This relationship has a specific material and textual history. In 1819, substantial portions of Cicero's treatise on politics, *De Re Publica* (ca. 55), were uncovered on a palimpsest of Augustine's *Commentary on the Psalms* in the Vatican Library by Angelo Mai, the library's keeper. The bulk of Cicero's fabled treatise had disappeared ca. 600, and Mai's recovery of long-lost sections of the work caused a sensation in intellectual circles throughout Europe and the Americas. It was fitting that the text was found underneath a work of Augustine's, for this leading early Christian interpreter of antiquity drew his influential definition of *commonwealth* in *The City of God* (ca. 420) from Cicero's work, where it is defined as "the concern of the people" based on "agreement on law and community of interest."[4]

In Book 2, Chapter 21, of *The City of God*, Augustine summarized key elements of Cicero's definition of the republic, and it was Augustine's paraphrase and selective quotation that was the main source of Cicero's thought on this topic until the recovery in 1819. After first establishing the incompatibility of a commonwealth with injustice, Augustine quoted Cicero's definition of the commonwealth as "the property of a people," that is, "an assembly united in fellowship by common agreement as to what is right and by a community of interest." The commonwealth can be a monarchy, an oligarchy, or a democracy, so long as its rule is just. In conditions of injustice, the commonwealth ceases to exist. Augustine quotes a lengthy passage from Cicero to the effect that, in his day, Rome had "fallen into decay" due to the corruption of morals and was no longer a true commonwealth. Augustine concedes that the Roman Republic was "a commonwealth of a sort; and it was certainly better administered by the Romans of more ancient times than by those who have come after them." Yet, he concludes, "true justice . . . does not exist other than in that commonwealth whose Founder and Ruler is Christ." With these words Augustine tied the definition of a commonwealth to the Christian tradition. His ideal Christian commonwealth influenced medieval Catholic theories of the polis, and Augustinian ideas later became important for Protestant political thinkers.[5]

At the time that Cicero's lost work was recovered, republics were proliferating, and the meaning of the term was sharply contested. Simón Bolívar promoted a form of republicanism in the South that differed in important ways from the republicanism of the United States, which found an influential spokesman in Daniel Webster, who treated it as a Puritan legacy. Bolívar stressed the racial heterogeneity, the imperial system, and the Catholic traditions that distinguished the southern republics from their northern sister. He concluded that a lifetime executive, a hereditary branch of the legislature, and a branch of government to monitor public morals and take the place of church authority were all necessary to the success of the newly independent southern republics. Bolívar's approach reflected the elastic nature of Roman republicanism, which allowed for its application to a wide array of states.

Meanwhile, Webster identified widely held private property, education, and Christian faith as the basis of republican self-governance, and celebrated the representative system modeled on the Roman Senate.[6]

The roots of Bolívar's republican themes can be traced in the early chronicles. MacCormack observes that, in the first years of Spanish conquest, "Cicero's notion of a host of settlements, each constituting for its inhabitants a little *patria*. . . . . found new life in Peru, the general homeland of people living in a multitude of villages, towns, and cities."[7] This translation was possible because it aligned with "a preexisting concept of Andean space," (25) shaped by the Inca imperial idea of the "Fourfold Domain" formed of "diverse language groups and ethnic polities" (26). Historians of the conquest commonly described these diverse collectivities as *repúblicas*. The first-generation historian Pedro Cieza de León concluded in his *Crónica del Perú* (1553) that "there is no better form of freedom than when republics live under royal government," which contributed to his appreciation for Inca rule (quoted in MacCormack, 91). MacCormack notes, "Rome became not only the filter that rendered the Inca achievement intelligible and credible, but also the yardstick whereby Cieza judged the deeds of his own countrymen" (16–17). Cieza's heirs include Bartolomé de Las Casas, who inherited his unpublished manuscripts, and whose manuscripts advocating a return of Inca rule in turn were extensively quoted by Jerónimo Román y Zamora, an Augustinian friar, who first published *Repúblicas del mundo* in 1575, followed by a revised and expanded edition in 1595. *Repúblicas del mundo* in its turn influenced Inca Garcilaso de la Vega, whose *Royal Commentaries of the Incas* (1609) has had a persistent influence on Andean society, including the rebellion headed by Tupac Amaru II in the 1780s, and the independence movements that Bolívar sought to steer in a republican direction.

Appreciation for Inca political organization did not require admiration for Inca religion. Cieza, Las Casas, and others agreed that Inca forms of worship were idolatrous, while at the same time emphasizing that, as with the Romans, false beliefs did not prohibit skill in statecraft. It was not unusual for Spanish historians to strike an Augustinian chord: they applauded Inca governance while calling for the destruction of Inca holy sites. It was also common for writers to note the coincidence of the Reconquista and Columbus's voyage and to see parallels between the peninsular conflict of Christians and Muslims, and the American conflict of Christians and pagans.[8]

These Ciceronian and Augustinian themes were present in works about British North America as well. John Smith's writings resemble the works of

Spanish chroniclers in their treatment of Powhatan and his "empire." Indeed, Smith may have been familiar with José de Acosta's *Naturall and Morall Histories of the East and West Indies*, which appeared in an English edition in 1604. Smith provides a description of "the Virginians Government" that resembles passages from Acosta and other Spanish chroniclers, writing, "Although the Country people be very barbarous, yet have they amongst them such government, as that their Magistrates for good commanding, and their people for due subjection, and obeying, excell many places that would be counted very civill. The forme of their Common-wealth is a Monarchicall government, one as Emperour ruleth over many Kings or Governours." In the section preceding this one, Smith describes the religious customs of the Algonquian communities with some specificity and interest, even as he repeatedly characterizes them as idolatrous. "To divert them from this blind Idolatry, we did our best endeavors," he notes, concluding that despite their attempts, "in this lamentable ignorance doe these poore soules sacrifice themselves to the Devill, not knowing their Creator."[9] Smith's own political views seem to have favored republican forms, and he expressly aimed to create commonwealths of English people in Virginia and New England. His commonwealth sentiments were nominally Christian, though the depth of this sentiment is debatable. Cicero's vision of the republic as an ordered polity based in natural law is consonant with Smith's approach to British colonialism.

By contrast, the Puritans who dominated the New England colonies were more Augustinian than Ciceronian in their approach to the founding of commonwealths. Perry Miller stressed the influence of Augustine on Puritan political theory in *The New England Mind* (1939), and it is everywhere in evidence in John Winthrop's "A Modell of Christian Charity." Miller effectively described the pressures faced by Puritan leaders in New England as they confronted the English Civil War: "In order to justify parliamentary opposition in England, they had to enjoin that rulers should seek the common welfare, but in order to maintain a Bible commonwealth in New England, they had to identify the common welfare with the glory of God. They had to demand that rulers look after the good of the people, but that God and not the people determine good." Miller aptly terms the underlying belief system "Augustinian," noting its consonance with the ideas expressed in *The City of God*.[10]

Puritan attitudes toward New England's Algonquian communities reveal additional layers of complexity. John Eliot's *The Christian Commonwealth: or, The Civil Policy Of The Rising Kingdom of Jesus Christ* (1659) offers a multivalent Augustinianism that calls for the stripping of all Native customs, including religious practices, in order to remake the Algonquians into Christians capable of forming commonwealths modeled on the ancient Israelites. David D. Hall notes that Eliot favored an Old Testament scheme "because it aligned the Indian communities with the earliest system of government practiced by the people of God." Even as he sought fundamental transformations in Indian societies, Eliot directed his sharpest critiques at the political and spiritual idolatry of England. It was Eliot's criticism of England, and not his plan for reforming the American Natives, that occasioned his ultimate decision to retract his pamphlet.[11]

Roger Williams showed greater interest than Eliot in indigenous forms of governance, though he shared Eliot's tendency to treat Native societies as vehicles to critique the English. Francis Jennings and James Axtell have noted that European observers sometimes characterized Indian government as both tyrannical and anarchic. Williams exemplifies this tendency in passages from *A Key into the Language of America* (1643), where he claims that "the Sachims . . . have an absolute Monarchie over the people" but that at the same time eloquent speakers will attract followers who "esteeme them Gods, as Herod among the *Jewes*." Williams also notes the central role of consultation and persuasion in Native communities. The leaders "will not conclude of ought that concernes all, either Lawes, or Subsides, or warres, unto which the people are averse, and by gentle perswasion cannot be brought." He describes a gathering of up to a thousand people seated in a circle, smoking and deliberating on a piece of news or a decision that would affect the community. Williams does not characterize these communities as republics or commonwealths. He does, however, say that the Natives are less sinful than their English neighbors. In the poem that concludes the section on Indian government, he adopts a Native perspective on the English colonies:

We weare no Cloaths, have many Gods,
And yet our sinnes are lesse:
You are Barbarians, Pagans wild,
Your Land's the Wildernesse.[12]

From these early hints, a more robust practice of treating indigenous communities as republics flowered among British writers a century later, notably in the work of Scottish-born, New York-based intellectual and diplomat Cadwallader Colden. Building on French sources, Colden presented the members of the Iroquois League as model republics: "Each Nation is an absolute Republick by its self, govern'd in all Publick Affairs of War and Peace by the Sachems or Old Men, whose Authority and Power is gain'd by and consists wholly in the Opinion the rest of the Nation have of their Wisdom and Integrity." Colden described the Iroquois republics as embodying "the most Ancient and Original Condition of almost every Nation" and manifesting "the Original Form of all Government." Like Williams, he lamented Indian barbarism and the debasing influence of the colonists, while calling on Christians to forward the civilizing project and multiply "the Number of good Men." His emphasis on civility and morality are more in accord with Cicero's republic than the Augustinian tradition that shaped Puritan writings. Colden's central goal in his 1727 and 1747 *History of the Five Indian Nations* was to provide a textured account of the Iroquois and their relations with the British colonial government. This focus on governance and diplomacy lent itself to a Ciceronian approach.[13]

Colden contributed to a developing image of American Indians as model republicans, which had influential champions in Benjamin Franklin and Thomas Jefferson. In "Remarks Concerning the Savages of North America" (1783), Franklin celebrated the deliberative traditions of American "savages," presenting their conduct at council meetings as more civilized than that of members of Parliament. Jefferson likewise admired Native oratory and diplomacy in his public writings and personal letters. Colden, Franklin, and Jefferson represent prominent instances of a broader phenomenon within the emergent republicanism of British North America and the early United States. The "savage" speaker who exerts power through persuasion rather than force came to be celebrated as a model of the new style of governance for the Revolutionary generation.[14]

Around the time when some prominent British Americans were embracing the label of "republican" to describe indigenous societies, Spanish and Spanish American historians became increasingly skeptical of the chronicle tradition that characterized indigenous societies as republics. In *How to Write the History of the New World* (2001), Cañizares-Esguerra describes the emergence of a new art of reading exemplified in the work of Cornelius de Pauw that privileged philosophical consistency over the authority of experience, and that treated indigenous Americans and Creoles as "degenerate and effete." Alexander von Humboldt built on Pauw's approach when he redefined Inca and Aztec polities as Oriental—and thus autocratic—rather than Roman.[15] The simultaneous rise of the republican Indian in British North America and eclipse of that figure in Spanish America reflect the differing paths taken by the British and Spanish empires in the Americas, as well as the shifting dynamics of post-Reformation religious conflict. In Spanish America the crown maintained stronger control and developed a more elaborate bureaucracy run by peninsular Spaniards and tied to the Roman Catholic Church. The church hierarchy was strongly European in orientation; indigenous Catholics were not accepted into convents and monasteries until the late eighteenth century.

The looser imperial structure of British America allowed for the significant autonomy granted to colonial governments and the proliferation of religious groups, mainly but not exclusively Protestant, which culminated in the constitutional separation of church and state, and pushed the new nation's republicanism in a more Ciceronian direction. For Cicero, religion was valuable as a basis of moral cohesion in civil society rather than offering an ultimate set of truths. Franklin Americanized and pluralized this view in his autobiography, where he described his youthful flirtation with atheism, followed by a conviction that religious belief was possibly true and definitely useful. As a young man he searched for the shared principles underlying the various moral and religious teachings that he encountered, and distilled them into his "Art of Virtue." Franklin personalized the broader social processes of religious pluralization that J. Hector St. John de Crèvecœur portrayed in *Letters from an American Farmer* (1782), where proximity dilutes the more extreme or idiosyncratic expressions of religious faith and intermarriage further blurs denominational boundaries. In "Remarks Concerning the Savages of North-America," Franklin gave the leading moral voice to a Susquehanna orator who chastised a Christian missionary for refusing to grant equal legitimacy to indigenous beliefs. The orator is offended by the minister's claim to possess an exclusive truth and berates the missionary for his lack of "common civility": "You saw that we . . . believed all your stories," he asserts, "Why do you refuse to believe ours?"[16] Highlighted by Franklin's mildly humorous tone, this anecdote serves to underscore the larger message of the essay: the "savages of North America" are more civilized than the British and other Europeans. The shift from Christianity to civility as a gauge of moral righteousness marks a transition from the Augustinian to the Ciceronian republic. Meanwhile, the rise of indigenous Christian churches led by Native ministers broadened the spectrum of Christian belief. Samson Occom and William Apess occupied the intersection point between Christianity and republicanism, pushing in the direction of a multiracial republic.[17]

The different trajectories of republican thought across the hemisphere should not obscure some important parallels. Native resistance to colonialism reached a peak in the second half of the eighteenth century in the American colonies of both Britain and Spain. Daniel Richter traces the emergence of parallel formations of pan-Indian and pan-colonial identity in British North America in *Facing East from Indian Country* (2001), while Gregory Dowd uncovers a significant religious dimension in this process, which he calls "The Indians' Great Awakening" and describes as the forging of shared spiritual practices and ideals that distinguished Native traditionalists from Christian believers. These religious and political identities crystallized in Pontiac's War, and they evolved into a fifty-year struggle for control of the continent, which overlapped with the Revolutionary War and ended only with the defeat of Tecumseh in the War of 1812. Meanwhile. in the Andes, Tupac Amaru II led a similar, though much briefer, resistance effort that posed a genuine threat to Spanish control of the region. The movement culminated in Amaru's brutal execution in 1781 and the swift suppression of his followers.[18]

Republican movements in the Americas embraced the iconography of indigeneity. Participants in the Boston Tea Party played Indian. The mestizo revolutionary leader José de San Martín sought to recruit Native support in Argentina by proclaiming, "I am an Indian too," and Bolívar ordered the reconstruction of the ancient temple Pachacamac, which had lain in ruins outside Lima since the conquest. Bolívar understood the irony—or hypocrisy—of Creole revolutionaries appropriating the indigenous past. He criticized a patriotic ode by José Joaquín Olmedo that featured an apparition of the Inca leader Huayna Capac blessing the independence movement and anticipating the success of the American republics. "It hardly seems proper for [the Inca] to praise indirectly the religion that destroyed him," Bolívar wrote to Olmedo, "and it appears even less proper that he does not desire the reëstablishment of his throne, but, instead, give preference to foreign intruders who . . . [are] the descendants of the destroyers of his empire." Bolívar's sensitivity to the place of religious differences in the formation of the southern republics perhaps reflects his attraction to French republican thought, which in its main contours rejected public expressions of faith and the political authority of the Catholic Church.[19]

Differences of race and religion did not resolve neatly in the early United States any more than in the republics of the South. Bolívar proposed to weld a shared national identity for the heterogeneous peoples of Spanish America by means of a strong executive and a secular body wielding moral authority. By contrast, Webster traced the origins of republicanism to local churches and town hall meetings. This localism manifested during the 1820s as support for both the Cherokee Republic and the American Colonization Society, which led to the foundation of the Republic of Liberia in 1847, when the colony gained its independence from the United States. Webster's commitments underscore a prominent feature of republicanism: the idea of the republic braids together the concept of a community, sometimes defined by race and religion, with an aspiration to self-governance. The blurring of identity and polis is visible in Spanish colonization writings, where descriptions of indigenous societies as "republics" often appear to collapse this distinction. Other sources suggest that identity alone is neither necessary nor sufficient for a republic.

Among these is Alexis de Tocqueville, who, near the end of the first volume of *Democracy in America* (1835), assessed "The Main Causes Which Tend to Maintain a Democratic Republic in the United States."[20] He considered the question first in a hemispheric perspective, noting that Spanish America had equal or superior geographic advantages to Anglo-America but had failed to establish stable republics. Next he reflected on the importance of law, and concluded that while law was more important than geography, it was not sufficient to explain the success of republican government in the United States: "Mexico, which is as fortunately situated as the Anglo-American Union, has adopted [U.S. federal] laws but cannot get used to a democratic form of government" (359). Mexico's diversity alone did not explain its comparative failure. Tocqueville went on to note that shared race and religion did not guarantee the success of a democratic republic, as evidenced by the disorder in the American West. Setting aside racial diversity in the North (which he treats in the succeeding chapter on the future of the "three races" inhabiting the United States), Tocqueville stated that "almost all the inhabitants of the Union have sprung from the same stock, speak the same language, pray to God in the same way, experience the same physical conditions, and obey the same laws." What, then, distinguished East from West in the United States? Unlike the chaotic West, the East was notable for the "customs, opinions, and social habits" that supported a "republican government" that was "strong and orderly, proceeding with mature deliberation." The customs, opinions, and social habits that made republicanism possible included "literary study and practical education" (360). Tocqueville also stressed the prevalence of religion united with liberty.

Running through *Democracy in America* is the question of the place that Catholicism would come to hold in the United States. Tocqueville, who describes himself in the work as a devoted Catholic, considers the issue repeatedly and with an eye to its implications for republican government in Europe and the Americas. He alludes to Augustine when he observes, "if the human mind is allowed to follow its own bent, it will regulate political society and the City of God in the same uniform manner and will, I dare say, seek to *harmonize* earth and heaven" (336). He notes the rising numbers of Catholic immigrants and stresses the compatibility of Catholicism with democratic republicanism, even claiming that Catholics "are the most republican and democratic class in the United States" (337). He claims further that Catholic laypeople were all equals in their subordination to the clergy, and that there were fewer differences of wealth among them. As for the clergy, they distinguish revealed truth, which is beyond discussion, and "political truth which they think God has abandoned to man's free inquiry." Thus, he concludes, "American Catholics are both the most obedient believers and the most independent citizens" (338). In a later section he projected that the United States would become increasingly Catholic as the appeal of its harmony and unity drew in converts.[21]

Tocqueville's analysis of the separation of church and state and his emphasis on the prominent role of religious faith in shaping the customs that made the republic successful are an important touchstone in recent discussions about the place of religion in the public square.[22] The nature of that relevance is twofold. On the one hand, Tocqueville offers a model for understanding how a religion sometimes thought to be antithetical to democratic republican values could instead be interpreted as manifesting and even fostering them. On the other, his assertion that nonwhites were incommensurable with American democracy and would either die or be pushed out (Indians) or would be the cause of persistent racial conflict and civil war (blacks), suggests the importance of attending to both racial and religious factors in the fashioning of the modern republic. The Irish Catholics, whose transformative impact on the United States was central to Tocqueville's predictions about the future of the republic, were able to become "white" in a way that Latino/a Catholics often were not, even long after the United States incorporated large numbers of Mexican Catholics in 1848. The American Catholic Church is still coming to terms with the indigenous difference symbolized by the Virgin of Guadalupe.[23]

Today, the relationship between the world's religions and the modern republican state remains volatile. The role of Islam in the Arab Republic of Egypt offers one highly visible set of conflicts, while the prolonged political and bureaucratic battles in the United States over the coverage of birth control mandated by the 2009 Affordable Care Act is another. A third instance involves the ability of American society to peacefully absorb a growing number of Muslim and other non-Christian immigrants. In a discussion of the so-called "Ground Zero Mosque," John T. McGreevy and R. Scott Appleby describe a revival of a strain of American nativism similar to the movement that developed in the nineteenth century in response to Catholic immigration. Underlying nativist attitudes is a line of thought associating modern republics with Protestantism, which Presbyterian minister Lyman Beecher articulated in *A Plea for the West* (1835). Beecher warned that Catholic attitudes toward the social and spiritual value of hierarchy threatened to undermine the American republic. Catholics in the United States were more loyal to the church than the nation, Beecher opined, and he urged his fellow citizens to love Catholics but hate Catholicism.[24]

McGreevy and Appleby recall anti-Catholic attitudes such as Beecher's in order to counter their contemporary "Islamophobic" equivalents. Noting certain parallels between Roman Catholicism and Islam (distinctive dress by clergy and religious women; preference for parochial over public schools; unfamiliar theology, holidays, and customs), they observe that "it took Catholics more than a full century to attain their current level of acceptance and influence," which includes Catholics serving as a majority of justices on the Supreme Court and having a substantial presence in both houses of Congress. As Catholics were absorbed into American society, the American Catholic Church came to have an important modernizing effect on the global Catholic Church. McGreevy and Appleby single out the contributions of the American Jesuit John Courtney Murray "in shaping *Dignitatis Humanae* (1965)—the Declaration on Religious Liberty, in which the Second Vatican Council endorsed religious freedom for all people." At the height of the Cold War, the Roman Catholic Church transformed itself from the agent of religious and political repression that it had represented to generations of American Protestants, becoming the most powerful global institution advocating religious liberty. The dialogical relationship between the Catholic Church and American republicanism resulted, in this regard at least, in transformation of both. The scope and meaning of religious liberty are at the heart of disputes over the birth control mandate in the Affordable Care Act.[25]

While scholars come to terms with the evident failure of secularization theory, as described most fully by Charles Taylor, the negotiation of religious claims in a multifaith society has emerged as a central challenge for the modern republic. The dynamic relationship between the republic as a political form and the world's religions took a new turn after December 2010, with the unfolding of the "Arab Spring" across the Middle East and northern Africa. As revolutionary movements ousted repressive regimes in Tunisia, Egypt, Libya, and elsewhere, the evolving relationship between Islam and republican self-government shaped public discussion about the future of the new regimes. Here the parallels in nineteenth-century Europe with the Roman Catholic Church were as pertinent as those in the United States. The republican tradition in France was built on a commitment to *laïcité*, or a secular state that allowed the government to limit the power of the church. The controversial ban of headscarves in French schools was based on the principles of *laïcité*. Even as France was implementing its ban, the secular Republic of Turkey moved in the opposite direction by *lifting* a ban on headscarves in universities, signaling the renewed importance of the headscarf within postcolonial Islamic societies. The Republic of India offers a further instance of the role that religious difference can play in a modern republic. Since its founding in 1950, India has experienced repeated, sometimes violent conflicts along sectarian lines, most often between Muslims and Hindus. The capacity to find common ground despite religious differences is a prominent theme in the recent work of Indian intellectuals, including Amartya Sen and Ramachandra Guha.[26]

Is the modern republic the City of God? Or Rome Reborn? Is *laïcité* or freedom of religion the order of the day? Can "agreement on law and community of interest" be established when law is rooted in a particular scripture, as is the case with Sharia law, or, conversely, when some members of the community believe that a law requires citizens to violate a particular religious doctrine, as with the Affordable Care Act? Cicero and Augustine help illuminate central questions about the modern republic. The tension between religious claims to transcendent authority and the assertion of the immanent authority of the state will not be resolved by the withering away of faith, as secularists once believed. These tensions can be illuminated, and strategies for addressing them perhaps devised, with greater awareness of the complex histories of the core concepts as they evolved in the early modern Americas.

NOTES

INTRODUCTION

1. In the compendium often recognized as the first global account of religion produced in Europe, Bernard Picart designed 250 plates of engravings covering disparate forms of worship throughout the world. In making his engravings, Picart drew from the long history of travel accounts and missionary reports that preceded his text, but in contrast to the accounts of world religion to come before his, Picart juxtaposed Christian ritual with Chinese, Jewish, and Indian, viewing these religions in tandem rather than through a hierarchical structure. *Ceremonies et coutumes religieuses de tous les peuples du monde, représentées par des figures dessinées de la main de Bernard Picart* (Amsterdam: J. F. Bernard, 1728–39). See Lynn Hunt, Margaret C. Jacob, and Winjnand Mijnhardt, *The Book That Changed Europe: Picart and Bernard's Religious Ceremonies of the World* (Cambridge, Mass.: Belknap Press of Harvard University Press, 2010), 211–46; and Ann Jensen Adams, "Reproduction and Authenticity in Bernard Picart's *Impostures Innocentes*," in *Bernard Picart and the First Global Vision of Religion*, ed., Lynn Hunt, Margaret C. Jacob, and Winjnand Mijnhardt (Los Angeles: Getty Research Institute, 2010), 75–99.

2. As the American Indian philosopher Viola F. Cordova remarks, it is very likely that "there are no literal correlates between concepts drawn from different cultures. Therefore, European and American populations of the early contact period would have understood entirely different things when discussing religious ideas such as "soul, good and evil, God, sin, and afterlife." Quoted in *How It Is*, ed. Kathleen Dean Moore, Kurt Peters, and Ted Jojola (Tucson: University of Arizona Press, 2007), 3, 5.

3. The literature on the ways that indigenous forms of worship blended with Christianity into complex forms of religious syncretism is vast. For example, see Linford D. Fisher, *The Indian Great Awakening: Religion and the Shaping of Native Cultures in Early America* (Oxford: Oxford University Press, 2012); James Ronda, "The European Indian: Jesuit Civilization Planning in New France," *Church History* 41, no. 3 (1972): 385–95; David Silverman, *Faith and Boundaries: Colonists, Christianity, and Community Among the Wampanoag Indians of Martha's Vineyard, 1600–1871* (Cambridge, UK: Cambridge University Press, 2005). For the colonial Latin American context, the following works offer interesting, and often conflicting, views on religious syncretism as well as its current value as a way of understanding complex processes of cultural mixing: Louise Burkhardt, *The Slippery Earth: Nahua Christian Moral Dialogue in Sixteenth-Century Mexico* (Tucson: University of Arizona Press, 1989); Solange Alberro, *El águila y la cruz: Orígenes religiosos de la conciencia criolla* (Mexico City: Fondo De Cultura Económica, 1999); Jaime Lara, *City, Temple, Stage: Eschatological Architecture and Liturgical Theatrics in New Spain* (Notre Dame, Ind.: University of Notre Dame Press, 2004); Joan Cameron Bristol, *Christians, Blasphemers, and Witches: Afro-Mexican Ritual*

Practice in the Seventeenth Century (Albuquerque: University of New Mexico Press, 2007); Serge Gruzinski, *Images at War: Mexico From Columbus to Blade Runner (1492–2019)*, trans. Heather MacLean (Durham, N.C.: Duke University Press, 2001).

4. José Acosta's *Natural and Moral History of the Indies*, ed. Jane E. Mangan, with an introduction and commentary by Walter D. Mignolo, trans. Frances M. López-Morillas (Durham, N.C.: Duke University Press, 2002). For example, in chapter 10, "Of a Strange Kind of Idolatry That Was Practiced by the Mexicans," Acosta writes of human sacrifice: "It is indeed painful to see how Satan holds these people in subjection, and is still master of many of them today, performing such mischievous and fraudulent tricks at the expense of the sad souls and miserable bodies that they offer him, while he laughs at the cruel pranks he plays on these unfortunates, whose sins justify Almighty God's leaving them in the power of the enemy whom they chose as god and protector" (275). For a discussion of the complexity of the devil and paganism in Acosta's work, see Fernando Cervantes's *The Devil in the New World: The Impact of Diabolism in New Spain* (New Haven, Conn.: Yale University Press, 1994).

5. According to Mangan, Acosta's text underwent "immediate translation" into a variety of European languages including English. *Natural and Moral History of the Indies*, xviii.

6. *History of the New World* was first published in Dutch in 1625 by Bonaventure & Abraham Elseviers in Leiden. A Latin edition came out in 1633, followed by a French edition in 1640. Quotes come from Joannes de Laet, *L'Histoire du Nouveau Monde* (A Leyde: Chez Bonaventure & Abraham Elseviers, 1640), 50–58. See Rolf H. Bremmer Jr. and P. G. Hoftijzer, "Johannes de Laet (1581–1649): A Leiden Polymath [introduction]," *Lias: Special Issue* 25, no. 2 (1998): 135–36.

7. The De Léry text is *Histoire d'un voyage faict en la terre du Brésil* (1578). Quote is from Marc Lescarbot, *The History of New France* (Toronto: Champlain Society, 1907), 108–9. The text was originally published as *Histoire de la Nouvelle-France* (1609), based on Lescarbot's expedition to Acadia in 1606–1607.

8. Thomas Thorowgood, *Jews in America* (London: Henry Brome at the Gun in Ivie-lane, 1660), 27.

9. Pliny, the Elder, *Natural History*, ed. Harris Rackham and William Henry Samuel Jones (Cambridge, Mass.: Harvard University Press, 1938–1963), Book 7.ii.30.

10. The Royal Society formed in 1660 but asked Charles II for an official charter in 1661; he issued it in 1662. Quoted from the "Translation of the First Charter, granted to the President, Council, and Fellows of the Royal Society of London, by King Charles the Second, A.D. 1662," London, Royal Society. A general correspondence between the new science and the New World has been amply explored. This exact quotation appears in a seminal text on this connection: Raymond Phineas Stearns, *Science in the British Colonies of America* (Chicago: University of Illinois Press, 1970), 90.

11. This understanding of the French Jesuits as somewhat removed from the politics of the French empire has been a commonplace in scholarship on New France since James Axtell and James P. Ronda's work. See Axtell, *The Invasion Within: The Contest of Cultures in Colonial North America* (New York: Oxford University Press, 1985), and Ronda, "The European Indian: Jesuit Civilization Planning in New France," *Church History* 41, no. 3 (1972): 385–95. More recently, see the introduction to *The Jesuit Relations: Natives and Missionaries in Seventeenth-Century North America*, ed. Allen Greer (Boston: Bedford/St. Martin's, 2000), and Peter A. Goddard, "Canada in Seventeenth-Century Jesuit Thought: Backwater or Opportunity?" in *Decentering the Renaissance: New Essays on Canada, 1500–1700*, ed. Germaine Warkentin and Carolyn Podruchny (Toronto: University of Toronto Press, 2002), 186–99.

12. For a discussion of the development of the Society of Jesus and its relationship with the crown, see Peggy Liss, "Jesuit Contributions to the Ideology of Spanish Empire in Mexico: Part II, The Jesuit System of Education and Jesuit Contributions to Ongoing Mexican Adhesion to Empire," *The Americas* 29, no. 4 (April, 1973): 449–70.

13. The literature of the Puritan migration is vast. The classic study is Perry Miller, *Errand into the Wilderness* (Cambridge, Mass.: Belknap Press of Harvard University Press, 1956). See also Andrew Delbanco, *The Puritan Ordeal* (Cambridge, Mass.: Harvard University Press, 1989) and Larzer Ziff, *Puritanism in America: New Culture in a New World* (New York: Viking Press, 1973). For a primary source that reveals Puritan anxiety about God abandoning England, see Thomas Hooker, *The Danger of Desertion: Or, A Farewell Sermon of Mr. Thomas Hooker* (London: Printed by G. M. for George Edwards, 1641).

14. In the case of New England, for example, the Seal of the Massachusetts Bay Colony (1629) depicts an American Indian poised on a docile and vacant landscape, with the slogan "Come over and help us," pouring out of his mouth.

15. Sarah Owens's recent translation and edition of *Journey of Five Capuchin Nuns* (Toronto: University of Toronto Press, 2009), sheds valuable light on the transit of Spanish nuns across the Atlantic. Kathleen Ross's book, *The Baroque Narrative of Carlos de Sigüenza y Góngora: A New World Paradise* (Cambridge, UK: Cambridge University Press, 1993), analyzes Sigüenza's chronicle of the founding of the convent of Jesús María in Mexico City. For the transit of Ursuline nuns traveling from France to Quebec to New Orleans, see Emily Clark, *Masterless Mistresses: The New Orleans Ursulines and the Development of a New World Society, 1727–1834* (Chapel Hill: University of North Carolina Press, 2007), and her edition of the voyage of Marie-Madeleine Hachard, *Voices from an Early American Convent* (Baton Rouge: Louisiana State University Press, 2007).

16. New Spanish convents remained bastions of white womanhood until the late eighteenth century, when the first convent for indigenous noblewomen was founded. Previously, indigenous and Afro-Hispanic women had formed part of convent populations as servants or slaves (in the case of some Afro-Hispanics).

17. For a collection of these confessions of faith, see Michael McGiffert, ed., *God's Plot: Puritan Spirituality in Thomas Shepard's Cambridge* (Amherst: University of Massachusetts Press, 1994). For discussions of the Puritan congregational community, see Edmund S. Morgan, *Visible Saints: The History of a Puritan Idea* (Ithaca, N.Y.: Cornell University Press, 1965); Charles Cohen, *God's Caress: The Psychology of Puritan Religious Experience* (Oxford: Oxford University Press, 1986), 137–62; Sarah Rivett, *The Science of the Soul in Colonial New England* (Chapel Hill: University of North Carolina Press, 2011), 70–125.

18. John Eliot formed the first Praying Town of Natick, Massachusetts, in 1652. During the winter of that year, ten Indian proselytes assembled in the meetinghouse to recount their experience of conversion. Eliot's *Tears of Repentance* contains the published record of these testimonies (London: Peter Cole in Leaden Hall, 1653). See also Jean M. O'Brien, *Dispossession by Degrees: Indian Land and Identity in Natick, Massachusetts, 1650–1790* (Lincoln: University of Nebraska Press, 1997).

19. Occasionally, of course, there were substantial doctrinal differences. Take, for example, belief in purgatory. Medieval theology built on the patristic theory of *limbus Patrum*, "the place where the souls of Old Testament patriarchs were detained." Christ would then deliver the souls at his ascension. Protestants rejected both this view of the underworld and the doctrine of purgatory. According to Jean-Louis Quantin, "they stressed that there was no middle state after death between damnation and blessedness," *The Church of England and Christian Antiquity: the Construction of a Confessional Identity in the 17th Century* (Oxford: Oxford University Press, 2009), 115. The point in

each case, whether it be of rhetorical inflation to cover up doctrinal similarities or key theological disputes, is that Roman Catholics, the English episcopacy, and nonconforming Protestants all used patristic evidence as a mechanism for legitimating the terms of dispute.

20. Here, saint refers to a church member, not one of those canonized by the Roman Catholic Church, reflecting a significant doctrinal difference between Catholics and Protestants. William Bradford, *Of Plymouth Plantation, 1620–1647,* ed. Samuel Eliot Morison (New York: Alfred A. Knopf, 1952), 3.

21. Ibid.

22. Ibid. Theodore Dwight Bozeman writes about the primitivist strain within Puritanism, positing that the Puritans sought to complete the Reformation project through an extreme focus on grace coupled with a Deuteronomic scheme of behavioral regulation. *The Precisianist Strain: Disciplinary Religion & Antinomian Backlash in Puritanism to 1638* (Chapel Hill: University of North Carolina Press, 2004).

23. In contrast to Perry Miller's account, Bernard Bailyn describes these migratory patterns in a comparative context in *The Peopling of British North America: An Introduction* (New York: Vintage Books, 1988). For a more recent comparative analysis of Atlantic migration, see Nicholas Canny and Philip Morgan, "Introduction: The Making and Unmaking of an Atlantic World," in *The Oxford Handbook of the Atlantic World, 1450–1850* (Oxford: Oxford University Press, 2011), 1–23.

24. Medieval Sourcebook, "Christopher Columbus: Extracts from Journal," Fordham University, http://www.fordham.edu/halsall/source/columbus1.asp.

25. Ibid.

26. The key bulls in the establishing of the *Real Patronato* are the ones issued by Pope Alexander VI on 4 May 1493 and on 16 November 1501, and Pope Julius II's bull of 28 July 1508, *Universalis Ecclesiae.* Anna L. Peterson and Manuel A. Vásquez, *Latin American Religions: Histories and Documents in Context* (New York: New York University Press, 2008), 59–60.

27. Cortés, *Letters from Mexico,* trans., ed., and with a new introduction by Anthony Pagden (New Haven, Conn.: Yale University Press, 2001), 332.

28. Ibid., 332–33.

29. Ibid., 334.

30. Indigenous noble youth received instruction in Latin grammar and theology with the idea that they would go on to pursue higher studies and train for holy orders at the Colegio de Santa Cruz de Tlatelolco, which was founded by the Franciscans in 1536.

31. The Dominicans were the next to arrive (1525), followed by the Augustinians (1533), and then the Jesuits (1571).

32. See Cervantes, *The Devil in the New World,* 13; and J. H. Elliott, *Empires of the Atlantic World: Britain and Spain in America 1492–1580* (New Haven, Conn.: Yale University Press, 2006), 185.

33. Daniel Reff reminds us that this seeming success must be contextualized within the population collapse that decimated the indigenous peoples of the region. Many of these several million converts died of diseases brought by the Spaniards. For more information on this topic, see chapter 3 of Daniel Reff's *Plagues, Priests, and Demons: Sacred Narratives and the Rise of Christianity in the Old World and the New* (Cambridge, UK: Cambridge University Press, 2005), 124, 127.

34. Viviana Díaz Balsera, *The Pyramid Under the Cross: Franciscan Discourses of Evangelization in Sixteenth-Century Mexico* (Tucson: University of Arizona Press, 2005).

35. Sabine MacCormack, *Religion in the Andes: Vision and Imagination in Early Colonial Peru* (Princeton, N.J.: Princeton University Press, 1993), 68.

36. Cervantes, *The Devil in the New World*, 25.

37. Elliott, *Empires of the Atlantic World*, 198.

38. Ibid.

39. See Pilar Gonzalbo Aizpuru for a detailed account of the efforts of various individuals to secure the arrival of the Jesuits. *Historia de la educación en la época colonial. La educación de los criollos y la vida urbana* (Mexico City: Colegio de México, Centro de Estudios Históricos, 1990) 146–50. As she points out, initially the idea was to have them support the Mendicants with their work with the indigenous since these first contacts were made in the 1540s, before their educational work was yet widely known.

40. Jerome V. Jacobsen remarks on the ascribing of the term "drudgery" to the educational work in the cities by some members of the Society, while their "more famous brethren" were out in the mission fields, which was seen as belonging to a more alluring "otro México." *Educational Foundations of the Jesuits in Sixteenth-Century New Spain* (Berkeley: University of California Press, 1938) 108. Jesuit missionary activity to indigenous populations began in earnest around 1580. Peggy Liss claims that historians' fascination with this aspect of the Society's New Spanish activities has served to "skew the corpus of Jesuit history in Mexico." "Jesuit Contributions to the Ideology of Spanish Empire in Mexico," 329.

41. Jacobsen, S. J. *Educational Foundations of the Jesuits in Sixteenth-Century New Spain* (Berkeley: University of California Press, 1938).

42. In her superb book on the representation of cities in colonial Latin American literature, Stephanie Merrim charts the development of the colonial city from its sixteenth-century beginnings to its baroque zenith in the seventeenth century. She evokes this urban space as "layered and spectacular," terming it the "generative motor of the viceregal world." *The Spectacular City, Mexico, and Colonial Hispanic Literary Culture* (Austin: University of Texas Press, 2010), 21.

43. Cortés, *Letters from Mexico*, 26.

44. Kelly Donahue Wallace, *Art and Architecture of Viceregal Latin America, 1521–1821* (Albuquerque: University of New Mexico Press, 2008), 82.

45. Ibid., 82.

46. Thomas M. Cohen, *The Fire of Tongues: Antonio Vieira and the Missionary Church in Brazil and Portugal* (Stanford, Calif.: Stanford University Press, 1998), 200.

47. Ibid., 212.

48. See, for example, George P. Fisher, *The Reformation* (New York: Scribner, 1887); and H. A. Enno Van Gelder, *The Two Reformations in the 16th Century: A Study of the Religious Aspects and Consequences of Renaissance and Humanism* (The Hague: Martinus Nijhoff, 1964).

49. Elliott, *Empires of the Atlantic World*, 41–48.

50. Quoted from Andrew Fitzmaurice, *Humanism in America: An Intellectual History of English Colonization 1500–1625* (Cambridge, UK: Cambridge University Press, 2003), 7–9, 41.

51. The quarto edition first appeared in 1588, printed by R. Robinson in London. The folio edition was printed by Theodor de Bry in 1590 in German, French, Latin, and English. The text was also printed in Richard Hakluyt's *Principal Navigations* (London: George Bishop, 1589). For the context on the Hakluyt edition, see Peter C. Mancall, *Hakluyt's Promise: An Elizabethan's Obsession for an English America* (New Haven, Conn.: Yale University Press, 2007).

52. Thomas Harriot, *Brief and True Report of the Newfound Land of Virginia* (Francoforti ad Moenum: Typis Ioannis Wecheli, sumtibus vero Theodori de Bry, 1590).

53. Ibid., 13–14.

54. For an extended reading along these lines, see: Karen Ordahl Kupperman, *Indians and English: Facing off in Early America* (Ithaca, N.Y.: Cornell University Press, 2000).

55. Ibid., 24.

56. Ibid., 24–25. Joyce Chaplin describes a comparable mode of rendering the unfamiliar familiar through her analysis of this section of the Harriot text as an attempt to carefully observe potential enemies, such that an "unfamiliar culture" could be successfully comprehended for the purpose of military intelligence. *Subject Matter: Technology, the Body, and Science on the Anglo-American Frontier, 1500–1676* (Cambridge, Mass.: Harvard University Press, 2001), 93.

57. Fitzmaurice, *Humanism in America*, 63–65.

58. Alexander Whitaker, "The Epistle Dedicatorie," in *Good Newes from Virginia Sent to the Counsell and Company of Virginia* (London: Felix Kyngston, 1613).

59. Of course the Puritans would write extensively about the native inhabitants of the land in later texts, such as Thomas Morton, *New English Canaan* (Amsterdam: Jacob Frederick, 1637); and Roger Williams, *A Key into the Language of America* (London: Gregory Dexter, 1643). The point here is that Cotton creates a powerful rhetorical fantasy of a divine right to the land that remains a major reference point for Puritan notions of sovereignty.

60. The doctrine of this sermon, 2 Samuel 7:10, reads "Moreover, I will Appoint a Place for my people Israel, and I will PLANT them, and they may dwell in a place of their OWN, and MOVE NO MORE." John Cotton, *God's Promise to His Plantation* (Boston: Reprinted by Samuel Green and are to be sold by John Usher, 1686). This sermon was originally printed in 1634 and originally preached in 1630. In his adamant insistence on the existence of a New World of divinely ordained vacancy, Cotton willfully ignored the violent and bloody history of English colonialism that preceded the Puritan migration. See Bernard Bailyn, *The Barbarous Years: The Conflict of Civilization, 1600–1675* (New York: Alfred A. Knopf, 2013), especially 3–62.

61. As David Hall succinctly explains, "apocalyptic hopes for purity and peace" repeatedly confronted the inconvenience of "social practice." David D. Hall, *A Reforming People: Puritanism and the Transformation of Public Life in New England* (New York: Alfred A. Knopf, 2011), 142.

62. Hall notes that the legal system that developed in New England was "remarkably different from its English counterpart." *A Reforming People*, 147.

63. On debates between Congregationalists and Presbyterians, particularly as they shaped the history of Protestantism in Scotland, see Margo Todd, *The Culture of Protestantism in Early Modern Scotland* (New Haven, Conn.: Yale University Press, 2002).

64. On the numbers of New England Puritans and Pilgrims who left for England during the war, see Susan Hardman Moore, *Pilgrims: New World Settlers & the Call of Home* (New Haven, Conn.: Yale University Press, 2007), 74–143.

65. For an analysis of the English Civil War as a primary motivation for the Puritan mission to the Massachusett and Wampanoag people of New England, see Kristina Bross, *Dry Bones and Indian Sermons: Praying Indians and Colonial American Identity* (Ithaca, N.Y.: Cornell University Press, 2004).

66. Roger Williams came to the Massachusetts Bay Colony in 1631, just one year after the great migration of 20,000 Puritans. He felt the pull of the New World for reasons very similar to the Puritans, but he came for different ideals. He believed in what became known as the "liberty of conscience," or the separation of religion from civil government so that individuals could worship according to their conscience. The Puritans jailed Williams for harboring dangerous opinions and endeavored to send him back to England, at which point Williams fled to the shores of the Narra-

gansett Bay, where he founded the colony of "Providence." Here, he strove to deal fairly with the Narragansett on the crucial issue of land, which was one of the main points of contention that he had with the Massachusetts government. He acquired a small parcel from the Narragansett chiefs in 1636 and set up a modest colony. Edwin S. Gaustad, *Roger Williams* (New York: Oxford University Press, 2005).

67. The clearest example of this is the millennial zeal surrounding John Eliot's mission to the Wampanoag Indians of southern Massachusetts. For the most famous case of the Indians as the sons of Adam, see Thomas Thorowgood, *Jews in America* (London: Henry Brome, 1660). For a complete set of the Eliot Tracts, published between 1643 and 1671, see Michael P. Clark, ed., *The Eliot Tracts: With Letters to Thomas Thorowgood and Richard Baxter* (Westport, Conn.: Praeger Publishers, 2003). On the millennial underpinnings of seventeenth-century social structures in England and America, see James Hulston, *A Rational Millennium: Puritan Utopias of Seventeenth-Century England and America* (New York: Oxford University Press, 1987).

68. Eliot referred to the *Wôpanâak* as the Massachusett. Here we are using the reclaimed spelling of Wampanoag, according to Jessie "little doe" Baird Fermino, the founder of the *Wôpanâak Language Reclamation Project* (http://www.wlrp.org).

69. On Christianity as ideologically static, see Axtell, *The Invasion Within*; Ronda, "The European Indian: Jesuit Civilization Planning in New France"; and Walter Mignolo, *The Darker Side of the Renaissance: Literacy, Territoriality, and Colonization* (Ann Arbor: University of Michigan Press, 2003). More recently, scholars have challenged this reading, demonstrating syncretic forms of faith in missionary communities where indigenous practices were not only accepted by priests and ministers but actively transformed the scope of Christianity. See David Silverman, *Faith and Boundaries,* who explains how the Wampanoag "transformed Christianity into a bulwark for Wampanoag communities and an expression of their own culture" (Cambridge, UK: Cambridge University Press, 2005), 10. Kathleen Bragdon argues that missionary texts record the "social world of native tribes" as well as "Native perceptions of land as morally and socially significant," *Native People of Southern New England, 1650–1775* (Norman: University of Oklahoma Press, 2009), 51, 52. See also Glenda Goodman, " 'But they differ from us in sound': Indian Psalmody and the Soundscape of Colonialism, 1651–75," *William and Mary Quarterly*, 3rd ser., 69, no. 4 (2012): 793–822; Margaret J. Leahey, " 'Comment peut un muet prescher l'evangile?': Jesuit Missionaries and the Native Languages of New France," *French Historical Studies* 19, no. 1 (1995): 105–31; Tracy Neal Leavelle, " 'Bad Things' and 'Good Hearts': Mediation, Meaning, and the Language of Illinois Christianity," *Church History* 76, no. 2 (2007): 363–94; Robert M. Morrissey, " 'I Speak It Well': Language, Cultural Understanding, and the End of a Missionary Middle Ground in Illinois Country, 1673–1712," *Early American Studies* (Fall, 2011).

70. David Silverman, "Indians, Missions, and Religious Translation: Creating Wampanoag Christianity in Seventeenth-Century Martha's Vineyard," *William and Mary Quarterly*, 3rd ser., 62, no. 2 (April, 2005): 146.

71. The *Indian Dialogues* of 1671, a late Eliot tract, reflects discrepancies between English and Massachusetts understanding of doctrine and faith. Eliot's later letters to both Baxter and Boyle try to present the mission in a positive light, but they are peppered with disappointment in the depleted state of the mission, which "contracted" greatly following King Philip's War. In the decades following Eliot's death, Mather would refuse to print the Indian Bible on the grounds that it was too costly and that he wanted to teach the Indians English. See his letter of 10 December 1712, to Sir William Ashurst in *Selected Letters of Cotton Mather,* ed. Kenneth Silverman (Baton Rouge: Louisiana

State University Press, 1971), 126–28. Natick is also described here as "our most languishing and withered Indian village." For a compelling account of the Protestant mission's revival during the First Great Awakening, see Linford D. Fisher, *The Indian Great Awakening: Religion and the Shaping of Native Cultures in Early America* (Oxford: Oxford University Press, 2012).

72. Mark Govier, "The Royal Society, Slavery and the Island of Jamaica: 1660–1700," *Notes and Records of the Royal Society of London* 53, no. 2 (1999): 203–17.

73. See, for example, the "Conversion of the Negroes in Barbados, 1670," which states that slaves should not be converted to Christianity, for this would make them "free & their several masters and owners loose property in them, it being against the grounds and rules of Christianity that one Christian should be a slave to another." "Conversion of the Negroes in Barbados (West Indies) & St. Hellena, 1670," The Boyle Papers, "Theology," vol. 4 (London: The Royal Society), 1–38.

74. Benjamin Braude, "The Sons of Noah and the Construction of Ethnic and Geographical Identities in the Medieval and Early Modern Periods," *William and Mary Quarterly*, ser. 3, 54, no. 1 (January, 1997): 138.

75. Vincent Carretta, *Unchained Voices: An Anthology of Black Authors in the English-Speaking World of the Eighteenth Century* (Lexington: University of Kentucky Press, 2004).

76. Elliott, *Empires of the Atlantic World*. Elliott references the further documentation of the arrival of 36,300 enslaved Africans between the years of 1550 and 1595. Their number, however, was certainly much higher owing to what he terms a "growing contraband trade." In 1595, the Spanish Crown awarded a monopoly contract to Pedro Gomes Reinel, a Portuguese slave trader who dominated the traffic in Angolan slaves, resulting in the shipping of a further 80,500 enslaved Africans, with another 50,000 transported to Brazil (100).

77. Cameron Bristol, *Christians, Blasphemers, and Witches*, 68.

78. John K. Thornton and Linda Heywood, "The Treasons of Dom Pedro Nkanga a Mvemba against Dom Diogo, King of Kongo, 1550," In *Afro-Latino Voices: Narratives from the Early Modern Ibero-Atlantic World, 1550–1812*, eds. Kathryn Joy McKnight and Leo J. Garafolo. (Indianaopolis, Ind.: Hackett Publishing Company, 2009), 3.

79. Alonso de Sandoval, S. J., *Treatise on Slavery: Selections from De instauranda Aethiopum salute*, ed. and trans., with an Introduction by Nicole von Germeten (Indianopolis, Ind.: Hackett Publishing Company, 2008), 112.

80. Cameron Bristol, *Christians, Blasphemers, and Witches*, 76.

81. Nicole Von Germeten, "Routes to Respectability: Confraternities and Men of African Descent in New Spain," in *Local Religion in Colonial Mexico*, ed. Martin Austin Nesvig (Albuquerque: University of New Mexico Press, 2006), 217.

82. Javier Villa-Flores "Voices from a Living Hell: Slavery, Death and Salvation in a Mexican Obraje" ed. Martin Austin Nesvig (Albuquerque: University of New Mexico Press, 2006), 235–249.

83. Sylvia Molloy's essay, "Latin America in the U.S. Imaginary: Postcolonialism, Translation, and the Magic Realist Imperative," offers an incisive look at the reasons behind the marginalization of Latin American history and culture within the U.S. academy. In *Ideologies of Hispanism*, ed. Mabel Moraña (Nashville, Tenn.: Vanderbilt University Press, 2005), 189–201. For a discussion of the persistence of these tenets in colonial Latin American studies, see Stephanie Kirk's "Nuevos itinerarios en un nuevo milenio: periodización, territorialización, e identidad," in *Estudios coloniales latinoamericanos en el siglo XXI: Nuevos itinerarios* (Pittsburgh: Instituto Internacional de Literatura Iberoamericana, 2011), 7–17. For a theoretical look at the early modern global imperial politics informing the Black Legend, see Margaret Greer, Walter Mignolo, and Maureen Quilligan's co-

edited essay collection, *Rereading the Black Legend: The Discourses of Religious and Racial Difference in the Renaissance Empires* (Chicago: University of Chicago Press, 2007).

CHAPTER 1

1. Cited in J. H. Elliott, *The Old World and the New* (Cambridge, UK, 1970; repr., 1992), 10.

2. See Alain Milhou, *Colón y su mentalidad mesiánica en el ambiente franciscanista español* (Valladolid, 1983).

3. J. W. O'Malley, *Giles of Viterbo and Church Reform* (Leiden, 1968), chap. 4; John Leddy Phelan, *The Millennial Kingdom of the Franciscans in the New World*, 2nd ed. (Berkeley, 1970).

4. For a wide-ranging survey of Protestantism in the context of the British Atlantic, see Carla Gardina Pestana, *Protestant Empire: Religion and the Making of the British Atlantic World* (Philadelphia, 2009).

5. For a useful introduction to the controversy over the question of how far Christianity should be adapted to traditional Chinese practices, see J. S. Cummins, *A Question of Rites. Friar Domingo de Navarrete and the Jesuits in China* (Aldershot, 1993).

6. See the Introduction to Francis J. Bremer and Lynn A. Botelho, eds., *The World of John Winthrop: Essays on England and New England 1588–1649*, Massachusetts Historical Society, Studies in American History and Culture, vol. 9 (Boston, 2005), 16–17. For a valuable attempt to consider the impact of religious developments in New England on the home country in the 1640s and 1650s, see Susan Hardman Moore, *Pilgrims: New World Settlers and the Call of Home* (New Haven, Conn., 2007).

7. George M. Foster, *Culture and Conquest* (Chicago, 1960), 191–98; Miri Rubin, *Corpus Christi* (Cambridge, 1991); Arturo Warman, *La danza de moros y cristianos* (Mexico City, 1972).

8. The standard work on evangelization in Mexico, Robert Ricard, *La 'conquête spirituelle' du Mexique* (Paris, 1933); The English translation *The Spiritual Conquest of Mexico: an Essay on the Apostolate and the Evangelizing Methods of the Mendicant Orders of New Spain* (Berkeley, Calif., 1966), still retains its value, although it has been supplemented and in part superseded by a vast amount of subsequent work. For a recent brief overview of the establishment of Christianity in Iberian America see John Lynch, *New Worlds: A Religious History of Latin America* (New Haven, Conn., 2012), chaps. 1 and 2.

9. For the millennial and apocalyptic tradition in general, see Marjorie Reeves, *The Influence of Prophecy in the Later Middle Ages: A Study in Joachimism* (Oxford, 1969).

For millenarian expectations aroused by the discovery of America, see Phelan, *The Millennial Kingdom of the Franciscans in the New World*; Georges Baudot, *Utopie et Histoire au Mexique* (Toulouse, 1977; Spanish trans., *Utopía e Historia en México* [Madrid, 1983]); David Brading, *The First America* (Cambridge, Mass., 1991), chap. 5.

10. Jaime Lara, *City, Temple, Stage: Eschatological Architecture and Liturgical Theatre in New Spain* (Notre Dame, Ind., 2004), 178.

11. Lara, *City, Temple, Stage*, chap. 4.

12. Fintan B. Warren, *Vasco de Quiroga and His Pueblo-Hospitals of Santa Fe* (Washington, D.C., 1963). For Paraguay, see Alberto Armani, *Ciudad de Dios y ciudad del sol. El 'estado' jesuita de los guaraníes, 1609–1768* (Mexico City, 1982; repr., 1987); Girolamo Imbruglia, *L'Invenzione del Paraguay* (Naples, 1983).

13. Guillermo Céspedes del Castillo, *América hispánica, 1492–1898* (Barcelona, 1983), 244.

14. J. H. Elliott, *Empires of the Atlantic World: Britain and Spain in America, 1492–1830* (New Haven, Conn., 2006), 199.

15. See, for example, Cayetana Álvarez de Toledo, *Politics and Reform in Spain and Viceregal Mexico: The Life and Thought of Juan de Palafox, 1600–1659* (Oxford, 2004); Oscar Mazín, *Entre dos majestades* (Zamora, Michoacán, 1987); William B. Taylor, *Magistrates of the Sacred: Priests and Parishioners in Eighteenth-Century Mexico* (Stanford, Calif., 1996).

16. Auke P. Jacobs, *Los movimientos migratorios entre Castilla e Hispanoamérica durante el reinado de Felipe III, 1598–1621* (Amsterdam, 1995), 93.

17. Jacobs, *Los movimientos*, 46.

18. For some fascinating examples of deviation, see Stuart B. Schwartz, *All Can Be Saved: Religious Tolerance and Salvation in the Iberian Atlantic World* (New Haven, Conn., 2008).

19. Cited in Elliott, *Empires of the Atlantic World*, 11.

20. Alexander Brown, *The Genesis of the United States*, 2 vols. (London, 1890), 1:366.

21. Geoffrey Parker, "Crisis and Catastrophe: The Global Crisis of the Seventeenth Century Reconsidered," *American Historical Review* 113 (2008): 1053–79, at 1074, citing Clarence S. Brigham, ed., *British Royal Proclamations Relating to America, 1603–1783* (1911, repr.; New York, 1974), 53.

22. James B. Bell, *The Imperial Origins of the King's Church in Early America, 1607–1783* (New York, 2004), 3–8; and see Rhys Isaac, *The Transformation of Virginia* (Chapel Hill, N.C., 1982), 58–65, and elsewhere for the gentry ethos in Virginia's churches.

23. Bell, *Imperial Origins*, chap. 9.

24. Elliott, *The Old World and the New*, 76–77.

25. D. B. Quinn, ed., *The Voyages and Colonising Enterprises of Sir Humphrey Gilbert*, Hakluyt Society, 2nd ser., vols. 83–84 (London, 1940), 1:71.

26. Edmund S. Morgan, *Visible Saints: The History of a Puritan Idea* (1963; repr., Ithaca, N.Y., 1971), 65.

27. See Richard J. Ross, "Puritan Godly Discipline in Comparative Perspective: Legal Pluralism and the Sources of 'Intensity,'" *American Historical Review* 113 (2008): 975–1002.

28. Cited by Charles M. Andrews, *The Colonial Period of American History*, 4 vols. (New Haven, Conn., 1934–38; repr., 1964), 2:8.

29. Cited by Richard Dunn, *Puritan and Yankee: The Winthrop Dynasty of New England, 1630–1717* (Princeton, N.J., 1962), 36.

30. See Seymour B. Liebman, *The Jews in New Spain* (Coral Gables, Fla., 1970), chap. 10.

31. Elliott, *Empires of the Atlantic World*, 48; Carole Blackburn, "The Wilderness," in *Harvest of Souls: The Jesuit Missions and Colonialism in North America, 1632–1650* (Montreal, 2000), chap. 3.

32. For Quakers and Baptists in New England, see Carla Gardina Pestana, *Quakers and Baptists in Colonial Massachusetts* (Cambridge, Mass., 1991). For Pennsylvania, see Richard S. and Mary Maples Dunn, eds., *The World of William Penn* (Philadelphia, 1986).

33. For the Jewish Atlantic diaspora, see, most recently, Richard L. Kagan and Philip D. Morgan, eds., *Atlantic Diasporas: Jews, Conversos and Crypto-Jews in the Age of Mercantilism, 1500–1800* (Baltimore, 2009).

34. Sir Josiah Child, *A New Discourse of Trade* (London, 1693), 191.

35. See Michele Gillespie and Robert Beachy, eds., *Pious Pursuits: German Moravians in the Atlantic World* (New York, 2007).

36. Cited by Thomas S. Kidd, *The Protestant Interest: New England after Puritanism* (New Haven, Conn., 2004), 1.

37. See especially Ruth H. Bloch, *Visionary Republic: Millennial Themes in American Thought, 1756–1800* (Cambridge, Mass., 1985).

38. Richard W. Cogley, *John Eliot's Mission to the Indians before King Philip's War* (Cambridge, Mass., 1999), chap. 1.

39. See, for New Spain, Robert Ricard, *La conquête spirituelle du Mexique*, 163–85, and, for Peru, Pierre Duviols, *La lutte contre les religions autochtones dans le Pérou colonial* (Paris, 1971), 248–63.

40. Elliott, *Empires of the Atlantic World*, 73–74.

41. David Hall and Alexandra Walsham, "'Justification by Print Alone?' Protestantism, Literacy, and Communications in the Anglo-American World of John Winthrop," in *The World of John Winthrop*, ed. Bremer and Botelho, (Boston, Mass., 2005) 334–85.

42. Nicholas Griffiths and Fernando Cervantes, eds., *Spiritual Encounters: Interactions Between Christianity and Native Religions in Colonial America* (Birmingham, Ala., 1999), 2–8.

43. For conquest societies and forced acculturation, see especially Foster, *Culture and Conquest*.

44. Iris Gareis, "Repression and Cultural Change: the 'Extirpation of Idolatry' in Colonial Peru" in *Spiritual Encounters*, ed. Griffiths and Cervantes, chap. 9; and see more generally Nicholas Griffiths, *The Cross and the Serpent: Religious Repression and Resurgence in Colonial Peru* (Norman, Okla., 1995); and Kenneth Mills, *Idolatry and Its Enemies: Colonial and Andean Religion and Extirpation, 1640–1750* (Princeton, N.J., 1997).

45. Lara, *City, Temple, Stage*, chap. 1.

46. James Axtell, *After Columbus* (New York, 1988), 98. For the French Jesuits, see also James Axtell, *The Invasion Within* (New York, 1985), chap. 6.

47. This point is well made in Blackburn, *Harvest of Souls*. See especially the Conclusion.

48. For examples, see Edward H. Spicer, *Cycles of Conquest* (Tucson, Ariz., 1962) and David J. Weber, *Bárbaros: Spaniards and Their Savages in the Age of Enlightenment* (New Haven, Conn., 2005).

49. Osvaldo F. Pardo, "Contesting the Power to Heal: Angels, Demons and Plants in Colonial Mexico," in *Spiritual Encounters*, ed. Griffiths and Cervantes, chap. 6.

50. Inga Clendinnen, "Ways to the Sacred: Reconstructing 'Religion' in Sixteenth Century Mexico," *History and Anthropology* 5 (1990): 105–41.

51. See, most recently, Jaime Lara, *City, Temple, Stage*, and his *Christian Texts for Aztecs: Art and Liturgy in Colonial Mexico* (Notre Dame, Ind., 2008).

52. Fernando Cervantes, *The Devil in the New World* (New Haven, Conn., 1994); Jorge Cañizares-Esguerra, *Puritan Conquistadors* (Stanford, Calif., 2006), chap. 2. For European diabolical thinking, see Stuart Clark, *Thinking with Demons* (Oxford, 1997).

53. Alejandra B. Osorio, "*El callejón de la soledad*: Vectors of Cultural Hybridity in Seventeenth-Century Lima," in *Spiritual Encounters*, ed. Griffiths and Cervantes, chap. 8.

54. *More Letters from the American Farmer: An Edition of the Essays in English Left Unpublished by Crèvecoeur*, ed. Dennis D. Moore (Athens, Ga., 1995), 82–83.

55. Carlos Alberto González Sánchez, *Los mundos del libro* (Seville, 1999), 71; and see Elliott, *Empires of the Atlantic World*, 206.

56. The deviations examined in Schwartz, *All Can Be Saved*, come from Inquisition records.

57. See especially Patricia V. Bonomi, *Under the Cape of Heaven: Religion, Society and Politics in Colonial America* (New York, 1986).

58. Jon Butler, *Awash in a Sea of Faith* (Cambridge, Mass., 1990), 127–28.

59. See Stephen Foster, *The Long Argument: English Puritanism and the Shaping of New England Culture, 1570–1700* (Chapel Hill, N.C., 1991); Paul R. Lucas, *Valley of Discord: Church and Society Along the Connecticut River, 1636–1725* (Hanover, N.H., 1976).

60. Pestana, *Quakers and Baptists*, 83–84. See also Michael Zuckerman, "The Fabrication of Identity in Early America," *William and Mary Quarterly*, 3rd ser., 34 (1977): 183–214.

61. Crèvecoeur, *More Letters*, 85.

62. Hall and Walsham, "Justification," in *The World of John Winthrop*, ed. Bremer and Botelho, 345, 349.

63. Nicholas P. Cushner, *The Jesuits and the First Evangelization of America* (Oxford, 2006), 88.

64. Lara, *City, Temple, Stage*, 197.

65. González Sánchez, *Los mundos del libro*, 89.

66. See Barry Shain, "Religious Conscience and Original Sin: An Exploration of America's Protestant Foundations," in *Liberty and American Experience in the Eighteenth Century*, ed. David Womersley (Indianapolis, Ind., 2006), 153–208.

67. Butler, *Awash in a Sea of Faith*, chap. 4.

CHAPTER 2

1. Christopher Columbus, "Diario," in *A Synoptic Edition of the Log of Columbus's First Voyage*, ed. Francesca Lardicci, textual editor Valeria Bertolucci Pizzorusso, trans. Cynthia L. Chamberin and Blair Sullivan. Repertorium Columbianum vol. VI (Turnhout, Belgium: Brepols, 1999), 48. José de Acosta, *The Natural and Moral History of the Indies*, ed. Jane Mangan; trans. Frances López-Morillas; introduction and commentary by Walter Mignolo (Durham, N.C.: Duke University Press, 2002), 330. For discussions of Acosta's demonological interpretation of Native American religions, see Fernando Cervantes, *The Devil in the New World: The Impact of Diabolism in New Spain* (New Haven, Conn.: Yale University Press, 1994); also Sabine McCormack, "Gods, Demons, and Idols in the Andes," *Journal of the History of Ideas* 67.4 (2006) 623–47; Cañizares-Esguerra, *Puritan Conquistadors: Iberianizing the Atlantic, 1550–1700* (Stanford, Calif.: Stanford University Press, 2006), 35–119; and Fermín del Pino Díaz, "Inquisidores, misioneros y demonios americanos," in *Demonio, religión y sociedad entre España y América*, ed. Fermín Pino Díaz (Madrid: Consejo Superior de Investigaciones Científicas, 2002), 139–160; and "Estudio introductorio," in *Historia natural y moral de las Indias*, by Josef de Acosta, ed. Fermín del Pino Díaz (Madrid: Consejo Superior de Investigaciones Científicas, 2008), xvii–lvi.

2. Cañizares-Esguerra, *Puritan*, 79, 76.

3. There is thus no argument in the observation made by Cañizares-Esguerra with regard to José de Acosta that his "treatise has been hailed as an ambitious essay on comparative ethnography and clear-eyed study of the natural history of the New World" while it is "actually a treatise on demonology" (*Puritan*, 120).

4. For discussions of this transformation in the perception of the Devil with an emphasis on northern Europe, see Stuart Clark, *Thinking with Demons: The idea of witchcraft in early modern Europe* (Oxford: Clarendon Press, 1997), especially 151–94; also Keith Thomas, *Religion and the Decline of Magic* (Oxford: Oxford University Press, 1971, rpt. 1997), especially 469–501; for an emphasis on southern Europe, see Julio Caro Baroja, *The World of Witches*, trans. O. N. V. Glendinning (Chicago: University of Chicago Press, 1964), especially 69–111; and for an emphasis on New Spain, see Cervantes, *The Devil*, 1–39.

5. See here especially Thomas, *Religion*, 469–501.

6. See Oberman, *The Two Reformations: The Journey from the Last Days to the New World*, ed. Donald Weinstein (New Haven, Conn.: Yale University Press, 2003), 1–43; also "*Via Antiqua* and *Via Moderna*: Late Medieval Prolegomena and Early Reformation Thought. *Journal of the History of Ideas* 48.1 (1987): 23–40.

7. Oberman, *The Two Reformations*, 24–25.

8. More recent scholarship on areas beyond New Spain has generally affirmed Cervantes's model but also suggested that there were often more local, rhetorical, and political forces at work in the representation of Native American religions. Thus, Kenneth Mills, in his work on the Andes, has pointed out that, frequently, the demonization of Native American religions was often "less tidy in practice" than suggested by Cervantes's study of the theological literature (219) and, on the ground, often particular to specific groups or individuals; Kenneth Mills, *Idolatry and its Enemies: Colonial Andean Religion and Extirpation, 1640–1750* (Princeton, N.J.: Princeton University Press, 1997), 219. Similarly, Sabine MacCormack, "Gods," 623–47, also focusing on Peru, has suggested that it was precisely the destruction of the physical idols, which forced Native deities into the invisible underground, so to speak, that drove home the point of their reality and inherent power in the eyes of the missionaries. While Europeans had, of course, had a long-standing acquaintance with idolatry from the Classical Greek and Roman pantheons, she argues, the recalcitrance of Native deities to be assimilated to classical models of idolatry enhanced their demonic power in the eyes of European ethnographers. In other words, while demonology was not the primary motivation of the early modern ethnographic project, ethnography in effect drove the project of demonology, as the more was learned about Native religions the more they appeared to resist assimilation to familiar classical models and the more demonic they appeared.

9. José Antonio Maravall, *Culture of the Baroque: Analysis of a Historical Structure*, trans. Terry Cochran (Minneapolis: University of Minnesota Press, 1986), 27. See also Monika Kaup and Lois Parkinson Zamora, "Baroque, New World Baroque, Neobaroque: Categories and Concepts," in *Baroque New Worlds: Representation, Transculturation, Counterconquest*, ed. M. Kaup and L. Parkinson Zamora (Durham, N.C.: Duke University Press, 2010), 1–40; and Gilles Deleuze, *The Fold Leibniz and the Baroque* (London: Athlone Press, 1993), 27–41.

10. The classic account of the philosophical questions raised by the colonial encounter in the context of Imperial Spain is still Anthony Pagden, *The Fall of Natural Man: The American Indian and the Origins of Comparative Ethnology* (Cambridge: Cambridge University Press, 1982), but see also MacCormack, *On the Wings of Time: Rome, the Incas, Spain, and Peru* (Princeton, N.J.: Princeton University Press, 2007).

11. On Eden, see Michael Householder, *Inventing Americans in the Age of Discovery: Narratives of Encounter* (Aldershot, UK: Ashgate, 2010); also Andrew Hadfield, "Peter Martyr, Richard Eden and the New World: Reading, Experience and Translation," *Connotations* 5.1 (1995–96): 1–22; also *Literature, travel, and colonial writing in the English Renaissance, 1545–1625* (Oxford, UK: Clarendon Press, 1998). Sixteenth-century England also had its own more direct experiences with colonial enterprises in Ireland, and some of the early English ideas about Native Americans were therefore colored, as Nicholas Canny and others have shown, by English ideas about the "wild Irish"; see Canny, "The Permissive Frontier: Social Control in English Settlements in Ireland and Virginia, 1550–1650," in *The Westward Enterprise*. ed. K. R. Andrews, N. P. Canny, and P. E. H. Hair (Detroit, Mich.: Wayne State University Press, 1979), 17–44.

12. Peter Martyr, "The Decades of the newe worlde," translated by Richard Eden (1555) in *The First Three Books on America*, ed. Edward Arber (Birmingham: n.p. 1885), 71, 78, 99.

13. Martyr, "Decades," 125.

14. Richard Eden, "The Preface to the Reader," in Peter Martyr, "The Decades," 57.

15. Sir Walter Ralegh, *The Discovery of the Large, Rich and Bewtiful Empyre of Guiana*, transcribed, annotated and introduced by Neil L. Whitehead (Norman: University of Oklahoma Press, 1997) 134.

16. Thomas Harriot, *A briefe and true report of the new found land of Virginia* (New York: Dover Publications, 1972), 25.

17. On "the Inca" Garcilaso de la Vega's Neoplatonic reading of Inca paganism, see Ralph Bauer, "Colonial Discourse and Early American Literary History: Ercilla, the Inca Garcilaso, and Joel Barlow's Conception of a New World Epic," *Early American Literature* 30, no. 3 (1995): 203–32; David Lupher, *Romans in a New World: Classical Models in Sixteenth-Century Spanish America* (Ann Arbor: University of Michigan Press, 2003); and Enrique Pupo-Walker,*Historia, Creación y Profesía en los Textos del Inca Garcilaso de la Vega* (Madrid: Ediciones José Porrúa Turanzas, S. A., 1982).

18. Harriot, *Briefe*, 25.

19. Harriot, *Briefe*, 26.

20. Harriot, *Briefe*, 26.

21. Thomas, *Religion*, 470.

22. For a discussion of the Elizabethan consideration of these legal issues, see Robert Miller, "The Doctrine of Discovery in American Indian Law," *Idaho Law Review* 42 (2005–2006): 1–122, espeically 15–19; also Anthony Pagden, *Lords of all the World: Ideologies of Empire in Spain, Britain, and France, 1500–1800* (New Haven, N.J.: Yale University Press, 1995), 90.

23. On the English challenges of Spanish claims to possession based on "mere discovery," see Miller, "Doctrine," 17–18; also Robert Miller, *Native America, Discovered and Conquered* (Westport, Conn.: Praeger, 2006), 9–58; and Lauren Benton and Benjamin Straumann, "Acquiring Empire by Law: From Roman Doctrine to Early Modern European Practice" *Law and History Review* 28 (2010): 1–38.

24. On the formation of the "Black Legend," see Charles Gibson, *The Black Legend. Anti-Spanish Attitudes in the Old World and the New* (New York: Knopf, 1971); on the history of the term, see also Margaret Greer, Walter Mignolo, and Maureen Quilligan, "Introduction," in *Rereading the Black Legend: The Discourses of Religious and Racial Difference in the Renaissance Empires* (Chicago: University of Chicago Press, 2008), 1–26.

25. Ralegh, *The Discoverie*, 134.

26. This terminology, however, dates only to the eighteenth century—to the bibliographer Charles d'Orléans de Rothelin. The de Brys and their colleagues in the book trade referred to the two series as "India Occidentalis" and "India Orientalis." The word "America" appears in the title beginning with volume two, about Florida.

27. Only the first six volumes of the series were published by de Bry senior. After his death in 1598, subsequent volumes published before 1617 were issued by his two sons, Johann Theodor and Johann Israel. After 1617, Johann Theodor worked by himself on the Voyages series. After 1623, the last two volumes of the Voyages were published by Johann Theodor's son-in-law, Matthaeus Merian. While the de Bry Voyages were long read primarily as Protestant anti-Spanish propaganda, more recently historians have emphasized also their broader allegorical, didactic, theological, and especially commercial dimensions. On anti-Spanish propaganda in the Voyages, see Bernadette Bucher, *La sauvage aux seins pendants* (Paris: Herman, 1977). For examples of the recent critical reappraisal, see Michiel van Groesen, *The Representation of the Overseas World in the De Bry Collection of Voyages (1590–1634)* (Leiden: Brill, 2008); Susanne Burghartz, ed. *Inszinierte Welten: Staging New World: Die west- und ostindische Reisen der Vergleger de Bry, 1590–1630. De Brys' Illustrated Travel Reports* (Basel: Schwabe Verlag, 2004); and Michael Gaudio, *Engraving the Savage: the New World and Techniques of Civilization* (Minneapolis: University of Minnesota Press, 2008).

28. See Kim Sloan, "Introduction," in *A New World: England's First View of America*, ed. Kim Sloan et. al. (Chapel Hill: University of North Carolina Press, 2007), 11–22; also Paul Hulton,

America 1585. The Complete Drawings of John White (Chapel Hill: University of North Carolina Press, 1984), 18; and Eric Cheyfitz, *The Poetics of Imperialism: Translation and Colonization from The Tempest to Tarzan* (New York: Oxford University Press, 1991), 188–98. On de Bry more generally, see Bucher, *La sauvage*; van Groessen, *Representation*; Gaudio, *Engraving*; and Patricia Gravatt, "Rereading Theodor de Bry's Black Legend," in *Rereading the Black Legend: The Discourses of Religious and Racial Difference in the Renaissance Empires*, ed. Margaret Greer, Walter Mignolo, Maureen Quilligan (Chicago: University of Chicago Press, 2007), 225–43.

29. Harriot, *Briefe*, 54.

30. See Gaudio, *Engraving*, especially 54–61. Despite the brilliance of Gaudio's reading of de Bry's smoke, he misses, I think, the ambivalence of Harriot's representation of Native shamanism, especially its partial debt to Italian Hermeticism.

31. Harriot, *Briefe*, 71.

32. On the impact of Italian Hermeticism in Renaissance England, see the classic study by Francis Yates, *Giordano Bruno and the Hermetic Tradition* (London: Routledge, 1964). On John Dee, see Yates, *The Occult Philosophy in the Elizabethan Age* (London: Routledge, 1979); also Nicholas Clulee, *John Dee's Natural Philosophy: Between Science and Religion* (London: Routledge, 1988); and Peter French, *John Dee: The World of an Elizabethan Magus* (London: Routledge & Kegan Paul, 1972); on the connections between Raleigh, Gilbert, and Dee, see Deborah Harkness, *John Dee's Conversations with Angels: Cabala, Alchemy, and the End of Nature* (Cambridge: Cambridge University Press, 1999) 124.

33. For a discussion of the alchemical motifs and plant symbolism in the *Primavera*, see Mirella Levi D'Ancona, *Botticelli's Primavera. A Botanical Interpretation including Astrology, Alchemy, and the Medici* (Florence: Olschki Editore, 1983).

34. Quoted in Stuart Clark, *Vanities of the Eye: Vision in Early Modern European Culture* (Oxford: Oxford University Press, 2007), 79.

35. Ibid.

36. This "folk" tradition of witchcraft is also implied in de Bry's depictions of the smoke of Native campfires, as Michael Gaudio's study of de Bry's engravings has shown (*Engraving*, 45–86).

37. Günther Mahal and Martin Ehrenfeuchter, eds. *Das Wagnerbuch von 1593*, 2 vols. (Tübingen: A. Francke Verlag, 2005), 239.

38. (My translation). The German reads here "Umb ire Religion hat es solche gestalt. Sie betten gar viel und mancherly Götter an / Etliche sind gemahlet / etliche geschnizt auss Kreyden oder Holz / oder aus Gold und Silber / seltsam geformiert / Etliche haben Vögel unn ander scheussliche Thier / wie wir den Teufel mahlen / mit Krawen Füssen und langen Schwänzen. . . . Der Teufel betreugt sie gar offt in mancherley gestalt / unnd verheiss bissweylen iren Priestern etwas / . . . Also verirt der die arme Leut der listige verlogne Schelm." Mahal and Ehrenfeuchter, eds. *Das Wagnerbuch*, 240, 250.

39. Theodor de Bry, [America. Pt. 3. German] *Dritte Buch Americae, darinn Brasilia durch Johann Staden auss eigener Erfahrung in teutsch beschrieben* (Frankfurt: Theodor de Bry, 1593), "Dem Durchleuchtingsten Hochgebornen . . . ," (t. 3, n.p.).

40. de Bry, [America. Pt. 3. German] *Dritte Buch Americae*, 160.

41. For a discussion of the dissemination of the Faust and Wagner stories in England, see Ernest Richards, "The English Wagner book of 1594," *PMLA*, 24, no. 1 (1909): 32–39.

42. For a discussion of Harriot's association in this circle and the accusations leveled against him as a mathematician, atomist, alchemist, and atheist, see Gordon Batho, "Thomas Harriot and the Northumberland Household," in *Thomas Harriot: An Elizabethan Man of Science*, ed. Robert Fox (Aldershot, UK: Ashgate, 2000), 28–47; also Joyce Chaplin, *Subject Matter: Technology, the*

Body, and Science on the Anglo-American Frontier (Cambridge, Mass.: Harvard University Press, 2001), 29–31.

43. James I, King of England, *Daemonologie in forme of a dialogue, diuided into three bookes* (Edinburgh: Printed by Robert Walde-graue printer to the Kings Majestie, 1597), n.p.

44. Stuart Clarke, *Thinking with Demons: The Idea of Witchcraft in Early Modern Europe* (Oxford: Clarendon Press, 1997), 445.

45. Not much is known about the translator, Edward Grimstone. He apparently translated various works from Spanish and French into English; see Andrew Hadfield, *Literature, Travel, and Colonial Writing in the English Renaissance, 1545–1625* (Oxford, UK: Clarendon Press, 1998), 105–8.

46. Joseph Mede, "A Coniecture Concerning Gog and Magog in the Revelation" (1627), in *The Works of the Pious and Profoundly-Learned Joseph Mede, BD* (London: Printed by James Flesher for Richard Royston, 1664), n.p.

47. Mede, "A Coniecture," n.p. For a discussion of Mede's place in the evolution of an imperialist ideology in Great Britain, see David Armitage, *The Ideological Origins of the British Empire* (Cambridge: Cambridge University Press, 2000), 94–97.

48. While Protestants in general identified the Antichrist with the papacy, the Puritans, especially, also saw the English episcopacy being infiltrated by the Kingdom of Evil; see Tuveson, *Millennium and Utopia: A Study in the Background of the Idea of Progress* (Berkeley: University of California Press, 1949), 23–70.

49. James Axtell, *The European and the Indian: Essays in the Ethnohistory of Colonial North America* (New York: Oxford University Press, 1981), 165. He points out that the Pequod War of 1637, for example, was essentially a conflict between two competing and incompatible concepts of farming and ownership of land. On John Eliot, see Richard Cogley, *John Eliot's Mission to the Indians before King Philip's War* (Cambridge, Mass.: Harvard University Press, 1999).

50. John Cotton, "God's Promise to His Plantations," in *The Puritans: A Narrative Anthology*, ed. A. Heimert and A. Delbanco (Cambridge, Mass.: Harvard University Press, 1985), 77. On the typological association of the Indians with the Canaanites, see also John Canup, *Out of the Wilderness: The Emergence of an American Identity in Colonial New England* (Middletown, Conn.: Wesleyan University Press, 1990), 79–87.

51. John Winthrop, *Winthrop Papers* (Boston: Massachusetts Historical Society, 1947), 5 vols. 3: 149.

52. John Winthrop, "Reason to be Considered," in *The Puritans*, ed. A. Heimert and A. Delbanco, 73.

53. Roger Williams, *A Key into the Language of America* (London: Gregory Dexter, 1643), n. p.

54. Williams, *Key*, n.p. On the early modern history of the idea of the "Jewish" origin of Native Americans, see Lee Eldridge Huddleston, *Origins of the American Indians, European Concepts, 1492–1729* (Austin: University of Texas Press, 1967).

55. Samuel Purchas, *Hakluytus Posthumus, or Purchas his pilgrimes* [London, 1625] (Glasgow: James MacLehose & Sons, 1905–1907), 20 vols, 19: 225.

56. For a discussion of "Virginia's Verger" as a "cant of conquest," see Francis Jennings, *The Invasion of America: Indians, Colonialism and the Cant of Conquest* (Chapel Hill: University of North Carolina Press, 1975).

57. Purchas, *Hakluytus*, 19: 231–32.

58. John Smith, *The Generall Historie of Virginia, New-England, and the Summer Isles with the Names of the Adventurers, Planters, and Governours from Their First Beginning* (London: Printed by I. D. and I. H. for Michael Sparkes, 1624), 48, 34.

59. Smith, *Generall Historie*, 38.

60. Mary Rowlandson, "The Goodness and Soveraignty of God," in *So Dreadfull a Judgment: Puritan Responses to King Philip's War, 1676–1677*, ed. Richard Slotkin and James K. Folsom (Middletown, Conn.: Wesleyan University Press, 1978), 326, 393.

61. Cotton Mather, *Wonders of the Invisible World*, ed. Reiner Smolinski (Lincoln: University of Nebraska Press, 2007), ix, 20, 104.

62. Mather, *Wonders*, x.

63. Anthony Grafton, *New Worlds, Ancient Texts: The Power of Tradition and the Shock of Discovery* (Cambridge, Mass.: Harvard University Press, 1995), 51.

64. For the case of Spain, see Christian; on England, see Thomas, *Religion*; on Continental Europe, see C. M. N. Eire, *War Against the Idols: The Reformation of Worship from Erasmus to Calvin* (Cambridge: Cambridge University Press, 1986). See also the October 2006 issue (vol. 67, no. 4) of *Journal of the History of Ideas*, especially the essay by Peter Miller ("History of Religion Becomes Ethnology: Some Evidence from Peiresc's Africa," 674–96), which considers the interaction between the history of religion in Europe and the history of colonial ethnography. Also, Joan Pau Rubié, in his contribution to the volume, notes the "peculiar relationship between events taking place in the 1520s in Mexico and Europe: while the Spanish were busy destroying the idols of freshly-conquered Mesoamerica, reformed writers from Lefevre to Calvin denounced the European cult of saints and relics as idolatrous, and incited the people to iconoclasm." Although he does not specifically investigate the impact of the Counter-Reformation on conceptions of idolatry in the Catholic world, he reminds us that "the difference between Catholic and Protestant responses was not over the conception of idolatry, which they shared, but its *range of application*" ("Theology, Ethnography, and the Historicization of Idolatry," 571–96, my emphasis).

65. Maravall, *Culture*, 77.

66. Hernando Ruiz de Alarcón, *Treatise on the heathen superstitions and customs that today live among the Indians native to this New Spain, 1629*, trans. and ed. J. Richard Andrews and Ross Hassig (Norman: University of Oklahoma Press, 1984), 39–40. For a discussion of Ruiz de Alarcón's treatise, see the editors' introduction to this edition (3–38).

CHAPTER 3

1. The Latin term *sanctitas* (sanctity) is perhaps intentionally less definite than the terms *sanctus* (a saint) and *martyr* (a martyr). In the texts discussed in these pages, Christians speak of people *cum sanctitatis fama* (with a reputation of holiness), as opposed to others *cum martyrii fama* (with a reputation of being martyrs). To avoid the annoyance of scare quotes, I refer to *saintly persons*, on one hand, and, on the other, to *saints* and *martyrs*, in the case of those formally canonized. Throughout these texts, the term *meritum* (merit) is used in the strict sense of something that brings honor not only to those upon whom God has bestowed his grace, but, more important, to God himself for having bestowed it. All translations from foreign languages are my own.

2. "De inuocatione, & veneratione, & reliquiis Sanctorum, & sacris imaginibus" (4 December 1563), in *Sacros. Concilii Tridentini canones et decreta: item declarationes* (Lyon: ex typis Simonis Rigavd, 1644), 636–37: "Sanctorum quoque martyrum, & aliorum cum Christo viuentium sancta Corpora, quæ viua membra fuerunt Christi, &c templum Spiritus sancti, ab ipso ad æternam vitam suscitanda, & glorificanda, à fidelibus veneranda esse: per quæ multa beneficia à Deo hominibus præstantur. . . . Illud verò diligenter doceant Episcopi, per historias mysteriorum nostræ redemptionis,

picturis, vel aliis similitudinibus expressas, erudiri, & confirmari populum in articulis fidei com-
memorandis, & assiduè recolendis: tum verò ex omnibus sacris imaginibus magnum fructum per-
cipi; non solùm quia admonetur populus beneficiorum, & munerû, quæ à Christo sibi collata sunt,
sed etiam quia Dei per sanctos miracula, & salutaria exempla oculis fidelium subiiciuntur: vt pro iis
Deo gratias agant, ad Sanctorúmque imitationem vita morésque suos component, excitentúrque ad
adorandum, ac diligendum Deum, & ad pietatem colendam" ("Saints and likewise martyrs, and
others living with Christ as a holy body, who were living members of Christ and a temple of the holy
Spirit, are for this reason to be called as witnesses to eternal life, and glorified and venerated by the
faithful, through which many services are rendered to God by men. . . . Bishops should indeed
diligently teach that, through stories of the mysteries of our redemption depicted in pictures or in
other likenesses, the populace is enlightened and confirmed, recalling and assiduously going over
the articles of faith. Similarly, there is surely great profit to be derived from all holy images, not only
because the populace is advised of the benefits and gifts that are conferred upon it by God, but also
because the miracles of God, and salutary examples, are set before the eyes of the faithful through
the saints, so that they might thank God for these and dispose their life and habits in imitation of
the saints, and be stirred to the adoration and devotion of God, and to the cultivation of piety.")

3. Philipp Melanchthon, *Apologia confessionis*, in *Confessio fidei exhibita invictiss. Imp. Carolo
V. Cæsari Avg. in comiciis Avgvstæ, anno M. D. XXX. Addita est Apologia Confessionis* (Wittenberg:
Impressum per Georgium Rhau, 1531), Kk2r: "Confessio nostra probat honores sanctorum. Nam
hic triplex honos probandus est. Primus est gratiarum actio. Debemus enim Deo gratias agere,
q[uod] ostenderit exempla misericordiæ. . . . Secundus cultus est, côfirmatio fidei nostræ, . . . vt
magis credamus. . . . Tertius honos est imitacio, primum fidei, deinde cæterarum virtutum quas
imitari pro sua quisq[ue] vocatione debet."

4. Tertullian, "Apologeticum," *Quinti Septimii Florentis Tertulliani Quae Supersunt Omnia*,
ed. Franciscus Oehler, 2 vols. (Leipzig: T. O. Weigel, 1853–54), 1:301: "semen est sanguis Christianorum" ("the blood of Christians is the seed [of the Church]").

5. John Foxe, "To the qvenes moste excellent Maiestie Quene Elizabeth," *Actes and Monuments of these latter and perillous dayes, touching matters of the Church, wherein ar comprehended and
described the great persecutions & horrible troubles, that haue bene wrought and practised by the Rom-
ishe Prelates, speciallye in this Realme of England and Scotlande, from the yeare of our Lorde a thou-
sande, vnto the tyme nowe present* (London: Iohn Day, 1563), B.1r.

6. Christopher Hales to Henry Bullinger (10 December 1550), ed. and trans. Hastings Robinson, *Original Letters Relative to the English Reformation, Written During the Reigns of King Henry
VIII, King Edward VI, and Queen Mary: Chiefly from the Archives of Zurich*, 2 vols. (Cambridge,
UK: University Press, 1846–47), 1:190. I thank my colleague at McGill, Torrance Kirby, for bringing Hales's correspondence to my attention.

7. Hales to Rodolph Gualter (between 12 June 1550 and 26 January 1551), *Original Letters*, 1: 191.

8. Hales to Gualter, *Original Letters*, 1:192. The quoted passage continues: "And if there be no
danger of this, I do not see why pictures may not be painted and possessed, especially when they are
not kept in any place where there can be the least suspicion of idolatry. . . . Supposing that there are
those who honour them when hung up in churches and sacred places, which I by no means approve;
yet where is the man so devoid of all religion, godliness, fear of the most high and Almighty God,
and so entirely forgetful of himself, as to regard with veneration a little portrait reposited in some
ordinary place in a museum?"

9. Hales to Bullinger (12 June 1550), *Original Letters*, 1:189.

10. Hales to Gualter, *Original Letters*, 1:193.

11. Hales to Gualter, *Original Letters*, 1:195.

12. Théodore de Bèze, "Serenissimo per Dei gratiam Scotiæ regi, Iacobo eivs nominis sexto," *Icones, id est Veræ imagines virorvm doctrina simvl et pietate illvstrivm, qvorvm præcipuè ministerio partim bonarum literaria studia sunt restituta, partim vera Religio in variis orbis Christiani regionibus, nostra patrúmque memoria fuit instaurata: additis eorundem vitæ & operæ descriptionibus, quibus adiectæ sunt nonullæ picturæ quas Emblemata vocant* (Geneva: apvd Ioannem Laonivm, 1580), *2r–v: "Sed erunt fortassis ex nostris nonnulli, qui præteritas imagines vel eam ob causam mallent, ne aduersariis, quos idolatriæ accusamus, calumniandi occasio præbeatur. Istis verò illud ipsum respondeo, quod minimè ignorant, neque picturam videlicet, neque cælaturam, cæterásue artes eiusmodi, per se reprehendi, quarum multiplicem esse vtilitatem constet. . . . Quid igitur vetat quominus sicut scripturæ beneficio doctos & pios homines, quáuis mortuos, quasi nobiscú adhuc loquentes audimus, ita quoque ex veris illorú imaginibus quos studiose viuos obseruauimus, hoc cósequamur vt eos ipsos adhuc intueri & amplecti videamur? Quod si qui vel in colendis viuis modú non tenêt, vel mortuorú imagines temerè & contra Dei mandatum in sacris locis collocatas tandem etiam superstitiosè, atque adeò impiè venerantur, atque adeò suas mutas imagines libros esse idiotarum nugantur, quid hoc ad nos, qui nedum vt tale quicquam admittamus, Christianorum quoque templa diligenter ab his sordibus repurgamus? Me quidem certè testari possum tantorum hominum non modò libros legentem, sed etiam expressos vultus intuentem, haud multò aliter affici, & ad santas cogitationes impelli, quàm si coram adhuc ipsos docentes, admonentes, increpantes his oculis aspicerem." This defense is even more impassioned and extensive in Simon Goulart's French translation, *Les vrais povrtraits des hommes illvstres en piete et doctrine, dv trauail desquels, Dieu s'est serui en ces derniers temps, pour remettre sus la vraye Religion en diuers pays de la Chrestienté* (Geneva: Iean de Laon, 1581), (♀)2r–3r.

13. Melanchthon, *Apologia confessionis*, in *Confessio fidei*, Kk3r: "vere faciant ex sanctis non tantum deprecatores sed propitiatores, hoc est, mediatores redemptionis."

14. Urban VIII, *Sanctissimus Dominus Noster* (13 March 1625), *Bullarum diplomatum et privilegiorum sanctorum Romanum pontificum Taurinensis editio* 13, ed. Aloysio Bilio (Turin: A. Vecco et Sociis Editoribus, 1868), 308–11. Before banning works of literature and art not officially authorized by the Church, Urban explains the abuses that he is seeking to correct, notably the depiction of those reputed to be saintly with halos or crowns of light that suggest God's grace: "Sanctissimus D. N. sollicite animadvertens abusus, qui irrepserunt et quotidie irrepere non cessant in colendis quibusdam cum sanctitatis aut martyrii fama vel opinione defunctis, qui, etsi neque canonizationis, neque beatificationis, honore insigniti ab Apostolica Sede, eorum tamen imagines in oratoriis, atque ecclesiis, aliisque locis publicis, ac etiam privatis, cum laureolis, aut radiis, seu splendoribus proponuntur, miracula et revelationes, aliaque beneficia a Deum per eorum intercessiones accepta." Urban later confirmed this decree in the bull *Caelestis Hierusalem cives* (5 July 1634), *Bullarum diplomatum et privilegiorum sanctorum Romanum pontificum Taurinensis editio* 14, ed. Aloysio Bilio (Turin: A. Vecco et Sociis Editoribus, 1868), 436–40.

15. Urban VIII, *Decreta Seruanda in Canonizatione, & Beatificatione Sanctorum* (Rome: Ex Typographia Reu. Cam. Apost., 1642), 17–18: "vt imprimi possint libri continentes gesta, miracula, seu reuelationes eorum, qui cum prædicta fama Sanctitatis, seu Martyrij decesserunt, non detur, nisi cum infrascriptis protestationibus in dictis libris, & historijs inferendis. Declarando etiam expressè . . . non admittantur Elogia Sancti, vel Beati absolutè, & quæ cadunt super personam, benè tamen ea, quæ cadunt supra mores, & opinionem." This obligatory statement is based on a papal decree allegedly issued on 5 June 1631 (although I have found no independent text to confirm its publication) and still appears at the start of many Catholic biographies.

16. Two examples of works with the obligatory caveat that were intended to promote beatification are Francisco Ignacio, *Vida de la venerable madre Isabel de Iesvs, recoleta agvstina* (Madrid: Francisco Sanz en la Imprenta del Reyno, 1672), and Françoise Madeleine de Chaugy, *Les vies de iv. des premieres meres de l'Ordre de la Visitation Sainte Marie* (Annecy: Iacqves Clerc, 1659). Another, designed to illustrate the benefits of *oración mental* (mental prayer)—a practice central to mysticism, is Antonio Arbiol y Diez, *Desengaños misticos a las almas detenidas, o engañadas en el camino de la perfeccion* (Zaragoza: Por Manvel Roman, 1706).

17. Cotton Mather, *Magnalia Christi Americana; or, The Ecclesiastical History of New-England, From Its First Planting in the Year 1620. unto the Year of our Lord, 1698. In Seven Books* 3.4.7 (London: Printed for Thomas Parkhurst, 1702), 3:224.

18. 2 Corinthians 3:2–3: "Ye are our epistle written in our hearts, known and read of all men: Forasmuch as ye are manifestly declared to be the epistle of Christ ministered by us, written not with ink, but with the Spirit of the living God; not in tables of stone, but in fleshy tables of the heart."

19. Cotton Mather, *Parentator: Memoirs of Remarkables in the Life and the Death of the Ever-Memorable Dr. Increase Mather* (Boston: Printed by B. Green, for Nathaniel Belknap, 1724), 1–2.

20. Mather appears to echo Thomas Vincent, *God's Terrible Voice in the City* ([London]: n.p., 1667), 136: "how few have got the Law of God written in their hearts, and the transcript thereof in their lives, exemplifying the precepts thereof in their conversations? how few in *London* have been like so many *Epistles* of Christ, in whom the will and grace of their Master might be read? who have troden in Christs steps, walking as he walked, and followed him in the way of obedience and self-denyal? who have shined like so many lights in dark places and times, adorning their profession, and living as becometh the Gospel?"

21. Mather, "A General Introduction," *Magnalia Christi Americana*, Civ.

22. Mather, *Magnalia Christi Americana* 3.2, 3:70.

23. Isaac Barrow, "Of Being Imitatours of Christ," *The Works of the Learned Isaac Barrow* 3 (London: Printed by M. Flesher for Brabazon Aylmer, 1686), 15–16: "Saint *Paul*, . . . being satisfi'd, that with integrity he did sute his conversation to the dictates of a good conscience, to the sure rule of God's Law, and to the perfect example of his Lord; that his intentions were pure and right; his actions warrantable, and the tenour of his life conspicuously blameless, doth . . . describe, and set forth his own practice, proposing it as a Rule, pressing it upon them as an argument, an encouragement, an obligation to the performance of several duties. . . . Thus . . . he urgeth the Christians, his disciples at *Corinth*, to fidelity and diligence in the charges and affairs committed to them, to humility, patience and charity; wherein he declareth himself to have set before them an evident and exact pattern. Which practice of Saint *Paul* doth chiefly teach us two things: That we be careful to give; and that we be ready to follow good example."

24. Foxe, "To the qvenes moste excellent Maiestie Quene Elizabeth," *Actes and Monuments*, B.1r–v.

25. "Regula non bullata," *Fontes Franciscani*, ed. Enrico Menesto, Stefano Brufani, et al. (Assisi: Edizioni Porziuncola, 1995), 193: "Omnes fratres studeant sequi humilitatem et pauperitatem Domini nostri Jesu Christi."

26. Text in Luke Wadding, *Annales Minorum seu trium ordinum a S. Francisco institutorum*, ed. José María Fonseca de Évora, 27 vols. (Florence: Ad Claras Aquas [Quaracchi], 1931–34), 16:187–88: "Quod profecto, ut a Christo, et discipulis beatissimus Pater noster Franciscus didicit, sic et vos opere docuit, dum non solum ad diversas mundi partes praedicationis causa ipse ibat, sed etiam ad gentium populos, suos destinabat Fratres, ut Apostolicae et Evangelicae Regulae, quam firmiter promisimus, veram nobis et puram manifestaret observantiam. . . . Et idcirco pro nunc duodecim

com uno omnium Praelato tantummodo mitto, quoniam hic fuit numerus discipulorum Christi pro mundi conversione, et numerus sociorum sanctissimi Patris nostri Francisci pro Evangelicae vitae publicatione."

27. Text in Joaquín García Icazbalceta, *Don fray Juan de Zumárraga, primer obispo y arzobispo de México*, ed. Rafael Aguayo Spencer and Antonio Castro Leal, 4 vols. (Mexico City: Editorial Porrúa, 1947), 3:77–79, doc. 29: "Quod si christianos omnes . . . subire tanquam pium et sanctam opus aggredi decet, nos certe, charissimi fratres, promptissime debemus munus arripere, si patriarchas nostros Franciscum et Dominicum, . . . non vestitu solum et nomine, sed vita et moribus referre velimus. Qui quantum laboris pertulerint, quantas ærumnas exanclarint; sitim, famem, algorem, incendia, injurias, opprobria ferentes, ut Christi regnum propagarent, notius est vobis. . . . Imitamini Christum ab infantia peregrinatum in Ægyptum et extra patriæ suæ fines, nec habentem ubi caput reclinaret. Imitamini et instituti nostri conditores Franciscum et Dominicum, nunquam fere in patria versatos, sed et alterum, scilicet Franciscum, ad Sultani usque regna progressum, ut Mahometi erroribus obcæcatos, veræ fidei flammis illustraret; alterum vero in Albigensium anfractus pro hujusmodi expungendis erroribus usque adeo invectum, ut minutatim membratimque discerpi anhelaret." This document is undated, yet appears to have been issued immediately after Zumárraga's consecration as bishop on 28 December 1533.

28. David A. Boruchoff, "New Spain, New England, and the New Jerusalem: The 'Translation' of Empire, Faith, and Learning (*translatio imperii, fidei ac scientiae*) in the Colonial Missionary Project," *Early American Literature* 43, no. 1 (2008): 5–34.

29. David A. Boruchoff, "*Tanto puede el ejemplo de los mayores*: The Self-Conscious Practice of Missionary History in New Spain," *Colonial Latin American Review* 17, no. 2 (2008): 161–83.

30. Jerónimo de Mendieta, *Historia eclesiástica indiana* (ca. 1596), ed. Francisco Solano y Pérez-Lila, 2 vols., Biblioteca de Autores Españoles 260–61 (Madrid: Atlas, 1973), 1:129: "Y maravilláronse de verlos con tan desarrapado traje, tan diferente de la bizarría y gallardía que en los soldados españoles antes habían visto. Y decían unos a otros: ¿Qué hombres son estos tan pobres?, ¿qué manera de ropa es esta que traen? No son estos como los otros cristianos de Castilla. . . . Llegados, pues, a México, el gobernador acompañado de todos los caballeros españoles y indios principales que para el efecto se habían juntado, los salió a recibir, y puestas las rodillas en tierra, de uno en uno les fue besando a todos las manos; haciendo lo mismo D. Pedro de Alvarado y los demás capitanes y caballeros españoles. Lo cual viendo los indios, los fueron siguiendo, y a imitación de los españoles les besaron también las manos. Tanto puede el ejemplo de los mayores." A strikingly similar account of how Cortés welcomed the first Dominicans to reach Tenochtitlán in 1526 is made by Agustín Dávila Padilla, *Historia de la fvndacion y discurso de la Prouincia de Santiago de Mexico, de la Orden de Predicadores, por las vidas de sus varones insignes, y casos notables de Nueua España* (Madrid: en casa de Pedro Madrigal, 1596), 4–5: "Regozijauanse todos en Dios con la venida de sus ministros, y mostraua su gozo y deuocion mas que todos el discreto Marques del Valle, auentajandose con sus muestras de reuerencia y contento. . . . Arrodillauase delante de cada Religioso, y besaule las manos y los abitos; poniendolos en los ojos y sobre su cabeça; assi por regalar su christiano pecho cõ los nueuos predicadores de Christo, como por dar bué exemplo alos Indios, para q[ue] tuuiessen en grande veneraciõ alos Religiosos" ("They all rejoiced in God with the coming of his ministers, and the discreet Marquis of the Valley [Cortés] showed his joy and devotion more than all [the others], surpassing [them] with his shows of reverence and contentment. . . . He kneeled before each man of religion and kissed his hands and habit, putting them to his eyes and upon his head, both to regale his Christian heart with the[se] new preachers of Christ, and to give a good example to the Indians, so that they might hold these men of religion in great veneration").

31. See, for example, Francisco López de Gómara, *Primera y segunda parte de la historia general de las Indias* (Zaragoza: Augustin Millan, 1552), 2:96v; Bernal Díaz del Castillo, *Historia verdadera de la conquista de la Nueva España* (ca. 1574), ed. Miguel León-Portilla, 2 vols. (Madrid: Historia 16, 1984), 2:245–46; Alonso de Zorita, *Relación de la Nueva España* (ca. 1578–84), ed. Ethelia Ruiz Medrano, Wiebke Ahrndt, and José Mariano Leyva, 2 vols. (Mexico City: Consejo Nacional para la Cultura y las Artes, 1999), 2:636; and Diego Muñoz Camargo, *Historia de Tlaxcala* (ca. 1594), ed. Germán Vázquez (Madrid: Historia 16, 1986), 233.

32. Mendieta, *Historia eclesiástica indiana*, 1:129: "Este celebérrimo acto está pintado en muchas partes de esta Nueva España de la manera que aquí se ha contado, para eterna memoria de tan memorable hazaña, . . . por cuyo medio el Espíritu Santo obraba aquello para firme fundamento de su divina palabra. . . . Y cierto esta hazaña de Cortés fue la mayor de las muchas que de él se cuentan, porque en las otras venció a otros, más en esta venció a sí mismo. El cual vencimiento, según doctrina de los santos y de todos los sabios, es más fuerte y poderoso y más dificultoso de alcanzar, que el de las otras cosas fortísimas del mundo."

33. Mendieta, *Historia eclesiástica indiana*, 2:129–30: "Memoria quedó en las divinas letras, cristiano lector, que aquel valeroso capitán de los ejércitos de Dios, Judas Macabeo, estando una vez para dar batalla a los enemigos del pueblo de Dios, viendo que los contrarios eran muchos y muy poderosos, esforzando y animando a los suyos, les dijo: 'Acordaos cómo . . . se salvaron nuestros padres y antepasados, cómo se esforzaron, cómo varonilmente pelearon contra sus enemigos y nuestros.' Palabras muy dignas de ser traídas y aplicadas a nuestro propósito, y de que nos debemos acordar, pues peleamos cada momento en la batalla espiritual. . . . Debemos, pues, traer a la memoria y ver cómo salvaron sus ánimas estos benditos padres y religiosos, cuyas vidas aquí tratamos. Cómo esforzadamente pelearon contra sus enemigos espirituales, mundo, demonio y carne. . . . Pues así, a imitación de Cristo nuestro Redentor, estos siervos suyos cuyas vidas aquí tratamos, con ferventísimo celo deseaban convertir a la fe de este mesmo Señor a sus incrédulos, ganar las almas perdidas, encaminar las descarriadas, doliéndose de las ofensas que a Dios se hacían, y si tuvieran mil vidas, las pusieran por la salvación de una ánima pecadora."

34. Agustín de Vetancurt, *Chronica de la provincia del Santo Evangelio de Mexico. Quarta parte del Teatro Mexicano de los successos Religiosos* (Mexico: por Doña Maria de Benavides Viuda de Iuan de Ribera, 1697), §§§v: "El Padre de los Machabeos queriendo esforzar à sus hijos à la defensa de la Ley, les acordò las obras de sus antecessores. . . . [C]on razon se deben escrevir las vidas de los Venerables, Padres de esta Provincia de el Santo Evangelio, para que à vista de su humilad, pobreza, y zelo de la conversion de las almas se muevan los animos à imitar las obras de tan Religiosos Varones. . . . [N]o fuera razon, que el castigo que da Dios à los mundanos, de que se acaven sus glorias con sus vidas, les diera nuestro descuydo à tan loables Religiosos, que aunque tienen el premio de estar escritos en el libro de la vida, y esto les basta, à nosotros nos hizieran falta sus virtudes, que para exemplares de nuestro Instituto las quiere Dios en los anales escritas, porque seamos lo que fueron, y subamos à lo que son."

35. In retelling the reception of the twelve Franciscans in Tenochtitlán, another eminent historian of the order, Fray Juan de Torquemada, not only borrowed heavily and at times verbatim from Mendieta, but indeed augmented the Christological parallels by inserting the following statement between those explaining how Cortés, Alvarado, and other Spanish captains kissed the friars' hands, and how the Indians followed their example: "Otro conquistador llamado Rafael de Trejo dexò escrito y firmado de su nôbre en vn breue memorial q[ue] hizo de algunas cosas dignas de memoria de aquellos tiempos, q[ue] no solo el Christianissimo capitan Fernando Cortes se auia hincado de rodillas para besar la mano a los religiosos, sino que tambien se auia quitado la capa y

puestola a los pies del santo fray Martin, caudillo y Custodio desta pequeñuela grey de Iesu Cristo, para que pusiesse sus pies sobre ella, y passasse, como hizieron el dia que Cristo nuestro Señor entrò triunfando en Ierusalen, rodeado de ramos, y pisando las ropas y vestidos de sus moradores" ("Another conquistador, Rafael de Trejo, left written and signed with his name, in a brief report that he made of some matters worthy of memory from those times, that not only did the very Christian captain Hernán Cortés kneel to kiss the hand of those men of religion, but he also took off his cape and placed it at the feet of holy Fray Martín, leader and custodian of that small flock of Jesus Christ, so that he might put his feet upon it and pass forward, as [the Apostles] did the day that Christ our Lord entered triumphant into Jerusalem, surrounded by branches and treading upon the clothes and dresses of its inhabitants.") Juan de Torquemada, *IIIa Parte de los Veynte y Vn libros Rituales y Monarchia Yndiana.Con el Origen y guerras de los Yndias Occidentales De sus publaçiones Descubrimiento Conquista Conuersion y Otras Cosas Marauillosas de la Mesma tierra distribydos En tres tomos* (Seville: Por Matthias Clauiso, 1615), 24.

36. Another Franciscan, Fray Toribio de Benavente, or Motolinía, also promoted the idea that both ordained and lay Christians might emulate the example of those who launched the evangelization of New Spain. While conceding that the success of the first friars was slow and sparse compared to that of others who followed, Motolinía insists that it is important to record their deeds for this very reason, for the difficulties that these friars overcame give proof of what the human spirit can achieve. See Motolinía, preface to book 2, *Historia de los indios de la Nueva España*, ed. Edmundo O'Gorman, 5th ed. (Mexico City: Editorial Porrúa, 1990), 77.

37. Sebastián de Covarrubias, *Tesoro de la lengva Castellana, o Española* (Madrid: Por Luis Sánchez, 1611), 74v: "Antiguallas, las cosas muy antiguas, y viejas, del otro tiempo." The term *antigüedades* appears in several of the censorial and official approvals published in Murúa's manuscript.

38. Royal directive of 22 April 1577 ordering the confiscation of Bernardino de Sahagún's writings, in Francisco Fernández del Castillo, comp., *Libros y libreros en el siglo XVI*, 2nd ed. (Mexico City: Archivo General de la Nación; Fondo de Cultura Económica, 1982), 513, doc. 25: "estaréis advertido *de no consentir que por ninguna manera, persona alguna escriba cosas que toquen a supersticiones y manera de vivir que estos indios tenían*" (italics in the original).

39. Martín Dominguez Jara, commissary of the Inquisition in Ylabaya (25 August 1611), in Martín de Murúa, *Historia general del Piru. Origen i deçendencia de los yncas. donde se trata, assi de las guerras çiuiles Suyas, como de la Entrada de los españoles, descripçion de las çiudades Y lugares del, con otras cosas notables*, Ms. Ludwig XIII 16, facsimile (Los Angeles: Getty Research Institute, 2008), 4r: "seran [*sic*] de muy gran prouecho el saberlas para los curas delos yndios deste r[ein]o."

40. Fray Balthasar de los Reyes, *comendador* of the Mercedarian convent in Cuzco (4 March 1613), in Murúa, *Historia general del Piru*, 6v: "La historia digna de ser sauida por su mucha curiosidad y bariedad de cassos rritos y gentilidades de donde se podra ynferir la mucha m[erc]ed q[ue] Dios a echo a este rreyno del piru por mano delos catholicos Reyes de españa, En ynbiar a este rreyno sus ministros Ecclesiasticos y seculares a la predicaçion Euangelica."

41. Bernardino de Sahagún, prologue, *Historia general de las cosas de Nueva España*, ed. Alfredo López Austin and Josefina García Quintana, 2 vols. (Madrid: Alianza Editorial, 1988), 1:31: "aplicar conveniblemente a cada enfermedad la medicina contraria." Similar is Diego Durán, *Historia de las Indias de Nueva España e Islas de la Tierra Firme* (1581), ed. Ángel María Garibay Kintana, 2 vols. (Mexico: Editorial Porrúa, 1967), 1:3: "Hame movido, cristiano lector, a tomar esta ocupación de poner y contar por escrito las idolatrías antiguas y religión falsa con que el demonio era servido, antes que llegase a estas partes la predicación del santo Evangelio, el haber entendido que los que nos ocupamos en la doctrina de los indios nunca acabaremos de enseñarles a conocer al

verdadero Dios, si primero no fueran raídas y borradas totalmente de su memoria las supersticiones, cerimonias y cultos falsos de los falsos dioses que adoraban" ("I was moved, Christian reader, to take on the task of putting and recounting in writing the ancient idolatries and false religion by which the devil was served before the preaching of the holy Gospel arrived in these parts because I understood that those of us who occupy ourselves in the indoctrination of Indians will never manage to teach them to know the true God, unless the superstitions, ceremonies, and false worship of the false gods that they adored are first rubbed out and obliterated from their memories.")

42. The passage from barbarism to civilization is arguably a key element in the self-portrayal of all major polities, serving not only to distinguish them from their neighbors, but also to make them explicitly advanced peoples. In addition to well-known examples such as China and Greece, this development may be seen in the disdain that the Nahua of central Mexico expressed toward the Chichimeca from whom they descended. On this issue more broadly, see David A. Boruchoff, "Indians, Cannibals, and Barbarians: Hernán Cortés and Early Modern Cultural Relativism," *Ethnohistory*, in press.

43. See in particular the final chapter of José de Acosta, *Historia natvral y moral de las Indias, en qve se tratan las cosas notables del cielo, y elementos, metales, plantas, y animales dellas: y los ritos, y ceremonias, leyes, y gouierno, y guerras de los Indios* (Seville: en casa de Iuan de Leon, 1590), 529–35.

44. On these developments in general, see Pierre Duviols, *La lutte contre les religions autochtones dans le Pérou colonial: "L'extirpation de l'idolâtrie" entre 1532 et 1660* (Lima: Institut Français d'Études Andines, 1971).

45. Alonso Remón, *Historia general de la Orden de N[uestra] Sª de la Merced Redencion de cautiuos* (Madrid: por Luis Sanchez, 1618). A second volume was published in 1633.

46. Rolena Adorno, "Censorship and Approbation in Murúa's *Historia general del Piru*," *The Getty Murúa: Essays on the Making of Martín de Murúa's "Historia General del Piru*," ed. Thomas B. F. Cummins and Barbara Anderson (Los Angeles: Getty Research Institute, 2008), 118–20.

47. Alonso Remón, "A Don Lorenzo Ramirez de Prado," *Historia Verdadera de la Conqvista de la Nueva España. Escrita Por el Capitan Bernal Díaz del Castillo, Vno de sus Conquistadores. Sacada a luz Por el P. M. Fr. Alonso Remon, Predicador y Coronista General del Orden de N. S. de la Merced, Redencion de Cautiuos* (Madrid: en la Emprenta del Reyno, 1632), n.p.: "en honra de los piadosos Oficios de mi sagrada Religion, y . . . de los notables hechos, y no pensados acaecimientos que se vieron en las primeras cõquistas de Nueva España."

48. On the redistribution of materials, see Rolena Adorno and Ivan Boserup, "The Making of Murúa's *Historia general del Piru*," *The Getty Murúa*, especially 24–27.

49. Murúa, *Historia general del Piru*, 331r: "Pastores Sanctisimos, y ques s[o]lo an atendido al ynteres espiritual y la ganancia de sus almas, olbidados de las temporales de hazienda y Riquezas." In this and subsequent quotations from Murúa's manuscript, I have separated into distinct words those arbitrarily fused together as an idiosyncrasy of the scribe's script. I have also changed to lowercase all initial letters that differ from both regular capitals and lowercase letters.

50. Murúa, *Historia general del Piru*, 324v: "A todo esto, sobrepujo el buen exemplo y s[an]ta Vida destos Religiosos, pues siempre procuraron pedricar [*sic*] mas con obras que con palabras. . . . Recieron el s[an]to ebangelio de tal modo que ya con gran feruor acudian a la yglesia a oyr misa . . . y aun biendo la Vida que aquellos santos barones habian dieron en hallarse en muchas particulares disciplinas y en otros exersiçios spirituales lleuados del buen exemplo que es el que mas suele mober los corazones."

51. Murúa, *Historia general del Piru*, 333v: "y ansi. si en el tiempo que sus yngas y Reies los rijieron y gouernaron fueran substentados en paz. tranquilidad y justiçia. y viuieron con seguridad y

quietud. el dia de oy que debajo de mando y monarchia de los catholicos Reyes de España mas guardados. defendidos y amparados estan con vn Rey tan zeloso de su bien, y tan piadoso y [Chris] tiano. . . . y así es su estado de los yndios del Peru. mas felize y dichoso que el antiguo. Puestos en carrera de salbaçion de sus almas y viuiendo devajo de leyes sanctos y justas y gouernados por Padres amantissimos que ansi se pueden dezir los Reyes y Prelados que tienen."

52. In the ellipsis of the passage cited in the preceding note, Murúa qualifies his praise for the virtues of Inca rule by adding "fuera de los castigos crueles y desapiadados que experimentaron de sus yngas por pequeños delictos" ("other than the cruel and merciless punishments that they experienced at the hands of their Incas for petty offenses"). This comment is clearly out of place within the chronological frame of the paragraph as a whole.

53. Murúa, *Historia general del Piru*, 328r: "no sin misterio e puesto estos . . . capitulos en este libro desta ystoria general del Peru que alguno le pareciera escusado y antes me escusara si echara de ver que leyendo la Sancta Vida que los Religiosos desta Sagrada Religion y viendo el fructo que en todo el y en todas las ciudades y pueblos hizieron los ancianos procuraremos hazer los presentes otro tanto, mobidos del buen exemplo y animados con el premio que Dios promete a los que como Valerosos Soldados en venzimiento de los ynfieles pelearen hasta el fin."

54. See, for example, Remón's interlinear revisions in Murúa, *Historia general del Piru*, 323v, 324v, 327r, 327v, and 328r. Moral and spiritual ideals of comportment also feature prominently in the *vitae* authored or revised by Remón to celebrate the examples set both by canonized saints (*Discursos elogicos y apologeticos: empresas y diuisas sobre las triunfantes vida y muerte del glorioso Patriarca San Pedro de Nolasco, primero Padre de la . . . Orden de Nuestra Señora de la Merced Redencion de Cautiuos*, 1628), and by other Christian noblemen (*La vida del sieruo de Dios Gregorio Lopez, natural de Madrid: añadida de nueuos milagros y doctrina suya*, 1617; *Relacion de la ejemplar vida y muerte del Caballero de Gracia*, 1620). I thank Jodi Bilinkoff, of the University of North Carolina at Greensboro, for bringing these writings to my attention.

55. Felipe Guaman Poma de Ayala, *El PRIMER nveva coronica i buen gobierno*, 905–6 [919–20]; facsimile of the autograph in the Royal Library of Denmark, http://www.kb.dk/permalink /2006/poma/info/es/frontpage.htm: "mira cristiano q[ue] mal y dano se me hizo como a pobre q[ue] me hara a otros pobres q[ue] no sauen nada y son mas pobres y cin fabor—despues dizen los p[adr] es—o q[ue] mala dotrina como no seran rricos se hazen todo esto dires q[ue] los protetores—a costa del rrey los pone para q[ue] defienda antes ellos hurta y rroba y se côseja conellos y no ay rremedio aci lo propio huzan los curacas principales y alcaldes y fiscales q[ue] todos hurtan y son soberbiosos enemigo de los pobres amigo de quitalle sus haziendas mucho mas los mestizos y mulatos y criollos espanoles como en mi presencia los maltrata alos yn[dio]s mira cristiano todo a mi se me a hecho— hasta querer me quitar mi muger un flayre merzenario llamado morua—en el pueblo de yanaca estos d[ic]hos agrauios y danos y males y no quieren uer a yn[dio]s ladinos cristianos hablando en castilla se le espanta y me manda echar luego de los d[ic]hos pueblos todo pretende q[ue] fueran bobos asnos para acauallo de quitalle quanto tiene hazienda muger y hija." In subsequent references, I use the abbreviated title *Nueva corónica* and give my own transcriptions. Because the manuscript is almost devoid of punctuation and has many incomplete or ungrammatical statements, my translations necessarily involve interpretation, while aspiring to keep as close as possible to the expression and sense of the original. In this effort, I have greatly benefited from the modernized transcription by Rolena Adorno, with John V. Murra and Jorge L. Urioste, on the Web site of the Royal Library of Denmark. Like other texts cited in this essay (see note 67 below), the *Nueva corónica* takes the terms *mestizo* and *mulato* in the narrow sense of what canon law called *descendentes in primo gradu*, that is, direct offspring of the unions of Europeans with Indians and blacks, respectively.

56. Guaman Poma, *Nueva corónica*, 647 [661]: "FRAILE MERZENARIO MORVA son tan brabos y justiciero y maltrata a los yn[dio]s y haze trauajar cõ un palo en este rreyno en las dotrinas no ay rremedio." Murúa's cruelty and excesses are narrated in detail on the following two pages.

57. Bernard of Clairvaux, *Sermones in Cantica canticorum* 66.12, *Opera genuina*, 3 vols. (Paris: Gauthier Fratrem et Soc., 1836), 3:369.

58. Pedro de Valencia, *Tratado acerca de los moriscos de España* (1606), ed. Joaquín Gil Sanjuán (Málaga: Editorial Algazara, 1997), 132: "si perseveran conocidos y apartados, siempre notados con infamia y desprecio, y gravados con tributos particulares, vendrán a quedar todavía en forma de siervos, y no verdaderos ciudadanos, y llevarán adelante el odio, y el deseo de la perdición de la república." This conclusion arises from a discussion of the practical difficulties faced by the Greeks and Romans in dealing with the Lacedaemonians (Spartans) and other subject peoples (*servi* in Latin), and of the challenge posed to Christian doctrine by discrimination between New and Old Christians, in that baptism is held to wash away one's former identity, so that, as Galatians 3:27–28 states: "There is neither Jew nor Greek, slave nor free, male nor female; you are all indeed one in Jesus Christ."

59. Guaman Poma, *Nueva corónica*, 702 [716]: "nos enoxeys cristiano letor de leer este libro leelda muy biẽ y enfrenaos con ella . . . los buenos se rriã del d[ic]ho libro los malos se enojaran y le pesaran deello y me desearan matarme pues digoos cristianos letores q[ue] no aues tenido ermano q[ue] os aya querido tanto de la saluacion de buestra anima y conci[e]ncia y q[ue] en el mundo os a librado de trauajos y pesadumbres y de pecados y os a honrrado tanto. tomareys este libro y lo leyres de en berbo en berbo y asentareys y llorares con buestra anima y uerís lo q[ue] es malo y lo que no es malo y quitado deellos hablares con tu s[eñ]or y perlado libremente y seres honrrado y cabres enel mundo con los chicos y grandes—y tratares conel papa y rrey y os tendra en los ojos y en la anima."

60. See Guaman Poma, *Nueva corónica*, 1–3, which repeatedly pairs the verbs *enseñar* (to teach) and *saber* (to know) with *enmendar* (to emend) and *enfrenar* (to restrain); for example, in the statement: "la d[ic]ha coronica es muy util y prouechoso y es bueno para las d[ic]has rrecidencias y becita generales de los d[ic]hos yn[dio]s tributarios y de la becita general de la s[an]ta madre yglecia y para sauer otras cosas y para enfrenar sus animas y consencias los d[ic]hos cristianos, como dios nos amenaza por la deuina escritura de dios por boca de los sanctos profretas heremias a q[ue] entremos a penitencia y mudar la uida como cristianos—como el profeta rrey dauid nos dize en el pezalmo—domine deus salutis meæ—dõde nos pone grandes miedos y desanparos de dios y grandes castigos q[ue] nos a de enbiar cada dia como el precursor san ju[an] bautista traxo los amenazos azotes y castigos de dios para que fuesemos en[frena]dos y emendados eneste mundo" ("The said chronicle is very useful and beneficial, and it is good for the said residences and general visits [reviews] of the said Indian tributaries of the said general visit [administrative jurisdiction] of the holy mother Church, and also to know other matters and restrain the spirits and consciences of the said Christians, as God warns us in God's divine scripture through the mouth of the holy prophet Jeremiah, that we might enter into penitence and change our lives as Christians, [and] as the prophet King David tells us in the psalm *Domine deus salutis meæ* [Lord God, my salvation], where he sets down for us the great frights and abandonments of God, and the great chastisements that he must send us every day, as [Christ's] precursor Saint John the Baptist brought threatening lashes and chastisements of God, so that we might be restrained and amended in this world").

61. Guaman Poma, *Nueva corónica*, 630 [644]: "los d[ic]hos rrebrendos padres todos ellos son sanctos y cristianicimos gran ubedencia y umildad y caridad amor de progimo . . . me parese estos sanctos de dios andubiese enlos pueblos delos yn[dio]s confesãdo todos los pobres yn[dio]s cin temor se allegarian y les buscariã y no se huyrian por q[ue] en deciendo q[ue] biene flayre franc[iscan]o luego todos acude a besar las manos . . . son sancticisimos cierbos de jesucristo y aci es muy justo

q[ue] sea amado y honrrado enel mundo la s[an]ta casa y conuento del s[eñ]or san fran[cis]co y ayga mucha limosna enel mundo eneste rreyno de las yn[di]as" ("The said reverend fathers [of the Order of Saint Francis] are all holy and very Christian, of great obedience, humility, charity, and love of others. . . . It seems to me that, were these holy men of God to go about hearing confessions in Indian settlements, all the poor Indians would come and seek them out without fear, and would not flee, because, upon saying that a good Franciscan friar is coming, everyone immediately comes to kiss his hands. . . . They are most holy servants of Jesus Christ and thus it is very just that the holy house and convent of Saint Francis be loved and honored in the world, and that it do much [work of] alms in the world in this realm of the Indies"). See also *Nueva corónica*, 599 [613]: "mira p[adr]e a los rrebrendos p[adr]es de la conpania de jesus y los rrebrendos p[adr]es flayres franc[iscan]os y hermitanos tan p[adr]es y rreligiosos son como bosotros hombres—con amor y caridad traẽ alos cristianos haziendo limosna alos hombres le llama hermanos como an uisto este bien le cigen los cristianos jamas se han uisto pleytos deellos jamas salen de su conuento aci abian de hazer los buenos saserdotes" ("Look, father, at the reverend fathers of the Company of Jesus and the reverend Franciscan father-friars and hermits, who are as much fathers and men of religion as you. They attract Christians with love and charity; giving alms to men, they call them brothers. As they have seen this good, Christians follow them. Never have lawsuits been seen of them; they never leave their convents. Good priests must act in this manner").

62. Guaman Poma, *Nueva corónica*, 11: "gaste mucho tienpo y muchos años, acordandome que a de ser prouechoso a los fieles cristianos para emienda de sus pecados y malas uidas y herronias."

63. Guaman Poma, *Nueva corónica*, 15: "le daua el d[ic]ho exenplo y castigo y dotrina q[ue] le dio a su entenado martin de ayala mestizo sancto y le enpuso y le metio a seruir a dios." According to Covarrubias, *Tesoro*, 209v, a *castigo* is the admonishment or correction given to a person so that he might adhere to the path of righteousness.

64. See in particular the chapter titled "Rastrearon los Incas al verdadero Dios nuestro Señor," in El Inca Garcilaso de la Vega, *Primera parte de los Commentarios reales, qve tratan del origen de los Yncas, reyes qve fveron del Perv, de sv idolatria, leyes, y gouierno en paz y en guerra: de sus vidas y conquistas, y de todo lo que fue aquel Imperio y su Republica, antes que los Españoles pasaran a el* (Lisbon: en la officina de Pedro Crasbeeck, 1609), 26r–27v. Although Garcilaso refers in general to the Andeans' old beliefs as "vana religión" and "idolatría," his detailed description of their practices and customs clearly echoes Christian and European ideals of spiritual and civic order. This practice is also commonplace in the works of Fernando de Alva Ixtlilxóchitl. See, for example, his account of the reign (1472–1515) of Nezahualpiltzintli, who was not only virtuous, but moreover foretold his people's submission to Spain and Christianity; "Compendio histórico del reino de Texcoco," *Obras históricas*, ed. Edmundo O'Gorman, 2 vols. (1975; rpt. Mexico City: Universidad Nacional Autónoma de México, 1985), 1:449: "Gobernó con grandísima quietud y paz. . . . Fue muy misericordioso con los pobres y gran justiciero . . . ; fue también muy valeroso. . . . Declaró a sus vasallos y a los demás reyes cómo esta tierra había de ser de los hijos del sol, hombres valerosos e invencibles, y que tenían un señor el mayor del mundo, y que su dios era el Tloque Nahuaque que era el creador de todas las cosas; y que a esta causa no convenía ser contra ellos, porque los que tal hiciesen habían de ser destruidos y muertos" ("He governed with the greatest quiet and peace. . . . He was very merciful with the poor and a great champion of justice . . . ; he was also very valiant. . . . He declared to his vassals and to the other kings that this land must belong to the children of the sun, valiant and invincible men who had the greatest lord of the world, and that their god was Tloque Nahuaque, the creator of all things; and for this reason, it was not right to oppose them, for those who might do so would have to be destroyed and killed").

65. Guaman Poma, *Nueva corónica*, 912–14 [926–28], avers that his ancestors, despite their idolatry, "guardaron los mandamientos y buenas obras de misericordia de dios en este rreyno lo qual no lo guarda agora los cristianos aues de conzederar cristiano ques la causa de los malos p[adr]es. . . . los yn[dio]s primeros aunq[ue] de los yngas fueron ydulatras tubieron fe y mandamiento de sus dioses y ley y buena obra guardaron y cumplieron. y tubieron rreys y señores grandes y capitanes y justicias y toda pulicia entero fe dela corona rreal y mag[esta]d del ynga y conseruación entre ellos aues de cózedrar - conzedera lo desta uida auiendo tantos buenos rreligiosos y justicias todos andan alborotados dela fe de jesucristo y dela ley del rrey y de sus señores grádes porq[ue] tienen tales maystros y aci se pierden las animas de los cristianos enesta uida aues de conzederar desto cristiano - conzedera de como los pobres yn[dio]s tienen tantos rreys yngas antiguamente tenia solo un rrey ynga y anci enesta uida ay muchos yngas—correg[id]or ynga doze tinientes son yngas ermano o hijo del correg[id]or y muger del correg[id]or y todos sus criados hasta los negros son yngas y sus parientes y escriuano son yngas . los encomenderos y sus ermanos o hijos y criados mayordomos y mestizos y mulatos negros y su muger yanaconas y chinaconas cocinaras son yngas—y los p[adr]es y sus ermanos y hijos y mayordomos yanaconas coseneras o amigos hasta sus fiscales y sacristanes cátores son yngas los susod[ic]hos hazen grandes danos y males a los yn[dio]s eneste rreyno tantos yngas aues de conzederar" ("they kept the commandments and good works of God's mercy in this realm, which Christians do not keep today. You must consider, Christian, that the cause of this are bad fathers. . . . The first Indians, though of the Incas, were idolaters, [yet] had faith and kept and fulfilled the commandment[s] of their gods and religion, and [did] good works. And they had kings, great lords, captains and justices; and there was complete political existence, firm faith in the royal crown and majesty of the Inca, and stability among them. Consider the state of life now: with so many good men of religion and justices, everyone goes about uneasy with the faith of Jesus Christ and the law of the king and his high lords, because they have such masters. And thus, the souls of Christians are lost in this life. You must consider this, Christian. Consider how poor Indians have so many inca kings [i.e., overlords]. In olden times, they had only one Inca king, yet now there are many incas: the *corregidor* is an inca; twelve lieutenants are incas; the brother or son of the *corregidor*, his wife, all his servants, and even [his] blacks [slaves] are incas; *encomenderos* and their brothers or sons, their servants, and majordomos; mestizos, mulattoes, and blacks; their wives, *yanaconas*, *chinaconas* [two categories of servants], and cooks are incas; priests and their brothers, sons, majordomos, *yanaconas*, cooks or friends, even their *fiscales* [those charged with ensuring religious observance], sacristans, and cantors are incas. The aforesaid do great damages and evils to Indians in this realm. You must consider [the effect of] so many incas").

66. Although hair type serves to distinguish between Indians (smooth), whites (wavy), and blacks (tightly curled), mestizos, despite having wavy hair, appear in various styles of dress in the *Nueva corónica*, in accordance with their status and degree of acculturation. A good example is the drawing depicting how priests "cruelly punish" and then indoctrinate five-year-old boys (585 [599]).

67. The unreservedly favorable portrait of Martín de Ayala has occasioned a good deal of curiosity due to Guaman Poma's harsh condemnation of mestizo priests elsewhere in the *Nueva corónica*. Indeed, he not only entreats the king to forbid the ordination of mestizos (978 [996]), but moreover blames their iniquity, arrogance and abuse of power for the backsliding of Indians. He demands: "Q[ue] los d[ic]hos yn[dio]s deste rreyno no puedan tener por p[adr]e y cura dotrinante a saserdotes mestizos ni criollos por los gran danos y capitulos q[ue] rrezultan de ellos y puede rrezultar y demas deeso se entran al uzo de sus tios antes es parte ellos de ello—y demas deeso son tan s[eño]res apsolutos y soberbiosos contra sus tios y enobidente a la justicia y a su perlado y de q[ue] se mete en gouernar y hazerse justicias y tener hijos y haziendas y sementeras" (That the said Indians

of this realm not be allowed to have as a father and doctrinizing priest mestizos nor *criollos* [Spaniards born in Spain] because of the great damages and recriminations that result and can result from them; and, in addition to this, they have a hand in that [Indians] enter unto the uses of their uncles [i.e., ancestors]. And moreover, they are such absolute lords and haughty toward thir uncles, and disobedient to justice and to their prelate [superior in the Church], and they set themselves to governing and to meting out justice and to having children and estates and plantations) (888–89 [902–03]). It is also curious that Martín de Ayala did not wish to serve in a *doctrina de indios*, but instead chose to work in the city of Huamanga, a regular parish, as reported in the following note. The ordination of mestizos was highly controversial due to persistent doubts as to the orthodoxy and *suficiencia* (suitability or competency) of neophytes, an offshoot of the notion of *limpieza de sangre* (purity of blood). Accordingly, the First Provincial Council of Mexico (1555) decreed that no one is to be admitted to the priesthood who "descendiere de Padres, ó Abuelos quemados, ó reconciliados, ó de linage de Moros, ó fuere Mestizo, Indio, ó Mulato" (might descend from parents or grandparents burned or reconciled [as heretics], or from the lineage of Moors, or might be a mestizo, Indian or mulatto). See "De el Examen que se debe hacer antes que sean ordinados los Clérigos," Cap. 44, *Concilios provinciales primero y segundo, celebrados en la muy noble, y muy leal ciudad de México . . . en los años de 1555, y 1565* (Mexico City: en la Imprenta de el Superior Gobierno, de el Br. D. Joseph Antonio de Hogal, 1769), 106. This ban was overturned by Pope Gregory XIII in the brief *Nuper ad Nos* (25 January 1577) as a means to compensate for the "maximam sacerdotum, qui idioma Indorum sciant, penuriam" ("great dearth of priests who know the language of Indians"). See Francisco Javier Hernáez, ed., *Colección de bulas, breves y otros documentos relativos a la Iglesia de América y Filipinas*, 2 vols. (Brussels: Alfredo Vromont, 1879), 1: 222. Far from settling the issue, Gregory's decree was opposed by King Philip II, who wrote a series of letters to bishops in both Mexico and Peru ordering that it not be put into practice. The ban on the ordination of mestizos therefore remained effective in Mexico, and was moreover reaffirmed by the Third Provincial Council of Mexico (1585). For the authoritative text of this decree, as edited by Archbishop Francisco Antonio Lorenzana, see *Concilium Mexicanum Provinciale III. Celebratum Mexici anno MDLXXXV* (Mexico City: Ex Typographia Bac. Josephi Antonij de Hogal, 1770). An excellent analysis of these developments is made by Stafford Poole, "Church Law on the Ordination of Indians and *Castas* in New Spain," *Hispanic American Historical Review* 61.4 (1981): 637–50. In contrast, observance of the crown's ban on mestizo priests was lax in Peru. Indeed, the Third Council of Lima (1583) approved their ordination specifically so that they might minister to Indians in *doctrinas*, that is, in temporary parishes set up to provide an initial indoctrination. See "Ad Titvlum Indorum posse promoueri etiam patrimonij expertem," Actio secvnda, Cap. 31, *Concilivm Limense. Celebratum anno. 1583 sub Gregorio XIII. Sum. Pont. autoritate Sixti Quinti Pont. Max. approbatum* (Madrid: Ex officina Petri Madrigalis, 1591), 38v–39r.

68. Guaman Poma, *Nueva corónica*, 18–20: "padre martin de ayala mestizo—despues de auerse ordenado de misa saserdote fue muy gran sancto hombre el qual no quizo dotrina nenguna cino toda su uida q[ue] auia deestar con los pobres del hospital dela ciudad de guamanga y fue capellan delos d[ic]hos pobres y hazia muy mucha penitencia enel dormir dormia poco y tenia por frezada y collchon estera tegida de paxa y tenia un gallo por rreloxo en la cauesera para quele despertase a la oracion y para uecitar delos pobres enfermos y rresaua sus maytines y nona uisperas y se daua muy muchas deseplinas en su carne toda su uida trayya selicio jamas trayya camisa enel cuerpo y no se rreyya en su uida jamas le miraua con los ojos alas mugeres hincaua los ojos y la cara al suelo quando le hablo alguna muger y hazia muy grandes limosnas y caridad temor de dios amor con los proximos jamas decia de malas palabras alos hombres ni alas d[ic]has mugeres ni a nenguna criatura no consentia

a animal fuese muerto ne q[ue]ria q[ue] le matasen a un piojo grandemente se holgaua q[ue] se casasen los pobres y les daua dote porque fuesen bien casados y serbiesen a dios los pobres y alas mañanas le uenian muchos paxaros a cantalle y a rrecibir su bendicion y los rratones se ahumillauan y no se meneauan mientras que staua en la dicha oracion los angeles del s[eñ]or cada noche les rreuelaua al s[an]to hombre y despues le ensenaua a su padrasto don martin de ayala . . . y a su madre y a sus ermanos el sancto mandamiento y el sancto euangelio de dios y las buenas obras de misericordia por donde uinieron a mas creser su padrasto dõ martin de ayala y su madre doña ju[an]a y cõ todos sus ermanos serbierõ a dios y tubieron mucha auilidad y fe en dios."

69. Bonaventure, *Legenda maior*, in *Legendae S. Francisci Asisiensis: saeculi XIII et XIV conscriptae ad codicum fidem recensitae*, 5 vols. (Ad Claras Aquas [Quaracchi], Florence: Typographia Collegii S. Bonaventurae, 1926–41), 5:577: "Cum igitur cerneret vir Dei Franciscus suo exemplo ad crucem Christi baiulandam ferventi spiritu plurimos animari, animabatur et ipse tamquam bonus dux exercitus Christi ad palam victoriae per culmen invictae pervenire virtutis."

70. Bonaventure, *Legenda maior*, in *Legendae S. Francisci Asisiensis*, 5:612: "subito tacuerunt, nec fuerunt motae de loco, donec fuit omnis praedicatio consummata. Omnes igitur, qui viderunt, stupore repleti, glorificaverunt Deum. Istius miraculi fama circumquaque diffusa multos ad Sancti reverentiam et fidei devotionem accendit."

71. Pedro de la Vega, *Flos sanctorum: la vida de Nuestro Señor Jesu Christo, de su sanctissima Madre, y de los otros sanctos, segun la orden de sus fiestas* (Seville: Fernando Diaz, 1580), 231v: "quien tanta compassion tenia d[e] los animales brutos, y sin razon, quan grande es de creer q[ue] era la q[ue] tenia delos hõbres." Vega's work was first published in 1521, with additions over the course of the sixteenth century. Other collections of *vitae* by Alonso de Villegas, Pedro de Rivadeneyra, and Francisco Ortiz Lucio also bear the title of *Flos sanctorum*. The great popularity of these *vitae* is evident in the number of copies sent to America in the latter decades of the sixteenth century and the first half of the seventeenth century. For detailed inventories and shipping manifests, see Irving A. Leonard, "Best Sellers of the Lima Book Trade, 1583," *Hispanic American Historical Review* 22, no. 1 (1942): 27; "*Don Quixote* and the Book Trade in Lima, 1606," *Hispanic Review* 8, no. 4 (1940): 298; and "On the Cuzco Book Trade, 1606," *Hispanic Review* 9, no. 3 (1941): 368. See also the cumulative figures for 1601–1649 in Pedro J. Rueda Ramírez, *Negocio e intercambio cultural: el comercio de libros con América en la Carrera de Indias (siglo XVII)* (Seville: Universidad de Sevilla; Diputación de Sevilla; Consejo Superior de Investigaciones Científicas, Escuela de Estudios Hispano-Americanos, 2005), 314.

72. Guaman Poma, *Nueva corónica*, 560 [574]: "EL PRIMERO COMIENZO DEL P[ADR]E que los padres cristianos y sanctos fue de jesucristo y de s[an] p[edr]o s[an] p[abl]o apostoles y de sãtos."

73. Guaman Poma, *Nueva corónica*, 562 [576]: "se dana alos espanoles y mas alos cristianos nuebos q[ue] son los yn[dio]s y negros teniendo una dozena de hijos como puede dar buen egenplo a los yn[dio]s deste rreyno—como los padres y curas de las dotrinas son muy colericos y señores apsolutos y soberbiosos y tienen muy mucha grauedad q[ue] conel miedo se huyen los d[ic]hos yn[dio] s y de q[ue] no se acuerda los d[ic]hos saserdotes de q[ue] n[uest]ro s[eñ]or jesucristo se hizo pobre y humilde para ajuntar y traer alos pobres pecadores y lleuallo a su sancta yglecia y dalli lleuallo a su rreyno del cielo."

74. Guaman Poma, *Nueva corónica*, 598 [612]: "p[adres] mios mira lo que manda dios el euangelio mira como ciguierõ los bienauenturados sanctos apostoles y otros s[anc]tos martires y confesores y uirgenes y para q[ue] mireys os muestra este hombre s[anc]to de dios p[adre] martin de ayala q[ue] fue mestiso y la uida de s[an] j[ua]n buenauentura negro y la bida q[ue] hizierõ estos sanctos." It would seem that the phrase "the life of Saint John Bonaventure" refers to a *vita* written

by Bonaventure, and not to the life story of Bonaventure himself, since the latter was rarely if ever recorded in menologies and other collections. Although Bonaventure composed a widely read *Meditationes vitae Christi*, it is doubtful that Guaman Poma had this theological treatise in mind, rather than the more famous *vita* of Francis of Assisi.

75. Guaman Poma, *Nueva corónica*, 598–99 [612–13]: "el mestizo desde nino comenso a serbir hecho hermitano enel hospital del cuzco de los naturales despues fue a seruir al hospital de la ciudad de guamanga alli fue hordenado de misa sazerdote q[ue] en los días q[ue] biuio ayunaua y deseplinaua y hazia penetencia y traya selicio en el s[ant]o cuerpo con el ojo lloraua y belaua cada noche becitaua alos d[ic]hos enfermos del d[ic]ho hospital y para ello tenia su selda muy serca dela enfermería y linpiaua con sus manos los seruidores delos enfermos y daua mucha limosna a todos los pobres de jesu cristo y tenia mucha caridad y humildad obra de misericordia amor temor de dios y anci se llegauan todos los pobres pecadores y biejos y enfermos y mosos y solteros y muchachos obedencia le hazia hasta los animales jamas se rreya y quando le hablaua muger hincaua los ojos al suelo jamas le miraua la cara de la muger y tenia un gallo ala cauesera q[ue] le cantaua la ora y despertaua y cada manana ala uentana cada paxaro le daua su salto al s[an]to hombre a su cuerpo y le echaua la uendicion y hazia otros milagros y jamas trayya cama para dormir por fresada una estera y collchon otra estera jamas dexaua entrar a la selda a muger ni aunq[ue] fuese hombre no lo cõsentia para q[ue] no fuese uisto su secreto de noche le rrebelaua angeles del s[eñ]or" ("As a child, this mestizo [Martín de Ayala], having become a hermit, began to serve in the native peoples' hospital in Cuzco and afterward went to serve in the hospital of the city of Huamanga. There, he was ordained to say mass as a priest. All the days that he lived he fasted, disciplined himself, did penitence, and wore a cilice on his holy body; he wept from his eyes and kept vigil every night; he visited the said patients of the said hospital, and to this end had his cell very close to the infirmary; he cleaned the patients' bedpans with his own hands and gave many alms to the poor of Jesus Christ, and had much charity and humility, work[s] of mercy, love, and fear of God. And thus all the poor, sinners, old, sick, young, unmarried men, boys, and even animals came and obeyed him. He never laughed and [always] fixed his eyes on the ground when a woman talked to him; he never looked a woman in the face. And he had a rooster at the head of his bed who would sing out the hour and wake him; and every morning every bird would come to his window and hop onto the body of this holy man; and he would bless it and do other miracles. He never brought [with him] a bed in which to sleep [and had] a fiber mat as a blanket, and another fiber mat as a mattress. He never let a woman enter his cell, and did not consent to this even if it were a man, so that his hiding place might not be seen. At night, the angels of the Lord revealed [themselves] to him").

76. Guaman Poma, *Nueva corónica*, 599 [613]: "aci abian de hazer los buenos saserdotes humillarse a dios y dexar toda la rriquiesa y uanidad del mundo echar la carne y al diablo de ci y ganar las animas para lo presentar ante los ojos dela santicima trinidad q[ue] para esto se unjio y se hizo cristo y se hizo apostol y uenauenturado antes aues de ser martir que confesor por rrecibir onrra como los sanctos de dios."

77. Lucius Annaeus Seneca, *Ad Lucilium epistulae morales*, ed. Richard M. Gummere, 3 vols., Loeb Classical Library (London: William Heinemann, 1917–25), 3:298: "O quam magnis homines tenentur erroribus, qui ius dominandi trans maria cupiunt permittere felicissimosque se iudicant, si multas milite provincias optinent et novas veteribus adiungunt, ignari, quod sit illus ingens parque dis regnum. Imperare sibi maximum imperium est" ("Oh, with what great errors are they possessed, who desire to extend the rule of their dominion overseas, who judge themselves most fortunate if they occupy many provinces by military force and join new provinces to old, ignorant that there is a kingdom as great as this and as valuable. The greatest mastery is the mastery of oneself").

This statement is included in Desiderius Erasmus, *Flores Lvcii Annei Senecae Cordvbensis svmmo labore selecti, ex omnibus illius operibus* (Antwerp: apud Martinum Caesarem, 1528), I6r, and translated, with Christian overtones that make the kingdom to be desired the kingdom of heaven, in *Flores de L. Anneo Seneca, tradvzidas de latin en romance Castellano, por Iuan Martin Cordero* (Antwerp: En casa de Christoforo Plantino, 1555), 103v: "O quan errados estan oy los hombres, que dessean ensanchar su mando aculla de las mares, y juzganse por bienauenturados si alcançan por fuerça de armas, y con soldados muchas prouincias, acrecentando con las nueuas, las viejas q[ue] tenian, sin saber que aquel reyno que les parece grande es muy pequeño. No ay mayor imperio que mandarse el hombre a si mismo" ("Oh, how mistaken are men today, who desire to extend their rule beyond the seas, and judge themselves blessed if they attain by force of arms and soldiers many provinces, increasing with [these] new provinces the old ones that they had, without knowing that the realm that seems great to them is very small. There is no greater empire than for man to command himself").

78. Without mentioning Seneca, Erasmus, in *Enchiridion militis christiani* (Strasbourg: apud Mathiam Schurerium, 1515), 26–27, conjoins his ideal of self-mastery to two precepts derived from Plato—"vnica ad beatitudinē via, primū, vt te noris" ("the only path to happiness is, first, that you know yourself") and "quæ pulchra sunt, eadē esse difficilia" ("things that are excellent are also difficult")—to assert: "Nihil fortius, q[uam] vt quis seip[su]m vincat. sed nullū maius p[rae]mium, q[uam] beatitudo" ("Nothing is more powerful than for one to defeat oneself; yet no reward is greater than beatitude"). The Spanish translation by Alonso Fernández de Madrid, *Enquiridio / o manual del cauallero Christiano* (Alcalá de Henares: En casa de Miguel de Eguia, 1528), 31r, underscores that the bliss of self-mastery is a gift from God: "No ay cosa de mayor esfuerço / que vēcerse el ōbre a si mesmo: p[er]o assi ningū galardō ay mayor que la biēauēturāça que por ello da dios" ("There is nothing of greater effort than for man to defeat himself; but, therefore, there is also no greater reward than the beatitude that God gives for it"). On the widespread use of the *topos* of self-mastery in early modern Spain, see David A. Boruchoff, "El Abencerraje de Antonio de Villegas: una revisión neocristiana," in *Lo converso: orden imaginario y realidad en la cultura española (siglos XIV–XVII)*, ed. Ruth Fine, Michèle Guillemont, and Juan Diego Vila (Madrid: Editorial Iberoamericana; Frankfurt: Vervuert, 2013), 187–215.

79. Vagad was *cronista mayor* of the kingdom of Aragon. For the publication history of the work in which his prologue appears, see José Aragüés Aldaz, "Trayectoria editorial de la *Leyenda de los santos*: primeros apuntes," in *À tout seigneur tout honneur: mélanges offerts à Claude Chauchadis*, ed. Mónica Güell and Marie-Françoise Déodat-Kessedjian (Toulouse: CNRS; Université de Toulouse-Le Mirail, 2009), 81–98.

80. Gualberto Fabricio de Vagad, "Prologue," *Leyēda delos sātos que vulgarmente Flos santorum llaman: agora de nueuo corregida: y en muchos y diuersos: passos donde del verdadero entendimiēto estaua elōgada* (Toledo: por Iuan Ferrer, 1554), A2r: "saco vn comun dezir: y vna cōforme hystoria."

81. Vagad, "Prologue," *Leyēda delos sātos que vulgarmente Flos santorum*, A2r: "A cuyo especial esfuerço \ amparo \lumbre y fauor: pudierō ellos ton [*sic*] alta \ virtuosa y marauillosamente vencer: no solo el mundo \ el diablo \ y la carne: mas . . . hasta los mas altos Principes del reyno del anima \ que son el entendimiento: y la voluntad \ que son los mas fuertes Principes \ y mas dificiles de vencer de todos los otros: porque son principios y causas mas reyes enteros y soberanos señores de todos nuestros libres acuerdos. . . . Vencer por ende su mesmo entendimiento y voluntad: no solo vencer mas sojuzgar \ y avn captiuar el entendimiento con la fee \ la volūtad con la tā por voto assentada: y tan para siempre prometida obediencia de religion \ . . . mucho mas es que vēcer el mundo \ y el infierno: y avn mas que sojuzgar los mas altos reyes y principes poderosos de aquellos. y para esso aprouecha mucho \ y es cosa muy saludable auer de recontar y leer la passion del . . . nuestro re-

demptor Jesu Christo. y avn las vidas y martyrios y milagros de los sanctos bienauenturados. Lo vno por la inmortal memoria y gloria \ por la qual siempre resplandescé. Lo otro por los exéplos de su buē biuir y perfecta vida sea doctrina y enseñamiento a nosotros para bien biuir."

82. *Leyēda delos sātos que vulgarmente Flos santorum llaman*, n.p.: "Materia es necessaria como vtilissima a las animas \ en el qual los que leyeren y oyeren las marauillosas vidas y sanctas obras y exercicios virtuosos de los sanctos se esforçaran a los seguir y imitar. Lo qual haziendo mereceran alcançar de christo nuestro redemptor el gualardon que ellos merescierő en la eterna gloria."

CHAPTER 4

1. E. Brooks Holifield, *The Covenant Sealed: The Development of Puritan Sacramental Theology in Old and New England, 1570–1720* (New Haven, Conn., 1974); Richard Lovelace, *The American Pietism of Cotton Mather: Origins of American Evangelicalism* (Grand Rapids, Mich., 1979).

2. On creolization and the struggles to define a term that seems remarkably unstable, see Peter Hulme, "Postcolonial Theory and Early America: An Approach from the Caribbean," in *Possible Pasts: Becoming Colonial in Early America*, ed. Robert Blair St. George (Ithaca, N.Y.: Cornell University Press, 2000), 33–48; and Verene A. Shepherd, "Unity and Disunity, Creolization and Marronage in the Atlantic World: Conceptualizing Atlantic Studies," *Atlantic Studies* 1, no. 1 (2004): 49–65, a reference I owe to Lawrence Buell.

3. The starting point for some discussions of lived religion has been the essay collection *Lived Religion in America: Toward a History of Practice*, ed. David D. Hall (Princeton, N. J.: Princeton University Press, 1997). See also Hall, "From 'Religion and Society' to Practices: The New Religious History," in *Possible Pasts*, ed. St. George, 149–59.

4. Alexander Walsham, *Providence in Early Modern England* (New York: Cambridge University Press, 1999). In *Print and Protestantism in Early Modern England* (Oxford: Oxford University Press, 2000), chap. 8, Ian Green demonstrates that certain "cheap" books described by Tessa Watt in *Cheap Print and Popular Piety* (Cambridge, UK: Cambridge University Press, 1991) as "godly" were in fact the doing of hack writers who created a hodgepodge of themes. Green's corrective is an acute reminder of how the workings of the book trade, unless attended to with precision, can fool most of us.

5. Arthur H. Williamson, *Scottish National Consciousness in the Age of James VI: The Apocalypse, the Union, and the Shaping of Scotland's Public Culture* (Edinburgh: J. Donald, 1979); Walsham, *Providence in Early Modern England*.

6. Francis J. Bremer, "The Heritage of John Winthrop: Religion Along the Stour Valley, 1548–1630," *New England Quarterly* 70 (1997): 515–47.

7. Harley, quoted in Jacqueline Eales, *Puritans and Roundheads: The Harleys of Brampton Bryan and the Outbreak of the English Civil War* (Cambridge, UK: Cambridge University Press, 1990), 43; Baxter, quoted in Andrew Cambers, *Godly Reading: Print, Manuscript and Puritanism in England, 1580–1700* (Cambridge, UK: Cambridge University Press, 2011), 22; about the Separatists, see Patrick Collinson, "The English Conventicle," in *Voluntary Religion*, ed. W. J. Sheils and Diana Wood, Studies in Church History 23 (Oxford: Published for the Ecclesiastical History Society by Basil Blackwell, 1986), 223–60.

8. See Collinson, *The Elizabethan Puritan Movement* (London, 1967); *The Religion of Protestants: The Church in English Society, 1559–1625* (Oxford, 1982); "The Downfall of Archbishop Grindal and Its Place in Elizabethan Political and Ecclesiastical History," in *The English Commonwealth 1547–1640*, ed. Peter Clark, Alan G. R. Smith, and Nicholas Tyacke (Leicester, 1979), 39–58; and the

essays collected in *Godly People: Essays on English Protestantism and Puritanism* (London, 1983). In my introduction to a 1970 reprinting of Perry Miller, *Orthodoxy in Massachusetts, 1630–1650* (Cambridge, Mass., 1933), I noted Miller's reliance on a denominational framework.

9. Foster's *The Long Argument: English Puritanism and the Shaping of New England Culture, 1570–1700* (Chapel Hill, N.C., 1991), remains the premier study of transatlantic influences and continuities.

10. Richard Bauckham, *Tudor Apocalypse: Sixteenth-Century Apocalypticism, Millenarianism and the English Reformation* (Appleford, 1978); Paul Christianson, *Reformers and Babylon: English Apocalyptic Visions from the Reformation to the Eve of the Civil War* (Toronto, 1978); and Jane Facey, "John Foxe and the Defence of the English Church," in *Protestantism and the National Church in Sixteenth Century England*, ed. Peter Lake and Maria Dowling (London, 1987), 162–92. Also pertinent is Adrian Chastain Weimer, *Martyrs Mirror: Persecution and Holiness in Early New England* (New York, 2012).

11. Peter Lake, *Anglicans and Puritans? Presbyterian and Conformist Thought from Whitgift to Hooker* (London, 1988).

12. *The Journal of John Winthrop, 1630–1649*, ed. Richard S. Dunn, James Savage, and Laetitia Yeandle (Cambridge, Mass.: Harvard University Press, 1996), 168–70.

13. *The Works of Thomas Shepard*, ed., John A. Albro, 3 vols. (Boston, 1853), 2:65, 20, 222. These paragraphs are borrowed from David D. Hall, *A Reforming People: Puritanism and the Transformation of Public Life in New England* (New York, 2011), 161–63.

14. David D. Hall, *The Faithful Shepherd: A History of the New England Ministry in the Seventeenth Century* (Chapel Hill, N.C., 1972), chap. 6.

15. Henry Vane, "A briefe Answer to a certaine declaration, made of the intent and equitye of the order of court, that none should be received to inhabite within this jurisdiction but such as should be allowed by some of the magistrates," in [Thomas Hutchinson], *A Collection of Original Papers Relative to the History of the Colony of Massachusetts-Bay* (Boston, 1769), 75.

16. Tensions and policies described in Hall, *A Reforming People*, chap. 3.

17. Ibid., chap. 2.

18. The truly amazing number of translations and reprints of English theologizing on the Continent is noted in Milton, "Puritanism and the Continental Reformed Churches."

19. John von Rohr, *The Covenant of Grace in Puritan Thought* (Athens, Ga., 1986); W. G. B. Stoever, *"A Faire and Easie Way to Heaven": Covenant Theology and Antinomianism in Early Massachusetts* (Middletown, Conn., 1978). Elsewhere in the scholarly literature (e.g., Andrew Delbanco's *Puritan Ordeal*), the story of religious debate in early New England is organized around a tension between a freer form of Spirit-centered piety and a repressive legalism, in a curiously American recasting of Max Weber's *Protestant Ethic*.

20. Anne S. Brown and David D. Hall, "'That Her Children Might Get Good': Family Strategies and Church Membership in Early New England," in *Lived Religion in America*, ed. Hall.

21. Leah Marcus, *Unediting the Renaissance: Shakespeare, Marlow, Milton* (London, 1996).

22. *Journal of John Winthrop*; and, for the broader context, Hall, *Ways of Writing*, chaps. 3–4. See also Margaret J. M. Ezell, *Social Authorship and the Advent of Print* (Baltimore, 1999).

23. Phillip H. Round, *By Nature and by Custom Cursed: Transatlantic Civil Discourse and New England Cultural Production, 1620–1660* (Hanover, N.H., 1999), 2, 6.

24. A fascinating demonstration of the possibilities for such transatlantic histories is Isobel Hofmeyr, *The Portable Bunyan: A Transatlantic History of The Pilgrim's Progress* (Princeton, N.J., 2004).

25. Susan O'Brien, "Eighteenth-Century Publishing Networks in the First Years of Transatlantic Evangelicalism," in *Evangelicalism: Comparative Studies of Popular Protestantism in North*

America, the British Isles, and Beyond 1700–1900, ed. Mark A. Noll, David W. Babbington, and George A. Rawlyk (New York, 1994), 38–57. See also the case study I provide of the Presbyterian minister Samuel Davies in Hall, "Afterword," *The Atlantic World of Print in the Age of Franklin, Early American Studies* 8, no. 1 (Winter 2010): 199–212.

26. Rachel Schneppers, "Jonas Cast Up at London: The Experience of New England Churches in Revolutionary England" (PhD diss., Rutgers University, 2010).

27. For an example, see Edwards, *The Second Part of Gangraena* (London, 1646), 174–75.

28. "Conclusions" refer to the arguments of the Antinomians.

29. Thomas Hutchinson, *A History of the Colony and Province of Massachusetts-Bay*, ed. Lawrence Shaw Mayo, 3 vols. (Cambridge, Mass., 1936), 1:60–61.

30. David D. Hall, *The Antinomian Controversy, 1636–1638: A Documentary History* (Middletown, Conn., 1968), 174.

31. Hall, *Ways of Writing*, 64–65.

32. Elizabeth Maddock Dillon uses gender to unpack the politics of a "transatlantic text," the *Short Story* in the version put together by Thomas Weld, although mistakenly attributing the text to an author, John Winthrop. Dillon, *The Gender of Freedom: Fictions of Liberalism and the Literary Public Sphere* (Stanford, Calif., 2004), chap. 2.

33. Preface to Cotton, *The Way of the Churches*, (London, 1645).

34. For the textual details of this intervention, see Jonathan Beecher Field, *Errands into the Metropolis: New England Dissidents in Revolutionary London* (Hanover, N.H.: University Press of New England, 2009).

35. Here again I borrow language from *Ways of Writing*, 94–95, where the appropriate references may also be found.

36. *The New England Company of 1649 and John Eliot* (Boston: Prince Society, 1920) 108; *Proceedings of the Massachusetts Historical Society*, 2nd ser. (1860–62), 5:376–77.

37. *Records of the Colony of New Plymouth in New England*, ed. Nathaniel B. Shurtleff and David Pulsifer, 11 vols. (Boston, 1855–61), 10:255–59. Here, I borrow passages from *Ways of Writing*, 169–71.

38. James C. Pilling, *Bibliography of the Algonquian Languages* (Washington, D.C., 1891), 136. This all too brief account of the materiality of the Eliot Bible is greatly expanded in Phillip H. Round, *Removable Type: Histories of the Book in Indian Country, 1663–1880* (Chapel Hill: University of North Carolina Press, 2010), chap. l. Where our narratives intersect is in our shared insistence that "all texts are produced in a composite way . . . [and] are the products of complex networks of publishers, printers, editors, audiences, and authors" (16). For Round, however, the ultimate goal of such closely contextual work is to demonstrate the "creativity" (agency) and possibilities for "resistance" within Native communities, a goal that runs the risk of downplaying the significance of becoming Christian and of relying on an essentialist concept of "Native" culture.

CHAPTER 5

1. Jerónimo de Mendieta, "Prólogo al Cristiano Lector," in *Historia eclesiástica indiana*, ed. Francisco Solano y Pérez-Lila, 2 vols., Biblioteca de Autores Españoles 260–61 (Madrid: Atlas, 1973), 2:227.

2. Mendieta, *Historia eclesiástica indiana*, 2:227–29.

3. Juan de Torquemada, "Prologue to Libro XXI," in *Tercera Parte de los veinte y un libros rituales: Monarchia Indiana* (Madrid: Nicolás Rodríguez, 1723), 606–7. "La primera es, que al

tormento recibido siga la muerte natural del cuerpo . . . La segunda . . . que sea por la defensión de la Fe de Jesu-Christo . . . La tercera, que el martirio sea voluntario; y esto ensena Santo Tomas . . . Pues que estos Benditos Religiosos hayan muerto de esta manera, quien lo dudara?" This is Torquemada's own argument, not present in Mendieta. I follow Mendieta in preference to Torquemada.

3. Mendieta, *Historia eclesiástica indiana*, 2:227–29.

4. On the activities of missionaries, especially Jesuits in the Far Orient, see Adriano Prosperi, "El misonero," in *El hombre barroco*, ed. Rosario Villari et al. (Madrid: Alianza Editorial, 1991), 201–39; and Charles R. Boxer, *The Christian Century in Japan, 1549–1650* (Berkeley: University of California Press, 1951).

5. Pedro Castillo Maldonado, "Prudencio y los mártires Calagurritanos," *Kalakorikos* 5 (2000): 65–75; A. González Blanco, "Los santos mártires y el Obispado de Calahorra," *Kalakorikos* 5 (2000): 77–86; Joaquín González Echegaray, "El culto a los santos Emeterio y Celedonio en Santander," *Kalakorikos* 5 (2000): 271–83.

6. Most authors base their narratives on the writings of Saint Eulogius, a ninth-century churchman who was beheaded in 859. See also Jessica A. Coope, *The Martyrs of Córdoba: Community and Family Conflict in an Age of Mass Conversion* (Lincoln: University of Nebraska Press, 1995); and C. R. Haines, *Christianity and Islam in Spain, A.D. 756–1031* (London: Kegan Paul, Trench and Co., 1889). Other narratives of martyrdom in the ninth century point to that of two hundred monks of the Order of Saint Benedict at the monastery of Cardeña, near Burgos, but this event seems to have been the product of a local cult rather than a true historical event. See Rafael Sánchez Domingo, "La narración de la memoria histórica y de la tradición: los mártires de Cardeña (Burgos) en la memoria colectiva de la Castilla medieval," in *El culto a los santos: cofradías, devoción, fiestas y artes: Actas del Simposio* (San Lorenzo del Escorial: Escurialenses, 2008), 571–91.

7. Morocco was the kingdom attracting the most intense missionary effort from the peninsula. Several Franciscan martyrs attested to the persistence of the order in rekindling Christianity in that kingdom since the thirteenth century. See Matías de San Francisco, *Relación del viaje espiritual y prodigioso que hizo a Marruecos el venerable Padre Fr. Juan de Prado* (Cádiz: Bartolomé Núñez, 1675). Fray Juan was a Franciscan martyred in Morocco in 1631. See also Manuel Pablo Castellanos, *Apostolado seráfico en Marruecos* (Madrid: Librería de D. Gregorio del Amo, 1896). As a matter of curiosity, the poet Robert Southey wrote a poem in honor of several Franciscans friars martyred in Morocco in 1217. See "Queen Orraca and the Five Martyrs of Morocco,"≈in *The Poetical Works of Robert Southey, Esq.*, vol. 13 (London: Longman, Hurst, Rees, Orme and Brown, 1823), 181, which was based on the Franciscan chronicle of Fray Manoel da Esperanza.

8. Mendieta, *Historia eclesiástica indiana*, 2:137. As a small child, Teresa of Avila left her home with her little brother to travel to the lands of the Moors. See Saint Teresa of Avila, *Libro de su vida* (Garden City, N.J.: Doubleday, 1961), 3.

9. Eusebio González de la Torre, *Chronica seraphica, sexta parte* (Madrid: Viuda de Juan García Infanzón, 1725), 325; Juan Abreu de Galindo, *The History of the Discovery and Conquest of the Canary Islands* (London: R. and J. Dodsley and T. Durham, 1764); Felipe Fernández-Armesto, *The Canary Islands After the Conquest: The Making of a Colonial Society in the Early Sixteenth Century* (Oxford: Oxford University Press, 1982). Officially the Castilian conquest ended in 1495 after contestatory struggles with Portugal and a slow conquest of the aboriginal Guanches; see L. J. Andrew Villalon, "San Diego de Alcalá and the Politics of Saint-Making in Counter-Reformation Europe," *Catholic Historical Review* 84, no. 4 (October 1997): 691–715.

10. John L. Phelan, *The Millennial Kingdom of the Franciscans in the New World* (Berkeley: University of California Press, 1970), 27. Juan de Torquemada was among those who believed that the conversion of the indigenous had been preordained by God. Torquemada, *Tercera Parte*, 131–32.

11. For a comparative study of martyrdom in early modern Europe, see Brad S. Gregory, *Salvation at Stake: Christian Martyrdom in Early Modern Europe* (Cambridge, Mass.: Harvard University Press, 1999); Lacey Badwin Smith, *Fools, Martyrs, Traitors: The Story of Martyrdom in the Eastern World* (Evanston, Ill.: Northwestern University Press, 1997); Antonio Rubial, *La justicia de Dios: La violencia física y simbólica de los santos en la historia del cristianismo* (Mexico: Educación y Cultura/Trama Editorial, 2011), 169–218.

12. See Gregory, "The New Saints: Roman Catholics and Martyrdom," in *Salvation at Stake*, 250–314; *De persecutioni Anglicana Libellus* (Rome: Francesco Zanetti, 1582); Dom Maurice Chauncy, *The History of the Sufferings of Eighteen Carthusians in England* (London: Burns and Oates, Ltd, 1896). This work is a translation of a 1539 Latin manuscript left by Dom Maurice Chauncey in 1539.

13. See Henk van Nierop, *Treason in the Northern Quarter: War, Terror and the Rule of Law in the Dutch Revolt* (Princeton, N.J.: Princeton University Press, 2001); Graham Darby, *The Origins and Development of the Dutch Revolt* (London: Routledge, 2001); Geoffrey Parker, *Spain in the Netherlands, 1555–1659* (London: Collins, 1979); and, by the same author, *The Dutch Revolt* (Ithaca, N.Y.: Cornell University Press, 1977). For English Catholics, see Richard Verntegan, *Theatrum Crudelitaru, Haereticorum* (Antwerp: Adrianum Huberti, 1592); Gregory, *Salvation at Stake*, 250–314. For Anabaptists, see Thielem J. Von Bracht, *Bloody Theatre of Martyrs Mirror* (Lancaster County PS: David Miller, 1837).

14. John Foxe, *Book of Martyrs: A History of the Lives, Sufferings and Triumphant Deaths of the Primitive as Well as Protestant Martyrs From the Commencement of Christianity to the Latest Periods of Pagan and Popish Persecution* (Improved by Important Alterations and Additions by Rev. Charles A. Goodrich) (Hartford, Conn.: Edwin Hunt, 1845). Goodrich added those martyrs not covered by Foxe, owing to his death.

15. *Relación de algunos martyrios que de nuevo han hecho los hereges en Inglaterra y de otras cosas tocantes a nuestra santa y Católica Religión*, trans. Roberto Personio (Madrid: Pedro Madrigal, 1590); Victor Houliston, *Elizabethan England: Joseph Person's Jesuit Polemic, 1590–1610* (London: Ashgate, 2007). See also Anne Dillon, *The Construction of Martyrdom in the English Catholic Community, 1535–1603* (London: Ashgate, 2002); and Nicolas Sander, *Rise and Growth of the Anglican Schism* (London: Burns and Oates, 1877).

16. The religious darts between England and Spain continued with the publication of Pedro de Ribadeneira, *Historia eclesiástica del cisma de Inglaterra* (1588) (Madrid: Imprenta y Librería de D Manuel Martin, 1781). Ribadeneira was a Jesuit who was said to have been inspired by the work of Nicholas Sander, an English Catholic author of a book on the English "schism." Although captured in England, Sander was allowed to return to France. While in the Tower he kept a diary of the tortures inflicted on Catholics. Sander did not live to see his work published, dying from a disease in France. Edward Rishton finished it in 1585 and published it in Cologne, adding materials on the reign of Elizabeth I. Rishton was one of the many Englishmen that took the priestly vows in France in the last quarter of the sixteenth century. He was a colleague of future Jesuit martyr Edmund Campion. See Sander, *Rise and Growth of the Anglican Schism*. Another distinguished English Catholic was poet Robert Southwell, whose works were widely read in the early seventeenth century.

17. Félix Lope de Vega y Carpio, *Triunfo de la Fe en los Reynos del Japón por los años de 1614 y 1615* (Madrid: Viuda de Alonso Martin, 1618); Pedro Calderón de la Barca, "La cisma de Inglaterra"

in *Comedias de D. Pedro Calderón de la Barca*, ed. Juan Jorge Keil, 4 vols. (Leipzig: Ernesto Fleischer, 1830), 4:136–58. Calderón de la Barca specialized in the writing of *autos sacramentales*, plays of a religious nature. Lope de Vega took the habit in his late years and wrote numerous sacred poems.

18. The literature on the expansion of Christianity in the Orient is vast. Here I offer a few select titles that incorporate information on martyrs. Most of them were published before the twentieth century. Alonso Franco, *Segunda parte de la historia de la provincia de Santiago de Mexico, orden de predicadores en la Nueva España* (1645; Mexico: Imprenta del Museo Nacional, 1900), 263–65, on the friars who died in the Philippines. See also 409–15; Francisco de Santa Inés, *Cronica de la Provincia de San Gregorio magno de religiosos descalzos de N. P. San Francisco*, vol. 1 (1676; Manila: Tipo-Litografia de Chofre y Comp., 1892). Spain established itself in the Philippines in 1565. For eighteenth-century Dominican missionaries and martyrs in the islands, see Evaristo Fernández Arias, *El Beato Sanz y compañeros mártires del orden de Predicadores* (Manila: Establecimiento Tipográfico de Santo Tomas, 1893); R. P. Charlevoix, *Historia del Cristianismo en el Japón* (Barcelona: Imprenta de Pablo Riera, 1858); Manuel Jiménez, *Mártires Agustinos del Japón* (Valladolid: Imprenta de D. Juan de la Cuesta, 1867); Francisco Carrero, *Triunfo del Santo Rosario en el Japón y Vida de Fr. Pedro Vázquez, Mártir*, 2nd ed. (1626; Manila Colegio de Santo Tomás, 1868). The Augustinians arrived in Japan in 1565, the Franciscans in 1578, the Jesuits in 1581, and the Dominicans in 1587: Eustaquio María de Nenclares, *Vidas de los mártires del Japón* (Madrid: Imprenta de la Esperanza, 1862); R. P. Giuseppe Boero, *Los Dosciento Cinco mártires del Japón* (Mexico: Imprenta de J. M. Lara, 1869); Manuel Jiménez, *Mártires Agustinos del Japón* (Valladolid: Imprenta de D. Juan de la Cuesta, 1867); Haruko Nawata Ward, *Women Leaders in Japan's Christian Century, 1549–1650* (London: Ashgate, 2009). See also José María Santos Rovira, "Estudio histórico-filológico de la crónica del viaje a China de fray Agustín de Tordesillas," *eHumanista* 6 (2006): 115–26; Charles R. Boxer, *The Christian Century in Japan, 1545–1650* (Berkeley: University of California Press, 1951); Anthony E. Clark, *China's Saints: Catholic Martyrdom During the Quin (1644–1911)* (Lanham, Md.: Lehigh University Press, 2011).

19. Mendieta, *Historia eclesiástica indiana*, 2:143–44. He tells his readers how the founding father Martin de Valencia—one of the original twelve missionaries who arrived in New Spain in 1524—had several visions or dreams on the conversion of infidels. In one of them he saw two women attempting to cross a river. The ugly one had much trouble in crossing; the beautiful one had no trouble at all. In his interpretation of the dream, the ugly woman was New Spain and its people, who reached the other shore (conversion) with much trouble. The beautiful woman was a new land whose people would convert willingly and achieve perfection. It was China, where the fruit of Christianity would be plentiful. In another vision, he had seen beasts, instead of women, experiencing similar problems of achieving the goal (New Spain) or achieving it effortlessly (China). In a third dream, he saw men with birds moving around them and almost touching their lips with their wings and giving them much consolation. They represented idolaters yet to be discovered, men of virile character capable of receiving the gifts of prayer and contemplation. These dreams betrayed his longing for an exotic kingdom of willing and spiritualized converts. Jerónimo de Mendieta was the first compiler of previous histories of the Franciscans that have disappeared. He finished writing in the first years of the seventeenth century but his history was not published. Juan de Torquemada, Agustín de Vetancurt, and José Arlegui—among other historians of the order—simply borrowed from his information, adding those who had died in the seventeenth century. Agustín de Vetancurt, *Teatro Mexicano: Crónica de la Provincia del Santo Evangelio de Mexico* (1698; Mexico: Editorial Porrúa, 1982). See *Menologio Franciscano*, as part of this work, for the lives of notable Franciscans; Joseph Arlegui, *Chronica de la Provincia de N.S.P.S. Francisco de Zacatecas* (Mexico: Joseph Ber-

nardo de Hogal, 1737). The attraction of the Far East was very strong through the first decades of the seventeenth century. Having established outposts in Manila, many peninsular recruits continued to pursue the dream of being "the" generation that world turn things around. See the story of Fray Pedro de Zúñiga, a member of a powerful family in Spain who became an Augustinian in 1604 and traveled through Mexico to the Philippines, landing in Japan where he perished in 1626 among other martyrs, in Joseph Sicardo, *Christiandad del Japón* (Madrid: Francisco Sanz, 1698), 164–204.

20. Alonso Franco, *Segunda parte*, 290, 301–2. In his dream, Gandullo climbed a tough path while a young man predicted that he would have harder work yet to come. His dream was interpreted by another friar as meaning there were greater hardships in China. Franco and other evangelizers considered the Philippines a lesser prize than China. However, the fact that the Jesuits had already made a dent in that empire made some turn to Japan, which remained a tantalizing challenge precisely because of its difficulty. Fray Luis Gandullo had the opportunity of visiting Macan in Sumatra, but owing to his incendiary preaching against local authorities and practices such as polygamy, he was expelled. After several incidents with Chinese and Portuguese authorities, he returned to Manila.

21. See Susan Deeds, "Legacies of Resistance, Adaptation, and Tenacity: History of the Native Peoples of Northwest Mexico," in T*he Cambridge History of the Native Peoples of the Americas*, ed. Richard E. W. Adams and Murdo J. Macleod, 2 vols. (Cambridge, UK: Cambridge University Press, 2000), 2:44–88; David Frye, "The Native Peoples of Northeastern Mexico," in *Cambridge History*, ed. Adams and Macleod, 2: 89–135; Eric Van Young, "The Indigenous Peoples of Western Mexico: From the Spanish Invasion to the Present," in *Cambridge History*, ed. Adams and Macleod, 2:136–86; David J. Weber, *The Spanish Frontier in North America* (New Haven, Conn.: Yale University Press, 1992).

22. Jerónimo de Mendieta, *Historia eclesiástica indiana*, 1:134–35; Agustín Dávila Padilla, *Historia de la Provincia de Santiago de Mexico de la Orden de Predicadores* (Bruselas: Casa de Francisco Vivien, 1648), 667; Robert Haskett, "Dying for Conversion: Faith, Obedience, and the Tlaxclan Boy Martyrs in New Spain," *Colonial Latin American Review* 17, no. 2:185–212.

23. Franco, *Segunda Parte*, 369. In less than two years after his death, Fray Sebastián's name had already been honored in the Dominican Chapter General celebrated in Lisbon. It was also mentioned by playwright and poet Lope de Vega in one of his works and in a sermon preached by the bishop of Córdoba, Fray Domingo Pimentel, on the occasion of the memorial service for Phillip III. He was also cited *inter alia* in a book on the miracles of the Holy Rosary published in 1627, and in the catalogue of the order's saints published in Rome in 1638.

24. Elizabeth A. Castells, *Martyrdom and Memory: Early Christian Culture Making* (New York: Columbia University Press, 2004), 7. She argues that spectacle is a crucial dimension of martyrology. In the New World there was no spectacle or audience, except the audience of readers and the spectacle created by the pen of the writer.

25. For the complex process of settlement of northern New Spain, see José Antonio Cruz Rangel, *Chichimecas, misioneros, soldados y terratenientes: Estrategias de colonización, control y poder en Querétaro y la Sierra Gorda*, vols. 16–18, (México: Secretaria de Gobernación/Archivo General de la Nación, 2003); Alfredo Jiménez, *El Gran Norte de Mexico: Una frontera imperial en la Nueva España (1540–1820)* (Madrid: Tébar, 2006).

26. Antonio Rubial, "Mártires y predicadores: La conquista de las fronteras y su representación plástica," in *Los pinceles de la Historia: De la Patria Criolla a la Nación Mexicana* (México: Conaculta, 2000), 50–71. When the representatives of the Spanish government re-entered the province of New Mexico in the 1690s [after the successful 1680 revolt], the missionaries were backed by

substantial military support. See J. Manuel Espinosa, ed., *The Pueblo Indian Revolt of 1696 and the Franciscan Missions in New Mexico: Letters of the Missionaries and Related Documents* (Norman: University of Oklahoma Press, 1988).

27. Thomas H. Naylor and Charles Polzer, eds., *The Presidio and Militia on the Northern Frontier of New Spain: A Documentary History, 1500–1700,* vol. 1 (Tucson: University of Arizona Press, 1986); Diane Hadley, Thomas H. Naylor, and Mardith K. Schuetz-Miller, eds., *The Presidio and Militia on the Northern Frontier of New Spain: The Central Corridor and the Texas Corridor, 1700–1765,* vol. 2 (Tucson: University of Arizona Press, 1997); Carlos Sempat Assadourian, *Zacatecas: Conquista y transformaciones de la frontera en el Siglo XVI. Minas de plata, guerra y evangelización* (México: El Colegio de México, 2008); Alberto Carrillo Cazares, *El Debate sobre la Guerra Chichimeca, 1531–1585,* 2 vols. (Zamora: el Colegio de Michoacán/ Colegio de San Luis, 2000); Philip Wayne Powell, *Soldiers, Indians, & Silver: The Northward Advance of New Spain, 1550–1600* (Berkeley: University of California Press, 1969).

28. Ida Altman, *The War for Mexico's West: Indians and Spaniards in New Galicia, 1524–1550* (Albuquerque: University of New Mexico Press, 2010); Felipe Castro, *La rebelión de los indios y la paz de los españoles* (Tlalpan: CIESAS, 1996). According to Castro, there were five rebellions between 1546 and 1585, four of them in Yucatán and Oaxaca and one in Nayarit, Chichimec territory. Of the nineteen rebellions in the seventeenth century, seventeen occurred in the northern territories. Of the eleven registered in the eighteenth century, nine were also in the north. See Castro, *La rebellion,* 124–27.

29. Susan Deeds, *Defiance and Deference in Mexico's Colonial North: Indians Under Spanish Rule in Nueva Vizcaya* (Austin: University of Texas Press, 2003), 23.

30. Deeds, *Defiance,* 3.

31. Deeds, *Defiance,* 31–38. For the report of the Bishop of Durango on this rebellion and the battle of Cacaria that determined the indigenous defeat, see Castro, *La rebelión,* 128–31.

32. Alonso de Benavides, "Memorial (1626])," *Bulletin of the New York Public Library* 3 (January–December 1899): 417–28.

33. J. Manuel Espinosa, *The Pueblo Indian Revolt,* 18, 24.

34. See, among others, John L. Kessel, *Pueblos, Spaniards and the Kingdom of New Mexico* (Norman: University of Oklahoma Press, 2010); Andrew L. Knaut, T*he Pueblo Revolt of 1680: Conquest and Resistance in Seventeenth Century New Mexico* (Norman: University of Oklahoma Press, 1995); Louis Baldwin, *Intruders Within: Pueblo Resistance to Spanish Rule and the Revolt of 1680* (New York: Franklin Watts, 1995). Ramón Gutiérrez describes the desire for martyrdom nurtured by New Mexico missionaries and the brutal and mocking treatment meted out to them during the revolt in *When Jesus Came, the Corn Mothers Went Away: Marriage, Sexuality, and Power in New Mexico, 1500–1846* (Stanford, Calif.: Stanford University Press, 1991), 127–37.

35. For a sample of different opinions, see David J. Weber, *What Caused the Pueblo Revolt of 1680* (Boston: Bedford/St. Martin's, 1999).

36. *Propaganda Fide* was founded by Pope Gregory XV in 1622 to strengthen the Catholic faith. In 1681 the Spanish king authorized the first institutions oriented to train missionaries in the New World, the *Colegios de Propaganda Fide,* which were in the hands of the Franciscan Order. In 1683, *Propaganda Fide* of Querétaro received its first trainees. See Isidro Félix de Espinosa, *Chronica Apostólica y Seraphica de todos los colegios de Propaganda Fide de esta Nueva España* (México: Viuda de D. Joseph Bernardo de Hogal, 1746). Other foundations followed: Guadalupe in Zacatecas by Fray Antonio Margil in 1707; San Fernando in Mexico City, 1734; San Diego, Pachuca, 1771; San José de Gracia, Orizaba, 1799. See Michael B. McCloskey, *The Formative Years of the Missionary*

College of Santa Cruz of Querétaro, 1683–1733 (Washington, D.C.: Catholic University of America, 1955); Román Gutiérrez et al., *Los Colegios Apostólicos de Propaganda Fide, su historia y su legado* (Zacatecas: Gobierno del Estado/Universidad Autónoma de Zacatecas/H. Ayuntamiento de Guadalupe, 2001–2004); Antonio Rubial García, "Estrategias de impacto. La llegada de los padres apostólicos de Propaganda Fide a Querétaro" in *Religión, poder y autoridad en la Nueva España*, eds. Alicia Mayer and Ernesto de la Torre Villar (México: UNAM, 2004), 263–73.

37. Juan Domingo Arricivita, *Crónica seráfica y apostólica del colegio de Propaganda Fide de la Santa Cruz de Querétaro en la Nueva España: Segunda Parte* (México: Felipe Zúñiga y Ontiveros, 1792), 426–31.

38. I focus on the mendicant orders only. The Jesuits were not a mendicant order.

39. Joseph Arlegui, *Chronica de la Provincia de N.S.P.S.*, 215–52. All who opposed Christianization were called "barbarians," a term we find applied to the Guanches in the Canary Islands, the Natives of the Philippine islands, and even the Japanese lords. See Richard Fletcher, *The Barbarian Conversion: From Paganism to Christianity* (Berkeley: University of California Press, 1999).

40. Mendieta, *Historia eclesiástica indiana*, "Prólogo al Cristiano Lector," 2:228–29.

41. Mendieta, *Historia eclesiástica indiana*, 2:228. He thanked the Tlaxcaltecans who went north to settle and teach the Chichimecs by example even though some had perished at Chichimecs' hands. At the time he was writing, it was his belief that viceregal policies and the work of the missionaries had helped to create the peace all were enjoying for the previous six or seven years.

42. Benavides, "Memorial," 419.

43. Frye, "The Native Peoples of Northeastern Mexico," 2:100. Frye quotes settler Gonzalo de Las Casas. See also Gaspar de Villagrá, *Historia de la Nuevo México, del Capitán Gaspar de Villagra* (Alcalá: Luys Martínez Grande, 1610). In this poem on the history of the first explorations of New Mexico, the author addresses the inhabitants as "*bárbaras gentes.*" In Canto Quince he writes: "Cuyos incultos bárbaros groseros / En la pasada edad, y en la presente / Siempre fueron de bronco entendimiento / De simple vida bruta, no enseñada / A cultivar la tierra, ni romperla / Y en adquirir hacienda, y en guardarla / También de todo punto descuidados / Sólo sabemos viven de la caza / De pesca y de raíces que conocen." The author suggested that such a life could be agreeable, having none of the problems found in cities, courts, and political kingdoms, but he continued to call the indigenous "barbarians."

44. Arlegui, *Chronica de la Provincia de N.S.P.S. Francisco*, 131–208. Arlegui praised their admirable sensory abilities, but he compared indigenous people's accurate knowledge of the land to that of animals, making them instinctual and close to nature, not born of cultivated intelligence. In fact, Arlegui believed that even those who had been Christianized were not to be trusted, as many persisted in their tribal habits. He could only explain the problems they confronted as having been permitted by God in His unfathomable designs. This total lack of understanding of tribal culture could not bode well for the future of evangelization.

45. J. Manuel Espinosa, "Report of Fray Francisco de Vargas," in *The Pueblo Indian Revolt*, 255.

46. Isidro Félix de Espinosa, *Chronica Apostólica*, 436. See also 419–38.

47. See the letters of Fray Damian Mazanet [1690] and Fray Benito Fernández de Santa Ana [1750], on the potential for the adoption of agriculture in pueblos in Texas in Hadley, Naylor, and Schuetz-Miller, *The Presidio and Militia*, 330–51, 482–99.

48. Arricivita, *Crónica seráfica y apostólica*, 505.

49. He reported to be elated with the *colegio* of Querétaro because it was more rigorous than those of the Carthusians. "In northern Mexico the possibilities of suffering martyrdom were greater than those imagined by so many Franciscan saints." See Arricivita, *Crónica seráfica y apostólica*, 537–38.

50. Thomas Gage, *The English-American: A New Survey of the West Indies* (London: G. Rout-ledge and Sons, 1928), 23. The same night, an attack by the islanders left three Jesuits dead and two wounded. A fourth one and a Dominican died of their wounds. Gage remarks that the zealous friars cooled down very fast.

51. Arricivita, *Crónica seráfica y apostólica*, 400. Father Juan Díaz, another casualty of the Colorado River revolt, who died in July 1781, was fully aware of the threatening situation into which he stepped, but, according to Arricivita (532–35), to preserve the honor of his order, he did not want to back off of the enterprise, and left for the planned establishment of two towns.

52. Mendieta, *Historia eclesiástica indiana*, 231–33.

53. Walking long distances was part of the European Mendicant tradition that was carried to the New World. Fray Martín de Valencia, a Franciscan founder in New Spain, had traveled from Spain to Rome on foot. See Mendieta, *Historia eclesiástica indiana*, 2:134. See also the life of Fray Antonio Margil, a notable Franciscan of the seventeenth century, whose trips to Guatemala and the Mexican north became a matter of hagiographical wonder: Isidro Félix de Espinosa, *El Peregrino Septentrional: Atalante delineado en la ejemplarísima vida del Venerable Padre F. Antonio de Margil de Jesús* (México: Joseph Fernando de Hogal, 1737).

54. Arlegui, *Chronica de la Provincia de N.S.P.S. Francisco*, 202–7, 253. Arlegui notes that the Indians of that zone were interested in clothes, animals, and merchandise. A missionary in Ato-tonilco witnessed an "attack" by over two hundred Indians, who did not touch him but took everything in his cell. The same friar was also attacked walking toward San Juan del Río. His two companions were hurt by arrows, but he succeeded in having their lives spared. The Indians gave him a horse to reach town and returned his clothes and his Breviary. The three rode the horse and reached the closest town. No date is given, but on narrating similar displays of charity by the indigenous, Arlegui commented that such charity required a prayer to God to "save them from falling into such bloody and harsh hands because such demonic piety is not to be desired but to run away from them," 204. One friar's life was disputed by two different parties, one in favor and one against. They decided to leave it to chance, and the friar was spared by a mere strike of luck. He was also described as full of "anguish and tribulation" while he prepared himself to die (255).

55. Manuel Espinosa, *The Pueblo Indian Revolt*, 254.

56. Arlegui, *Chronica de la Provincia de N.S.P.S. Francisco*, 207.

57. Ibid., 255–56.

58. Arlegui, *Chronica de la Provincia de N.S.P.S. Francisco*, 215, 217. In 1555, after the deaths of two of his missionaries, Fray Pedro thanked God for the grace of such "benefice" and quickly "determined to send two new workers to the new enterprise" in Sinaloa, populated at that time by "numberless barbarians."

59. Mendieta, *Historia eclesiástica indiana*, 2:248.

60. Arlegui, *Chronica de la Provincia de N.S.P.S. Francisco*, 209–15; Mendieta, *Historia eclesiástica indiana*, 237. Mendieta maintained that the first Franciscan martyr was Fray Juan Calero, while Arlegui claimed that honor for Bernardo Cossin.

61. Arlegui, *Chronica de la Provincia de N.S.P.S. Francisco*, 224. These friars had first destroyed the "idols" of the Indians.

62. Arlegui, *Chronica de la Provincia de N.S.P.S. Francisco*, 212–13.

63. Ibid., 239.

64. Mendieta, *Historia eclesiástica indiana*, 244. Fray Francisco Lorenzo, preacher among the Chichimecs of Nueva Galicia, had been told he would die among them. Thus, when in his last trip he

heard that the rebels had attacked a town, he prepared himself to die. He told his companion: "It is time to win heaven." He knelt before the altar, lit some candles, and died there from the blow of a *macana*.

65. Torquemada, *Tercera Parte*, 620. Mendieta, *Historia eclesiástica indiana*, 242. Torquemada borrows line for line from Mendieta. The over two hundred Indians surrounding them changed their minds, which the writer attributed to the miraculous and charitable intercession of God. Unfortunately, Fray Francisco Lorenzo died a martyr some years later. Neither Mendieta nor Torquemada are precise with their chronology and forget to give dates.

66. Bernardo De Lizana, *Historia de Yucatán: Devocionario de Ntra. Sra. De Izmal y Conquista Espiritual* (1633; México: El Museo Nacional de México, 1893), 121–22. In both instances, the attack was deemed treacherous by the chronicler because the Spaniards had been received amicably and with expressions of joy, or at least that is how they misinterpreted the situation. Fray Juan Enríquez had gone to the interior of the peninsula obeying orders of his provincial, but had taken the precaution of making a final confession before leaving because he did not expect to return. Like others, he was concerned about his salvation, not death.

67. Gregory, *Salvation at Stake*, 97–138.

68. Alonso Franco, *Segunda parte*, 367–80.

69. Mendieta, *Historia eclesiástica indiana*, 2:240.

70. In his work on Christianity in Japan, Augustinian Fray Joseph Sicardo, who resided in New Spain, used martial metaphors in a fashion similar to that of other chroniclers of the seventeenth century. See his *Christiandad del Japon*. He frequently called them "valiant soldiers" of the Christian militia.

71. Arlegui, *Chronica de la Provincia de N.S.P.S. Francisco*, 221–22, 227, 235.

72. Ibid., 221, 227, 235, 251–52.

73. González de la Puente, *Primera Parte*, 276–300. Martyrdom created a bond of empathy and support among men who saw themselves as members of a brotherhood of faith facing similar risks. In his history of the Dominican Order in Mexico, González de la Puente included the stories of those of those martyred in the Far East as part of their collective memory.

74. For more about Felipe de Jesús, see Balthasar de Medina, *Vida, Martyrio y Beatificación del Invicto Proto-Martyr de el Japón, San Felipe de Jesús*, 2nd ed. (Madrid: Imprenta de los Herederos de la Viuda de Juan García Infanzon, 1751); Marcelo de Ribadeneyra, *Historia de las Islas del Archipelago y Reynos de la Gran China* (Barcelona: Emprenta de Gabriel Graells y Giraldo Dotil, 1601); *San Felipe de Jesus Protomártir Mexicano: Extracto de las informaciones auténticas para la beatificación de los veintiséis Mártires del Japón* (Mexico: Talleres de la Librería Religiosa, 1898); Iván de Santa María, *Chronica de la Provincia de San Joseph de los Descalzos de la orden de los Menores de nuestro seráfico Padre San Francisco, Parte Segunda* (Madrid: Imprenta Real, 1618); Cornelius Conover, "Catholic Saints in Spain's Empire," in *Empires of God: Religious Encounters in the Early Modern Atlantic*, ed. Linda Gregerson and Susan Juster (Philadelphia: University of Pennsylvania Press, 2011), 87–105, and "Saintly Biography and the Cult of San Felipe de Jesús in Mexico City, 1597–1697," *The Americas* 67, no. 4 (April 2011): 441–66; Norma Durán, "La retórica del martirio y la formación del yo sufriente en la vida de San Felipe de Jesús," in *Historia y Grafía* 26 (2006): 77–107.

75. *Breve resumen de la vida y martirio del ínclito mexicano y protomartyr del Japón, el Beato Felipe de Jesús* (Mexico: Oficina Madrileña, 1802); Balthasar de Medina, *Chronica de la Santa Provincia de San Diego de México* (México: Juan de Ribera, 1682), 3:113–21.

76. De Ribadeneyra, *Historia de las Islas*, 631.

77. Ibid., 482, 633. His willingness to die is still an object of discussion. See, Cornelius B. Conover, "A Saint in the Empire: Mexico City's San Felipe de Jesús, 1597–1820." Doctoral Dissertation, University of Texas, Austin, 2008.

78. Sicardo, *Christiandad del Japon*, 239–64. Sicardo wrote his work following strict lines of historical corroboration, including letters of the friars and reports from the Manila province. Doubtless, the rules for writing about martyrs had been tacitly acknowledged and followed by writers of this new "genre," whether Catholic or Protestant. See also Antonio Rubial "El Mártir colonial. Evolución de una figura heroica," in *Coloquio Internacional: El héroe, entre el mito y la historia* (México: Educación y Cultura/Trama Editorial, 2010), 169–218.

79. J. Manuel Espinosa, *The Pueblo Indian Revolt*, 242. He continued: "Put aside, my sons, the fear of those who can only kill the body . . . there can be no greater charity than to risk one's corporal life to convert an idolater and maintain in the faith those who have already converted."

80. Arricivita, *Crónica seráfica y apostólica*, 411–13.

81. Arricivita, "Parecer de Fray Juan Antonio Chaves," in *Crónica seráfica y apostólica*, n.p.

CHAPTER 6

The author thanks Ralph Bauer, Nicole Gray, Sandra Gustafson, Russ Leo, Alyssa Mt. Pleasant, Sarah Rivett, David Shields, Bryce Traister, Edlie Wong, the anonymous readers for the University of Pennsylvania Press, and the participants at the series of Religious Transformations meetings for their help in shaping this essay.

1. Max Weber, *The Protestant Ethic and the Spirit of Capitalism* (New York: Charles Scribner's Sons, 1958). Amanda Porterfield, arguing for the social power of female piety in colonial New England, goes so far as to say that the "religion of female piety was largely responsible for the social cohesion that existed in seventeenth-century New England," which by extension "made possible the economic success of the merchant class." Porterfield, *Female Piety in Puritan New England: The Emergence of Religious Humanism* (New York: Oxford University Press, 1992), 9.

2. For some of the scholarly landscape summarized here, see Perry Miller, *Errand into the Wilderness* (Cambridge, Mass.: Harvard University Press, 1956); Edmund S. Morgan, "The Historians of Early New England," in *The Reinterpretation of Early American History*, ed. Ray Allen Billington (San Marino, Calif.: Huntington Library, 1966), 41–63; Michael McGiffert, "American Puritan Studies in the 1960s," *William and Mary Quarterly*, 3rd ser., 27, no. 1 (January 1970): 36–67; David D. Hall, "On Common Ground: The Coherence of American Puritan Studies," *William and Mary Quarterly*, 3rd ser., 44, no. 2 (April 1987): 193–229; and Steven Foster, *The Long Argument: English Puritanism and the Shaping of New England Culture, 1570–1700* (Chapel Hill: University of North Carolina Press, 1991).

3. Michel Serres, *The Parasite* (Baltimore: Johns Hopkins University Press, 1982).

4. Joel W. Martin and Mark A. Nicholas, eds. *Native Americans, Christianity, and the Reshaping of the American Religious Landscape* (Chapel Hill: University of North Carolina Press, 2010), 8–9; David Silverman, *Faith and Boundaries: Colonists, Christianity, and Community among the Wampanoag Indians of Martha's Vineyard, 1600–1871* (New York: Cambridge University Press, 2005).

5. Jill Lepore, *The Name of War: King Philip's War and the Origins of American Identity* (New York: Knopf, 1998); Nancy Shoemaker, *A Strange Likeness: Becoming Red and White in Eighteenth-Century North America* (New York: Oxford University Press, 2006). The argument for cultural

similarity as driver of differentiation is taken farther in Erik Seeman, *Death in the New World: Cross-Cultural Encounters, 1492–1800* (Philadelphia: University of Pennsylvania Press, 2010). Seeman claims that similarity was the matrix of understanding for Europeans in the New World, and that from just after the beginning of colonization, similarities were put to exploitative use.

6. Nicholas Thomas, *Colonialism's Culture: Anthropology, Travel and Government* (Cambridge, UK: Polity, 1994), 8.

7. Daniel Mandell, "Eager Partners in Reform: Indians and Frederick Baylies in Southern New England, 1780–1840," in *Native Americans*, ed. Martin and Nicholas, 38–66; Douglas L. Winiarski, "Native American Popular Religion in New England's Old Colony, 1670–1770," in *Native Americans*, ed. Martin and Nicholas, 93–124; Joanna Brooks, "Hard Feelings: Samson Occom Contemplates His Christian Mentors," in *Native Americans*, ed. Martin and Nicholas, 23–37.

8. Robert O. Keohane, "Reciprocity in International Relations," *International Organisation* 40, no. 1 (1986): 1–27.

9. Paine, *Rights of Man: Being an Answer to Mr. Burke's Attack on the French Revolution* (London: Printed for J. S. Jordan, 1791), 1:121; see Kant, *The Metaphysic of Morals, Divided into Metaphysical Elements of Law and of Ethics*, trans. John Richardson, 2 vols. (London: William Richardson, 1799), 1:viii, "The reciprocity of the obligation from an universal rule."

10. See Malinowski, "Kula: The Circulating Exchange of Valuables in the Archipelagoes of Eastern New Guinea," *Man* 20 (1920): 97–105; Polanyi, *The Great Transformation* (New York: Rinehart, 1944); Aberle, *The Peyote Religion Among the Navaho* (Chicago: University of Chicago Press, 1982); and Mauss, *The Gift: Forms and Functions of Exchange in Archaic Societies* (1922; London: Routledge, 1990).

11. Barre Toelken, "Seeing with a Native Eye: How Many Sheep Will It Hold?" in *Seeing with a Native Eye: Essays on Native American Religion*, ed. Walter Holden Capps (New York: Harper Forum, 1976), 9–24.

12. Lincoln, *Native American Renaissance* (Berkeley: University of California Press, 1983), 16.

13. Brooks, *The Common Pot: The Recovery of Native Space in the Northeast* (Minneapolis: University of Minnesota Press, 2008); Brooks, "Digging at the Roots: Locating an Ethical, Native Criticism," in *Reasoning Together*, ed. Craig Womack, et al. (Norman: University of Oklahoma Press, 2008), 234–64.

14. Vine Deloria, Jr., *God Is Red: A Native View of Religion*, 2nd ed. (1972; Golden, Colo.: Fulcrum, 1992), 3.

15. See, N. Scott Momaday, "Native Attitudes to the Environment," in Capps, *Seeing with a Native Eye*, 79–85.

16. Deloria, *God Is Red*, 1–2.

17. Deloria, *God Is Red*; and Deloria, *Custer Died for Your Sins: An Indian Manifesto* (New York: Macmillan, 1969). For a delightfully compact hint at the reputation of the concept of piety among many American Indian writers, see N. Scott Momaday's short story (originally titled "Can a Dog Be Pious?") titled "An Element of Piety," in *The Man Made of Words: Essays, Stories, Passages* (New York: St. Martin's, 1997), 193–95.

18. Garrison, *Pietas from Vergil to Dryden* (University Park: Pennsylvania State University Press, 1992), 2. My discussion of *pietas* is indebted largely to Garrison.

19. Dryden, *The Works of John Dryden*, ed. Edward Niles Hooker, H. T. Swedenberg, Jr., and Vinton A. Dearing (Berkeley: University of California Press, 1956–2000), 5:288.

20. The title page of the 1697 London edition features a quotation from Book 12 of the *Aeneid*, "Discite Virtutem ex Hoc, verumque Laborem," or "Learn virtue/valor and true toil from this

man." See an analysis rooted in the myth-symbol school in John Shields, *The American Aeneas: Classical Origins of the American Self* (Knoxville: University of Tennessee Press, 2001); an unusual treatment of *pietas* and Mather in Christopher Felker, *Reinventing Cotton Mather in the American Renaissance: Magnalia Christi Americana in Hawthorne, Stowe, and Stoddard* (Boston: Northeastern University Press, 1993); and Jane Donahue Eberwein, " 'In a Book, as in a Glass': Literary Sorcery in Mather's Life of Phips," *Early American Literature* 10, no. 3 (1975): 289–300.

21. Augustine, *De civitate Dei contra paganos*, ed. and trans. George E. McCracken et al., 7 vols. (Cambridge, Mass.: Harvard University Press, 1957), 2:82.

22. Qtd. in William Bradford, *Of Plymouth Plantation, 1620–1647*, ed. Samuel Eliot Morison (New York: Modern Library, 1967), 197–98.

23. Swift, *The Prose Works of Jonathan Swift*, ed. Herbert Davis, 14 vols. (Oxford: Oxford University Press, 1941), 11:278.

24. Miller, *The New England Mind: The Seventeenth Century* (Boston: Beacon, 1968), 4, ix.

25. Walter D. Mignolo, *The Darker Side of the Renaissance: Literacy, Territoriality, and Colonization* (Ann Arbor: University of Michigan Press, 1995).

26. Knight, *Orthodoxies in Massachusetts: Rereading American Puritanism* (Cambridge, Mass.: Harvard University Press, 1994); Matthew P. Brown, *The Pilgrim and the Bee: Reading Rituals and Book Culture in Early New England* (Philadelphia: University of Pennsylvania Press, 2007), 179–207; Stein and Murison, "Introduction: Religion and Method," *Early American Literature* 45, no. 1 (2010): 1–29, quot. 7. For other exemplary works formed around the concept of piety, see Charles Hambrick-Stowe, *The Practice of Piety* (Chapel Hill: University of North Carolina Press, 1982); and Charles Cohen, *God's Caress: The Psychology of Puritan Religious Experience* (New York: Oxford University Press, 1986).

27. Saba Mahmood, *Politics of Piety: The Islamic Revival and the Feminist Subject* (Princeton, N.J.: Princeton University Press, 2005), 145.

28. Tessa Watt, *Cheap Print and Popular Piety, 1550–1640* (Cambridge, Mass.: Cambridge University Press, 1991).

29. Matthew P. Brown, *The Pilgrim and the Bee*, 4–5; Mayhew, *A Brief Narrative of the Success Which the Gospel Hath Had Among the Indians* (Boston: B. Green, 1694), 12.

30. The role of John Eliot's "Praying Indians" in King Philip's War is a cardinal instance of the mutually inflecting relation between piety (as a set of codes, a performance, and a feeling) and law; see, for example, J. Patrick Cesarini, " 'What Has Become of Your Praying to God?' Daniel Gookin's Troubled History of King Philip's War," *Early American Literature* 44, no. 3 (2009): 489–515; and Jenny Hale Pulsipher, *Subjects unto the Same King: Indians, English, and the Contest for Authority in Colonial New England* (Philadelphia: University of Pennsylvania Press, 2006).

31. Woodward, *Prospero's America: John Winthrop, Jr., Alchemy, and the Creation of New England Culture, 1606–1676* (Chapel Hill: Omohundro Institute and the University of North Carolina Press, 2010).

32. Archaeological investigations of Narragansett burials and residential sites from the seventeenth century suggest the intensification of spiritual practices over the course of the century. See Paul A. Robinson, et al., "Preliminary Biocultural Interpretations from a Seventeenth-Century Narragansett Indian Cemetery in Rhode Island," in *Cultures in Contact: The Impact of European Cultures on Native American Cultural Institutions, AD 1000–1800*, ed. William W. Fitzhugh (Washington, D.C.: Smithsonian Institution Press, 1985), 107–30; Michael S. Nassaney, "Men and Women, Pipes and Power in Native New England," in *Smoking and Culture: The Archaeology of Tobacco Pipes in Eastern North America*, ed. Sean Rafferty and Rob Mann (Knoxville: University of

Tennessee Press, 2005), 125–41; and Diana DiPaolo Loren, *In Contact: Bodies and Spaces in the Sixteenth- and Seventeenth-Century Eastern Woodlands* (Lanham, Md.: AltaMira Press, 2008), 50–53.

33. Silverman, *Faith and Boundaries.*

34. Matthew P. Brown, *Pilgrim and the Bee*, 102.

35. Hugh Amory, *Bibliography and the Book Trades: Studies in the Print Culture of Early New England*, ed. David D. Hall (Philadelphia: University of Pennsylvania Press, 2005).

36. Woodward, *Prospero's America*, 93–137.

37. Amory, *Bibliography and the Book Trades*, 29; Nicholas Thomas, *Entangled Objects: Exchange, Material Culture, and Colonialism in the Pacific* (Cambridge, Mass.: Harvard University Press, 1991).

38. Kevin A. McBride, "Bundles, Bears, and Bibles: Interpreting Seventeenth-Century Native 'Texts,'" in *Early Native Literacies in New England: A Documentary and Critical Anthology*, ed. Kristina Bross and Hilary E. Wyss (Amherst: University of Massachusetts Press, 2008), 135.

39. See my longer discussion of the relations between kinship and systematicity in Matt Cohen, *The Networked Wilderness: Communicating in Early New England* (Minneapolis: University of Minnesota Press, 2009), esp. chap. 4; and on the complexities of the region's indigenous politics in the seventeenth century, see Michael Leroy Oberg, *Uncas: First of the Mohegans* (Ithaca, N.Y.: Cornell University Press, 2006).

40. McBride, "Bundles, Bears, and Bibles," 136.

41. Frank Chouteau Brown, "'The Old House' at Cutchogue, Long Island, New York: Built in 1649," *Old-Time New England* 31, no. 1 (July 1940): 11–21; John and William Blye, qtd. in Robert Blair St. George, *Conversing by Signs: Poetics of Implication in Colonial New England* (Chapel Hill: University of North Carolina Press, 1998), 188.

42. David. D. Hall, *Worlds of Wonder, Days of Judgment: Popular Religious Belief in Early New England* (New York: Knopf, 1989).

43. George F. Horton, compiler, *Horton Genealogy; or Chronicles of the Descendants of Barnabas Horton, of Southold, L.I., 1640* (Philadelphia: Home Circle Publishing Co., 1876).

44. Keith Thomas, *Religion and the Decline of Magic: Studies in Popular Beliefs in Sixteenth and Seventeenth-Century England* (New York: Penguin, 1978). As in the case of Benjamin Horton's rats, there are more parasitic or transferential agents here than just Pequots and English settlers. First, the text in the Pequot bundle was illegally printed in Holland and smuggled into England for sale, eventually reaching the colonies and the Pequots. There is a temporal transference as well: the page fragment in the bundle "was preserved by contact with an iron ladle, which converted the cloth and paper to a lump of iron salt known as a pseudomorph, because it *exactly reproduces the form and structure of the original in a different material*" (Amory, *Bibliography and the Book Trades*, 13, emphasis mine). An English form and a Native structure, then, are preserved for the archive only because of a third material transaction with no "culture" associated with it—and subsequently resurrected for analysis by the Pequots themselves, who many non-Indians in Connecticut today consider to be not only parasites, but posers—Indians in form and structure, but not "material." For a particularly intense version of this position, see Jeff Benedict, *Without Reservation: The Making of America's Most Powerful Indian Tribe and Foxwoods the World's Largest Casino* (New York: HarperCollins, 2000).

45. Joanna Brooks, "From Edwards to Baldwin: Heterodoxy, Discontinuity, and New Narratives of American Religious-Literary History," *American Literary History* 45, no. 2 (2010): 425–440, cit. 429.

46. Brown, *The Reaper's Garden: Death and Power in the World of Atlantic Slavery* (Cambridge, Mass.: Harvard University Press, 2008), 11. In this passage, Brown quotes Grey Gundaker, "Discussion: Creolization, Complexity, and Time," *Historical Archaeology* 34, no. 3 (2000): 124. See also Christopher

C. Fennel, "Conjuring Boundaries: Inferring Past Identities from Religious Artifacts," *International Journal of Historical Archaeology* 4, no. 4 (2000): 281–313, which delineates a parallel concern in African-American studies. "Ethnographic studies show that an ethnic group is typically defined by a limited constellation of cultural traits selected to function as membership criteria for the group," Fennel writes. "We should attempt to assess the degree to which one or more of those criteria were communicated, in intergroup or intragroup settings, through artifacts expressing benevolent, protective, or malevolent religious practices" (309).

47. Dillon, "Religion and Geopolitics in the New World," *Early American Literature* 45, no. 1 (2010): 198.

48. Carlo Ginzburg, *Clues, Myths, and the Historical Method*, trans. John and Anne C. Tedeschi (Baltimore, Md.: Johns Hopkins University Press, 1989), 106. Piety and reciprocity, it could be argued, belong to that arsenal that Ginzburg describes as "the powerful and terrible weapon of abstraction" (115).

49. "We are always," writes Michel Serres, "simultaneously making gestures that are archaic, modern, and futuristic." Michel Serres and Bruno Latour, *Conversations on Science, Culture, and Time*, trans. Roxanne Lapidus (Ann Arbor: University of Michigan Press, 1995), 60.

CHAPTER 7

This chapter is part of a longer research project entitled "The Return as Mission: The Mulatto Priests Vicente Ferreira Pires e Cipriano Pires Sardinha and their *Viagem de África em o Reino de Daomé*," financed by CNPq and FAPEMIG, to whom I am grateful and also PRPq/UFMG that financed the translation.

1. Pierre Verger, *Fluxo e refluxo: Do tráfico de escravos entre o golfo do Benin e a Bahia de Todos os Santos* (Salvador: Corrupio, 2002), 251–93.

2. Adanruzâ was a title that all kings of Dahomey inherited. Luis Nicolau Parés, "Cartas do Daomé: Uma introdução," *Afro-Ásia* 47 (2003), 311.

3. Robin Law, "Religion, Trade and Politics on the 'Slave Coast': Roman Catholic Missions in Allada and Whydah in the Seventeenth Century," *Journal of Religion in Africa* 21, no.1 (1991), 44.

4. Ibid., 42–77.

5. António Brásio, *Monumenta missionaria Africana*, 14 vols. (Lisboa: Agência Geral do Ultramar, 1952–85).

6. See Robin Law, "Dahomey and the Slave Trade: Reflections on the Historiography of the Rise of Dahomey," *The Journal of African History* 27, no. 2, Special Issue in Honour of J. D. Fage (1986): 237–67; and "Ideologies of Royal Power: The Reconstruction of Political Authority on the 'Slave Coast,' 1680–1750," *Africa* 57, no. 3 (1987): 321–44.

7. Clado Ribeiro de Lessa, *Viagem de África em o Reino de Dahomé* (São Paulo: Companhia Editora Nacional, 1957), 103.

8. Luiz Felipe de Alencastro, *O trato dos viventes: Formação do Brasil no Atlântico sul* (São Paulo: Companhia das Letras, 2000).

9. Sanjay Subrahmanyam, "Connected Histories—Notes Towards a Reconfiguration of Early Modern Eurasia," *Modern Asian Studies* 31, no. 3 (1977): 735–62.

10. João José Reis, *Slave Rebellion in Brazil: The Muslim Uprising of 1835 in Bahia* (Baltimore, Md.: Johns Hopkins University Press, 1993); Júnia Ferreira Furtado, "Black Pearls: Freed Women of Color in the Diamond District," *Società e storia*, no. 119 (2008): 149–62.

11. Lessa, *Viagem de África em o Reino de Dahomé*, 25. On the ambassadorial visit, see "Lisbon," Arquivo Histórico Ultramarino (AHU), Manuscritos Avulsos da Bahia (MAB), Caixa 100, docs. 19.560–19.572 (20 November 1799); Caixa 107, docs. 20.931–20.936 (12 November 1800); Caixa 147, docs. 29.494–29.499 (13 January 1806). Hereafter, AHU-MAB.

12. Lessa, *Viagem de África em o Reino de Dahomé*, 28–29.

13. Alberto da Costa e Silva, *Um rio chamado Atlântico: A África no Brasil e o Brasil na África* (Rio de Janeiro: Nova Fronteira/Ed. UFRJ, 2003), 66–67.

14. Regarding the embassies to Dahomey, see J. F. de Almeida Prado, "A Bahia e suas relações com o Dahomé," in *O Brasil e o colonialismo europeu* (São Paulo: Companhia Editora Nacional, 1956), 122–23; Verger, *Fluxo e refluxo*, 251–307; Silvia Hunold Lara, "Uma embaixada africana na América Portuguesa," in *Festa: Cultura e sociabilidade na América portuguesa*, ed. István Jancsó e Íris Kantor (São Paulo: Edusp, 2000), 131–65; Silvia Hunold Lara, "Significados cruzados: as embaixadas de congos na Bahia setecentista," in *Carnavais e outras f(e)estas*, ed. Maria Clementina P. Cunha (Campinas: Ed. Unicamp, 2002), 1:71–100; Ana Lucia Araujo, "Images, Artefacts and Myths: Reconstructing the Connections Between Brazil and the Bight of Benin," in *Living History: Encountering the Memory of the Heirs of Slavery*, ed. Ana Lucia Araujo (Newcastle upon Tyne: Cambridge Scholars Publishing, 2009), 180–202; Ana Lucia Araujo, "Dahomey, Portugal and Bahia: King Adandozan and the Atlantic Slave Trade," *Slavery & Abolition: A Journal of Slave and Post-Slave Studies* 33, no.1 (2012): 1–19.

15. Alberto da Costa e Silva, *Francisco Félix de Souza, mercador de escravos* (Rio de Janeiro: Nova Fronteira/Ed Eduerj, 2004), 44.

16. "Letter of Agonglo of 20th March, 1795," in Verger, *Fluxo e refluxo*, 289–91.

17. Lessa, *Viagem de África em o Reino de Dahomé*, 30.

18. Júnia Ferreira Furtado, "The Journey Home: A Freed Mulatto Priest, Cipriano Pires Sardinha, and His Religious Mission," in *Slaves and Religions in Graeco-Roman Antiquity and the Modern Americas*, ed. Stephen Hodkinson and Dick Geary, (Newcastle upon Tyne: Cambridge Scholars Publishing, 2012), 149–73.

19. Law, "Religion, Trade and Politics on the 'Slave Coast,' " 45–46.

20. Ibid., 51.

21. Parés, "Cartas do Daomé: Uma introdução," 299.

22. Verger, *Fluxo e refluxo*, 290.

23. Parés, "Cartas do Daomé: Uma introdução," 302.

24. Verger, *Fluxo e refluxo*, 251.

25. Law, "Religion, Trade and Politics on the 'Slave Coast,' " 45.

26. In the case of Angola, see Roquinaldo Amaral Ferreira, *Cross-Cultural Exchange in the Atlantic World: Angola and Brazil During the Era of the Slave Trade* (Cambridge, UK: Cambridge University Press, 2012).

27. Marina de Mello e Souza, *Reis negros no Brasil escravista: História da festa de coroação de rei Congo* (Belo Horizonte: EdUFMG, 2002), especially "A conversão da corte congolesa," 52–62.

28. Of course the Catholicism in Africa experienced changes and adaptations. See Wyatt Mac-Gaffey, *Religion and Society in Central Africa* (Chicago: University of Chicago Press, 1986); John Thornton, *The Kingdom of Kongo: Civil War and Transition, 1641–1718* (Madison: University of Wisconsin Press, 1983); Anne Hilton, *The Kingdom of Kongo* (Oxford: Oxford University Press, 1985).

29. Robin Law, "Religion, Trade and Politics on the 'Slave Coast,' " 58.

30. Robin Law, "Slave-Raiders and Middlemen, Monopolists and Free-Traders: The Supply of Slaves for the Atlantic Trade in Dahomey c.1715–1850," *Journal of African History* 30, no. 1 (1989): 45–68.

31. Evergton Sales Souza, "Jansénisme et réforme de l'Eglise dans l'Amérique portugaise au XVIIIᵉ siècle," *Revue de l'histoire des religions* 226, no. 2 (2009): 201–26.

32. Ibid., 207.

33. "Au contraire du jansénisme français qui a une histoire profondément marquée par des conflits avec le pouvoir royal, le jansénisme portugais se développe avec la bienveillance du pouvoir royal."

34. Renato Pinto Venâncio, *Famílias abandonadas* (Campinas: Papirus, 1999).

35. AHU-MAB, doc. 16.780.

36. The prince and his half-brother, Simão Pires Sardinha, were also friends of Father Joaquim Veloso de Miranda (later author of the magnificent *Brasiliensium Plantaram*, describing several plant specimens), a distinguished botanist. Arquivo Histórico Ultramarino (AHU), Reino, Pacote 26, Letters from Dom Rodrigo de Sousa Coutinho to Manoel José Correa da Serra of 08/11/1797 and to Maria José Correa da Serra and Anna José Correa da Serra of 06/04/1798.

37. Lessa, *Viagem de África em o Reino de Dahomé*, 31.

38. Parés, "Cartas do Daomé: Uma introdução," 307.

39. Law, "Religion, Trade and Politics on the 'Slave Coast,'" 47.

40. Lessa, *Viagem de África em o Reino de Dahomé*, 31.

41. AHU- MAB, Caixa 100, docs. 19.563–19.565.

42. AHU-MAB, Caixa 100, doc. 19.562.

43. On 22 September 1799, Father Antônio Pimenta said three masses for his soul at the Brotherhood of the Mercies in Tejuco. Diamantina, Arquivo Eclesiástico da Arquidiocese de Diamantina (AEAD), Caixa 520, f. 14v.

44. Arquivos Nacionais da Torre do Tombo (ANTT), Mesa da Consciência e Ordens (MCO). Ordem de Cristo, Padroado do Brasil, Bispado de Mariana. Caixa 6, maço 6. Requerimento de Vicente Ferreira Pires, Hereafter, ANTT-MCO.

45. AHU-MAB, Caixa 100, doc. 19.562.

46. AHU-MAB, Caixa 100, doc. 19.560.

47. Cônego Raymundo Trindade, *Breve notícia dos seminários de Mariana* (Mariana: Archdiocese of Mariana, 1951), 19.

48. Lessa, *Viagem de África em o Reino de Dahomé*, 103.

49. AHU-MAB, Caixa 100, doc.19.560.

50. AHU-MAB, Caixa 107, doc. 20.931, f.1–iv.

51. Parés, "Cartas do Daomé: Uma introdução," 295–395.

52. Verger, *Fluxo e refluxo*, 256; Parés, "Cartas do Daomé: Uma introdução," 304.

53. Verger, *Fluxo e refluxo*, 291.

54. Parés, "Cartas do Daomé: Uma introdução," 312.

55. Lessa, *Viagem de África em o Reino de Dahomé*, 11.

56. Lisbon, Biblioteca da Ajuda, Cota 51/IV/37.

57. Lessa, *Viagem de África em o Reino de Dahomé*.

58. Ibid., 34.

59. In Portuguese, *pátria* (country or native land). At the time, this notion of *patria* referred mainly to one's place of birth.

60. Renato Cymbalista, "Martírios de jesuítas e a construção de uma territorialidade cristã na América portuguesa," in *Contextos missionários: religião e poder no Império* português, ed Adone Agnolin et ali (São Paulo: Fapesp, 2011) 160.

61. Ibid., 160–86.

62. Charles R. Boxer, *The Church Militant and Iberian Expansion: 1440–1770* (Baltimore, Md.: Johns Hopkins University Press, 1978).

63. Sheila Moura Hue, "Introdução," in *Primeiras Cartas do Brasil: 1551–1555* (Rio de Janeiro: Zahar, 2006), 13.

64. Boxer, *The Church Militant and Iberian Expansion*, 97–106.

65. Marina de Mello e Souza, *Reis negros no Brasil escravista*, 61.

66. Sebastião Monteiro de Vide, *Constituições Primeiras do Arcebispado da Bahia*, ed. Bruno Feitler and Evergton Sales Souza (1720; São Paulo: Edusp, 2010).

67. Bruno Feitler and Evergton Sales Souza, "Estudo introdutório," in Vide, *Constituições Primeiras do Arcebispado da Bahia*, 17–24, 61, 68.

68. Feitler and Souza, "Estudo introdutório," 22–24, 29, 66.

69. Feitler and Souza, "Estudo introdutório," 53.

70. Cônego Raimundo Trindade, *Breve notícia dos Seminários de Mariana* (Mariana: Archdiocese of Mariana, 1951), 9–20.

71. Regarding the performance of the bishops teaching in the Catholic seminaries under Jansenism in Brazil, see Evergton Sales Souza, "Jansénisme et réforme de l'Eglise dans l'Amérique portugaise au XVIIIe siècle," 201–26.

72. Frei António do Rosário, "Notícia de frades pregadores em serviço diplomático. Séculos XIII-XVII," in *A Diplomacia na História de Portugal*. (Lisboa: Academia Portuguesa da História, 1990), 29–58.

73. Edgar Prestage, *Frei Domingos do Rosário, diplomata e político* (Coimbra, 1926).

74. The Portuguese Kingdom was created out of the opposition between a Christian monarchy and the Muslims then invading the Iberian Peninsula. The kingdom's founding act was the Battle of Ourique, fought in the Algarve. On the eve of the confrontation, João I had a vision in which Christ assured him of victory, even though the Portuguese army was vastly outnumbered. Thus the Portuguese Crown was born with a catechizing mission. A next stage in this predestination occurred with the discovery of transoceanic lands, whereupon the crown took it upon itself to bring Christianity to the New World.

75. Trindade, *Breve notícia dos seminários de Mariana*, 12–20; Leandro Pena Catão, "Sacrílegas palavras: Inconfidência e presença jesuítica nas Minas Gerais durante o período pombalino" (PhD diss., Belo Horizonte: Universidade Federal de Minas Gerais, 2005).

76. Valéria Maria Pena Ferreira, "Retórica das lágrimas, sermões e orações fúnebres na Bahia do século XVIII" (PhD diss., Belo Horizonte: Universidade Federal de Minas Gerais, 2007).

77. Lessa, *Viagem de África em o Reino de Dahomé*, 25.

78. Padre Inácio Felizardo Fortes, *O pregador instruído nas qualidades necessárias para bem exercer o seu ministério* (Rio de Janeiro: Imprensa Régia, 1818).

79. Quoted in Maria Renata da Cruz Duran, *Ecos do púlpito: Oratória sagrada no tempo de D. João VI* (São Paulo: Unesp, 2010), 105.

80. Trindade, *Breve notícia dos seminários de Mariana*, 39.

81. Quoted in Cruz Duran, *Ecos do púlpito*, 105.

82. Andréa Daher, *O Brasil francês: As singularidades da França Equinocial* (Rio de Janeiro: Civilização Brasileira, 2007), 186.

83. Lessa, *Viagem de África em o Reino de Dahomé*, 34.

84. Ibid., 36–37.

85. Ibid., 55.

86. Ibid., 71.

87. Daher, *O Brasil francês: As singularidades da França Equinocial*, 6.

88. Ibid., 62.

89. Daher, *O Brasil francês: As singularidades da França Equinocial*, 186–88.

90. Lessa, *Viagem de África em o Reino de Dahomé*, 62.

91. Cymbalista, "Martírios de jesuítas e a construção de uma territorialidade cristã na América portuguesa," 161.

92. Ibid., 160–85.

93. According to Renato Cymbalista, in 1675, the Jesuit martyrology counted 304 brothers killed worldwide. Cymbalista, "Martírios de jesuítas e a construção de uma territorialidade cristã na América portuguesa," 166.

94. Cymbalista, "Martírios de jesuítas e a construção de uma territorialidade cristã na América portuguesa," 167.

95. Ibid., 168.

96. Daher, *O Brasil francês: As singularidades da França Equinocial*, 186–88.

97. Lessa, *Viagem de África em o Reino de Dahomé*, 103, 121–22.

98. Ibid., 122.

99. Júnia Ferreira Furtado, *Chica da Silva: A Brazilian Slave of the Eighteenth Century* (Cambridge, UK: Cambridge University Press, 2009), 41–52.

100. Verger, *Fluxo e refluxo*, 253.

101. See Marina de Mello e Souza, *Reis negros no Brasil escravista*.

102. José Ramos Tinhorão, *Os sons dos negros no Brasil. Cantos, danças, folguedos: origens*. 2nd ed. (São Paulo: Editora 34, 2008), 108.

103. Marina de Mello e Souza, *Reis negros no Brasil escravista*, 257.

104. Auguste de Saint-Hilaire, *Viagem pelas províncias de Rio de Janeiro e Minas Gerais* (São Paulo: Companhia Editora Nacional, 1938).

105. Nuno Marques Pereira, *Compêndio narrativo do peregrino da América* (Rio de Janeiro: Academia Brasileira de Letras, 1939), 1:128.

106. Ramos Tinhorão, *Os sons dos negros no Brasil*.

107. Júnia Ferreira Furtado, "Piccola Africa: Il mondo degli schiavi nel Distretto Diamantino e nel villaggio di Tejuco, (Minas Gerais, Brasile)", *Terra d'Africa*, 14 (2005): 143–59.

108. Marina de Mello e Souza, *Reis negros no Brasil escravista: história da festa de coroação do rei Congo* (Belo Horizonte: Ed.UFMG, 2002).

109. See Furtado, *Chica da Silva*.

110. Lessa, *Viagem de África em o Reino de Dahomé*, 86.

111. Ibid., 60.

112. Ibid., 51.

113. Ibid., 86.

114. Ibid., 53.

115. Ibid., 18.

116. Marina de Mello e Souza, *Reis negros no Brasil escravista*.

117. Lessa, *Viagem de África em o Reino de Dahomé*, 25.

118. Ibid., 32.

119. ANTT- MCO, Ordem de Cristo, Padroado do Brasil, Bispado de Mariana, maço 5.

120. Lessa, *Viagem de África em o Reino de Dahomé*, 62.

121. Ibid.

122. Law, "Religion, Trade and Politics on the 'Slave Coast'," 47–48. See also H. Labouret and P. Rivet, *Le Royaume d'Ardra et son évangélisation au XVII siècle* (Paris, 1929), which includes the text of the *Doctrina Christiana*.

123. Lessa, *Viagem de África em o Reino de Dahomé*, 66–67.

124. Marina de Mello e Souza, *Reis negros no Brasil escravista*, 229.

125. Lessa, *Viagem de África em o Reino de Dahomé*, 94.

126. Ibid., 108.

127. Marina de Mello e Souza, *Reis negros no Brasil escravista*, 62–71.

128. Lessa, *Viagem de África em o Reino de Dahomé*, 105.

129. Verger, *Fluxo e refluxo*, 291.

130. Parés, "Cartas do Daomé: Uma introdução," 342–43.

131. Cruz Duran, *Ecos do púlpito*, 13.

CHAPTER 8

1. With regard to the emergence of geography at the service of the sixteenth-century Spanish Empire, see John M. Headley, "Geography and Empire in the Late Renaissance: Botero's Assignment, Western Universalism and the Civilizing Process," *Renaissance Quarterly* 53, no. 4 (winter 2000): 1119–55.

2. In this respect, see, for example, Thomas Bender, "Foreword," in *The Atlantic in Global History 1500–2000*, ed. Jorge Cañizares-Esguerra and Erik R. Seeman (Upper Saddle River, N.J.: Pearson Prentice Hall, 2007), xvii–xxi.

3. See Amy Bushnell and Jack P. Greene, "Peripheries, Centers, and the Construction of Early Modern American Empires," In *Negotiated Empires: Centers and Peripheries in the Americas, 1500–1820*, ed. Christine Daniels and Michael V. Kennedy (New York: Routledge, 2002), 1–14. Bushnell and Greene discuss, Wallerstein and the dependency theory of the 1960s and 1970s in connection to the center-periphery dichotomy.

4. Jorge Cañizares-Esguerra, "Iberian Colonial Science," *Isis* 96, no. 1 (March 2005): 64–70.

5. This has been argued, for example, by Carlos Espinosa in a recent publication. See Carlos Espinosa, *Historia del Ecuador en contexto regional y global* (Barcelona: Lexus Editores, 2010), 412–13.

6. Steven J. Harris. "Jesuit Scientific Activity in the Overseas Missions, 1540–1773," *Isis* 96, no. 1 (March 2005): 71–79.

7. Juan de Velasco, *Historia del Reino de Quito en la América Meridional: Historia moderna III* (Quito: Casa de la Cultura Ecuatoriana, 1979), 139, 140, 194. Juan de Velasco also provides a list of the Jesuit missionaries working in the Amazon during what he calls the first period, and which ends in 1683. Of a list of thirty-two missionaries, fourteen were born in Spanish America. See 386–87.

8. Pedro de Mercado, *Historia de la Provincia del Nuevo Reino y Quito de la Compañía de Jesús*. vol. 3 (Bogotá: Empresa Nacional de Publicaciones, 1957).

9. Jacinto Morán de Butrón, "La Azucena de Quito, la Virgen Mariana de Jesús Paredes y Flores," in *Letras de la audiencia de Quito* [Período Jesuítico], ed. Hernán Rodríguez Castelo (Caracas: Biblioteca Ayacucho, 1984), 70–71.

10. Manuel Rodríguez, *El descubrimiento del Marañón*, ed. Ángeles Durán (Madrid: Alianza Editorial, 1990), 313–25.

11. Gaspar de Carvajal, *Relación del descubrimiento del Río Grande* (Quito: Superintendencia de Bancos, 1995).

12. I am borrowing this idea from Stephen Greenblatt, *Marvelous Possessions: The Wonder of the New World* (Chicago: University of Chicago Press, 1991).

13. The voyage of the two Franciscans to Pará is recounted by authors of the same order. See, for example, José de Maldonado, *Relación del descubrimiento del Río de las Amazonas, por otro nombre, del Marañón, hecho por la religión de nuestro Padre San Francisco, por medio de los religiosos de la provincia de San Francisco de Quito*. Biblioteca Amazonas, vol. 5 (Quito: Imprenta del Ministerio de Gobierno, 1942); and Laureano de la Cruz, *Nuevo descubrimiento del Río de las Amazonas hecho por los misioneros de la provincia de San Francisco de Quito el año 1651*. Biblioteca Amazonas, vol. 7 (Quito: Imprenta del Ministerio de Gobierno, 1942).

14. As noted by Hugo Burgos Guevara, there are two manuscript versions of the same account. One is kept in the National Library in Paris, and the other one in the National Library in Madrid. Attached to the latter is the first individual cartographic depiction of the Amazon. The account was first attributed to Don Martín de Saavedra y Guzmán, president of the Real Audiencia de Santa Fe, who had sent it to the Royal Council of the Indies along with an introductory letter. Later on, however, Marcos Jiménez de la Espada attributed it to the Jesuit priest Alonso de Rojas. More recently, Burgos Guevara argued that the author of the account was the Jesuit Cristóbal de Acuña, who traveled along the Amazon with Pedro de Texeira and the Portuguese Army on their trip back to Pará, as will be seen later. This argument is based on the fact that Acuña borrows a few paragraphs from the anonymous text in his own narrative. This may only suggest that Acuña knew its author, who was probably also a Jesuit. Moreover, the anonymous text focuses on third-person eyewitness testimonies of the Amazon Basin, provided mostly by the pilot major of the Portuguese expedition, and does not recount the trip made by Acuña along the Amazon, as Burgos Guevara seems to suggest. See Hugo Burgos Guevara, *La crónica prohibida: Cristóbal de Acuña en el Amazonas* (Quito: FONSAL, 2005). In this chapter I use the following version, attributed to Saavedra y Guzmán: Martín de Saavedra y Guzmán. *Relación del descubrimiento del río Amazonas y hoy San Francisco de Quito*. *Biblioteca Amazonas* (Quito: Ministerio de Gobierno, 1942).

15. Saavedra y Guzmán,, *Relación del Descubrimiento*, 59–66.

16. Ibid., 59.

17. "Tiene esta ciudad para su defensa un castillo fabricado sobre un peñol, a la boca del río que hace cara al mar, y una ensenada delante en figura de herradura. Tiene parapetos que caen al río y a la ensenada, cubiertos de teja . . . para la defensa de las cureñas en que están encabalgadas veinte piezas de artillería . . . y en la plaza de armas, aunque pequeña, casa de vivienda para el capitán y otra casa separada para la munición, labrada de piedra. Está labrado todo el fuerte con muralla de terrapleno sobre cimientos de cantería y con foso, y en la puerta no hay puente levadizo, pero tiene reducto de a dos puertas con troneras." Saavedra y Guzmán, *Relación del descubrimiento*, 55.

18. "Hasta este castillo ha llegado algunas veces el enemigo olandés [*sic*]." Saavedra y Guzmán, *Relación del descubrimiento*, 56–57.

19. Ibid., 51.

20. Ibid., 61–62.

21. Ibid., 51.

22. "Como la embarcación es fácil, apacible el río, los mantenimientos abundantes y los indios poco belicosos, será fácil al enemigo navegar este río y aprovecharse de las riquezas y frutos de la tierra." Saavedra y Guzmán, *Relación del descubrimiento*, 67.

23. Ibid.

24. "Bien se pueden gloriar Babilona de sus muros, Nínive de su grandeza, Athenas [sic] de sus letras, Constantinopla de su imperio, que Quito las vence por llave de la Cristiandad y por conquistadora del Mundo." Saavedra y Guzmán, *Relación del descubrimiento*, 50.

25. "el mayor y más célebre río del Orbe." Saavedra y Guzmán, *Relación del descubrimiento*, 53.

26. Saavedra y Guzmán, *Relación del descubrimiento*, 54.

27. "Corriendo el río grande de las Amazonas más de 2.500 leguas, no se avecinda tanto ninguna ciudad de las Indias, cuyos muros llegara a besar a no impedirlo las ásperas montañas." Saavedra y Guzmán, *Relación del descubrimiento*, 50.

28. An inscription on the map states precisely that it is a reproduction of the said painting. The inscription reads: "Este plano es reducción de una copia del que acompaña al AM Q 196 de la Biblioteca Nacional titulado 'Descubrimiento del Río Amazonas y sus dilatadas provincias' dirigido al Presidente del Consejo de Indias en 1639 por Don Martín de Saavedra y Guzmán, Gobernador y Capitán General del Nº Reino de Granada y Presidente de la Rl Audiencia de Chancillería de Sta. Fé de Bogotá."

29. Saavedra y Guzmán, *Relación del descubrimiento*, 50.

30. Ibid., 51.

31. "Como persona que lo había marcado y tanteado bien." la Cruz, *Nuevo descubrimiento del Río de las Amazonas*, 26.

32. "Que si desde el aire dejaran caer una aguja, ha de dar en cabeza de indio y no en el suelo." Saavedra y Guzmán, *Relación del descubrimiento*, 51.

33. The following edition is cited in this chapter: Cristóbal de Acuña, "Nuevo descubrimiento del Gran Río del Amazonas en el año de 1639," in *Informes de Jesuitas en el Amazonas 1660–1684*, Monumenta Amazónica, Francisco de Figueroa, Cristóbal de Acuña et al. (Iquitos: IIAP–CETA, 1986), 37–107.

34. Acuña, "Nuevo descubrimiento del Gran Río del Amazonas en el año de 1639," 40.

35. Ibid., 48.

36. Ibid.

37. For a discussion of monstrous races in the Middle Ages, see, for example, Michael Camille, *Image on the Edge: The Margins of Medieval Art* (Cambridge, Mass.: Harvard University Press, 1992); and John Block Friedman, *The Monstrous Races in Medieval Art and Thought* (Cambridge, Mass.: Harvard University Press, 1981). Diaries of explorers such as Columbus and, later on, Sir Walter Raleigh show the persistence of the medieval literary tradition, as suggested by their expectations regarding the finding of monstrous races.

38. "Son gigantes de diez y seis palmos de altura, muy valientes, andan desnudos, traen grandes patenas de oro en las orejas y narices." Acuña, *Nuevo descubrimiento*, 81.

39. "Viven, entre otras, dos naciones, la una de enanos, tan chicos como criaturas muy tiernas, que se llaman Guayazís la otra de una gente que todos ellos tienen los pies al revés, de suerte que quien no conociendo los quisiese seguir sus huellas, caminaría siempre al contrario que ellos, llámanse Mutayus." Acuña, *Nuevo descubrimiento*, 90.

40. "Por ser nacidos y criados en aquellas costas." Acuña, *Nuevo descubrimiento*, 90.

41. "Parece más cierto por ser dicho más común . . . el tiempo descubrirá la verdad, y si éstas son las Amazonas afamadas de los historiadores, tesoros encierran en su comarca para enriquecer a todo el mundo." Acuña, *Nuevo descubrimiento*, 93.

42. Ibid., 57.

43. Ibid., 58.

44. "Son muy altas, de lindas campiñas, y yerbas para ganados, arboladas no muy cerradas, abundantes lagos y que prometen muchas y buenas comodidades a los que la poblaren." Acuña, *Nuevo descubrimiento*, 79.

45. "El mayor y más hermoso río." Acuña, *Nuevo descubrimiento*, 83–84.

46. Ibid., 78.

47. "Los ritos de toda esta gentilidad, son casi en general unos mismos; adoran ídolos, que fabrican con sus manos, atribuyendo a unos el poder sobre las aguas . . . a otros escogen por dueños de las sementeras, y a otros por valedores de sus batallas." Acuña, *Nuevo descubrimiento*, 62.

48. "Con cierto género de veneración, como si fueran las reliquias de santos, van recogiendo todos los huesos de los hechiceros que mueren, los cuales tienen colgados en el aire, en las mismas hamacas en que ellos dormían en vida." Añade que ellos son "sus Maestros, sus predicadores, sus consejeros y sus guías." Acuña, *Nuevo descubrimiento*, 65.

49. "De las que puedo dar fe, nombrándolas con sus nombres, y señalándoles sus sitios, unas de vista, y otras por informaciones de todos los indios que en ellas habían estado, pasan de ciento cincuenta, todas de lenguas diferentes." Acuña, *Nuevo descubrimiento*, 60.

50. "Que ni la comodidad ni el ingenio los pudiera fingir mejores." Acuña, *Nuevo descubrimiento*, 81.

51. "Que tuvieran bien que aprender de ellos muchos de nuestros escultores." Acuña, *Nuevo descubrimiento*, 82.

52. Ibid., 71.

53. "Es esta gente la de más razón y mejor gobierno que hay en todo el río." Acuña, *Nuevo descubrimiento*, 72.

54. "No sólo tejidos de diversos colores, sino pintados con estos mismos tan sutilmente, que apeas se distingue lo uno de lo otro." Acuña, *Nuevo descubrimiento*, 73.

55. "Son todos de cabeza chata, que causa fealdad en los varones, si bien las mujeres mejor lo encubren con el mucho cabello . . . desde que nacen las criaturas, se las meten en prensa, cogiéndoles por la frente con una tabla pequeña, que sirviendo de cuna, recibe todo el cuerpo del recién nacido, el cual puesto de espaldas sobre ésta y apretado fuertemente con la otra, queda con el cerebro y la frente tan llanos como la palma de la mano." Acuña, *Nuevo descubrimiento*, 73.

56. "Que casi todos tienen agujereadas, y en las orejas lo afectan tanto, que a muchos les cabe todo el puño por el agujero que en la parte de abajo, donde suelen pender los zarcillos, tienen trayéndole de ordinario ocupado con un mazo de ajustadas hojas, que en él por gala acostumbran." Acuña, *Nuevo descubrimiento*, 78.

57. Barbara Mundy, *The Mapping of New Spain: Indigenous Cartography and the Maps of the Relaciones Geográficas* (Chicago: University of Chicago Press, 1996), 1–159. See also Headley, "Geography and Empire," 1129.

58. Acuña, *Nuevo descubrimiento*, 87.

59. Ibid., 38–40.

60. "Dieron los dos religiosos noticia de su viaje, que fue como de personas que venían cada día huyendo de las manos de la muerte, y lo que más pudieron aclarar, fue decir que venían del Perú, que habían visto muchos indios." Acuña, *Nuevo descubrimiento*, 41.

61. "Noticia suficiente y la más clara que se pueda, de las naciones que en él habitan, ríos que se le juntan y lo demás necesario para que en el Real Consejo de las Indias se haga pleno concepto de esta empresa." Acuña, *Nuevo descubrimiento*, 86.

62. Ibid., 84.

63. See, for example, Sanjay Subrahmanyam, "Holding the World in Balance: The Connected Histories of the Iberian Overseas Empires, 1500–1640," *American Historical Review* 112, no. 5 (December 2007): 1359–85.

64. See Francisco Javier Ullán de la Rosa, "Jesuitas, omaguas, yurimaguas y la guerra hispano-lusa por el Alto Amazonas: Para un posible guión alternativo de 'La misión,' " *Anales del Museo de América* 15 (2007): 181. Samuel Fritz states that it was the Cuchivara River. Cited in Pablo Maroni, *Noticias auténticas del famoso Río Marañón (1738)*, ed. Pierre Chaumeuil (Iquitos: IIAP–CETA, 1988), 334.

65. "Si los portugueses que están en la boca de este río (que todo se puede presumir de su poca cristiandad, y menos lealtad) quisiesen, ayudados de algunas naciones belicosas que tienen sujetas, penetrar por él arriba hasta llegar a lo poblado del Perú, o Nuevo Reino de Granada, aunque es verdad que por algunas partes hallarán resistencia, por otras muchas la hubiera muy poca, por salir a pueblos muy faltos de gente, y en fin pisarán aquellas tierras vasallos desleales de Vuestra Majestad." "Memorial presentado en el Real Consejo de las Indias, sobre el dicho descubrimiento después de la rebelión de Portugal," in *Informes de Jesuitas en el Amazonas 1660–1684*, ed. Figueroa, Acuña et al., 106.

66. Ibid., 103.

67. With regard to Samuel Fritz's contribution to modern cartography, see André Ferrand de Almeida, "Samuel Fritz and the Mapping of the Amazon," *Imago Mundo* 55 (2003): 113–19. The manuscript version was taken to France by Charles Marie de La Condamine in 1745. Almeida attributes two other ink drawings of the Amazon to Fritz. One is kept in the Archivum Romanum Societatis Iesu in Rome, and the other in the National Library in Paris.

68. This essay was reproduced by Maroni, *Noticias auténticas*, 332–35.

69. Juan Magnin, *Descripción de la provincia y misiones de Mainas en el Reino de Quito* (Quito: Biblioteca Ecuatoriana 'Aurelio Espinosa Pólit' and Sociedad Ecuatoriana de Investigaciones Históricas y Geográficas, 1998).

70. "En particular cada cual se diferencia en costumbres, géneros, oficios y mantenimientos." Magnin, *Descripción de la provincia*, 159.

71. "Los Yameos engastan en la perilla de la oreja un trozo redondo de madera que tiene a veces cuatro dedos de diámetro y más de uno de espesor. La carne crece entonces en forma tan extraordinaria que al quitar ese taruguito, levantan la extremidad inferior de la oreja para colgarla de la superior . . . . Engastarse otro palito redondo, como medio real, en el labio superior, es de Yurimaguas, quienes también solían henderse las orejas . . . . Los Iquitos o Coronados se rapan lo alto de la cabeza, deforman el cráneo y se lo pintan de colorado." Magnin, *Descripción de la provincia*, 159–60.

CHAPTER 9

1. For the most recent and complete study of the multiple local and imperial contexts in which William Phips lived his short, active life, see Emerson W. Baker and John G. Reid, *The New England Knight: Sir William Phips, 1651–1695* (Toronto: University of Toronto Press, 1998). See also two important early essays by Viola F. Barnes: "Phippius Maximus," *New England Quarterly* 1 (1928): 532–53; and "The Rise of William Phips," *New England Quarterly* 1 (1928): 271–94. Scholars focused on Phips's "exceptionalism" fail to consider the text's initial English publication in 1697. Mather is clearly trying to address at least two audiences in this text.

2. For a recent discussion of secularization that similarly describes the traditional understanding of the term, see Vincent Pecora, *Secularization and Cultural Criticism: Religion, Nature, and Modernity* (Chicago: University of Chicago Press, 2006), especially 1–66. Pecora offers a useful bibliography of a range of past and current disputes over the meaning and application of the term. For a collection of recent essays, see Craig Calhoun, Mark Juergensmeyer, and Jonathan Van Antwerpen, eds., *Rethinking Secularism* (Oxford: Oxford University Press, 2006).

3. See T. H. Breen's magisterial *The Character of a Good Ruler; A Study of Puritan Political Ideas in New England, 1630–1730* (New Haven, Conn.: Yale University Press, 1970.) Breen focuses on the "evolution" of Puritan ideas about governance found in multiple discussions of the "good" ruler. For Breen, this evolution involves the separation of features of Puritan religious thought from thinking about governance, as colonial interests "shift" from piety to property. While he offers thick descriptions of contexts in which such shifts occur, including the time after the Glorious Revolution and Phips's brief governorship, Breen's concern is the larger move to secularization that he sees in such separations, not in the ways in which such separations might be figured, reconfigured, and framed in religious terms by specific historical actors. For Breen, *Pietas in Patriam* is Mather's failed attempt to justify both the new charter and its first governor largely because of the erratic and angry political behaviors of the "real" Phips.

4. For important arguments about the discrepancies between the rhetorical and real Phips, and how Mather's depictions of his public service subsume or replace religious conversion, see, for example, Jane Eberwein, " 'In a Book, as in a Glass': Literary Sorcery in Mather's *Life of Phips*," *Early American Literature* 10 (1975–1976): 282–300; Philip Gura, "Cotton Mather's *Life of Phips*: 'A Vice with the Vizard of Vertue Upon It,' " *New England Quarterly* 50 (1977): 440–57; and Stephen Carl Arch's extended discussion of how Mather attempts to persuade readers to see his own version of Phips as one converted not simply to God, but also to New England: Stephen Carl Arch, *Authorizing the Past: The Rhetoric of History in Seventeenth-Century New England* (DeKalb: Northern Illinois University Press, 1994), 164–73. See also David H. Watters, "The Spectral Identity of Sir William Phips," *Early American Literature* 18 (1983–1984): 219–32. Perry Miller long ago interpreted the shift from behavior emanating from a conversion experience to behavior that masks inner motives (a key issue in the battle over "spectral evidence") as another episode in the declension of later generation Puritans from the more organic thought and practices of the first generation. See Perry Miller, *The New England Mind: From Colony to Province* (Boston: Beacon Books, 1968). For this reading of the spectrality of writing itself, see Watters, "The Spectral Identity of Sir William Phips." For a discussion of spectral evidence in its relation to transformations in global credit, see Michelle Burnham, *Folded Selves: Colonial New England Writing in the World System* (Lebanon, N.H.: University Press of New England, 2007). Rejecting accounts of the Puritans' evolution to secularization (whether this is defined in Weberian or anti-Weberian terms), Burnham locates a kind of secularization before the fact in a capitalist world system toward which she sees New English Puritans throughout the seventeenth century manifesting a very similar ambivalence strikingly locatable at the moments when they seem most to dissent from it. This world system forms, in her Marxist reading, the determining context within which "embedded" rhetorics and practices of commerce and religion intersect. Burnham offers a fascinating discussion of how debates over the relation of paper money to "real" specie inform Mather's discussion of colonial debt and spectral evidence in *Pietas in Patriam*, but her analysis assumes the preeminence of an economic over any religious understanding of the witchcraft controversy.

5. See Pecora, *Secularization and Cultural Criticism*. I am borrowing some of Pecora's language of the "twisting and reversals" involved in secularization itself to describe Mather's *rhetorical*

twists and turns as he addresses his own understanding of the "process," 18 and 23. Pecora mentions, for example, the works of Bernard Lewis, Peter Berger, Robert Bellah, and, especially, Talal Assad in formulating different understandings of secularization in its non-Western as well as Western dimensions. See Pecora, 12–15 and 25–67.

6. See Bruno Latour, *Reassembling the Social: An Introduction to Actor-Network Theory* (Oxford: Oxford University Press, 2007), especially 1–17 and 43–55. I am not asserting congruence between actor-network theory and rhetorical analysis of the kind I do here. I do not focus on what Latour would call "figurations" of groups in the nonhuman world, for example, although Mather's scientific writings, especially on witchcraft, might be considered using Latour. Still, Latour's method more generally construed can infuse rhetorical analysis with a sense of the provisional and shifting quality of the descriptions used by mediators like Mather as well as focus new critical attention on the ways rhetorical overlaps and their dissociations function in particular historical situations.

7. Arch, *Authorizing the Past*, 166.

8. For important discussions of the history, theology, language, and structure of the Puritan conversion narrative, see, for example, Edmund Morgan, *Visible Saints: The History of a Puritan Idea* (Ithaca, N.Y.: Cornell University Press, 1965); and Patricia Caldwell, *The Puritan Conversion Narrative: The Beginnings of American Expression* (Cambridge, UK: Cambridge University Press, 1986). For a comprehensive summary of the sources of and disputes over the nature of the conversion experience that specifically considers Cotton Mather's conception of it, especially in its relation to an active external holiness, see Richard Lovelace, *The American Pietism of Cotton Mather: Origins of American Evangelicalism* (Grand Rapids, Mich.: Christian University Press, 1979), 73–109.

9. See Cotton Mather, *Magnalia Christi Americana; or, The Ecclesiastical History of New England* (Hartford, Conn.: Silas Andrus and Son, 1855), 172. (Subsequent parenthetical page references in the text are to this work.) David Watters reads parallels with the conversion experience in Phips's making of a covenant with his loyal crew to put down a mutiny in Section 5 of *Pietas in Patriam*. The notion of a church covenant, for him, also pervades Phips's later promise to share with his crew once they reach England. I read the discovery of the treasure itself as the place where the language and structure of the conversion narrative are mostly clearly demonstrated. See Watters, 226.

10. The Dominion of New England was the new colonial administrative system put into effect by English policymakers after the vacating of the Massachusetts charter in 1684. The Dominion administratively yoked Massachusetts with Rhode Island, Plymouth, Connecticut, and New Hampshire, and later, with New York and New Jersey. All were under the control of a single appointed royal governor. For details on how the Dominion operated and colonial reactions to it, see Breen, *The Character of a Good Ruler*, 138–41.

11. Mather is drawing on his own work, *The Declaration of the Gentlemen, Merchants and Inhabitants of Boston, and the Country Adjacent, 1689*. See Charles M. Andrews, ed., *Narratives of the Insurrections, 1675–1690* (New York: Charles Scribner's Sons, 1915), 175–82.

12. For some major discussions of the second charter and the political battles over it in which William Phips, Increase Mather, and Cotton Mather confronted fellow ministers and other colonials opposed to the "real" Phips's high-handed use of his new powers, see Breen, *The Character of a Good Ruler*; Richard Johnson, *Adjustment to Empire: The New England Colonies, 1675–1715* (New Brunswick, N.J.: Rutgers University Press, 1981); and William Pencak, *War, Politics, and Revolution in Provincial Massachusetts* (Boston: Northeastern University Press, 1981).

13. For an important discussion of the ways in which a variety of seventeenth- and eighteenth-century thinkers configured and reconfigured their understanding of the economic and noneconomic

meanings and relations of self-interest and public-interest in their connection to "good" and "bad" passions, see A. O. Hirschman, *The Passions and the Interests: Political Arguments for Capitalism Before Its Triumph* (Princeton, N.J.: Princeton University Press, 1977). Mather, who elsewhere in *Pietas in Patriam* takes issue with both Hobbes's and Machiavelli's notions of the basis of governance, attempts here to suggest that Phips, as both the people's and the king's man, encompasses in himself private and public interests that, given his conversion, will be conditioned by moral, and in Mather's presentation of them, ultimately *religious* purposes. Phips is described as remaining deferential to ministers of the "standing order" in spite of his politically mandated religious tolerance toward other religious groups.

14. While the image of Phips as angel has obvious providential connotations—Providence is showing how God continually watches over/guards New England through the person of Phips, it also intersects with Mather's interest in more explicit political readings of angels, both in scripture and in texts ranging from the "ancients" through Calvin to Dutch political theorist, Hugo Grotius: "The Scripture itself does plainly assert it: and hence the most learned Grotius, writing of commonwealths, has a passage to this purpose. *His singulis, suos Attributoes, esse Angelo, ex Daniele, magno consensus, et Judoei et Christiani veteres colligebant.*" (*Pietas in Patriam*, 203–4.) Mather is not quoting from Grotius's work on commonwealths, but from his commentary on the New Testament, *Annotationes in Novum Testamentum: denuo emendatius editae* (BiblioBazaar, 2011). This edition is a copy of an 1827 text published by W. Zuidema. The passage Mather quotes appears on page 83. Strikingly, both Cotton Mather and his father were increasingly concerned with the nature and role of angelic mediators in their own lives during the 1690s, both before and after the death of Phips. See, for example, Kenneth Silverman, *The Life and Times of Cotton Mather* (New York: Harper and Row, 1984); and Michael G. Hall, *The Last Puritan: The Life of Increase Mather* (Middletown, Conn.: Wesleyan University Press, 1988). Phips is presented as a quasi-angelic mediator between God and people.

15. See *Pietas in Patriam*, 206–7 for these descriptions. Like David Watters, my interest is in how and why Mather is re-using earlier comments on witchcraft just following his description of the new charter. As noted above, while *Pietas in Patriam* can obviously be read chronologically, it should also be read as a series of dialogues between its different sections. What seems crucial in this context is to see the variety, not the singleness of the ways in which Mather relates the witchcraft controversy to problems of governance, beginning with the unauthorized "little sorceries" of the "young people." Witchcraft is implicitly presented as yet another kind of mutiny against legitimate authority that Captain Phips is best qualified to quell.

16. For an example of a younger Phips's earlier "sailing away" with the "people" to preserve them from Indian attack, see *Pietas in Patriam*, 168. The use of the classical images is striking at this point, suggesting as they do Phips's role as a defender of civil society who cuts the "knot" or "sails away" from religious conflict that threatens to rend the social order. At this moment in *Pietas in Patriam* this technique seems in contrast to Mather's well-known practice elsewhere in the text (and in the *Magnalia* more generally) to more consciously *yoke* Christian and classical images. But such separation is then itself reinscribed in a larger providential rhetoric. In the late 1680s, defending his father's charter negotiations against colonial detractors such as Elisha Cooke and Thomas Danforth, Mather had similarly turned to classical imagery. For a discussion of Mather's manuscript "Political Fables," see David S. Shields, *Oracles of Empire: Poetry, Politics and Commerce in British America, 1690–1750* (Chicago: University of Chicago Press, 1990), 100–112. Thanks to David Hall for reminding me of the "Fables."

17. See Michael Winship, *Seers of God: Puritan Providentialism in the Restoration and Early New England* (Baltimore, Md.: Johns Hopkins University Press, 1996). Winship offers a rich discussion of Calvinist understandings of God's watchful and omnipresent general providence, both in its relation to God's hidden aims, and in its relation to elite and popular understandings of God's periodic revelation of his aims as they are displayed in particular "special" providences. He also usefully discusses how providence manifests itself in internal as well as external phenomena. His larger focus falls, however, on the conflicts and eventual diminishment of transatlantic Dissenter notions of providence in the face of their cultural confrontation with the "new" philosophy. Mather's re/turn to providential mystery in the Phips biography as well as his re/turn to readable providences in the two angry jeremiads that follow it could be read as consciously anomalous and defiant in Winship's terms or, as in much of his writing, could also be seen as yet another example of Mather's unceasing efforts to engage and interpret all phenomena, even the "new" science, in religious terms. For an important revisionary discussion of this tendency in Mather and other New Englanders, see Sarah Rivett, *The Science of The Soul in Colonial New England* (Chapel Hill: University of North Carolina Press, 2011). See also Cotton Mather, *Terribilia Dei* (Boston, 1697). For general definitions and specific understandings of the concept of providence during the period at issue, see also *The Westminster Dictionary of Christian Theology*, ed. Alan Richardson and John Bruder (Philadelphia: Westminster Press, 1988), 478–79. Mark Valeri's excellent recent study, *Heavenly Merchandize: How Religion Shaped Commerce in Puritan America* (Princeton, N.J.: Princeton University Press, 2010), similarly focuses on how New English providentialism transforms as it encounters political and especially commercial change. Valeri traces how certain New English ministers come over time to align political loyalty to William and Mary and morally construed commercial ventures with God's providential, and increasingly readable, plan for an ecumenical, even millennial Protestantism. I came upon Valeri's study as I completed this essay. In my reading, *Pietas in Patriam* attempts to associate and to balance rather than to integrate its different rhetorics, only to see these attempts mysteriously fail in the case of Phips. Mather's turn to the will of a traditionally more mysterious and sovereign providence could help account for the Phips biography's inclusion in the *Magnalia*. Whereas *Pietas in Patriam* suggests Mather's disappointment with local politics in its relation to providence, it also suggests how providential aims might be glimpsed or furthered in arenas outside the political—in "doing good" for the public through projects. Mather's disenchantment with local New English magistrates as God's instruments and his belief that other civic groups can often more usefully further the public good appears clearly in his *Bonifacius* of 1709. See Cotton Mather, *Bonifacius: An Essay upon the Good*, ed. David Levin (Cambridge, Mass: Belknap Press of Harvard University Press, 1966.) See particularly chap. 7, "Magistrates," 91–96.

18. I am referring here to Milton's "Samson Agonistes," and the at once humiliating and humbling relinquishment of the dream of Puritan *political* hegemony in England as well as New England. Of interest, too, are the ways in which the character of Samson, to whom Phips is also compared, moves from being a figure of heroic courage to a figure forced to learn to wait patiently for the will of providence to reveal itself. For a discussion of the transformation of the heroic ideal in Milton and other early modern English writers, see Mary Beth Rose, *Gender and Heroism in Early Modern English Literature* (Chicago: University of Chicago Press, 2002). As his quotation from *Paradise Lost* suggests, Milton seems to be on Mather's mind as he composes *Pietas in Patriam*, both in the epic context of "good" and "bad" angels and in the context of religious responses to a changed form of human governance. Mather's baroquely punitive images at the end of the Phips biography in which, drawing on a number of traditional and classical tales, he imagines a skull

hurling stones back at those who throw them, and statues of good men falling on those who malign them, do not call for human redress, but represent various fantasies about the ways in which providence may yet unexpectedly and indirectly strike those who have slandered and brought down Governor Phips. See, for example, *Pietas in Patriam*, 228–29.

19. Many of the details of Phips's character, including the comparison with Fabius Maximus, his drive to exhibit *pietas in patriam* by doing good for God's people, and his special concern for the ministry of the standing order, already made their appearance in *Optanda*, the sermon Cotton Mather directed to him upon his arrival in New England in the spring of 1692. Seeking in *Pietas in Patriam* to show English and New English readers the fulfillment by Phips of the qualities Mather had argued that an "excellent spirit" should possess, Mather omits his earlier overt and covert instructions to Phips about how such a spirit must deal coolly and calmly with a fractious people, who are similarly described in *Optanda* as demanding their "country pay." *Optanda* also warns against split interests and factions. See Cotton Mather, *Optanda, or Good Men Described* (Boston, 1692). In *Pietas in Patriam*, Phips is described such that he both fulfills the image of himself with which Mather had earlier presented him, and yet, by the mysterious will of providence, fails anyway.

20. Richard F. Lovelace has meticulously traced the way in which Mather's Calvinist theology works its way through his many exhortations to *practical* piety. In Lovelace's view, Mather early on developed positions akin to that of many German Pietists. Both late seventeenth-century Puritans like Mather and certain Pietists "affirmed the importance of assent to creedal propositions drawn from Scripture but sought to balance this emphasis on the illuminating and transforming work of the Holy Spirit and the resulting human response of faith and holy living." Both attempted to balance "a one-sided doctrine of justification by a thrust toward sanctification." Those who read Phips's public service as erasing or subsuming his religious conversion may wish to reconsider Mather's own understanding of sanctification. See Lovelace, *The American Pietism of Cotton Mather*, 37.

21. See Mark Valeri, *Heavenly Merchandize: How Religion Shaped Commerce in Puritan America* (Princeton, N.J.: Princeton University Press, 2010). See also note 17. Even though the earlier sections of *Pietas in Patriam* present Phips's successful projecting as indicative of his providentially inflected capacities for politics, his "failure" as governor does not discount his projecting, but instead makes it rhetorically available as a divinely directed instrument of a public service distinct from any institutionalized political structure.

22. Mather's positive image of the projector, earlier denigrated as a self-interested schemer and speculator, shares characteristics with English Dissenter Daniel Defoe's attempts to transform understandings of projecting in his *Essay Upon Projects*. William Phips himself is more ambiguously described by Defoe as one whose project would have been dismissed as sheer lunacy had it not succeeded. Still, Defoe shares with Mather a sense of the providential, even millennial, intentions driving a productive projecting in which self-interest and community interest could both be furthered. See Daniel Defoe, *An Essay Upon Projects*, ed. Joyce D. Kennedy, Michael Seidel, and Maximillian E. Novak (New York: AMS Press, Inc., 1999), 11–12, 15. For a discussion of Defoe's understanding of English projecting and commerce in their relation to God's providential plan, see Katherine Clark, *Daniel Defoe: The Whole Frame of Nature, Time, and Providence* (Houndmills: Palgrave Macmillan, 2007).

23. Richard Lovelace points to Mather's early desire to shape reforming societies of laymen under ministerial oversight in sermons such as "Address to Old Men, and Young, and Little Children," (Boston, 1690), and "Unum Necessarium" of 1693 (*The American Pietism of Cotton Mather*, especially chapter 6). Mather's urge to suggest how those in different callings can do public good can obviously be seen in *Optanda* and its accompanying sermon, "Good Things Proposed" of 1692.

In these sermons, he is of course discussing the good to be done by those in political power. Mather's sermon "Faith at Work: A Brief and Plain Essay upon Good Works by Which the Faith of a Christian Is to Be Evidenced" appeared in 1697, the same year as *Pietas in Patriam*, and was also published in London. Mather's focus on the reforming capacities of ministerially guided *lay* Protestant groups on politics as well as in all other arenas of "humane society" reaches its apotheosis in his *Bonifacius* of 1709.

24. Mather neatly circumvents his disappointment at local politics and his own diminished political role in it through the intensity of his rhetoric in support of William and Mary. For the provincial tendency more generally to fight the king's appointees while fulsomely claiming allegiance to the king himself, see Brendan McConville, *The King's Three Faces: The Rise and Fall of Royal America, 1688–1776* (Chapel Hill: University of North Carolina Press, 2006).

CHAPTER 10

1. J. G. A. Pocock, *The Machiavellian Moment: Florentine Political Thought and the Atlantic Republican Tradition* (Princeton, N.J.: Princeton University Press, 1975); J. H. Elliott, *Empires of the Atlantic World: Britain and Spain in America 1492–1830* (New Haven, Conn.: Yale University Press, 2006), 398–99.

2. Sabine MacCormack, *On the Wings of Time: Rome, the Incas, Spain, and Peru* (Princeton, N.J.: Princeton University Press, 2007); MacCormack, "Limits of Understanding: Perceptions of Greco-Roman and Amerindian Paganism in Early Modern Europe," in *America in European Consciousness 1493–1750*, ed. Karen Ordahl Kupperman (Chapel Hill: University of North Carolina Press for the Institute of Early American History and Culture, 1995), 79–129; MacCormack, *Religion in the Andes: Vision and Imagination in Early Colonial Peru* (Princeton, N.J.: Princeton University Press, 1991). On the influence of American and French republicanisms, see John Lynch, *Simón Bolívar: A Life* (New Haven, Conn.: Yale University Press, 2006).

3. Jorge Cañizares-Esguerra, *Puritan Conquistadors: Iberianizing the Atlantic, 1550–1700* (Stanford, Calif.: Stanford University Press, 2006).

4. Cicero, *On the Commonwealth and On the Laws*, ed. James E. G. Zetzel (Cambridge, UK: Cambridge University Press, 1999), xx, 18. *De Re Publica* is variously translated as *The Republic, On the Republic*, and *On the Commonwealth*. For the purposes of this discussion I am treating *republic* and *commonwealth* as interchangeable terms.

5. Augustine, *The City of God Against the Pagans*, ed. and trans., R. W. Dyson (Cambridge, UK: Cambridge University Press, 1998), Book 2, chap. 21, 78–80.

6. Webster followed the English commonwealth philosopher James Harrington. In these paragraphs I draw on the discussion in my *Imagining Deliberative Democracy in the Early American Republic* (Chicago: University of Chicago Press, 2011), especially chap. 2, Part 1, and pages 71–72.

7. MacCormack, *On the Wings of Time*, 25. Subsequent parenthetical page references in the text to MacCormack are to this work.

8. MacCormack discusses the perceived parallels between Moors and Incas in "The Fall of the Incas: A Historiographical Dilemma," *History of European Ideas* 6 (1985): 421–45.

9. John Smith, et. al., *The Generall Historie of Virginia, New-England, and the Summer Isles*, in *The Complete Works of Captain John Smith (1580–1631) in Three Volumes*, ed. Philip L. Barbour, (Chapel Hill: University of North Carolina Press for the Institute of Early American History and Culture, 1985), 2:125–26. On Smith's possible familiarity with Acosta, see 1:124. For a discussion of

the influence of Spanish chronicles on English writers, see Ralph Bauer's essay in this volume. Bauer notes that "When Richard Hakluyt, for example, the most prolific Elizabethan collector of English travel literature, translated, in the 1598 edition of his *Principal Navigations*, parts of one of the most important texts in Spanish Counter-Reformation demonology and ethnography, José de Acosta's *Historia natural y moral*, he did not select a single passage that linked Native religions with diabolic perversions."

10. Perry Miller, *The New England Mind: The Seventeenth Century* (1939; Cambridge, Mass.: Belknap Press of Harvard University Press, 1983), 430, 417. Miller's approach has recently been recuperated and updated. David D. Hall situates the New England Puritan project of creating "Godly rule," in the form of a Christian commonwealth, in the context of Reformation biblical exegesis in *A Reforming People: Puritanism and the Transformation of Public Life in New England* (New York: Alfred A. Knopf, 2011), chap. 3. Michael Winship provides an account of New England republicanism focused on the interactions of Puritans and Separatists in *Godly Republicanism: Puritans, Pilgrims, and a City on a Hill* (Cambridge, Mass.: Harvard University Press, 2012).

11. John Eliot, *The Christian Commonwealth: or, The Civil Policy Of The Rising Kingdom of Jesus Christ*, http://digitalcommons.unl.edu/libraryscience/19/, accessed 25 July 2013. Hall discusses Eliot in chap. 3 of *A Reforming People*; the quoted sentence is on page 120.

12. Roger Williams, *A Key into the Language of America*, in *The Complete Writings of Roger Williams*, 7 vols. (New York: Russell & Russell, 1963), 1:83, 164, 167. This discussion of Williams draws on my analysis in *Eloquence Is Power: Oratory and Performance in Early America* (Chapel Hill: University of North Carolina Press, 2000), 33–39.

13. Cadwallader Colden, *The History of the Five Indian Nations Depending on the Province of New-York* (Ithaca, N.Y.: Cornell University Press, 1958), xx, xxi, vii.

14. See my discussion in *Eloquence Is Power*, chap. 3. I elaborate the connections between Franklin and Cicero in *Imagining Deliberative Democracy*, 78–79.

15. Jorge Cañizares-Esguerra, *How to Write the History of the New World: Histories, Epistemologies, and Identities in the Eighteenth-Century Atlantic World* (Stanford, Calif.: Stanford University Press, 2001), 13.

16. Benjamin Franklin, "Remarks Concerning the Savages of North-America" (1783), in *Writings* (New York: Library of America, 1987), 969–74. The quotation is on 972.

17. Nathan O. Hatch, *The Democratization of American Christianity* (New Haven, Conn.: Yale University Press, 1989); Gustafson, *Imagining Deliberative Democracy*, chap. 5.

18. Daniel K. Richter, *Facing East from Indian Country: A Native History of Early America* (Cambridge, Mass.: Harvard University Press, 2001); Gregory Evans Dowd, *A Spirited Resistance: The North American Indian Struggle for Unity, 1745–1815* (Baltimore, Md.: Johns Hopkins University Press, 1993). On the Tupac Amaru rebellion, see J. H. Elliott, *Empires of the Atlantic World*, esp. 360.

19. Ralph Bauer, "The 'Rebellious Muse': Time, Space, and Race in the Revolutionary Epic," *Creole Subjects in the Colonial Americas: Empires, Texts, Identities*, ed. Bauer and José Antonio Mazzotti (Chapel Hill: University of North Carolina Press for the Omohundro Institute of Early American History and Culture, 2009), 442–64; see esp. 442–44, 446; Philip J. Deloria, *Playing Indian* (New Haven, Conn.: Yale University Press, 1998).

20. Alexis de Tocqueville, *Democracy in America*, trans. Gerald E. Bevan (London: Penguin Books, 2003). Subsequent parenthetical page references in the text to Tocqueville are to this work.

21. On conversion to Catholicism among Tocqueville's contemporaries, see Jenny Franchot, *Roads to Rome: The Antebellum Protestant Encounter with Catholicism* (Berkeley: University of California Press, 1994).

22. A central work in this debate is Richard John Neuhaus, *The Naked Public Square: Religion and Democracy in America* (Grand Rapids, Mich.: Eerdmans, 1984).

23. Noel Ignatiev, *How the Irish Became White* (New York: Routledge, 1995); Timothy Matovina, *Latino Christianity: Transformation in America's Largest Church* (Princeton, N.J.: Princeton University Press, 2011). Matovina discusses the differences between the ultramontane posture of many nineteenth-century European immigrant clergy to the United States and the practices of Mexican Catholics on page 18.

24. John T. McGreevy and R. Scott Appleby, "Catholics, Moslems, and the Mosque," *New York Review of Books* (27 August 2010); http://www.nybooks.com/blogs/nyrblog/2010/aug/27/catholics-muslims-mosque-controversy/, accessed 25 July 2013; Lyman Beecher, *A Plea for the West* (New York: Leavitt, Lord, 1835).

25. McGreevy describes the trajectory of American Catholicism in relation to republican politics in greater detail and notes the sometimes tense relationship between American Catholics and the Vatican in *Catholicism and American Freedom: A History* (New York: Norton, 2003).

26. Charles Taylor, *A Secular Age* (Cambridge, Mass.: Belknap Press of Harvard University Press, 2007). Olivier Roy discusses France in *Secularism Confronts Islam*, trans. George Holoch (New York: Columbia University Press, 2007). Leila Ahmed characterizes the renewed attraction of the veil to Islamic women as a postcolonial testament in *A Quiet Revolution: The Veil's Resurgence, from the Middle East to America* (New Haven, Conn.: Yale University Press, 2011). Amartya Sen, *Identity and Violence: The Illusion of Destiny* (New York: Norton, 2006); Ramachandra Guha, *India After Gandhi: The History of the World's Largest Democracy* (New York: HarperCollins, 2007). In his anthology of writings about politics by Indian intellectuals, *Makers of Modern India* (Cambridge, Mass.: Belknap Press of Harvard University Press, 2011), Guha includes a number of selections concerned with religious differences.

CONTRIBUTORS

RALPH BAUER is associate professor of English and comparative literature at the University of Maryland, College Park. His publications include *The Cultural Geography of Colonial American Literatures: Empire, Travel, Modernity* (2003, 2008), *An Inca Account of the Conquest of Peru* (2005), and (coedited with José Antonio Mazzotti) *Creole Subjects in the Colonial Americas: Empires, Texts, Identities* (2009). He is currently completing a monograph entitled *The Alchemy of Conquest: Discovery, Prophecy, and the Secrets of the New World*.

DAVID A. BORUCHOFF is associate professor of Hispanic studies at McGill University in Montreal. He is completing a book titled *Renaissance Exploration and the Invention of a New World* and a critical edition and translation of the newly found manuscript of the *Vida y sucesos de la Monja Alférez* (The Life and Exploits of the Lieutenant Nun).

MATT COHEN is associate professor of English at the University of Texas at Austin. He is the author of *The Networked Wilderness: Communicating in Early New England* (2009) and, with Jeffrey Glover, coeditor of *Colonial Mediascapes: Sensory Worlds of the Early Americas* (2014).

SIR JOHN ELLIOTT (J. H. Elliott) is Regius Professor Emeritus of Modern History at the University of Oxford and a specialist in the history of early modern Spain, Europe, and the Americas. His books include *Empires of the Atlantic World: Britain and Spain in America, 1492–1830* (2006), and, most recently, *History in the Making* (2012).

CARMEN FERNÁNDEZ-SALVADOR is professor of pre-Columbian and colonial art history at the Universidad San Francisco de Quito, in Ecuador. She earned her PhD from the University of Chicago and has published a number of works dealing with the historiography of art history and colonial and nineteenth-century art. Her current research analyzes the iconographic program of the Church of La Compañía in Quito in connection to the Jesuit missionary enterprise in the Amazon basin during the seventeenth century.

JÚNIA FERREIRA FURTADO is professor of modern history at the Universidade Federal de Minas Gerais, Brazil. She has held visiting professorships at Princeton University and the École des Hautes Études en Sciences Sociales, Paris, and has been a visiting scholar at both Princeton and the Universidade de Lisboa. From 2011 to 2012 she held the Joaquin Nabuco Chair in Brazilian Studies at Stanford University. She has published a number of books and articles on colonial Brazil and slavery including *Chica da Silva: A Brazilian Slave of the Eighteenth Century* (2009). The Brazilian edition of this book received an award from the Casa de las Américas, Cuba, in 2004.

SANDRA M. GUSTAFSON is professor of English and concurrent professor of American Studies at the University of Notre Dame. She is the author of *Eloquence is Power: Oratory and Performance in Early America* (2000) and *Imagining Deliberative Democracy in the Early American Republic* (2011). She edits the MLA-affiliated journal Early American Literature and is coeditor of the collection *Cultural Narratives: Textuality and Performance in America Culture before 1900* (2010). She is writing a book about conflict and democracy in classic American fiction with funding from the National Endowment for the Humanities.

DAVID D. HALL is the Bartlett Research Professor of New England Church History at Harvard Divinity School. He has been interested for many years in popular or lived religion, the workings of Reformed theology and the Reformed international, and the history of the book. His most recent book is *A Reforming People: Puritanism and the Transformation of Public Life in New England* (2011).

STEPHANIE KIRK is associate professor of Spanish at Washington University in St. Louis. She is the author of *Convent Life in Colonial Mexico: A Tale of Two Communities* (2007). Recently, she edited the volume *Estudios coloniales latinoamericanos en el siglo XXI: Nuevos itinerarios* (2011). Currently, she is completing a book entitled *Sor Juana Inés de la Cruz and the Gender Politics of Culture in Colonial Mexico*.

ASUNCIÓN LAVRIN is emerita professor of history at Arizona State University. She is the author and coeditor of six books on gender issues, sexuality, and religious history in colonial and post-independence Spanish America. Among her titles are *Brides of Christ: Conventual Life in Colonial Mexico* (2008) and *Women, Feminism and Social Change: Argentina, Chile and Uruguay, 1890–1940* (1995).

SARAH RIVETT is assistant professor of English at Princeton University. She is the author of *The Science of the Soul in Colonial New England* (2011), and is currently completing a book entitled *Unscripted America: Writing Indigenous Tongues from Colony to Nation*.

TERESA A. TOULOUSE is professor of English at the University of Colorado. She is the author of *The Art of Prophesying: New England Sermons and the Shaping of Belief* (1987), and *The Captive's Position: Female Narrative, Male Identity, and Royal Authority in Colonial New England* (2006). She is currently working on a comparative study of the rhetoric of exemplarity in New England, New France, and New Spain.

INDEX

Abandozan (King of Dahomey), 188
Abbeville, Nicolas Sanson d', 216, *217*
Aberle, David, 167
Acaxees, 140
Acevedo, Pablo de, 152
Acosta, Benito de, 211, 215
Acosta, José de: C. Mather and, 75;
   European views of spirituality of Native
   peoples, 46–47; *Historia natural y moral*,
   2–3, 49–51, 69–70, 256, 266nn4–5
Actes and Martyrs (Foxe), 80
Acts and Monuments (Foxe), 83, 114–15, 135
Acuña, Cristóbal de, 206, 208, 216–23,
   318n14
*Admiranda narratio, fida tamen, de
   commodis et incolarum ritibus Virginiæ*
   (de Bry), *14*
Admonition to the Parliament (1572), 111, 116
Adorno, Rolena, 90
Aeneid (Vergil), 169
Africa, 19, 181, 183, 188, 191–92, 197–200, 261.
   See also Dahomey (later Benin)
Afro-Brazilians, 181, 197–200
Afro-Christians, 20
Agonglo (king of Dahomey), 180–82, 188,
   199, 201–2
Aguirre, Lope de, 210, 222
Ahmed, Leila, 328n16
Alcalá, Diego de, 134
alchemy, 172–73
Alemán, Mateo, 190
Alexander VI (Pope), 54, 268n26
Algonquians: burial bundles, 174–76,
   311n34; described by Harriot, 13, 15;
   illustrations of, 57; Puritan attempts to
   remake, 256–57; religion of, 52–53, 171–72,
   299n38; translation of Bible, 129. *See also*
   Pequots
Allada, 181, 184, 201

altruism, 168
Alva Ixtlilxóchitl, Fernando de, 96
Alvarado, Pedro de, 85–86, 286–87n35
Amaral, Francisco Xavier Alvarez do, 188
Amazon Basin, 4, 11, 205–27, 317n7, 319n28
ambassadors, 186, 199–200
America (de Bry), *59*, *66*, *68*, 278n26
American Colonization Society, 261
Amory, Hugh, 174–76, *178*
Anabaptist Church, 110
Andros, Edmond, 237–38
angels, 324n14
Anglican Church, 12, 32, 42, 111, 116
Angola, 181, 183
Antichrist, 280n48
Antinomian controversy, 124–25
Apaches, 141
Apess, William, 259
apostolic model. *See* missionaries and
   missions
Appleby, R. Scott, 263
Aquinas, Thomas, 48
Arab Spring, 264
Arch, Stephen Carl, 234
architecture, 10–11
Argentina, 4
Arlegui, Joseph, 144, 147–49, 153, 302–3n19,
   305n44, 306n54
Arricivita, Juan Domingo, 144–45, 146, 156
art and the Catholic Church, 79–81, 135,
   283n14. *See also* portraits
Artieda, Andrés de, 216
Ashley, Anthony, 56
Assinais, 144
astrology, 247
Augustine, Saint, 48, 169–70, 253–54,
   256, 262
Augustinian order, 4, 29
Axtell, James, 257

Ayala, Martín de (father of Guaman Poma), 96, *97–98*
Ayala, Martín de (half-brother of Guaman Poma), 96, *97–99*, 100–101, 103–4, 292–93n67, 295n75

Bacon, Francis, 61
Bahia, Salvador de, 222
Baillie, Robert, 123, 127
Baldung, Hans, 57
Bale, John, 114
baptism, 18–19, 117–18, 121, 201–4
Baptists, 34
Barca, Calderón de la, 301–2n17
Barebones Parliament, 119
Barrow, Isaac, 83
Basílio da Gama, José, 189
Bastos Varella, Manoel de, 187
Battle of Ourique, 314n74
Bauer, Ralph, 327–28n9
Baxter, Richard, 112
bear paw, 175–76
Beecher, Lyman, 263
Beltrán de Caicedo, Diego, *99*
Benavente, Toribio de. *See* Motolinía
Benavides, Alonso de, 140, 144
Benedictine order, 191
Benin. *See* Dahomey
Benítez, Esteban, 152
Benzoni, Girolamo, 67
Bèze, Théodore de, 80–81
Bible: talismanic function of, 174, 176, 311n34; translations of, 17, 43, 111, 129, 271–72n71, 299n38
Bishop, Bridget, 176
Black Hills, 167
Black Legend, 55
Boa Morte Seminary (Minas Gerais, Brazil), 192–94
Bobadilla, Francisco de, 89
Bolívar, Simón, 254–55, 260
Bonaventure, John, Saint, 101, 104, 294–95n74
Bonhoeffer, Dietrich, 115
Book of Common Prayer, 111
Book of Martyrs (Foxe), 80, 83
books, 122–23, 297n4. *See also* printing
Boston Tea Party, 260
Botticelli, 61, *62–63*
Boyle, Robert, 129–30
Bozeman, Theodore Dwight, 268n22

Bradford, William, 4–5, 115
Bradwardine, Thomas, 248
Bragança, João Carlos de, 186, 199
Braude, Benjamin, 18
Brazil: African customs and traditions, 198–99; Amazon Basin, 205–27, 317n7, 319n28; missionaries and missions, 4, 181, 191–92; Tupinambá people, 65, *66*, 218
Breen, T. H., 232, 322n3
Brevíssima relación de la destrucción de las indias (Las Casas), 55
Briefe and true report of the new found land of Virginia (Harriot), 13, 52–53
Briera, Domingo de, 210
British America, 12–13, 22, 27–28, 41–43, 258–60. *See also individual states, settlements or religions*
Brito, Bernardo Gomes de, 190
Brooks, Joanna, 165, 178–79
Brooks, Lisa, 167
Brown, Frank, 176–77
Brown, Matt, 171–72
Brown, Vincent, 179
Bruno, Giordano, 61
Buena, Mariano, 156
burial bundles, 174–76, 311n34
burial rituals, 310n32
Burnham, Michelle, 322n4
Bushnell, Amy, 207

Cabot, John, 54
Calderón de la Barca, Pedro, 135
Calero, Juan, 146, 306n60
Calvert family, 33
Calvin, John, 111, 115–16
Calvinism (Reformed Tradition), 35, 111–21
Cambridge Platform, 117
Camões, 190
Canary Islands, 134
Cañizares-Esguerra, Jorge, 47, 207, 253, 258, 276n3
cannibalism, 39–40
capitalism, 322n4
Caripunás, 219
Carmelite order, 191
Carretta, Vincent, 18
Cartas de relación (Cortés), 10
cartography, 205–8, 213, *214*, 215–16, *217*, 223–27, 224, 226, 319n28
Cartwright, Thomas, 116
Carvajal, Garpar de, 219, 221

Casas, Francisco de las, 153
Casas, Juan de las, 153
Cassacinamon, Robin, 173, 174
Catechism to the Slaves (Vide), 192
Catedral Metropolitana de la Asunción de María (Mexico City), 10–11, *11*
Catholic Church: among slaves, 198; authorization of art and literature, 79–81, 135, 283n14; challenges to, 134; convergence of economic and religious interests, 180–85, 191–92; conversion strategies, 184, 203; and development of modernity, 22; ecclesiastical government, 30; and godly rule, 5; and individual sanctity, 79–83; institutionalization of, 41–42; martyrs and martyrdom, 79, 135, 196; missionaries, 133; New World as religious refuge, 33; pageantry and outward manifestation of religion, 41; on purgatory, 267–68n19; secularization of, 184; similarities with Protestantism, 28; transatlantic transfers, 27–28; uniformity of worship, 41; in the U.S., 262–63. *See also* Jesuits; Spanish Christianity
center-periphery dichotomy, 207
Cervantes, Fernando, 47, 48
Cervantes, Miguel de, 190
Charles I (King of England), 32
Charles II (King of England), 3, 266n10
Charles V (Holy Roman Emperor), 7, 19
Cherokee Republic, 261
Chichimec peoples, 139–40, 143, 288n42
Child, John, 128
Child, Josiah, 35
children, liminality of, 175
China, 136, 153
chorography, 205–8, 216–23
Christian Commonwealth, The (Eliot), 256–57
Christianity: among slaves, 18–20, 198; and commonwealths, 254; convergence of economic and religious interests, 180–85; and Native ministers, 259; native religions paving the way for, 53; primitive, 4–5, 30; redefining of, 3; rejection of, 5, 140–45, 157; republics and republicanism, 253–64; and self-mastery, 104–5; syncretic versions of among Native peoples, 8, 17–18, 38, 164; transatlantic transfers, 27–28; transformations of, 19–21, 161–65, 232–51; westward march of, 134, 155

Chronica de las provincia del Santo Evangelio de Mexico (Vetancurt), 87
Chronology of the Life of Saint Ignatius of Loyola (Vide), 192
Church of England, 12, 32, 42, 111, 116
Cicero, 253–55, 259
Cieza de León, Pedro, 255
City of God, The (Augustine), 254, 256
City on the Hill, 42–43
civilization, passage from barbarism, 89, 288n42
Clark, Stuart, 48, 61
Clear Sun-Shine of the Gospel, The (Shepard), 128–29
Cohen, Thomas, 12
Colden, Cadwallader, 257–58
Colegios de Propaganda Fide, 141, 144, 304n30
Collinson, Patrick, 113–14
Colonialism's Culture (N. Thomas), 164
colonies and colonization, 6, 12–13, 16, 21, 232–53, 277n11. *See also individual countries or regions*
Columbus, Christopher, 6, 25, 46–47, 51–52, 319n37
Commentary on the Psalms (Augustine), 253
Commissioners of the United Colonies, 129
Common Pot, The (L. Brooks), 167
commonwealths, 254. *See also* republics and republicanism
confessionalization, 28
confraternities, 20
Congo, 19, 181, 183, 191–92
Congregational Churches, 16, 42, 74–75, 116–17, 173, 237–38
congregational system of government, 33–34
Congregational Way, 127–28
"Coniuerer, The" (de Bry), 57, *59–60*
"Conjecture Concerning Gog and Magogs in the Revelations, A" (Mede), 70
"Conjurer, The/The Coniueuer" (de Bry), 57, 61
Conmutá settlement, 211
Connecticut, 16
Constituições Primerias do Arcebispado de Bahia (Vide), 192, 196
Constitution, U.S., 44

contractual rhetoric, 233, 236–39, 244–51, 323n9

convents, 4, 267n16

conversion: acceptance of converts, 95, 290n58; of Africans, 19, 181, 191–92; of ambassadors, 186; and conquest societies, 37; of Dahomey king and subjects, 180–82, 184–89, 194–97, 201–4; decimation from diseases among converts, 268n33; Eliot and, 17, 70, 256–57; of Jews, 36; and millenarian expectations, 29; narratives, 235–41, 267n18; Praying Indians and Towns, 4, 17, 37, 172, 267n18, 310n30; of slaves, 18–20, 272n73. *See also* Dahomey; missionaries and missions

Córdoba, Spain, 133

Cordova, Viola F., 265n2

Corpus Christi, feast of, 28

Correa, Antônio, 187

Cortés, Hernán, 7, 10, 85–86, 104–5, 285n30, 286–87n35

Cossin, Bernardo, 148, 306n60

Cottington, Francis, Baron, 34

Cotton, John: on baptism, 118; and the Congregational Way, 127–28; and divine right to the land, 15–16, 70, 270nn59–60; *God's Promise to His Plantations*, 15–16, 70, 270n60; and loyalty to crown, 113; unauthorized printing of sermons or letters, 122, 127–28

Council of the Indies, 30

Council of Trent, 79, 192

Counter-Reformation, 43, 50, 77

Covarrubias, Sebastián de, 88

Crashaw, William, 15, 31

Creoles, 208

Crèvecœur, J. Hector St. John, 41, 43, 259

Cromwell, Oliver, 119

Crónica del Perú (Cieza de León), 255

Crown, English, 31–33, 113, 238–39, 240–41

Crown, Portuguese, 19, 181, 191–92

Crown, Spanish, 6–7, 8–9, 30–31, 88–89, 272n76

Cruz, Laureano de la, 215

Cruz, Manuel da, 192

Cuchiguará River, 218

cultural congruences, 174, 178

Curiguerés, 218

Curi Ocllo, Juana, *97–98*

Curse of Ham, 18

Custer Died for Your Sins (Deloria), 168

Daemonologie (James I), 69

Dahomey (later Benin), 180–82, 184–89, 194–97, 201–4

dancing, 198–99

Danger of Tolerating Levellers in a Civill State (Winslow), 128

Davenport, John, 117

Death in the New World (Seeman), 175, 309–10n5

de Bry, Johann Israel, 278n27

de Bry, Johann Theodor, 67, 278n27

de Bry, Theodor: *Admiranda narratio, fida tamen, de commodis et incolarum ritibus Virginiæ*, 13, 14; *America*, 49–50, *59, 66, 68*, 278n26; "Der Schwarzkünstler oder Zauberer," 57, *60*, 61; folk tradition of witchcraft, 279n30; "The Conjurer/The Coniuerer," 57, *59–60*, 61; "Voyages" series, 55–68, 278n27

Decades (Peter Martyr), 51

Deeds, Susan, 140

Defoe, Daniel, 326n22

De instauranda Aethiopum salute (Sandoval), 19

De Laet, Joannes de, 2

Delgado, Diego, 150

Deloria, Vine Jr., 168

Democracy in America (Tocqueville), 261

De Re Publica (Cicero), 253–54

"Der Schwarzkünstler oder Zauberer" (de Bry), 57, *60*, 61

devil: and astrology, 247; European views on Native religions, 47, 50–54, 57, 63–68, 70–77; and human governance, 243; pacts with, 61, 63; Protestant belief in, 54; Western perceptions of, 47–48. *See also* Satan

diabolism, 69, 70

Díaz, Juan, 306n51

Díaz del Castillo, Bernal, 74, 77, 90

"Digging at the Roots" (L. Brooks), 167

Dignitatis Humanae, 263

Dillon, Elizabeth Maddock, 179

Diretório dos Índios, 184

Discovery of the Large, Rich and Beautiful Empire of Guiana (Raleigh), 52

Dissuasive from the Errours of the Time, A (Baillie), 127

Divers Voyages Touching the Discoverie of America (Hakluyt), 56–57
Doctrina Christiana (Naxara), 201–2
doctrinas de indios, 89–90
dolls as talismans, 176–78, *177*
Dominican order, 4, 9, 29
Dominion of New England, 323n10
Don Quixote (M. Cervantes), 190
d'Orléans, Charles, 278n26
Dowd, Gregory, 260
drums, 198–99
ˈDryden, John, 169
Duns Scotus, John, 48
Durán, Diego, 89
Dutch (Holland), 183, 211–12, 222

Eden, Richard, 50–51
educational opportunities, 9–10, 12, 19–20, 36, 192–94
Edwards, Thomas, 123, 127
Egypt, 262, 264
El descubrimiento del Marañón (Rodríguez), 209
Eliot, John: and building a holy community, 37, 271n67; *Christian Commonwealth, The*, 256–57; conversion of Native peoples, 17, 70, 256–57; the "Eliot Tracts," 128; *Indian Dialogues* (Eliot), 17, 271–72n71; Praying Towns, 267n18; translation of Bible into Algonquian, 129, 299n38
"Eliot Tracts" (anon), 128
Elizabeth I (Queen of England), 12, 111–14, 119
Elliott, J. H., 252
El primer nueva corónica i buen gobierno (Guaman Poma), 88, *94, 97–99*, 289n55
Emeterio, 133
emigration to the New World, 33–35, 34. *See also individual groups*
Empires of the Atlantic World (Elliott), 252
empiricism, 191
Encabellados, 220
Enchiridion militis Christiani (Erasmus), 104–5
England: Calvinism in, 111–14; Civil War, 17, 27, 34, 123, 256; diabolism, interest in, 69; English Revolution, 126–27; Glorious Revolution, 232, 237; and godly rule, 119–25; justification for conquest of New World, 54–55; Marian exiles, 111, 113–14; martyrs and martyrdom, 135, 301n16;

practical divinity, 120–21; Puritans in, 113–14; and reciprocity, 172; Toleration Act (1684), 42; transatlantic exchanges of religion, 27–28; and two kingdom theory of authority, 118–19; written texts compared to Colonial texts, 123
Engratia, Saint, 133
Enlightenment, age of, 28, 191
Enríquez, Juan, 150, 307n66
Equiano, Olaudah, 18
Erasmus, 104–5, 296n78
Erastian civil state, 111
Esperanza, Manoel da, 300n7
Espinareda, Pedro de, 148, 306n58
Essay Upon Projects (Defoe), 326n22
Estrapajosos, 211
Étienne, Saint, 190–91
Eulogius, Saint, 300n6
Eurosia (Orosia), Saint, 133
Eusebius of Caeserea, 80
Euthyphro (Plato), 170
evangelization. *See* missionaries
excommunication, 116
exemplarity, 83–88, 90–93, 101–2
Exhortacam I em vespora do Espíritu Santo (Vieira), 12
exploration narratives, 205–27
expostos, 185

Facing East from Indian country (Richter), 260
"Faith at Work" (C. Mather), 326–27n23
Far East as ultimate goal of missionaries, 136, 153, 302n18
Faust legend, 61, 63, 68
Felipe de Jesús, Saint, 136, 153–55
Felix de Espinosa, Isadro, 144
Felizardo Fortes, Inácio, 194
Ferreira, Valéria Maria Pena, 194
Ferrer, Rafael, 209
Ficino, Marsilio, 76
Field, John, 113
Fiore, Joachim, 8
First Amendment, 44
Florida, 9
Flos sanctorum (anon), 105–6
Flos sanctorum (Vega), 101, 294n71
"Flyer, The" (White), *58, 59*
Fonseca Aragão, Francisco Antônio da, 188
Fort Williams, Whydah, 183

Foxe, John, 80, 83, 114–15, 135
Franciscan order: Amazon Basin explora-
    tion, 209–13, 222; in Brazil, 191;
    conversions of Native peoples, 8; disputes
    with Dominicans, 9; and exemplarity,
    83–88; martyrs and martyrdom, 131–32,
    136–41, 306n60; millenarianism of, 8;
    missionary complexes, 4; in Morocco,
    300n7; reception of by Cortés, 7–8, 10,
    85–86, 285n30, 286–87n35; respect for, 95,
    147, 306n54
Francisco de los Ángeles, 83–84
Francis of Assisi, Saint, 101
Franco, Alonso, 137, 150
Franklin, Benjamin, 258–59
Fritz, Samuel, 223–25

Gage, Thomas, 145
Gálvez, Joseph de, 156
Gandullo, Luis, 136, 303n20
Gangraena (Edwards), 123, 127
Garrison, James, 169
Gaudio, Michael, 57
General History of the Indies (López de
    Gómara), 25
Generall Historie of Virginia, The (Smith),
    16, 72, 73
geography, scientific, 205–8, 213, 214, 215,
    223–27
Gilbert, Humphrey, 13
Ginzburg, Carlo, 179
Glorious Revolution, 232, 237
God, 66–67, 173, 248–51. See also providen-
    tial rhetoric
God is Red (Deloria), 168
god-parentage, 199
God's Promise to His Plantations (Cotton),
    15–16, 70, 270n60
God's Terrible Voice in the City (Vincent),
    284n20
Gómara, Francisco López de, 25
Gomes, Maria, 199
"Good Things Proposed" (C. Mather),
    326–27n23
governance, human, 243–47, 246, 322n3,
    324–25nn17–18, 325–26n18
grace, covenant of, 4, 117–18
Grafton, Anthony, 76
Great Awakening, 18, 35
Great Transformation, The (Polanyi), 166
Green, Ian, 297n4

Green, Samuel, 129
Greene, Jack, 207
Gregory, Brad, 150
Gregory XIII (Pope), 292–93n67
Gregory XV (Pope), 304n30
Grimstone, Edward, 69–70, 280n45
Gronniosaw, Ukawsaw, 18
Grotius, Hugo, 324n14
Guachichiles, 140
Guaman Poma de Ayala, Felipe, 88, 92–104,
    94, 97–99, 103, 289n55, 295n75
Guaraní Indians, 4
Guayazís, 218
Guevara, Hugo Burgos, 318n14
Guiana, 54–55
Gulliver's Travels (Swift), 170
guns, 203
Gutiérrez, Bartolomé, 155
Guzmán de Alfarache (Alemán), 190

hagiography, 101, 137, 149–53, 209
Hakluyt, Richard, 13, 31, 52, 55–57, 72,
    327–28n9
Hales, Christopher, 80, 282n8
Hall, David, 169, 176
Harley, Brilliana, 112
Harrington, James, 252
Harriot, Thomas: accusations of sorcery,
    68–69; Briefe and true report of the new
    found land of Virginia (Harriot), 13, 52–53;
    justification for New World conquests, 55;
    on shamanism, 59, 279n30; specificity of,
    13, 15
Harris, Benjamin, 75
Harris, Steven, 208
Henry VIII (King of England), 114
Hermetic tradition, 59
Hernández, Francisco, 207
Higginson, John, 124–26
Historia de la Nueva México (Villagrá), 74
Historia del Mondo Nuovo (Benzoni), 67
Historia del origen y genealogía real de los
    reyes ingas del Piru (Murúa), 88
Historia de los Indios de la Nueva España
    (Motolinía), 2
Historia eclesiástica indiana (Mendieta),
    85–86, 302–3n19
Historia general del Piru (Murúa), 88
Historia Indica (Sarmiento de Gamboa), 77
Historia natural y moral (Acosta), 2–3, 49–51,
    69–70, 256, 266nn4–5

História trágico-marítima (Brito), 190
Historia verdadera de la conquista de la Nueva España (Díaz del Castillo), 74, 77, 90
Historia von D. Johann Fausten (Spies), 61, *64*
historiography, 83–88
History of the Five Indian Nations (Colden), 258
Holifield, E. Brooks, 117
Holland, 183, 211–12, 222
Hooker, Thomas, 117, 124
Horton, Benjamin, 176
How to Write the History of the New World (Cañizares-Esguerra), 258
Huayna Capac, 260
Hubbard, William, 74
Huguenots, 35
Huitzilopochtli, 67, 75
human sacrifice, 39–40
Humboldt, Alexander von, 258
Humfrey, John, 122
Hutchinson, Anne, 34, 124–26
Hypocrisie Unmasked (Winslow), 128

iconography, 57, 59, 61
idolatry, 38, 39–40, 80–81, 277n8
Ignatius of Loyola, 191. *See also* Jesuits
Image of Both Churches, The (Bale), 114
imitatio Christi, 89, 284n23
Incas, 89, 253, 255, 260. *See also* Peru
India, 136, 264
Indian Church of New Spain, 84–85
Indian Dialogues (Eliot), 17, 271–72n71
Indians. *See* Native peoples
Indigenous peoples. *See* Native peoples
individual sanctity, 79–83
Inquisition, 20, 31
interpreters, 188. *See also* translation
Iquitos, 225
Ireland, 277n11
Irish Catholics, 262
Iroquois League, 258
Islam, 28–29, 133–34, 171, 262–64, 314n74

Jacobsen, Jerome V., 269n40
James I (King of England, former James VI of Scotland), 69, 119
James II (King of England), 236–39
James VI (King of Scotland, later James I of England), 69, 119
Jamestown Settlement, 31–32

Jansenism, 181, 184–85, 192
Japan, 136, 153–56, 208, 303n20
Jefferson, Thomas, 258
Jemez, 141
Jennings, Francis, 257
Jesuits: accommodation and selective adaptation, 38; Amazon Basin exploration, 4, 11, 205–6, 225–27, 317n7; apostolic and scientific works, 208; Boa Morte Seminary, 192–94; in Brazil, 191–92; educational opportunities, 9–10, 12, 269n40; in Florida, 9; identity formation, 6, 208–9; martyrs and martyrdom, 140, 191, 196, 208–9, 225–27, 316n93; in Mexico, 9–10; missionary complexes, 4; New World as desert or wilderness, 5, 34; and Portugal, 181, 184; praise for, 95; urbanization, 10. *See also* missionaries and missions
Jesus, 39, 79, 83, 89, 104, 284n23
Jews, 31, 34, 36
Jews in America (Thorowgood), 2, 71
Jiménez de la Espada, Marcos, 206, 318n14
João (regent of Portugal, later King João VI), 182, 185, 203
João II (King of Portugal), 184
João III (King of Portugal), 191
Johnson, Carina, 47
Johnson, Marmaduke, 129
justice, 254

Kant, Immanuel, 166
Key into the Language of America (Williams), 71, 173
Keyes of the Kingdome (Cotton), 127
King Philip's War, 18, 129, 172, 310n30
Knight, Janice, 171

Laïcité, 264
Lake, Peter, 116, 120
land grants or patents, 12–13, 16
language, 38, 188, 199–200. *See also* translation
Larson, Pier M., 123
Las Casas, Bartolomé de, 8–9, 46–47, 51–53, 55, 255
Last Judgment, The (de Olmos), 29
Latour, Bruno, 233–34, 323n6
Laud, William, Archbishop of Canterbury, 12, 34, 128–29
Laudonniere, Rene Goulaine de, 63

law, 261
Law, Robin, 180
Legenda aurea (Voragine), 101, 105
Legenda major (Bonaventure), 101
Leguedés, 199–200
Le Moyne, Jacques, 64
Lepore, Jill, 164
Léry, Jean de, 65
Lescarbot, Marc, 2
Lessa, Clado Ribeiro de, 189
Letters from an American Farmer
  (Crèvecœur), 259
L'histoire notable de la Floride (Laudonniere),
  64–65, 65
Liberia, Republic of, 261
liberty of conscience, 270–71n66
Libya, 264
Lima, Peru, 40–41
Linken, Kenneth, 167
literacy, 172
literature, 81, 189–90, 205–27, 233, 283n14
Lizana, Bernardo de, 150
Lord's Supper, 115–16, 118, 127
Lorenzo, Francisco, 149, 151,
  306–7nn64–65
Lusíadas (Camões), 190
Luther, Martin, 79

MacCormack, Sabine, 47, 253, 255
Machiavellian Movement, The
  (Pocock), 252
magic, 69, 176–78. *See also* supernatural
Magnin, Juan, 225, 226, 227
Magnalia Christi Americana (C. Mather),
  81–83, 232
Mahmood, Saba, 171
Mai, Angelo, 253
malaria, 197
Malinowski, Bronislaw, 166
Mandell, Daniel, 165
Manifest Destiny, 42–43
maps of Amazon Basin, 213, 214, 215–16, 217,
  223–27, 224, 226, 319n28
Maravall, José Antonio, 49, 77
Margil, Antonio, 306n53
Maria I (Queen of Portugal), 182
Marian, Marthaeus, 278n27
Marian exiles, 111, 113–14
Mariana de Jesús, Saint, 209
Mariner's Mirror, The (Waghenaer), 55–68
Marlowe, Christopher, 68

Marrant, John, 178
Martha's Vineyard, 128, 164. *See also*
  Wampanoags
Martin, Joel, 163, 165
Martín de Valencia, 83–84
Martyr, Peter, 51
martyrs and martyrdom: celebration of,
  79–80; death rituals, 149; in England, 135,
  301n16; Franciscan, 131–32, 136–41,
  306n60; hagiography, 101, 137, 149–53;
  209; historical context of the New World,
  133–36; *imitatio Christi*, 150; Jesuit, 140,
  191, 196, 208–9, 225–27, 316n93; in
  Mexico, 136–39; miracles after death, 152;
  missionaries as, 5, 194–97; in New Spain,
  131–33, 136–42, 145–57; Puritan, 114–15;
  requirements of, 132; and spectacle, 138,
  303n24; strengthening commitment of
  others, 155–57, 307n73; and treason, 135
Martyrs' Mirror (Weimer), 115
Mary I (Queen of England), 114, 135
Maryland, 33
Massachusetts Bay Colony, 16, 267n14
Massachusetts Bay Company, 33–34,
  36, 127
Massachusetts charters, 239, 245, 249
Massachusetts General Court, 125–26
Mather, Cotton: classical imagery, use of,
  243, 324n16; on conversion of slaves, 18;
  "Faith at Work," 326–27n23; "Good
  Things Proposed," 326–27n23; on
  honoring exemplary people, 81–83;
  Magnalia Christi Americana, 81–83, 232;
  Negro Christianized, 18; *Optanda*, 246,
  326n19, 326–27n23; on Phips' governance,
  323–24nn13–14; *Pietas in Patriam*, 169,
  232–51; practical piety, 326n20; *Seasonable
  Discourses*, 75; transformation of colonial
  religious beliefs, 232–51; on witchcraft and
  Native religions, 74–75, 324n15; and
  witchcraft in Salem, 243; *Wonders of the
  Invisible World*, 74
Mather, Increase, 74, 238, 239
Mauss, Marcel, 167
Mayhew, Matthew, 17, 172
Mayhew family, 164
Mayhew, Thomas, 128
McBride, Kevin, 174–75, 178
McGreevy, John T., 263
Mede, Joseph, 70
Medina, Baltasar de, 154

Melanchthon, Philip, 79
Mello e Souza, Marina, 199–200, 202
Mendicant orders, 9, 38, 306n53. *See also* Dominican order; Franciscan order
Mendieta, Jerónimo de: on Franciscan welcome by Cortés, 85–86, 286–87n35; *Historia eclesiástica indiana*, 85–86, 302–3n19; on martyrs and martyrdom, 131, 149; on missionary practices, 148; on Native peoples, 142–43; and self-mastery, 104–5
Mennonites, 35
Mercado, Pedro de, 208–9
Mercedarian order, 89–92
Merrim, Stephanie, 269n42
messianism, 28–29
mestizos, 100, 292n66
Mexico: Felipe de Jesús, 153–55; and martyrs and martyrdom, 136–39; militancy of Spanish Christianity, 28; missionaries and missions, 4, 9–10, 138; rebellions by Native peoples, 40, 304n28; republics and republicanism, 253, 261. *See also* New Spain
Mezquia, Marcos de, 147
Middle East, 264
Mignolo, Walter, 171
military: Amazon Basin defenses, 211, 222–23, 225; as protectors for missionaries, 139, 152, 156, 210–11
millenarianism, 8, 29, 35–36, 87, 271n67
Miller, Perry, 120, 170, 256, 322n4
Mills, Kenneth, 277n8
Milton, John, 246, 325–26n18
ministers, 32, 37, 112, 124–25, 259. *See also* priests
miracles, 152–53
missionaries and missions: accommodation and selective adaptation, 38; in Africa, 19; apostolic model, 195; as authors, 83–88; in Brazil and the Amazon Basin, 4, 181, 191–92, 205–27, 317n7, 319n28; Catholics fueled by the Protestant Reformation, 133; convergence of economic and religious interests, 180–85; and exemplarity, 83–88, 93, 102; Far East as ultimate goal, 136, 302n18; and imperial policy, 205; imperial policy and mission work, 210–15, 221–23; and language, 149, 188; martyrs and martyrdom, 5, 194–97; military support for, 139, 152, 156, 210–11; missionary

complexes, 4; syncretic versions of Christianity, 3, 8, 17–18, 38, 164; as warriors for Christ, 139, 151–52; zeal of, 145–53. *See also* Dominican order; Franciscan order; Jesuits; *individual missionaries*
Mixton rebellion, 140
"Modell of Christian Charity, A" (J. Winthrop), 256
Mohegans, 164–65
Montaño, Sebastian, 137, 150, 303n23
Monzabal, Manuel de, 156
Moomaday, N. Scott, 168
Moors, 28–29, 31. *See also* Islam
moral projecting, 233, 246–51, 326n19
Morán de Butrón, Jacinto, 208
Moravians, 35
More, Thomas, 135
Moreno, Joseph Matías, 145
Moriscos, 95
Morocco, 300n7
mortuary rituals, 174–76
Motolinía, 2, 8–9, 35, 287n36
mulattos as priests, 181, 185
Mundy, Barbara, 221
Murison, Justine, 171
Murray, John Courtney, 263
Murúa, Martín de, 88–92
music, 198–99
muskets, 203
Muslims. *See* Islam
Mutayus, 218
mutinies, 235, 238, 323n9
Muy Rica Villa de la Vera Cruz, Mexico, 10
mythological creatures, 218, 319n37

Nahua peoples, 39, 288n42
Nahuatl, 43
Nameaug plantation, 174
Narragansetts, 173, 270–71n66, 310n32
Narrative of the Troubles with the Indians, A (Hubbard), 74
Narváez, Juan de, 223, 224, 225
Natick, Massachusetts, 267n18
Native American Renaissance (Linken), 167
Native Americans, Christianity, and the Reshaping of the American Religious Landscape (Martin and Nicholas, eds.), 163

Native peoples: accommodation and selective adaptation, 38; of the Amazon Basin, 218–20; Arricivita on, 144–45; assumption of welcome by, 16; belief systems in conflict with Christianity, 39–40; as blank slates, 1–2, 51–52; as Canaanites, 71; cruelty towards, 93, *94*, 129; decimation from diseases, 268n33; demonization of, 2, 253, 255–58; diabolism, 70; European views of, 2, 46–47; houses as contested spaces, 176–78; and idolatry, 277n8; illustrations of, 56–61; internecine territorial wars, 143; on martyrs, 156–57; and the Massachusetts Bay Company, 36; Mendieta on, 142–43; and millenarianism, 29, 35–36; as ministers, 259; mistreatment of, 9; as model republics, 258; native religious paving the way for Christianity, 53; and piety, 172–76; Praying Indians and Praying Towns, 4, 17, 37, 172, 310n30, 367n18; rebellions in Mexico, 140, 304n28; receptivity of communities, 39; and reciprocity, 167–68; rejection of Christianity, 5, 140–45, 157; religious and political identities, 260; resettlement of, 36; resistance strategies, 37–38; respect for Franciscans, 95, 147, 306n54; seminomadic tribes, 132, 137–39; spiritual transformations, 20–21, 161–65; and the supernatural, 171–72, 176–78; syncretic versions of Christianity, 8, 17–18, 38, 164; views of God, 66–67, 73–74, 79–80. *See also individual cultures or tribes*

Natural and Moral Histories of the East and West Indies (Acosta), 2–3, 51, 69–70, 256, 266nn4–5

nature, 168, 218–19

Navigational et Viaggi (Ramusio), 56–57

Naxara, Joseph de, 201–2

Negro Christianized (C. Mather), 18

New Discourse of Trade, A (Child), 35

New England, 20–21, 116–17, 119, 161–65, 232–51, 256

New England Company, 129–30

New England Mind, The (Miller), 120, 256

New England Salamander (Winslow), 128

New Englands Jonas Cast Up (Child), 128

New France, 34

New Galicia, Mexico, 137

New Jerusalem, 30

New Mexico, 140

Newport, R.I., 34

New Spain: alleged Judaizers in, 34; institutionalization of Christianity, 30–31; institutionalization of Spanish Christianity, 30–31; linguistic concessions, 38; martyrs and martyrdom in, 131–33, 136–42, 145–57; missionary authors, 83–88; spiritual and ceremonial traditions of Native peoples, 39–40. *See also* Mexico; missionaries and missions; Peru; Spanish America

New World, conquest and colonization: as experimental field for philosophical inquiry, 50; historical context of, 133–36; and identity formation, 6, 208–9; link with Biblical Promised Land, 15–16, 30, 70, 270nn59–60; messianic overtones, 28–29; millenarianism, 8, 29, 35–36, 87, 271n67; native religious paving the way for Christianity, 53; Papal allocation of to Spain and Portugal, 6, 29, 54, 268n26; primacy of religious aspects, 25–26; as religious refuge, 33–35; restrictions on emigration to, 31; settlement patterns and demographic characteristics, 36; and transformation of Christianity, 5–6, 20–21, 27; vulnerability of, 132

Nicholas, Mark, 163, 165

Nieuwe wereldt, ofte, Beshrijvinghe van West-Indien (De Laet), 2, 266n6

Nominalism *vs.* Realism, 48

nonconformity, 112

Nuevo descubrimiento del Gran Río de las Amazonas . . . (Acuña), 206, 216–23

O Araguai (Basílio da Gama), 189

Oberman, Heiko, 48

Occom, Samsom, 178, 259

Oceans of Letters (Larson), 123

Of Plymouth Plantation (Bradford), 4–5, 115

Oliveira Mendes, Luís Antônio de, 198

Olmedo, Bartolomé de, 89

Olmedo, José Joaquín, 260

Olmos, Andrés de, 29

Omaguas, 211, 220

"On the Invocation and Veneration of Saints and Their Relics, and on Holy Images," 79

Optanda (C. Mather), 246, 326n19, 326–27n23
oración mental, 284n16
Orellana, Francisco de, 210, 221–22
original sin, 40
Orsúa, Pedro de, 210, 222

Padilla, Augustín Dávila, 285n30
Padroado, 191
paganism, 50
Paine, Thomas, 166
paintings. *See* portraits
Pames, 140
Pané, Ramón, 7
Paracelsus, 76
Paraguay, 4
Pará settlement, 211, 215
patents or land grants, 12–13, 16
Paul, Saint, *103*
Pauw, Cornelius de, 258
Peckham, George, 33
Penn, William, 34
Pennsylvania, 34, 35
Pequots, 164–65, 173–76, 280n49. *See also* Algonquians
Perea, Estevan, 140
Perkins, William, 54
Personius, Robert, 135
Peru: alleged Judaizers in, 34; idolatry, 38; Lima, 40–41; militancy of Spanish Christianity, 28; missionary complexes, 4; in Murúa's writings, 89; republics and republicanism, 253; syncretic versions of Christianity, 8. *See also* New Spain
Peter, Saint, *103*
Peyote Religion Among the Navaho, The (Aberle), 167
Phelan, John, 134
Philip II (King of Spain), 9–10, 207, 221–22, 292–93n67
Philip IV (King of Spain), 201
Philippines, 136, 154
Phips, William, 231, 235–38, 240–50, 323–24nn13–14, 323n9, 324n16, 326n19
Picart, Bernard, 265n1
Pico della Mirandola, Giovanni, 76
Pietas in Patriam (C. Mather), 169, 232–51
Pietism, 250, 326n20
piety, 161–62, 169–76, 179, 308n1
Pilgrim and the Bee, The (Brown), 171–72

Pilgrims, 16, 33, 42–43
Pimenta, Antônio, 314n43
Pimentel, Domingo, 303n23
Pinzón, Martín Alonzo, 6
Pinzón, Vincent Yáñes, 6
Pires, Francisca da (Chica da Silva), 199
Pires, Vicente Ferreira, 181–82, 185–89, 194–97, 201–4
Piumbubou, 17
Platforme of Discipline Gathered out of the Word, A, 117
Plato, 170
Plea for the West, A (Beecher), 263
Pliny, 2
Plymouth Colony, 16, 33, 42–43
Pobre, Juan, 154
Pochohontas, 74
Pocock, J. G. A., 252
Polanyi, Karl, 166
politics, secularization of, 6, 239–51, 325n18
Politics of Piety (Mahmood), 171
Pontiac's War, 260
Popes and the Papacy, 6, 29, 54, 268n26, 280n48. *See also individual Popes*
poppets as talismans, 176–78, *177*
Porterfield, Amanda, 308n1
portraits, 80–81, 135, 281–82n2, 282n8
Portugal, 180–85, 191–92, 205–6, 222, 272n76, 314n74
Portugal, José de, 187
Powhattans, 72, 74
practical divinity, 120–21
practical piety, 326n20
Praying Indians, 17, 172, 310n30
Praying Towns, 4, 37, 267n18
"Preface to the Reader" (Eden), 51
"'Preparation for Salvation' in Seventeenth-Century New England" (Miller), 120
Presbyterians, 16, 33
"Prestigiator" (White), 57, 61
priests, 93, 102, 292–93n67. *See also* ministers; missionaries and missions
Primavera (Botticelli), 61, 62–63
Prince, Thomas, 35
Principal Navigations, Voiages, Traffiques and Discoueries of the English Nation (Hakluyt), 13, 52, 56
printing, 122–23, 127–28, 297n4. *See also* books
Propaganda Fides, 141, 144, 304n30

Protestantism: and conversion of Native peoples, 37; and development of modernity, 22; and freedom of religion, 44; and individual sanctity, 79–83; lack of institutional structure, 42; Luther and Melanchthon as examples to emulate, 79; on magic and witchcraft, 69, 74–75; martyrs and martyrdom, 80, 135; New World as religious refuge, 33; on portraits and idolatry, 80–81; on Purgatory, 267–68n19; and republics and republicanism, 252; similarities with Catholic Church, 28; work ethic, 43. *See also individual nominations*

Protestant Reformation, 12, 50, 54, 77. *See also* Anabaptist Church; Calvinism

protonationalism, 111–12

providential rhetoric, 233, 235–38, 240–41, 243–51, 324–25nn17–18

Pueblo Indians, 141

Purchas, Samuel, 15, 72

purgatory, 267–68n19

Puritan Conquistadors (Cañizares-Esguerra), 253

Puritans: and Algonquians, 256–57; as Augustinian commonwealths, 256; and building holy communities, 37; and capitalism, 322n4; dissension within, 124–25; emigration to the New World, 34; evangelism of, 111; and exemplarity, 85; and governance, 4–5, 119–25, 232–51, 325–26n18; on governance, 322n3; as kingdom of heaven on earth, 116–17; lack of institutional structure, 42; martyrs and martyrdom, 114–15; and piety, 170, 172–73, 326n20; primitivist strain within, 268n22; protection from factionalism, 16; protonationalism of, 111–12; and reciprocity, 172–73; refusal to accommodate or adapt, 38; separation of church and state, 16; in seventeenth-century England, 113–14; syncretism within, 176; and U.S. societal icons, 42–43; and the visible Church, 115–16; and visible saints, 4, 116, 232, 235, 248

Quakers, 34

Quiroga, Vasco de, 30

Quito, 209, 210–16

Quran, 171

race and republicanism, 261–62

Raleigh, Walter, 13, 52, 55, 319n37

Ramusio, Giovanni Battista, 56–57

Realism, 48, 54

Real Patronato, 6, 268n26

reciprocity, 162, 165–68, 172–73

Recuerdos históricos y políticos de los servicios que los generales y varones ilustres de la religión de Nuestra Señora de la Merced . . ., 90

Reformed tradition (Calvinism), 35, 111–21

Reinel, Pedro Gomes, 272n76

Relación de las antigüedades de los indios (Pané), 7

Relación del descubrimiento del Río de las Amazonas . . . (anon), 206, 210–15, 318n14

Relaciones geográficas de Indias, 207–8, 221

Relation of the Troubles with the Indians, A (Mather, I.), 74

religion, 4, 6, 22, 121, 253–64. *See also* transformations, religious; *individual cultures or religions*

"Remarks Concerning the Savages of North America" (Franklin), 258

Remón, Alonso, 90

Rentería, Joseph de, 148

Repúblicas del Mundo (Román y Zamora), 255

republics and republicanism, 252–64

resistance strategies, 37–38

Revelation, 115

revivalist movements, 35

rhetoric, 194–95, 233–51

Rhode Island, 16, 34, 71, 270–71n66

Ribadeneira, Pedro de, 155, 301n16

Ribault, Jean, 64

Rich, Charles, Earl of Warwick, 128

Richter, Daniel, 260

Rights of Man (Paine), 166

Río, Juan del, 152

Río Negro, 219

Rishton, Edward, 301n16

Robinson, John, 170

Rodríguez, Manuel, 209

Rojas, Alonso de, 206, 208, 318n14

Román y Zamora, Jerónimo, 255

Rome, ancient, 254

Rosary Brotherhood festivals, 198

Round, Philip H., 122–23

Rowlandson, Mary, 74

Royal Academy of Sciences of Lisbon, 186, 191

Royal African Company, 18

Royal Commentaries of the Incas (Vega), 255

Royal Society of London, 3, 266n10
Ruiz de Alarcón, Hernando, 77
Rump Parliament, 36, 120

Saavedra y Guzmá, Martín de, 318n14
Sahagún, Bernardino de, 89, 287n38
Saint Louis de Grégoy, Whydah, 183
saintly persons, 281–82nn1–2. *See also* visible
    saints
saints and exemplarity, 79, 101, *103,* 104
Salem Witch Trials, 74–75, 232, 241–43
Sales Souza, Evergton, 185
"Samson Agonistes" (Milton), 246, 325–26n18
sanctitas, 281–82nn1–2
Sander, Nicholas, 301n16
Sandoval, Alonso de, 19
San Luis de Marañón, settlement, 211, 216
San Martín, José de, 260
Santacruz, Raimundo de, 209
Santander, Juan de, 140
Sâo João Baptista de Ajudá, 182–84
Sardinha, Cipriano Pires, 181–82, 185–89,
    192, 194–97, 201–4
Sarmiento de Gamboa, Pedro, 77
Satan, 39–40, 46–47, 280n48. *See also* devil
scientific developments, 3, 207–8
scientific exploration, 205–8, 218–19, 223–27
Scotland, 118, 120–21
scribal publication, 122
Seasonable Discourses (Mather, C.), 75
secularization, 184, 232–51, 263, 325n18
Seeing with a Native Eye (Toelken), 167
Seeman, Erik, 175, 308–9n5
selective membership, 116–17
self-mastery, 104–6, 296n78
seminomadic tribes, 132, 137–39
Seneca, 104
Separatists, 112–13, 127
Seris, 141
sermons, 15–16, 122, 191–95, 246,
    270nn59–60, 326–27n23, 326n19
Serres, Michael, 162–63
settlement patterns, 36
Shepard, Thomas, 116–17
shipwrecks, 190
Shoemaker, Nancy, 164
*Short Story of the Rise, Reigne, and Ruine of
    the Late Antinomians, Familists and
    Libertines, A.* (anon), 123–27
Sicardo, Joseph, 155, 307n70
Silverman, David, 17, 163–65, 167, 173

silver mines, 138–40, 222
Sioux, 167
slaves and the slave trade, 18–20, 181–83, 198,
    203, 272n73, 272n76
Smith, Arleen M., 74
Smith, John, 16, 72, *73,* 255–56
social changes in colonies, 232–51
Society for the Propagation of the Gospel in
    New England, 36
Society of Jesus. *See* Jesuits
Sousa Sepúlveda, Manoel de, 190
South America, 253. *See also* New Spain;
    Spanish America; *individual countries or
    cultures*
Southey, Robert, 300n7
Souza, Tomé de, 191
Soveraignty and Goodness of God, The
    (Rowlandson), 74
Spain: defeat of Muslims, 134; imperial
    policy and mission work, 205, 210–15,
    221–23; justification for conquest of New
    World, 54–55; militancy of Church,
    28–29; saints and martyrs, 135; scientific
    developments, 207–8; transatlantic
    transfers of religion, 27–28; unification
    with Portugal, 222
Spanish America: cartography, 205–8;
    decimation of converts from diseases,
    268n33; and development of modernity,
    22; ecclesiastical government, 30–31; as
    holy experiment, 30; integrationist
    approach, 44–45; pageantry and outward
    manifestation of religion, 41; religious and
    imperial goals of colonization, 6–7, 185,
    205, 210–15, 221–23; republics and
    republicanism, 253, 258–60, 261; role of
    religion compared to British America, 41,
    43; urbanization of, 10, 269n42
specificity, 13, 15, 218–21
spectacle and martyrdom, 138, 303n24
spectral evidence, 241–43, 245, 322n4.
    See also supernatural
Spies, Johann, 61, *64*
spiritual transformations, 161–62.
    See also conversion
spiritual vacuums, 39–40
Staden, Hans, 65
Stephen, Saint, 190–91
St. George, Robert, 176–77
Stien, Jordan, 171
Stuart, Mary, 111

Sun worship, 39–40
supernatural, 171–72, 176–78, 241–43, 245, 322n4
Swift, Jonathan, 170
syncretic versions of Christianity, 8, 17–18, 38, 176
Synod of 1637, 124–26

Tacanaga, 155
Tamayo, Juan, 154
Taos, 141
Tapia, Juan de, 152
Taycozam (Emperor of Japan), 154
Taylor, Charles, 263
Tecumseh, 260
Tenochtitlan, Mexico, 7, 10, 85, 286–87n35
Tepehuanes, 140
Teresa of Avila, 300n8
Tertullian, 80
Tesoro de la lengua Castellana, or Española (Covarrubias), 88
Texas, 141
Texeira, Pedro de, 210, 215–16, 223
Thomas, Keith, 54, 177
Thomas, Nicholas, 164
Thorowgood, Thomas, 2, 71
Tinhorão, José Ramos, 198
tobacco, 182
Tocqueville, Alexis de, 261
Toelken, Barre, 167
Toledo, Andrés de, 210
Toleration Act (England, 1684), 42
Tonantzin, 39
Torquemada, Juan de, 286–87n35, 301n10, 302–3n19
trade, 19, 180–85, 191–92
transatlantic exchanges, 21, 27–28, 122–30, 181
transformations, religious, 5–6, 19–21, 27, 161–65, 232–51. See also conversion; missionaries and missions
translation, 17, 50–51, 199–200, 265n2, 271–72n71, 299n38. See also language
Trapajosos, 212
Tratado de las supersticiones y costumbres gentílicas que hoy viven entre los indios naturales de esta Nueva España (Ruiz de Alarcón), 77
treason, 135
Trejo, Rafael de, 286–87n35
Tribunal of Conscience and the Orders (Portugal), 191

Tunisia, 264
Tupac Amaru II, 255, 260
Tupinambá people, 65, 66, 218
Turkey, Republic of, 264

urbanization, 10, 40–41, 141, 269n42
Urban VII (Pope), 81, 284n14

Vagad, Gualberto Fabricio de, 105, 296n79
Valencia, Martín de, 134, 286–87n35, 302–3n19, 306n53
Valencia, Pedro de, 95
Valentine (Saint), 133
Valeri, Mark, 250
Valle, Juan del, 150
Vargas, Francisco de, 148
Veen, Gijsbert van, 57
Vega, Garcilaso de la "El Inca," 53, 96, 255
Vega, Lope de, 135, 303n23
Vega, Pedro de la, 101
Velasco, Juan de, 208–9, 317n7
Veloso de Miranda, Joaquim, 314n36
Vergil, 169
Vetancurt, Agustín de, 87, 302–3n19
Via Antigua, 48
Viagem de África em o Reino de Dahomé (Pires), 189–91, 195–97, 202–4
Via Moderna, 48
Vicente Ferreira Pires. See Pires, Vicente Ferreira
Vida del pícaro Guzmán de Alfarache (Alemán), 190
Vide, Sebastião Monteiro de, 192, 196
Vieira, António, 11–12
Villagrá, Gaspar de, 74
Vincent, Thomas, 284n20
Virginia Company, 15, 31–32
"Virginia's Verger" (Hakluyt), 72
Virgin Mary, 39
visible Church, 115–16
visible saints, 4, 116, 232, 235, 248
vitae, 101, 294n71
Voragine, Jacobus de, 101, 105
"Voyages" series (de Bry), 55–68, 278n27
Voyage to Dahomey (Pires), 189–91, 195–97, 202–4

Waghenaer, Lucas, 56
Wagner, Christoff, 61, 63
Wampanoags (Wôpanâak), 17–18, 164, 173, 271n67. See also Martha's Vineyard

Watt, Tessa, 171
Way of the Churches of Christ in New England, The (Cotton), 127–28
Way of the Churches of Christ in New England . . . Cleared, The (Cotton), 127
Ways of Writing (Hall), 123
weapons, 203
Webster, Daniel, 254–55, 261
Weimer, Adrian, 115
Weld, Thomas, 124, 126
West Africa, 183
Wheatley, Phillis, 18
Wheelwright, John, 124
Whitaker, Alexander, 15
White, John, 56–57, *58*, 59, 61, 113
Whitfield, George, 18
Whole Booke of Psalmes, The, 111
Whydah, 181–83
wilderness, New World as, 5, 34
Wilhelm of Ockham, 48
William and Mary (King and Queen of England), 239, 325n18
Williams, Roger: and Baillie, 123; banishment of, 124; conversion of Native peoples, 17; holy experiment of, 34; *Key into the Language of America*, 71, 173; and liberty of conscience, 270–71n66; on Native forms of government, 257; Rhode Island charter, 128
Winiarski, Douglas, 165
Winship, Michael, 324–25nn17–18
Winslow, Edward, 128
Winthrop, John: "A Modell of Christian Charity," 256; denial of the Lord's Supper, 127; on God's approval of settlements, 71; and loyalty to crown, 113; on ministers as nonconformists, 112; Nameaug plantation, 174; on printing of Cotton's sermons, 122; and the *Short Story of the Rise . . .*, 124
Winthrop, John Jr., 172–73
witchcraft, 69, 74–75, 232, 241–43, 279n30, 324n15
women, 4, 121, 171, 267n16, 308n1
Wonders of the Invisible World (Mather, C.), 74
Woodward, Walter, 172–73
Wôpanâak (Wampanoags), 17–18, 164, 173, 271n67. *See also* Martha's Vineyard
Wright, Goodman, 172
writing and publishing, 122–30, 188. *See also* books; literature; printing

Xavier, Francisco, 191
Xiximes, 140

Yameos, 225
Yquiari, 219
Yumas, 141
Yurimaguas, 225
Yurupazi River, 219

Zacatecos, 140
Zemes, 51
Zumárraga, Juan de, 10, 84
Zurinas, 219
Zwingli, Huldrych, 80

ACKNOWLEDGMENTS
<hr>

We began our collaboration on this project several years ago through conversations about our own work on religion in our respective fields of Early American and Colonial Latin American Studies. We began to identify provocative points of contact and divergence in our work on New England Puritanism and colonial Mexican Catholicism and concluded rather quickly that religion offered an important yet underexplored rubric of comparative analysis. From these conversations, we initiated a long and fruitful collaboration that now culminates with this essay collection. This volume would not have been possible without the generous support that we received from numerous institutions as well as the exemplary scholarship and critical debate offered by our contributors.

Since the inception of this project in 2007, we have hosted a speaker series and a conference at Washington University in St. Louis (2009), a conference at the Huntington Library in San Marino, California (2010), and a joint workshop between Princeton University and the McNeil Center for Early American Studies at the University of Pennsylvania (2011). At each of these events, leading experts in the field of religion in the early modern Americas joined our conversations from universities throughout the United States, the United Kingdom, Brazil, Ecuador, France, and Canada. A disciplinarily diverse crowd, these scholars represent the perspectives of the fields of English, History, Divinity, Art History, and Anthropology. We are extremely grateful to all of them for the ways that their work has impacted our thinking on this topic and advanced our discussions.

We received generous funding from these institutions in hosting these events. At Washington University, we are grateful to the Program in American Culture Studies and its then-director, Wayne Fields, to Provost Edward Macias, and to the English Department and its then-chair, David Lawton, for offering financial help to bring the spring 2008 event to fruition. We were also the lucky recipients of a series of internal grants from the Center for Joint

Programs, International and Areas Studies, and the Center for Ethics and Human Values. A matching grant from the Program for Cultural Cooperation between Spain's Ministry of Culture and United States Universities also helped fund part of this event. We received excellent logistical support from the staff of the Program in American Culture Studies. We were very fortunate to have the Huntington's backing for our conference in the fall of 2009. We wish to thank Peter Mancall and Roy Ritchie in particular, as well as the wonderful staff that facilitated such a great event. Fredrika Teute attended the Huntington conference and has offered keen insights on the volume. In the fall of 2011, we hosted a workshop for the contributors of this volume through the generous support of Princeton University and the McNeil Center for Early American Studies at the University of Pennsylvania. This conference was funded by the Stewart Fund for Religion and the Council of the Humanities, the Center for the Study of Religion, and the American Studies Program at Princeton University. We would like to extend our thanks to Hendrik Hartog, the then-director of American Studies, and the director of the McNeil Center, Daniel Richter. The staff at each of these hosting institutions was magnificently helpful in organizing this event. Robert Lockhart attended the McNeil Center conference and has offered invaluable advice as we have worked to bring this volume to fruition.